# Overlanders

# Overlanders

## Richard Thomas Wright

Winter Quarters Press

Cover illustration: "Camping on Plains" 1862. Watercolour on pencil by William George Richardson Hind, (1833-1899), Overlander. PAC C-13974

Copyright ©1985 and 2000 Richard Thomas Wright

All rights reserved. No part of this book may be reproduced or transmitted in any form by any means without written permission from the publisher, except by a reviewer, who may quote brief passages in a review.

Winter Quarters Press
Box 15 Miocene, Williams Lake, B.C. Canada V2G 2P3
Email:cwellner@grassrootsgroup.com
http://goldrushbc.com

Distributed by: Sandhill Book Marketing Ltd.
    #99 – 1270 Ellis Street
    Kelowna, B.C. Canada V1Y 1Z4
    (250) 763-1406; fax: (250) 763-4051

Canadian Cataloguing in Publication Data

Wright, Richard Thomas 1940-
    Overlanders

Includes bibliographical references and index.
ISBN 0-9696887-3-3

1. Overland journeys to the Pacific. 2. Northwest, Canadian—Description and travel—1822-1870. 3. Cariboo (B.C.: Regional district)—Gold discoveries 4. Fraser River Valley (B.C.)—Gold discoveries. I Title.

FC3213.W74 2000        971.2'01    C00-900744-X
F1060.8.W74 2000

Publishing history: First published 1985 by Western Producer Prairie Books, Saskatoon, Saskatchewan, with sub title 1858 Gold.

Printed in Canada

This book is dedicated to the memory of my
Mother and Father:


Thomas Stanley Wright
1913 – 1999
who keenly followed and supported
the careers of his children.

E. Audrey Wright
1912 – 1999
A generous, courageous, inspirational woman.
A mother who encouraged and supported her three sons
and grandsons and who, while she could not understand
"why we did not have real jobs", accepted, encouraged and
supported our artistic endeavors

History is not like some individual person, which uses man to achieve its ends.
History is nothing but the actions of men in pursuit of their ends.

>Karl Marx
>*Die Heilige Familie* (1845)

# Contents

| | |
|---|---|
| Acknowledgements | ix |
| Prologue | xi |
| Maps | xiii, xiv |

CHAPTER ONE
    The El Dorado     1
    Approaches     4
    The Expansionists     7

CHAPTER TWO
    The Men of Faribault     12
    The Red River Settlement     20
    A Journey on the Plains     24

CHAPTER THREE
    "Pampered Bastards of English Barons"     41
    A Winter's Journey in the Rocky Mountains     45
    Washington Territory     54
    Winter This Side of the Mountains     58
    The Faribault Party     61

CHAPTER FOUR
    The Man From Brechin     65

CHAPTER FIVE
    The British Imperialist     77

CHAPTER SIX
    The Northwestern Exploring Expedition     89

CHAPTER SEVEN
    Across the Rocky Mountains     108
    "A Summer's Jaunt"     120

CHAPTER EIGHT
    1860     130
    1861     132

| | |
|---|---|
| Dr. Reid and Red River | 133 |
| Fort Edmonton to Victoria | 136 |

## CHAPTER NINE

| | |
|---|---|
| The 1862 Prelude | 141 |
| Canada West to St. Paul | 145 |
| "Ho! For Cariboo" | 149 |
| In Camp at Georgetown | 154 |
| The British Overland Transit Company | 161 |

## CHAPTER TEN

| | |
|---|---|
| Fort Garry –"Big Bugs and Little Bugs" | 166 |
| McMicking Party to Fort Ellice | 174 |
| McMicking Party— Fort Ellice to Fort Edmonton | 180 |
| St. Peters Party to Fort Edmonton | 187 |
| Saskatchewan Gold Expedition to Fort Edmonton | 189 |

## CHAPTER ELEVEN

| | |
|---|---|
| McMicking Party –at Fort Edmonton | 202 |
| McMicking Party—Fort Edmonton to Tete Jaune Cache | 205 |
| St. Peters Party—Fort Edmonton to Tete Jaune Cache | 211 |
| Saskatchewan Gold Expedition – Fort Edmonton to Tete Jaune Cache | 212 |
| Fraser River Parties | 215 |
| Thompson River Parties | 223 |

## CHAPTER TWELVE

| | |
|---|---|
| London, Canada West, to Fort Edmonton | 231 |
| The Rock | 234 |
| In the Colonies in 1862 | 242 |
| Epilogue | 247 |

## APPENDIX ONE

| | |
|---|---|
| Party Rosters | 251 |

## APPENDIX TWO

| | |
|---|---|
| The Overlanders – An Annotated List | 256 |

## APPENDIX THREE

| | |
|---|---|
| 2000 Edition updates | 272 |
| Notes | 277 |
| Bibliography | 299 |
| Index | 307 |

# Acknowledgements to the 2000 edition

"Overlanders" and the people who helped in the research, writing and publishing go back to the book's 1975 inception and the initial support of Rick Antonson, then publisher of Antonson Publishing. Also a special thanks to Rob Sanders, former publisher of Western Producer Prairie books who first published this book.

In these early years I was helped by Jim Stanton, who read sections for me and visited some sites, and Yorke Edwards, then with the British Columbia Provincial Museum.

The Canada Council, God bless them, moved the research a long way to completion with grants in 1977 and 1979, which allowed the research to be expanded to include the pre-1862 overlanders.

In 1977 the National Film Board filmed the Wright family retracing the Overlanders' route in the film titled Family Down the Fraser, a film that is still seen late at night on obscure television channels. This journey enabled me to visit sites, travel the Fraser River portion of their trek, and experience it firsthand.

The Hudson's Bay Company archivists, in particular Shirlee Ann Smith, were of great help, as was the staff of the BC Archives, the Alberta Archives and the Manitoba Archives. The United Church Archives helped with the Woolsey letters; the Public Archives of Canada staff were particularly resourceful in finding newspapers and photographs; and the Whitman College library, Washington, located information and photos of Dr. Thibodo. The Glenbow Museum; the Public Records Office, London, England; the Oregon Historical Society; the Newberry Library in Chicago; the Montana Historical Society; and the Jasper Yellowhead Historical Society also provided information.

Elaine C. Everyly, Military Archives Division, U.S. National Archives, found records of several Overlanders. Ruby Shields and Brigid Shields of the Minnesota Historical Society answered many letters and on visits to St. Paul were most helpful. Mary Balf, Kamloops Museum, answered queries about Thompson country overlanders and Andree S. Vajda-Janyk translated OMI documents.

Thanks also to those who sent family information, in particular Helen Warren Wood, a niece of Robert Warren, who sent the Erastus Hall letters; A.E. Moore of Chambley, Quebec, who sent three letters of William Hugill; John E. Potts of the Mickle family; historian James McGregor who answered questions about Edmonton; George Thorman of St. Thomas, and Mr. E.W. Elliott of Gooderich.

My thanks to those who read the first printing of Overlanders and offered reviews and sent additional family information: Isabel Eddy, re Robert Harkness; John Stevenson re: Eady Stevenson; and James E. Connell re William McCormick; Peter Dady on the Halpennys.

History thanks Ken Faverholdt, formerly of the Kamloops Museum, who rescued from the Kamloops landfill Dr. Wade's collection including the lecture notes of William Wattie, diary extracts of James Wattie, the letters of Archibald Thompson and more, after the book first went to press.

The most recent thanks goes to Lana Fox, Quesnel, and George Hebenton of Scotland, who helped identify the anonymous Man from Brechin as Alexander Hebenton, a 24-year-old Scot from Brechin.

Through the years of research and writing several friends offered a variety of support. Reshard Gool sounded ideas of Victorian times; Eugene Benson, the late Thomas York, Michel Gilbert and many other members of the Writer's Union of Canada offered the kind of support only writers can give.

For help with the Cariboo story thanks goes to all the Barkerville Historic Townsite staff, in particular Ken Mather, former curator, the only other person I know who knows Jamey Jock Bird.

As the book neared completion I was helped by those who read the manuscript—Keith Maillard, David John Smith, Rick Antonson and George Payerle, who also copy edited and typed several chapters. Cyndi Turvey and Susan Chernov helped keyboard the manuscript.

My two sons lived with the Overlanders for years. Richard unknowingly offered encouragement by asking each day after school, "How's Overlanders coming Dad?" He spent hours over a computer inputting the raw data for rosters and final editing changes. Now, a decade later, as a partner in Winter Quarters press, he still gives support and encouragement.

Raven asked the questions that needed answers, with rare insight. While following the route he once said, "Wouldn't it be great if we met one of the Overlanders? Then we would really know what it was like." He also helped in last-minute research while living with me in Barkerville.

Acknowledgement and thanks goes to Rochelle Farquhar who for many years helped with research, sounded my theories and shared the excitement of research.

As this new publication of Overlanders was wrestled to completion and publication, my wife and partner Cathryn Wellner helped with final production, publication and has remained my rock of support.

To all these folks, and the Overlanders themselves who have given me some great times, my thanks. This book is yours.

# Prologue

There was an allurement, an enchantment, to the vision of an overland journey. To cross the continent by land—by train, paddle wheeler, stagecoach, and then finally, ultimately, thousands of miles on foot. To contemplate such a journey you had to stretch your vision to the far horizon, to accomplish it you had to force your body to its physical limits.

The journey was bold and broad; a composite of sights and feelings were etched into the traveler: the sweep of prairie grassland, the fastness of mountain valleys, nights of interminable cold, and days when treeless plains simmered in a pan of sweat. Moccasined feet would tread a grass-bound land festooned in spring with a weaving of wild flowers and herbs, and in fall with thickets of wild rose. There were days when one would smell the musty dung and fetid heat of a buffalo herd passing, and that evening savor the succulent steaks and roasts.

Out there in a lonely land roamed the nomads of the great plains— the Oglalla Sioux, the Assiniboines, Gros Ventres, and Blackfeet, who roamed a land still free from reservations, fences, boundaries, and laws —and travelers trespassed at some risk.

West of the Mississippi and the Red River of the North lay the immense solitude of the prairie, a shallow ocean of waving grass, an engulfing remoteness so vast it bewildered the mind, so endless it frightened. Beyond the plains lay the formidable mountain barriers of rock, ice, snow, and treacherous rivers, overwhelming peaks that closed the adventurer in a stratum of time. And waiting there on the plains or in some mountain pass was "the Elephant," a lurking, unseen hulk of fear, sensitive to failure and unforgiving of weakness.

In the populated eastern towns the Elephant was a myth, at most a good story. It began, unbelievers said, with the circus. Everyone wanted to see a circus elephant, and with the parade in town a farmer drove to market, his wagon loaded with produce. The circus elephant scared his horse and trampled the produce, but the farmer didn't care; he had "seen the elephant," he had seen it all. The metaphor found its way into print, song, and speech.

To those who crossed the plains the Elephant was a reality. The beast was there all right, waiting over the horizon by day and outside the fire's light at night. You had to meet him face to face, on his own ground, or be crushed beneath an awesome foot. Some experienced him early in a trip and retreated before his immensity. The rest went forward.

Before this overland journey ended thousands of miles and many months would pass. And when the plains were crossed, the mountains climbed, the rivers swum, well then, by damn, these men and women were not mere gold-seekers or fortune hunters. They were distinctive amongst those who went west, people of singular mettle: overlanders.

The golden banks of Fraser River were the lure that drew them on this westward odyssey. But they went, not for the getting there, but for the going.

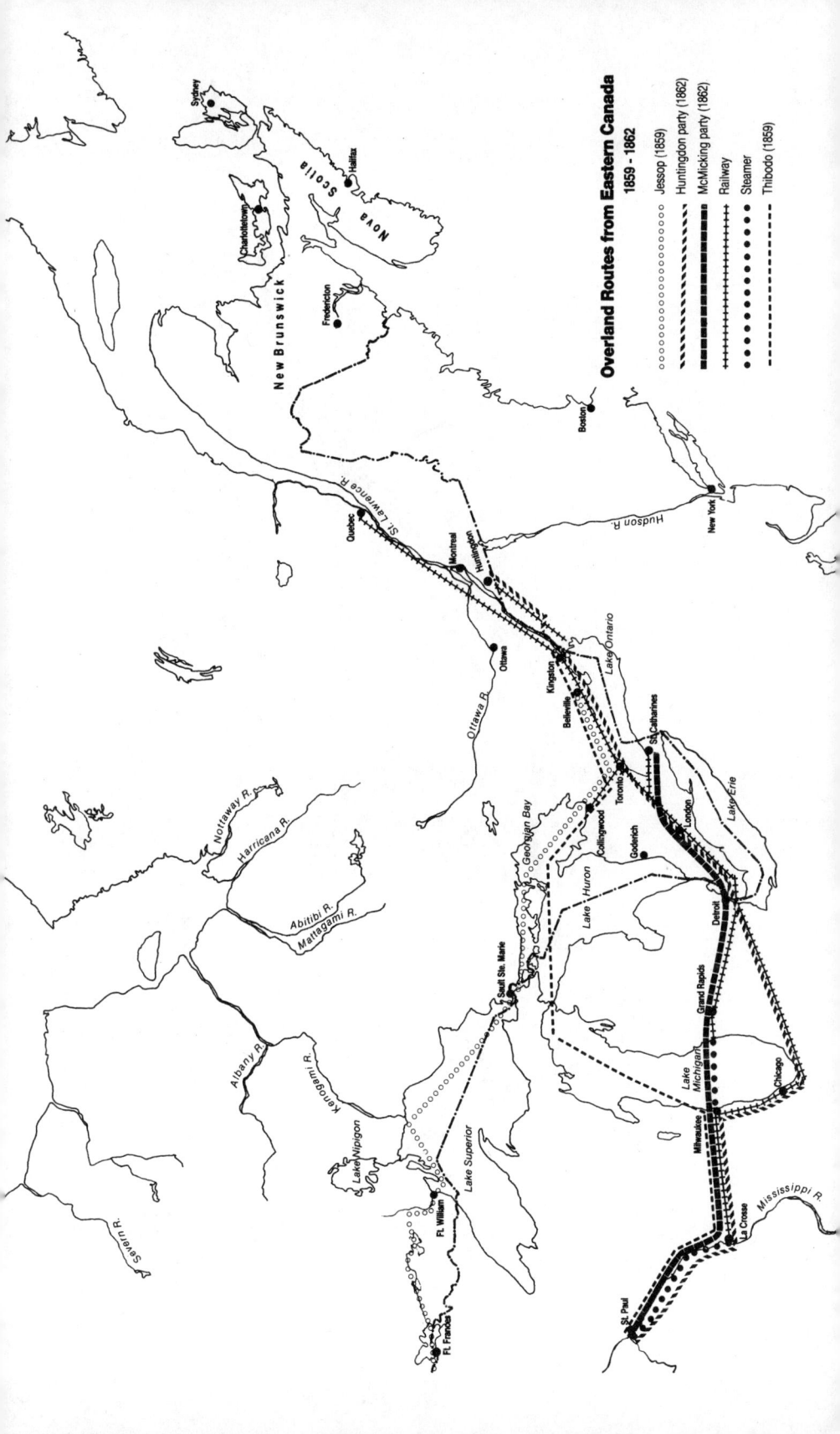

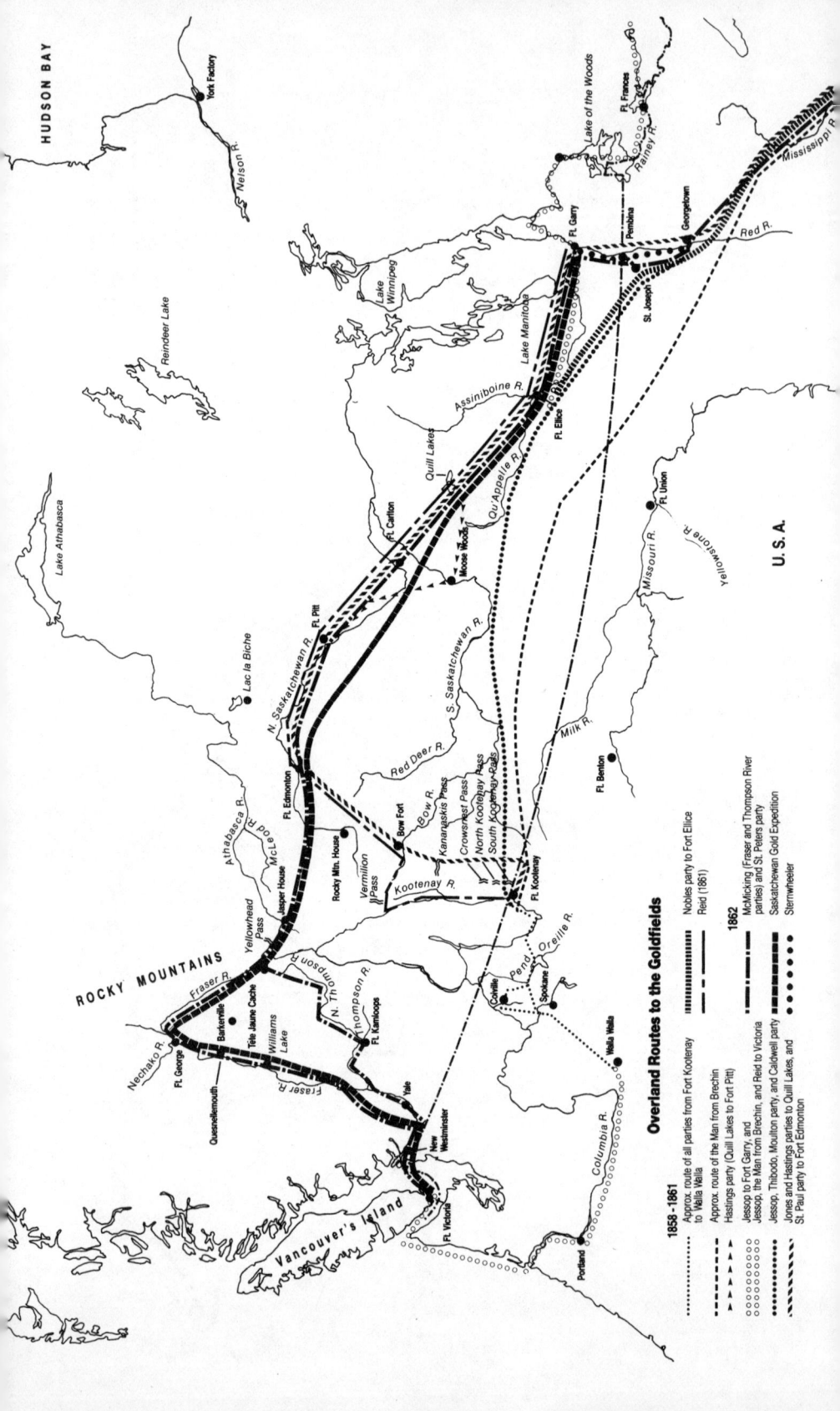

# Chapter One

## The El Dorado

The inflammatory words spread down the coast like gossip about the parson at a church social. From each port the message reverberated, building, until at San Francisco the docks literally screamed the words, "Gold! Gold on Fraser's River!"

The reports had miners sluicing twenty-five to fifty dollars per day, a month's wages, and even Indian women panning ten to twelve dollars a day. The new El Dorado was north, in British territory.[1]

News of the strike met with momentary bewilderment. "The Fraser River—where was it? No one knew," miner Thomas Seward later wrote. "It was known only that gold could be found there, and that was enough to send hundreds of men into the wilderness to make their fortunes or to die in the attempt. . . . I did not even know that Great Britain had any 'possessions' on the Pacific Coast of North America, and my fellow miners were no better informed."[2]

Miners found the Fraser River and came by the thousands. Alfred Waddington, a Vancouver Island merchant, wrote in 1858 that "never perhaps was there so large an immigration in so short a space of time into so small a place. Unlike California, where the distance from the Eastern States and Europe precluded the possibility of an immediate rush, the proximity of Victoria to San Francisco . . . afforded every facility, and converted the whole matter into a fifteen dollar trip."[3]

The gold news emptied San Francisco. On April 20, 1858, an estimated seventeen hundred men left between 4:00 and 5:30 P.M. At the Pacific Street dock the steamer *Commodore* loaded while besieged by friends and acquaintances of the adventurers. At the head of the wharves steamboat runners harangued passengers "in screams of manufactured rage in favor of their employers." Miners pushed and squeezed their way on board the steamers, loaded with blankets, canteens, tin pots, wash pans, picks, shovels, spades, and firearms; dressed in coarse wool, flannel shirts, and heavy boots still caked with California mud.

At 5:30 the cry "all aboard" came; the gangplanks were hauled in, hawsers dropped, and the *Commodore* steamed out in a strong northwest wind to cries of "Write for sure," "Good luck," and general cheers being tossed between ship and shore. The *Columbia* left the Folsom Street dock at the same time. Between them they carried 600 miners. Another 725 were aboard the *Golden Age* and 350 on the *Stockton* and *Sacramento*. The streets were empty. Montgomery Street "looked as deserted as on a Sabbath Day." The rush for Fraser River was on.[4]

The El Dorado of the Americas had challenged men's visions long before Spanish *Conquistadores* rode roughshod over native populations in search of the legendary Seven Cities of Gold, ever searching for the Goddess of Dawn—the Gilded One. In reality the Cities of Gold that Coronado sought were seven humble villages of sunbaked mud. He retreated southward to Mexico City in 1542 and the gold discovery had to wait another three centuries.

In the 1840s Swiss-born John Sutter was fashioning "New Helvetica" in California's Sacramento Valley, a fortified estate where he was self-appointed ruler, on a Mexican land grant of thousands of acres. He sent James Marshall to build a mill on the American River, forty miles northwest. There, in January 1848, Marshall discovered California gold.

Within days San Francisco and Monterey were deserted. Strikes on other streams like the Feather, Stanislaus, and Tulomne quickly followed. By the close of 1848 an estimated ten thousand men were washing gold on Sierra Nevada foothills' streams.[5]

The trek of the forty-niners the following year was something the like of which had never been seen. They came seeking riches, few intending to stay and make a home. Five years (hopefully less) was what they were prepared to offer in their search for money to set them up in business, pay off debts, or free the family home from mortgages. Tens of thousands ballooned the sleepy village of San Francisco into a teeming seafront metropolis, then raced upstream to spawn in gold-rich gravel towns such as Morman Island, Long Bar, Marysville, Volcano, Ophir, Ground Hog's Glory, Hangtown, Downieville, and Mariposa. On the Feather River seven miners panned 275 pounds of gold in two weeks. A claim near Yuba City yielded $75,000 in three months. Men became wealthy overnight, yet died as paupers.

As the creeks were ravaged and stripped of their wealth the men moved, upstream, south, north, or over the next mountain. The search continued and each year new strikes were made farther and farther afield.

When gold was found at Ophir, Australia, in 1851 California miners raced across a dateline following the rainbow's spectrum in search of the Golden Fleece. Then the Queen Charlotte Islands in British North

America gave false hope in 1852 and men sped north for a few wet, fruitless months. Gold fever had lodged in men's veins, a sickness that manifested itself in a restless, relentless urge to seek new streams.

By 1852 the population of California was over 250,000. Many were miners impatiently seeking and listening for a new strike. Their search spread north, up the Columbia to the Snake, John Day, and Salmon rivers and the Nez Percé mines, and east to the territories that later became the states of Arizona, Utah, Colorado, and Montana. Gold was there, but you had to *rush*, be first to lay claim, or end up shoveling gravel from a creek bed or mud from a shaft for someone else.

By late 1853 small samples of gold had begun to turn up at Hudson's Bay Company posts in Washington Territory and New Caledonia. The HBC, however, had an aversion to miners and settlers, farmers and ranchers—in fact anyone or anything that might upset the delicate balance of the fur trade. News of strikes by HBC servants were neither publicized nor encouraged, and the local Indians were urged to sell any gold they found to the Company. By late 1857 the HBC had accumulated approximately eight-hundred ounces at sixteen dollars per ounce, which it shipped south to the San Francisco mint aboard the SS *Otter*. Other freighters picked up the news. Gold rushes were generated not by discovery but by a sense of drama and excitement, and the gold shipment was catalyst enough. The word was out.[6]

James Douglas, HBC governor and governor of Vancouver's island colony, realized that miners would soon pour across the border and it would be necessary to establish British sovereignty over the claims but there was no legislative body, no person or body of authority. As the sole west coast British authority, Douglas, based on Australian example, assumed that role until such time as someone was appointed.

On December 28, 1857, he issued a proclamation that Fraser and Thompson River gold belonged to the Crown and announced a system of mining licenses to be instituted in February 1858, the fee to be twenty-two shillings, five dollars American. Anyone removing gold without authorization would "be prosecuted, both criminally and civilly, as the law allows."

He had moved just in time. By March 1858 newspapers were spreading the gold excitement in sensational front-page stories. The *Pioneer and Democrat* of Olympia, Washington, was one of the first. The March 5 issue headlined "Reported Gold Discoveries."

> We learn from Capt. Jones of the schooner Wild Pigeon ... that much excitement exists on Vancouver's Island, in consequences of the alleged discovery of rich gold deposits to the Northward—in the British Possessions ... located between Fort Hope and Thompson's River, and not to exceed four or five days journey from the mouth of Frazier's River. It is represented that persons with canoes can approach within ten or twelve miles of the diggings, although, in so doing, some pretty strong rapids will have to be encountered. ... Captain Jones has no doubt of the existence of rich gold fields. ... Nearly all the French and half-bloods on this Island had either started to this new El Dorado, or were preparing to start. Fort Langley is said to be almost entirely deserted;—the

Chief Factor having gone to the diggings with provisions, merchandise, etc., leaving but one clerk and a few Kanakas in charge. The company's blacksmith at Victoria is employed day and night in manufacturing picks, shovels, etc., for the mines.

A new strike, a new search, a new destination—another gold rush. By mid-summer ten thousand men had headed up the Fraser River. Between April 1 and November 30 over twenty-seven thousand men left San Francisco ports for British Columbia, plus those arriving from other ports or via inland routes. Miners had invaded New Caledonia whether the HBC liked it or not. Initially reluctant, traders turned from furs to mining supplies and raked in huge profits in a matter of weeks.[7]

The first rush came from the West Coast but soon news reached the eastern seaboard. After some hesitation the reports of a new goldfield were accepted. *Harper's Weekly* ran an inaccurate article and map in July 1858 entitled "The New El Dorado in British America":

... there seems to be little room for doubting the truth of the accounts which are extensively circulated about the recent gold discoveries on the shores of Frazer's and Thompson's rivers, in the territories of the Hudson's Bay Company....
It need hardly be said that the climate is severe. Lying many miles to the north of the most northerly civilized settlement on the continent, the future El Dorado will resemble more closely the northern gold-fields of the Ural Mountains than any that have been worked in California or Australia. The climate has seconded the efforts which the Hudson's Bay Company has made to preserve a monopoly of the country. There are no settlements on or near Frazer's River save the Company's trading posts....
It must be painful to the conventional Jonathan [American] to reflect that these new goldfields are in a foreign country ... the Hudson's Bay Company's hours are numbered; and their territories—with all the furs, and all the ice, and all the gold they contain—will soon pass under the control of the British Government. ... Nor can he hope ... that all that is worth having in the land of foreigner will soon pass under the talon of the American eagle. If Frazer's River be worth keeping, John Bull will keep it ... and if the miners go for annexation to the United States (as they naturally will, being mostly of American breed), he will spend millions rather than let them go. Ah! what a blunder it was to make such a fuss about "54'40" or fight," and then to be satisfied after all with 49'.

Similar sentiments were expressed by many American newspapers, a chorus of regret that the U.S.A.'s loss of the border dispute had cost her the new goldfields.

## Approaches

In 1846, the Oregon Boundary Treaty ratified the border between American- and British-claimed lands at the 49th parallel of latitude, with a jog around the end of Vancouver Island. The British region north of that line was referred to by the old fur-trade name of New Caledonia, with the exception of the new British colony of Vancouver Island, one of over one hundred colonies forming the British Empire.

The obstacle to settlement and development of central and western British North America was "The Governor and a Company of Adventurers of England Trading into Hudson's Bay Company" or simply "The Company"—as if there could be any other. Less respectful traders called it "Old Here Before Christ," referring to its existence since 1670 when his Majesty King Charles II had so graciously bestowed the charter granting exclusive trade to all lands draining into Hudson's Bay. For nearly two hundred years the HBC had controlled the vast region of Rupert's Land as the "true and absolute Lordes and Proprietors." In the 1700s a rival Canadian firm, the North West Company, began to reach its tentacles into the fringes of the HBC's trading area. In 1821 "The Company" absorbed the NWC, almost doubling its posts and trading area and securing a monopoly. As their influence spread west from the Canadian Shield to the Pacific Ocean the Company governors became rulers of all trade, and thereby the population.

By the mid-1800s there was growing dissatisfaction with the Company and solidifying opposition to its monopoly. Its trade license was up for renewal in 1859 and the Canadian government wanted more information than fur traders were willing to give about the interior territory. Knowledge of the interior regions of the British territories was scant. Was the land suitable for agriculture? Was travel practical? Where were the Rocky Mountain passes? Did the interior have gold deposits? In 1857 the Imperial Parliament responded to a petition of the Canadian Parliament and set up a parliamentary select committee on the HBC "to consider the state of those British possessions in America which are under the administration of the Hudson's Bay Company or over which they possess a license of trade."[8]

North of the 49th parallel there were only two established routes west: a northern water route following the various rivers and then crossing the Rockies via the Peace River; and the prairies' new-born Carlton Trail linking Fort Garry to Fort Edmonton that then crossed the Athabasca Pass to the Columbia River posts. Either took months to travel east to west. The alternative route to the West Coast was by sea, a voyage of long, uncomfortable weeks confined aboard a sailing ship.

To answer the questions of potential routes west and a hundred other queries two exploring expeditions were mounted, one by each concerned government. The British government sent Capt. John Palliser accompanied by geologist Dr. James Hector, Captain Sullivan, and Capt. Thomas Blakiston. They spent the years 1857, 1858, and 1859 exploring the trails and passes from the Red River to New Caledonia, assessing the resource potential. This British North American Exploring Expedition "produced voluminous reports and an accurate map of the area traversed."[9]

The Canadian-sponsored expedition was undertaken over two years. In 1857 the Canadian Red River Exploring Expedition crossed the Canadian Shield by the old fur-trade route to survey the valley of the Red River. Though George Gladman was the titular head, it was Henry Youle

Hind, a thirty-five-year-old professor of chemistry and geology at the University of Toronto, who provided the leadership. In 1858 Hind himself led the Assiniboine and Saskatchewan Exploring Expedition "to ascertain the practicability of establishing an emigrant route between Lake Superior and Selkirk Settlement, and to acquire some knowledge of the natural capabilities and resources of the Valley of the Red River and the Saskatchewan."[10]

Palliser's and Hind's preliminary reports appeared in the daily presses beside news of gold discoveries. Clearly an overland route would be a boon to westward expansion.

Until this time British North America, the vast expanses of wasteland and wilderness that stretched west from the settled banks of the St. Lawrence in the Canadas across the Rockies to the west coast fiords, was of little interest to the merchants, financiers, and politicians of Victorian England. Except for the minor income from furs it was the commerce of Asia and India that was bringing wealth to the motherland. Then the colonial secretary, Lord Stanley, resigned to take charge of the Governments of India Bill, a result of the Sepoy rebellion that would transfer British East India Company property to the Crown. Sir Edward Bulwer Lytton, a sometime novelist, succeeded him, prepared to take strong action. He saw this as the time to open free trade by ending HBC monopoly. Within three weeks he presented a bill establishing the Crown colony of New Caledonia, soon changed to British Columbia.[11]

The bill received royal assent August 2, 1858. The territory included all land from the Rockies to the Pacific and from the 49th parallel to the waters of the Findley and Nass rivers in the North. (The northern boundary would later be pushed north.) The Queen Charlotte Islands were to be included, but Vancouver Island would remain separate. James Douglas, after thirty-seven years with the HBC, was offered, and accepted, joint governorship of the two colonies.[12]

At the time of their emergence as colonies, Vancouver Island and British Columbia were isolated from contact with the outside world, for few had reason to go there. The white population of less than one thousand had only a superficial coating of civilization. There were no roads, no government except the HBC, no public institutions, and little communication. The outside world, which was marching to a different drummer, could be contacted only through the HBC steamers. Miners were rushing into a colony being wrenched out of a state of monopolistic feudalism under a factoral system transplanted from the highlands of Scotland. The colonies existed solely because of the fur trade and any exploration or trade routes worn into the landscape had the singular goal of increasing fur-trade profits.

The westward push from Canada and the pull of the goldfields was drawing British North America into a time of transition. The era of the independent fur trader and plainsman was ended as fashion shifted from clipped beaver-felt hats to silk hats. The HBC monopoly was dissolving and for the country-born people of Rupert's Land the end of a nomadic life closely linked with the buffalo was coming to a close. A time of limitlessness was giving way to one of boundaries. Frontiers of space and culture were being erased. Fraser River gold was the catalyst that brought all these parameters into focus.

The most common approach to the new goldfields was by sea, up the coast from the long-established port of San Francisco, a voyage lengthy and expensive. The California rush of 1849 had, however, shown a new possibility. By wagon, wheelbarrow, cart, on horseback and on foot thousands trekked west from the eastern seaboard and the more recently settled regions east of the Mississippi. Those who traveled this often dangerous, always difficult route were unique: they were overlanders.

Overland journeys prior to 1858 were confined to three major groups. First were the transcontinental journeys of explorers like Alexander MacKenzie in 1794, Simon Fraser in 1808, and Lewis and Clark in 1805. They were followed by the fur traders, who established the routes taken by the first "tourists"—artists such as Paul Kane and botanists such as David Douglas, who traveled under the sponsorship and care of the HBC. Third were the large transcontinental migrations that had taken place in the United States since 1840; the movements to California and Oregon made legendary by Indian attacks, blizzards, and deserts. James Sinclair's movement of Red River settlers to Oregon in 1841 and 1854 was similar in motive but had little effect on the whole. The explorers had opened the country for exploitation; the "tourists" had studied and recorded its vegetation, geology, and peoples; the third group would bring commerce, settle, and make it home.

# The Expansionists

When news of British Columbia gold filtered east to the major papers many saw wealth not in terms of gold but in terms of the commerce and trade that would develop as an adjunct. Nowhere was this idea more prevalent and more aggressively pursued than by the businessmen and merchants of St. Paul in the newly formed state of Minnesota. Their frontier optimism sprang from need as well as desire, for like the rest of the country Minnesota was prostrated by the financial panic and depression of 1857.

Minnesota expansionists were not so naive as to consider annexing British Columbia, but they did see an east-west route to the mines as a poultice drawing people and business to the state. If an inexpensive, safe, and reliable route could be found logically linking the Mississippi and Fraser River then St. Paul would become the supply and jumping-off point to the Fraser gold rush as Independence, Missouri, had been to the Great Migration to Oregon. Should gold discoveries on the Fraser begin a similar movement, St. Paul merchants would be wealthy.

Already St. Paul had lines of communication east and south. In 1854 a rail line was completed to the Mississippi in Illinois; sternwheelers plied the Mississippi south to many ports; the opening of the Sault Ste. Marie Canal had made direct ship passage to the head of the Great Lakes possible; and a telegraph service was on its way. For links west the federal government had explored several possible railway routes since 1853, and any wagon roads west would serve as the ax mark where the iron-horse wedge would be driven. A Fraser link, however, would likely take a northern route. Here St. Paul had the advantage of already being at a trail head because of the foresight of a Britisher half a century before.[13]

In 1812 the Earl of Selkirk, Thomas Douglas, had begun a settlement of Scots, crofters removed from the land during the Highland Clearances, five hundred miles north of St. Paul in Rupert's Land. Douglas observed, "The great facilities which nature offers, for a commercial intercourse between the country which I propose to establish, and the American settlements ... from whence our people might draw their supplies of many articles, by way of the Mississippi, and River St. Peters, with greater facility than from Canada or from Europe."[14]

Selkirk's predictions were indeed visionary. Despite the HBC's initial reluctance to develop a transport link through the U.S.A., important commerce now rolled along the cart trails between Fort Garry and St. Paul.

In the beginning these trails had a southern orientation as their importance lay in linking the Red River settlement to the Mississippi valley civilization. This orientation shifted during the 1850s and the tracks worn into the prairie soil pointed the direction to fur-trade riches of the North, new lands for settlement, and routes to the western ocean. The HBC changed their supply routes as Selkirk had seen they would. Trains of hundreds of carts brought goods from St. Paul, rather than via the arduous canoe and York boat trip across the Canadian Shield or through Hudson Bay and York Factory. As furs were shipped south St. Paul grew to be second only to St. Louis as the largest fur market in the United States.

By the late 1850s a variety of trails crisscrossed the St. Peters (now Minnesota) River, Mississippi, and Red River valleys, all trending toward the north. The St. Paul trail head was more than a jumping-off point, it was an end and a beginning. An end to civilization; a beginning of wilderness.[15]

Fraser gold "revived to the verge of practical solution the favorite Minnesota project of a northern emigrant route to the Pacific," wrote Earle S. Goodrich, St. Paul *Pioneer and Democrat* editor. Businessmen took the lead in finding this solution and convened the "Fraser River Convention" on July 1, 1858, "for the purpose of considering the best measures for establishing an immigrant route through the Red River and Saskatchewan Valleys, to the Gold Mines on Fraser and Thompson Rivers in British Oregon." Col. William H. Nobles was appointed chairman and Joseph A. Wheelock elected secretary.[16]

Nobles was forty-two years old and had been lobbying government and business for a northern wagon road for several years. A native of New York, he was a skilled machinist who after serving as an officer with General Houston in the Mexican-American War came to the small village of St. Paul in 1848. On Robert Street he opened the first blacksmith and wagon shop and built Minnesota's first wagon. In the early 1850s he discovered the Nobles cutoff through the Sierras—a pass still bearing his name. Returning to Minnesota he and a group of land speculators promoted a western route, obtaining fifty thousand dollars from Congress for a road from Fort Ridgely in central Minnesota across the Missouri to the overland roads in present-day Wyoming. After some grading, surveying, and construction of river fords the project ground to a halt in 1858 under political and financial problems. In the meantime Nobles had been elected a member of the House of the fifth territorial legislature in 1855 and the seventh in 1857. Western gold gave new life to Nobles's proposals—a renewed opportunity to promote his ideas.[17]

Nobles found ready support in James Wickes Taylor, a thirty-nine-year-old lawyer and journalist who moved from New York to Minnesota in 1856. His passion was the North West and he became a prolific writer and lecturer on the subject. Taylor was appointed special agent of the treasury department, charged with the "investigation of reciprocal relations of trade and transportation between the United States and Canada." Overland routes were part of his study mandate.[18]

Joseph A. Wheelock was a journalist, younger than the others at twenty-eight, and had been described as "an invalid." He was born in Canada, at Bridgtown, Nova Scotia in 1831; and came to Minnesota in 1850 to work as a sutler's store clerk at Fort Snelling across the river from St. Paul. In 1856 he became editor of the *Real Estate and Financial Advertiser*. In his many years as an editor he was known as a straight shooter. In June 1858 he closed the *Advertiser* and joined the staff of the St. Paul *Pioneer and Democrat*.[19]

The second convention meeting was held in Fuller House on Wednesday, July 7, at 8:00 P.M.; Nobles chairing. Taylor presented an over-long committee report on the overland route and the natural features of the region connected with it. A second report estimated the supplies needed by an exploratory party of ten for a journey to Fraser River, assuming six months' supply of food:

| | |
|---|---:|
| 10 barrels of flour cost $4 per barrel | $ 40 |
| 5 barrels of pork cost $18 per barrel | 90 |
| 450 pounds sugar | 54 |
| 40 pounds tea, cost $.60 per pound | 24 |
| Sundries | 100 |
| Powder and Lead | 100 |
| 10 pairs of blankets | 100 |
| Tools and implements | 100 |
| Teams and Vehicles | 1000 |
| Total | $1608 |

Both reports were accepted and Martin McLeod then presented resolutions that would affect overland journeys for the next five years.

Resolved. That the overland emigration to British Oregon, attracted by the gold discovery on Frazer and Thompson Rivers, will find Minnesota the most desirable point of departure and supply for the following reasons.

First. The emigrant has a choice of three routes, far more easy and direct than any south of St. Paul, to wit: (1) By Pembina, Carlton, Edmonton, Athabasca Portage and the Boat Encampment of the Columbia. (2) By the South Saskatchewan and the Kootanais Pass to Fort Colville; and (3) By Gov. Stevens' well known Rail Road route on the American side of the international Boundary.

Second. Either of these routes has more water, timber, game and is less difficult than those which start from the Missouri River.

Third. Supplies of all kinds are very cheap in Minnesota.

Fourth. Faithful guides and attendants are easily obtained on our frontiers, and in the territory of the Hudson's Bay Company.

Fifth. There is no danger of molestation from Indians on these Northern routes.

Resolved. That the citizens of Minnesota will join heartily with the people of Canada in the policy of colonizing the Western districts of British America, which is about to be established; and that relations of reciprocal trade with the United States, if not now existing, should be extended over that region of North America.

Resolved. That our citizens be urged to encourage the formation of parties over either of the routes above designated.

These resolutions were unanimously adopted and the meeting adjourned to Saturday, July 10.[20]

The third meeting dealt with routes, presenting the advantages and disadvantages of each. McLeod concluded that the best route for the average party was the northern Carlton Trail, estimated to take between sixty and seventy-five days.

Col. John H. Stevens suggested that existing rivers made steamboat navigation to Edmonton possible and practical. "This was surely the most economical and the fastest transportation presently available," he thought, and "it would open up the area to settlement, agriculture and general commerce."

Gov. Alexander Ramsey advocated American settlement of the fledgling colony: "This is a trade which belongs to us in Minnesota. It cannot be diverted from us."

Taylor agreed that the northern Saskatchewan route was a good one but thought that a "route from Pembina, far more to the South, has every advantage of the route above named, except that a party might be annoyed by the Blackfeet Indians; and there are no trading posts as a resource against unforeseen accidents." His advice, and comments on being "annoyed by Indians," would be regretted by at least one 1858 overland party.[21]

Taylor was suggesting the Kootanais Pass, later termed the North Kootenay, British Kootenay, or Railway Pass, based on information from Jamey Jock Bird, a plainsman who had lived with the Blackfeet for many years.[22] Bird knew the Bears River, Chief Mountain, Bad Back Fat, Medicine Rock, and Crows Lodge passes.[23]

"The Medicine Rock is the best pass," he figured.

From St. Paul, let a good strong party go straight across the plain to the upper head of Cypress Mountain—then rather northwest, west more than north, about eight days travel—then enter the mountains, and, with moderate travelling, four days reach the Columbia River.
Medicine Rock pass comes out on Tobacco Plains, near the border. . . .
Medicine Rock must be the best, for the Kootanais prefer it—travel it in winter. They carry packs on their backs, with snow shoes and kill buffalo on eastern plains. Then, when they have made their provisions they go back on the Crow's Lodge route. . . . Medicine Rock or Kootanais Pass had been passed by me in one day's ride on horseback. . . . I estimate the distance as about 70 miles—3 or 4 days journey on foot.[24]

Taylor edited Bird's cryptic notes in proposing the North Kootenay Pass route:

This whole route is very favorable, consisting of an extensive prairie, or buffalo range, and easily travelled by carts. The pass thus reached known as the Kootanais Pass, rises gradually and is only three days' walk, one day on horseback, to the border of the Kootanais, McGillivray or Flatbow river now the Kootenay River. . . . Beyond the pass the route to Fort Colville . . . is circuitous and difficult, so much so, as to add 500 miles before reaching the gold district. If a more direct connection should be discovered, this route might be found more advantageous than any other.

A fourth meeting was held one week later. After a brief recap of the previous proceedings, various resolutions were passed, and it was resolved "that Martin McLeod be requested to organize and conduct a party of ten men for the purpose of exploring the best route from Minnesota to the Fraser River Gold District, through the valleys of the Red River of the North and the Saskatchewan." A committee was to raise the funds needed through subscriptions from individuals, though the State and City of St. Paul were asked to guarantee any money that might be put up.

The St. Paul meetings did not go unnoticed in the eastern press. The *New York Herald* published a full report of the meetings and said, "The opening of these routes will ensure in a greater degree to the English than to us; but with the reciprocal feeling existing between the two countries, we shall have our share of the trade, and perhaps, with the superior energy and activity of our frontier settlers, a trifle more. At any rate the people of St. Paul are bound not to be the last in the field."

The *N.Y. Journal of Commerce* remarked on the funds that had already been collected and concluded that "the whole matter seems now to be in shape, that it is probable that all the plans and expectations of the originators of the enterprise will soon be realized."

By July 25 the *Pioneer and Democrat* reported: "Several parties have been formed at considerable expense of preparation, in the different interior towns of this State, for the purpose of going overland to the gold mines of Fraser River."

The Minnesotan expansionist-led rush to the gold mines of Fraser River in British North America had begun. The first overlanders were on their way.

# Chapter Two

## The Men of Faribault

St. Paul, Minnesota, was not the only crucible of gold excitement galvanizing men to action. While Nobles and his cohorts met in St. Paul with lengthy oratory and laborious resolutions, men in Mankato, Woodsville, Shakopee, Hastings, and Faribault, eastern Canada, and in the Atlantic settlements of New Brunswick were becoming caught in the seductive web of potential riches spun over the continent. By the time the bitter winds of winter swept the plains and the Mississippi was blockaded by ice, seven parties of Fraser River–bound gold-seekers, totalling eighty-six men, would have passed through frontier St. Paul and headed north on the Red River trails.[1]

South of St. Paul, sixty-five miles west of the Mississippi, lay the prairie town of Faribault. The town's land office was booming with speculators engaged in legal and illegal preemptions of lands recently opened. But the land grab did not attract everyone's attention. A party of determined, experienced plains travelers was forming to seek Fraser River gold. They were destined to become one of the most important overland companies, the only party to cross the Rocky Mountains in 1858.[2]

This Faribault party of nine divided into two messes, a common practice that eased tenting and cooking chores. Edward (Ned) Hind, a saddler and California forty-niner, petulant and irascible, was the leader of one mess that included J. S. Houck, Jim Ellhi Smith, a correspondent for the *New York Times*, and John W. Jones. The second mess was led by William Amesbury and included Ira Emihiser, "Dutch" John Schaeffter, John R. Sanford, and John Palmer.[3]

The men of Faribault were a mixed lot. Palmer was described by John

Jones as a "queer specimen of humanity. A native of England, he had long served as jockey at races, footman and servant in general to some corpulent and gouty beef-eater."

John W. Jones was the primary journalist for the Faribault party. More complete than most, Jones's journal offers the greatest insight of all and presents a distinctively American viewpoint. He was born in Pleasant Grove, Iowa, in 1831, and in 1858 was a clerk in the receiver's office in Chatfield, Minnesota, where he was known by the nickname Taffy.[4]

Jones had a gift for calligraphy, often decorating scrolls for his Masonic lodge. But if he was a clerk by trade and calligrapher in skill he was an adventurer and plainsman by choice. His journal reflects a man who paid attention to detail, noticing and recording the color of ptarmigan's feet; a sensitive man who picked mountain bluebells to press in his diary and who was moved to tears by the kindness of Indian women; a man in love with life, enjoying the companionship of good friends and remarking on the beauty of Métis girls and Indian women. He also had a tragic love for the bottle. Jones felt comfortable with himself. He knew who he was, believed there were rules to life's game, and had little regard for those who broke them. It is fortunate that it was this man who chose to keep a journal of the Faribault company's trek "Across the Plains."[5]

The small, jubilant party left Faribault on Tuesday, July 20, 1858. In the waning afternoon sun they bid relatives and friends goodbye. It was a short day. Six miles later Camp No. 1 was pitched. While they were cooking their first dinner friends arrived, reluctant to bid adieu.

The dozen or so guests, friends, town merchants, and relatives had, with admirable forethought, brought a full supply of liquids, from sparkling champagne to tangle-legged whiskey. "We soon commenced to attack the enemy, nor did we cease till the grey tint of morn appeared in the horizon." It was a fine farewell for comrades who in many cases would never tip a glass together again. Hind's and Houck's two brothers, who were amongst the revelers, decided to ride as far as St. Paul.

Two days later the party arrived at St. Paul's Franklin House and, as the merchants had hoped, here completed their outfit. As the first of many hoped-for migrants, their arrival was noted in the town papers. On Saturday, Jones dashed off letters to friends then packed up and headed north, camping near St. Anthony, a mill town just north of St. Paul at the falls made famous in Longfellow's epic poem *Hiawatha*. Here they had a last drink with their Faribault relatives, who left with shouts of "Ho! for the goldfields! Don't forget to write," and "Watch out for the Elephant!"

Also camped at St. Anthony was another party bound for the Fraser. An inauspicious party off to a halting start. The July meeting in Minnesota had made Indian trader McLeod responsible for leading a party of ten men, financed by the merchants of the state, in the exploration of a route west. The idea had been greeted with enthusiasm; the prospect of profits was anticipated with robust cries of "Westward Ho!" Action and commitment, though, were reluctant and slothful. McLeod's success in raising a party was abysmal. He backed out of leadership. Only three men were heading west on behalf of the expansionists: Charles Goodrich, W. Ellis Smith, and George C. Burnham.

Little is known of Goodrich, though he and other members were described as being "well fitted by experience and natural qualifications." W. Ellis Smith, C.E. (not to be confused with Jim Ellhi Smith of the Faribault party), an engineer and surveyor, had been on previous Nobles expeditions and made at least one later trip west. He was a "big-hearted man strongly addicted to gazing at the sun and moon through a long necked bottle," and would have enjoyed the Faribault farewell festivities. Burnham was a returned California miner. Amongst their equipment was an odometer to measure mileages as an aid to future travelers. It was believed that this would be the first accurate measurement of the route.[6]

The St. Paul party was too small to tackle safely a cross-country journey and likely hoped to join up with other adventurers or a Red River cart brigade. Fortunately on Sunday, July 25, they linked up with the men of Faribault, making a total of twelve in the group. They continued north up the Mississippi's east bank. Often eager young men, enthused with the vision of heading west, approached asking for permission to join, but each was turned down.

At Anoka, a village of three hundred inhabitants, they stopped at a match factory to purchase a large supply, and near the villages of Orono and Elk Town, Jones and Jim Smith were very nearly caught by an irate farmer while "foraging a potato patch." Wednesday the twenty-eighth was a noteworthy date—as they approached the town of St. Cloud the last of the wine disappeared.

On July 30, northwest of St. Joseph (not the St. Joseph on Pembina River), where some "thieving heartless Dutchman" had stolen their frying pan, and north of Richmond, where they purchased a new one, they arrived at Lake George. A northbound Red River cart brigade was encamped, awaiting reinforcement. Sioux had been harassing settlers and stealing stock near Pembina and St. Joseph, and rumors reported four hundred waiting in ambush.

Jones remarked on the carts as every early journalist did. Similar carts had been in use since 1801 when North West Company trader Alexander Henry's men constructed a solid-wheel cart modeled after the two-wheeled charettes of Quebec. Modifications resulted in the present cart: four- to six-foot-high spoked wheels, the wide rim offset from the hub, an open box set on the axle between the wheels, and two long tongues between which an ox was yoked. Each cart could carry nine hundred pounds, the equivalent load of three horses, and the wide rims prevented the cart from sinking in the prairie soil. The remarkable feature was the absence of any metal, the construction being entirely of native wood and therefore easily repaired along the trail. The wheels were bound with green hide, shagganappi, that was replaced as it wore out. While not as majestic and romantic as the southern Conestoga, the cart was inexpensive. Depending on demand, the price was about ten dollars, compared with several hundred for the Conestoga. When horse-drawn, the animals were usually hitched in tandem, one in front of the other. Oxen, the more common stock, were yoked side by side. Should there be only one draft animal, the driver would walk.

The carts were cheap, efficient, convenient—and noisy. "Hellish, horrifying and nerve-wracking," one traveler wrote. "The creaking of the wheels is indescribable. It can be heard six miles away. It is like no other sound you ever heard in all your life and it makes your blood run cold." In the thirty to forty days it took the average train to travel from St. Paul to Fort Garry the unlubricated axles (for grease attracted dust) could drive men to distraction.

It was a beautiful land the men were traveling. Small lakes surrounded by oaks and rolling grass-covered hills lent a feeling of serenity, a feeling that was not to last.

The country continued in a similar vein for many miles along the Middle Trail. They angled northwest across a wide prairie dotted with pothole lakes, each ringed with gnarled oak, willow, and cattails. They were attractive, pretty one might say, and they reminded the men of the girls they left behind. With little hope the names would be perpetuated, two were named Charlotte and Mary, for "dear Ones." These small lakes were the headwaters of rivers like the Little Chippewa, Rapid, and Pomme-de-Terre, all of which had to be forded. The fords, along with showers that broke the usually clear skies, kept the men wet. At Otter Trail River the crossing was three feet deep and eighty feet wide. The travelers encountered a few problems in the soft and miry bottom, but crossed and camped on the north shore on August 3.[7]

The next stage was the negotiation of twenty-five miles of woodless, waterless prairie, part of the ancient bottom of prehistoric Lake Agassiz, evidenced by the trail being thickly covered by small shells in some places. The temperature was one hundred degrees Fahrenheit, and humid; a wet sticky day when the men longed for another river crossing to cool off. By three o'clock they reached the Red River crossing below Graham's Point. As Jones noted in his journal, this point was a major landmark on the Red River Trail. Here they met a man from Breckenridge who had brought goods down in a bateau. Jones's party decided to lighten their horses' loads, purchased the boat for thirty dollars, and chose the two Smiths, Sanford, and Burnham as crew. The idea was for the boat to freight the bulk of their provisions, twenty-five hundred pounds, downstream to Pembina.

"Crossed the river at eve and camped on its banks. Having now come to the heart of the Indian country, we concluded to set night watches, first from dark till 12 m. the second from 12 m. to daylight." Near midnight the guard aroused them with cries of alarm. He pointed out a fire at Graham's Point. Each man supposed it to be the signal for an attack "by the thieving red dogs." They broke out their guns and loaded, ready for action. Nothing happened. After several minutes someone suggested that perhaps it was the campfire of the bateau man from Breckenridge. They agreed, but their fears were not dispelled enough to allow sound sleep. It was a warning. From here to the goldfields they would have to be wary of Indians, usually posting a watch, always cautious of scouting parties, taking care to have rifles and pistols at the ready. For men like Hind who had seen action it would be second nature. To others the readiness was an experience in itself. For the next several weeks they would face the constant threat of attack and death.

Over the next few days they were attacked, both men and animals suffering sorely, but the enemy were more numerous and more difficult to combat than Sioux, Chippewa, or Blackfeet. Their enemy were of the tribes *Anophelini* and *Culicini*. Jones's journal, Thursday, August 5:

During my travels throughout the different sections of the States, and especially in the swamps of Louisiana and other southern states, I harbored the idea that I had seen a few mosquitoes, but there is no comparison between the two. The air was perfectly darkened with them, our poor animals were perfectly frantic, and in spite of the continual switching with a brush they still clung to us with annoying tenacity, for several miles, and in fact, we travelled till about eleven at night in order to get away from the mosquitoes empire. Our animals feeling the effect of hard driving, we concluded to stop, and cut up our tents and cover them with it. Camped on the prairie—grass very tall, built smudges with dry grass. The animals laid down, and in a measure relieved themselves of the pestilence, as we found that the mosquitoes did not come very low down. I never, in the whole course of my life saw any species of insects that were so bloodthirsty as these rapacious devils were.

The party continued their northward journey, the steady twenty-five-mile-per-day trek broken by a stampede of their stock one morning and losing the trail a few times. In several places wood was scarce and they used the plainsman's fuel—buffalo chips—the dried dung left scattered across the plains by the vast herds of bison. When they did see their first buffalo their reaction was that of every prairie traveler who believed the herds would go on forever. Buffalo were to shoot.

Aug. 9th, Monday—Soon after we started this morning, one of our party happening to look ahead saw a black object, what he thought at first a small clump of bushes, but on watching he saw it move. Soon it became apparent it must be a buffalo. Houck and Hinds immediately took their guns, mounted their horses, and gave pursuit, the chase was exciting. Houck upon coming within range of his unerring rifle, dismounted and fired, and as he fired his horse left him frightened. The bull was seen to stagger, and at this moment, Hinds came up and let him have the contents of both barrels in a ticklish part, which brought him to the ground.

We soon dispatched him, and replenished our larder with the most choice portions, leaving the rest to the wolves and vultures. We afterwards learned that the Red River train which preceded us killed a drove of seventy buffalo at this place, and he was evidently the only one that escaped.

Minor adventures continued. Men and horses were persistently plagued by mosquitoes, horseflies, and buffalo gnats; biting, drawing blood, and raising welts and open sores on man and beast alike. There were streams and swamps to be crossed, including one marsh over seven miles in width with water lapping at the wagon beds. Prairie chickens and ducks added to their hunting recreation and ultimately the food pot.

One night Dutch John became particularly annoyed and pestered by mosquitoes and in an effort to find relief at the risk of asphyxiation kept piling grass on the smudge fires. Busy swatting and whisking flies he let the fire spark to the dried grass of the campsite and before he could stamp it out a fire raged. While some men moved the stock and provisions to a safer area the others grabbed water and blankets and with some difficulty beat the flames out, all the while afraid of another stampede of stock.

On Friday, August 13, just before noon, they ferried across the Pembina River and were welcomed into the shanty border town of Pembina by U.S. customs agent James McFetridge. It was an inauspicious town: three mud huts, a half-dozen log shanties, the American Fur Company post, and on the north side of the river the HBC's stockaded Fort Pembina.

The settlement had begun in 1793 as Grant's House, a Canadian Independent post in opposition to the HBC. Five years later the North West Company built a second post and then around 1812-14 Métis began drifting into the area from the Red River colony. Not until settlement was well established half a century later, in 1845, did the Company open Pembina Post. The HBC move was in part a response to severe competition that developed when Norman Kittson challenged the HBC's monopoly in 1844 by opening an American Fur Company post. In 1852, however, severe flooding caused settlers to begin moving, seeking drier land. They moved west thirty miles and founded St. Joseph (now Walhalla, North Dakota) on the north bank of the Pembina River in the Pembina Hills. The Catholic mission established at Pembina by Father George-Antoine Bellecourt in 1848 also moved and Pembina became something of a ghost town.[8]

Jones's party arrived to a bustle of activity. Surveyors were laying out a new town in anticipation of a railroad. The previous year the Minnesota legislature had approved the construction of several railways, with the usual monetary grants and colossal land grants. The Minnesota and Pacific was to run a line to St. Vincent, on the opposite shore of the Red River. Although ten years was allowed for completion under the act, Pembina settlers were optimistic the railroad would arrive well in advance.[9]

Joseph Rolette Jr. watched the development with interest. Son of the legendary "King" Rolette, Rolette Jr. had been instrumental in establishing the Red River routes to draw furs south. He had been in charge of Pembina Post, burned the HBC post to the ground, been elected a territorial council representative, and become independently wealthy by the time he was thirty-seven. He lost everything in the 1857 financial panic. Attempting a comeback he agreed to supply the St. Paul party. Neither he nor the supplies had arrived. Nor had the Faribault bateau party. At a good campsite, the land contingent settled in to wait, while Hind and McFetridge rode to Fort Garry to visit Hind's cousin.[10]

Meanwhile progress on the river was slow and tedious. On August 5 the party of W. Ellis Smith, Jim E. Smith, Sanford, and Burnham had pushed off from Graham's Point for the long downstream drift to Pembina. They soon realized this was a tiring, boring way to travel. The current was only three miles per hour. With a distance of four to five times that of the trail they had to keep moving twenty-two monotonous, bug-tortured hours per day. It took seventy-eight hours to reach the mouth of the Sheyenne River, a distance of fifty land miles. Engineer W. Ellis Smith reckoned that this was the effective head of navigation for the Red River, and he was not far out, for the mouth of the Buffalo River just a few miles downstream later became Georgetown, the site of sternwheeler construction.[11]

The tension of the tedious trip was increased by the fear of Sioux catching them in the bateau, unable to escape. When a few days later they passed what the old traders had called La Grande Fourche, where Red Lake River flows in from the east (now Grand Forks, North Dakota), their fear increased. The fur post had recently been attacked and burned.[12]

Now more aware of the Sioux, Smith's group drifted on, the countryside and possible attack beyond the ten-foot-high bank hidden by a fringe of oak, maple, and willow leaning over to form a tunnel, casting ominous shadows in the summer moonlight. Only at their infrequent stops could they stretch cramped legs and make a hot meal. For every mile forward they sidled a mile east, then west, in a sinuous, frustrating voyage.

Boredom was relieved by short walks along the banks and on one such solitary occasion Jim Smith wandered ahead of the boat, planning to meet it downstream. He cut across the meander bends, through groves of tall trees and grass, flushing grouse and ducks and sending squirrels scurrying in the acorns of the oaks. Lost in reflection and rumination, time passed him by until, weary and winded, he sat on the bank to await the boat. A few minutes passed, then an hour, then two. The boat did not appear. Perhaps it had traveled faster than he expected. He set off downstream at a fast pace. Frustrated by the tortuous progress of the river he again cut across the sweeping meander bends, crashing through thickets and tangles, until surprised and chagrined at his own incompetence, he had to admit he was lost. With acceptance came solution. South was the sun and east the river. So with the sun on his right he should eventually reach the muddy flow. And soon he did. He decided to stick to the river's bank. He would not be lost, he just wouldn't know where he was. Night came. His moccasins wore out, so he went barefoot, sharp grass and brambles tearing at his feet. He flushed birds but with no gun he went hungry. Another night and another day passed. Three days and nights of walking brought him finally, torn and tattered, to the Pembina River and the camp of the advance land party. He had beat the boat. Jones wrote: "He was a miserable looking specimen of the genus homo when he made his entre into our camp. His feet were badly lacerated. He soon had a meal cooked for him by Mrs. Rolette, and the way he made the viands disappear was truly astonishing to the natives. He never strayed away from the party after that."

The boat party arrived one day after Smith, early on August 16, cursing "like devils at the tediousness of the voyage and the crookedness of the river." Despite troubles with water only a foot deep and numerous sandbars and riffles, W. Ellis Smith felt that downstream of the Sheyenne River steamers of the Minnesota River class could be used most of the season and from Grand Forks the larger Mississippi steamboats such as the *Grey Eagle* or *Milwaukee*. Their downriver voyage had taken eleven and half days, traveling twenty-two hours per day, a total of 350 hours, over 630 miles, compared to the trail length of approximately 250 miles.

Monday, August 16, was spent unloading the bateau and reloading the wagons. They traded one American horse for an Indian pony and Red River cart and then headed to the HBC post for a final drink. The Chippewa Indians who were waiting outside in hopes of stealing the rum were as disappointed as the overlanders. The rum keg was dry.

Rolette had still not arrived with the remainder of the St. Paul party's outfit so it was decided that the original Faribault party of nine would press on alone. Goodrich, W. Ellis Smith, and Burnham would have to wait in Pembina, hoping that their supplies would arrive in time for them to cross the mountains before winter.

On Tuesday they crossed the Scratching River, twenty-six miles downstream, on a ferry built by Adam Klyne (the mail carrier between the river settlements and Pembina), who had built it and a tavern of sorts the year before. He was one of a growing number of settlement people farming along the Red and Assiniboine rivers.[13]

On the stretch of road entering the sprawling Selkirk settlement, poor Jim Smith, who had been lost on the river, became the object of much hilarity. He and Jones were lagging behind, taking their time and Smith decided to take off his pants and mend them while he rode. Jones's horse became stuck in a small slough and no matter what he could not make the "obstinate and obstreperous beast" move. He hollered at Smith to give him a hand. They unharnessed the Indian pony and took him to dry land, then tied long ropes back to the cart, easily pulling it out. As the cart reached solid ground Jim Smith's team bolted down the trail at a dead gallop. Smith took off after them, pantless, his shirt flapping in the breeze while Jones goaded "old obstinacy" into a gallop after the pair. For half a mile Smith ran and Jones galloped. Then, rounding a corner they found the team being brought back by another traveler. Smith, embarrassed and frantic, donned his pants "and vented his wrath on the poor beast in such a manner that he soon got tired. I think, however," Jones wrote, "that it taught the horse a lesson, for he was never known to run away after." Such was the party's entry into the Red River settlement on August 19, 1858.

## The Red River Settlement

John W. Jones and the Faribault men arrived at the Red River settlement during a time of transition, when the two-hundred-year-old fur trade was giving way to agriculture and settlement. The HBC's charter had only been renewed in the northern forest. Vancouver Island and British Columbia were to become colonies; the North West was to be left open for annexation by Canada. The monopoly was losing its hold, the fingers of trade pried loose by aggressive freetraders. Difficulties and arguments between the Métis and the HBC had caused many of the Métis to move to the U.S.A. Some even considered inviting the U.S. to annex the valley of the Red River.

The settlement at the forks had been in existence for close to fifty years and the population around the two rivers had increased, according to the census of 1856, to 6,523. Time and people had changed the prairie and the area had an air of permanency about it. Scattered along the river were nine missions or churches with congregations numbering up to 1,500. On the east side of the Red stood the Roman Catholic cathedral and the warehouses of the American merchants, surrounded by land now devoid of timber or bush but patterned with fields. Houses and farm buildings, usually white, dotted the landscape, breaking the otherwise static horizon. Windmills rose high above the rich land, their whirling arms kept in motion by the ever-present wind that swirled through the buildings and around the walls of the fort. The fields and plots lay carefully divided by fences. Vertical crop lines stretched from house to river, slashes of brown, gold, yellow, and black delineating the long, narrow river lots reminiscent of the farms of eastern Canada that gave each landholder access to water, field, and bush lot.[14]

Two rope ferries crossed the Red and Assiniboine rivers, that over the latter landing on the bank below the imposing structure of Fort Garry. Forts of varying parentage, size, and construction had been located near the forks of the Red and Assiniboine since La Vérendrye built Fort Rouge here in 1738.

Disastrous floods in 1826 damaged the HBC's Fort Garry to such an extent that Governor Simpson decided to establish a new post miles down river, the Stone Fort or Lower Fort Garry. His choice of location, far from the established trade around the older fort, was purported to be because of the new site's high position and an abundance of wood and stone. However, he was unsure enough about the move that he did not report his plans to the Company directors until construction was well under way. Simpson's real reason for moving the fort may have been more subtle. The governor was bringing his eighteen-year-old cousin and bride, Frances, from England. The gracious new surroundings would suit her sensibilities better, and more importantly, keep her distant from his mistresses and illegitimate offspring, his "commodities" and "bits of brown" as he called them.[15]

Despite Simpson's wishes, trade did not move to the new stone fort. Business was a failure and the move left the gate open for other traders at the forks. So in 1835 the rebuilding of Upper Fort Garry on the north side of the Assiniboine and west of the Red was given top priority. By 1837 Alexander Christie, the governor of Assiniboia, had completed the work. The fort soon became the focal point of the settlement.

Jones, an observant traveler, fortunately recorded his impressions and meetings with people, and despite biases gives a rich feeling for Fort Garry in 1858:

Mr. McTavish, the chief Factor of the District and master of the Fort, upon learning of our arrival, came to us to extend his hospitality and invite us to take quarters at the Fort. Upon meeting us he enquired who was the gentleman of the party, entertaining I have no doubt of English customs, and the idea that there was but one gentleman, and the rest were servants. Hinds informed him that we were all gentlemen—it proved too obtuse for him—he then enquired how many servants we had with us, and the reply was that we had no servants, that every one had to serve for himself. This also proved to be rather curious to him, as he remarked that, when we travel we are always accompanied by servants. . . .

For Geary [Garry] is situated at the junction of the Assiniboin and Red Rivers, and holds a commanding position. The barracks is surrounded with a stone wall, with two towers mounted with guns of small calibre at each corner. It was occupied by two companies of the Canadian Royal Rifles, and the Hudson's Bay Company's attaches. . . . Among the soldiers, we noticed three or four veterans wearing the Victoria medal [cross] upon their left breast for their gallant conduct in the Crimean War [1854-1856].

The Hudson Bay Stores, warehouses, Chief Factors residence, officers and privates quarters, magazines, and everything pertaining thereto, are all enclosed within this fortification. On the inside and near the top of the wall, are placed sentry walks. The parade grounds is very small, not being room enough for the two companies to make their evolutions with ease. I should judge that these poor soldiers faces [fare is?] pretty hard, as they complained considerably to us. We saw two or three groups outside of the fort, cooking their dinner and on examining the "flesh pots," we could observe nothing but fresh water herrings, or hickory shads as some term them, but there [here?] they are known as "silver sides" and "gold eyes." They are small, very bony and contain but little meat.

The Captain commanding, introduced himself to us—(his name [Major George Seton] has slipped my memory)—during our conversation and the top of conversation was the British and American armies, during which he uttered the treasonable wish that if he held the same position in the American army, he would be perfectly satisfied and contented with his lot.

Major Seton and his force of 120 officers and men of the Royal Canadian Rifles had been sent to Fort Garry "to serve as a counterpose to the growing influence of the United States in the North-West Territory," after an American army detachment under Col. C. F. Smith came to Pembina in 1856 and prohibited British Territory halfbreeds from hunting south of the border, a tradition that had lasted several generations and was important to their way of life. One month after Jones and the Faribault party left Fort Garry, a minor incident over the officers' mess brought Seton to his breaking point. He "resigned by sale of his Commission," September 24, 1858, and a month later he was on his way back to England. The troops had to wait much longer for their relief. Not until 1861 were they recalled to Quebec.[16]

While Seton stewed inside the stone walls of the fort, Jones and company busied themselves in the hot August sun gathering supplies for their journey across the plains to the Rockies. They spoke to everyone they could, asking about trails, passes, routes, distances. "They have no conception of miles," Jones wrote, "they measure by the day, or if it is less than a day, it is then so many 'smokes' from point to point; from this we would judge they have stated times for smoking." It had long been the practice of the fur trade to measure distance by "smokes," or more commonly "pipes." Voyageurs smoked almost continuously while paddling and stopped for five to ten minutes every two hours to refill.[17]

The Faribault party decided to follow the cart trail linking the HBC posts across the northern prairies, where there were fewer buffalo and therefore fewer Indians. In preparation they traded their American four-wheeled wagons and horses for oxen, Indian horses, and Red River carts. Oxen had proved themselves to be indispensible for long marches and had become the preferred beast of burden. "More wind, but less drizzle," the old teamsters said. Oxen were about one-third the price of good horses. They were docile and did not sink into mud as narrower-hooved horses would. Furthermore, should they become mired, they would simply flop and wait to be eased out. Horses would panic, rear, and thrash about under a load or in harness. The harness of an ox was a simple wooden yoke, cheap, easily made from local materials, and quick to fit. If the going got really rough oxen could be eaten with much more relish than horse meat. As a final consideration, prairie travelers learned that Indians seldom raided a wagon train for oxen, whereas horses were their symbol of wealth and the reason for many skirmishes.

There were, however, certain concessions that had to be made. Oxen suffered greatly from heat. They liked to walk, not run, and stayed in good condition only if there were water and feed at each stopping point. Travel schedules conformed to the needs of the oxen, not the travelers. A start was made at dawn and during the heat of the day a "nooning" of two or three hours was made during which stock could rest and feed while the men made a hot meal. The march then continued until camp was pitched late in the evening.

In the three days the Faribault party spent in the Red River settlement they also replenished supplies and completed their outfits. One of the items was two-hundred pounds of pemmican, dried meat and sometimes Saskatoon berries and fat pounded into an animal stomach or other casing for preserving. Jones did not find it particularly palatable, but nutritionally it was unsurpassed.

The HBC's gradual release on trading allowed merchants to set up legal trading stores in the settlement, giving the overlanders a choice of over fifty outlets to buy from. These stores were nothing like a modern shop, nor even a country general store. The "store" was usually a lean-to outbuilding or secondary part of the house, seldom recognizable as a place to trade. With no regular business hours prospective customers had first to find the proprietor. Once inside, it was evident that merchandise was not laid out in logical groupings; in fact, only a third of the goods might be visible. The rest would be in the cellar, under a pile of goods or in the attic, and only on specific request would a recondite item be hunted out. When the proprietor returned with a pair of pants or a pail, the buyer took whatever size was offered, and paid what was asked. In winter, business was concluded quickly for no firewood was wasted in heating the establishment, nor tallow in lighting it. Such conveniences as coal-oil lamps were still half a decade away.[18]

Jones found clothing cheaper than in the States, but was annoyed at having to pay 2 pounds 10 shillings for a tea kettle and similar prices for a frying pan and a miscellaneous pots. Jones's kettle cost him $12.50. His annoyance is understandable. For the same amount he could have bought a Red River cart or two hundred pounds of flour. For the price of a few pots he could have had a yoke of oxen, a cart, and several weeks' provisions. Complain about the prices though and the trader would say, "It's the freight from St. Paul" to justify the high cost.

Jones was more pleased with the gunsmith who repaired his Colt Bulldog revolver. It was done "in a very neat and satisfactory manner, and charged very reasonably." While talking to the gunsmith, a native of Scotland who had been in North America for many years, "so long that he has almost forgotten everything connected with the old country," Jones learned more of the ways of the Red River settlers.

The old Scot said, "I like Americans, they are punky, and can not be domineered over by the Hudson's Bay Company, nor any other body of men, but are ever ready to maintain, at the risk of their lives, their own independence. I admire them for that. I admire you. I hope I see the day when this country is under the U.S. government." Obviously one of the settlers that Governor Simpson had been concerned about inviting annexation, this man went on to say that he had long been under the employment of the HBC and "consequently was well informed of their tyrannical actions to their employees."

He had a further inducement for Jones. As his daughter entered the room he pointed to her and "informed me that I might have her for a partner. . . . She was I judge about sixteen, dark, quadron [quarter Indian] medium height and somewhat pretty . . . the very personification of retired simplicity, gay but modest, no intellectual refinement could be discerned."

"What do you think girl. Would ye consent?" the father asked.

She blushed and gave an evasive answer. The old man did not like it and "demanded a peremtory answer, but she was equally resolute and the only answer received was a quick and silent retreat, much to my relief . . . I took my departure with the promise that I would call again, one that I never fulfilled."

While visiting the fort the man witnessed Governor George Simpson's departure for Montreal. Sixty-year-old Simpson's forty-year reign was drawing to a close along with that of the Company.

They made great hubbub at the Fort to-day, fired their guns, played "God Save the Queen," just because the Governor of Prince Rupert's Land was going to leave for Canada. He had a glimpse of the Governor—he was a very good specimen of the "beef-eating and port-loving" John Bull—looked as though he might make a good alderman for some ward in a large city, if obesity is the qualification necessary. . . . It being near dinner time, we were pressed by several of the privates to dine with them.

The dinner fare Jones had seen cooking in the soldiers' "flesh pots" the previous day remained in his memory and the offer was refused with no reluctance. The Faribault party were then fortunate enough to be invited to dinner with Messrs. Sergeant and C. Cavalier, partners of the American Fur Company stationed here. The men had a "very sociable time." Mrs. Cavalier retired early and "left the field clear, and receiving an assurance that no petticoat would intrude" the men settled down to some serious drinking. Their revelry ceased only when they fell to the floor in besotted oblivion. Drunk as brewer's farts, as Palmer might have said, they snored into the warm prairie dawn.

## A Journey on the Plains

The drunken carousal that preceded the Faribault party's farewell to Fort Garry on August 21 had taken its toll. Hind was sleeping it off in his cousin's home. Jones and Amesbury, "being somewhat influenced by the rosy loitered in the rear." After trudging with leaden feet and thick heads for three miles the two Lochinvars "met a couple of blooming half-breed damsels searching for cows. Pretending to have lost the track of our company we enquired for the nearest house."

The ploy was successful, or at least the girls chose to let them think it was successful, and the girls agreed to lead them in return for help in rounding up the cows. "Oh, charming rural simplicity," Jones wrote, "my mind was now confused and chaotic, continually wandering from the Eldorado we had in view to the dusky hue of our fair guides. Amesbury enjoyed himself immensely." The two overlanders were captivated and had fallen, if not in love, at least in lust. The girls led them home, where the two men accepted an invitation to dinner, and then spent the evening passing the jug the girls' father produced. They reached their companions' camp late that night, full of tales of their enviable escapade.

Westward they rode through St. James and St. Francis Xavier parishes, through the farms and the settlements that were ever spreading up the Assiniboine. If the farms were not as large as might have been expected it was not for want of good soil or industrious farmers. John Gowler, a pioneer farmer, said, "If I found it worth my while, I could enclose 50, 100 or 500 acres, and from every acre get 30 to 40 bushels of wheat, year after year. I could grow Indian corn, barley, oats, flax, hemp, hops, turnips, tobacco, anything you wish, and to any amount, but what would be the use? There are no markets." To the farmers of the Assiniboine and Red rivers a route south was also important. As it was they grew little extra and any influx of people, like soldiers or travelers, caused a shortage in food and supplies and a jump in prices.[19]

Beyond the settlements were the White Horse Plains, then Lane's Post and, after fifty miles, Portage la Prairie, an HBC post. The post had marked the site of the portage or carry from Lake Manitoba to the Assiniboine River and although La Vérendrye had built a post here as early as 1738, it was known before that, perhaps by Radisson and Groseilliers. The site marked a change in vegetation for this was the northern limit of the Bur oak, which had so far lined the river banks. It was therefore the last supply of good repair material for the wagons and carts, so a midday halt was called to make spare axles.

They met two American plainsmen here, a Virginian and a Missourian, both married to Blackfeet women, who had just returned from a yearly expedition to the Missouri headwaters to trap and hunt. The trappers passed word that a freetrader, that is one not attached to a company, by the name of Pierre C. Pambrun, was just two days ahead; and the moccasin telegraph, or rumor, had it that two gold-seekers from Mankato, Minnesota, were in the vicinity.

While pitching camp, Hind for some reason "vented his spleen" on Jones, one more incident in a long continuing run of skirmishes. Jones was on his feet and swinging almost before Hind had finished speaking. The bare knuckle exchange lasted until the rest of the camp pulled them apart. Jones flattered himself that he could have won if let go. More importantly, the argument shifted the mess organization considerably.

Leaders of any mess or train were chosen by election, by general agreement, or by having put the expedition together. Any of these circumstances made for an apprentice leader, not a monarchy for the journey's duration. The appointed leader must show concern for the train as a whole and each man as an individual. He must have a certain knowledge of the country and know how to travel, be prepared to solve problems and look after the company's finances. While shouldering these responsibilities, he had to treat individuals with respect. Should a leader not prove up to the challenge, he was out. Hind had shown himself to be incapable of handling the role. He was voted out and "the mantle of authority" placed on Joe Houck. A further shift occurred when John Palmer, who had previously had some conflicts with the Amesbury mess, switched to Houck's.

From Portage la Prairie the party traveled due west, taking the middle cart track to Fort Ellice rather than the northern section of the Carlton Trail, which crisscrossed the White Mud River. They now left behind all vestiges of settlement and civilization.

Ahead of them the plains, the tall-grass and short-grass prairie, marched west for over a thousand miles to the Rocky Mountains. From the Missouri River north to the beginning of the northern parkland along the North Saskatchewan River was five hundred miles. This half a million square miles of grass and aspen groves was divided by three main rivers: the Assiniboine and the North and South Saskatchewan. Feeder streams like the Red Deer, Bow, Belly, Battle, and the Qu'Appelle flowed into these eastward-coursing arteries.

Along the eastern and northern limits of these vast plains was a chain of nine Hudson's Bay Company posts: Fort Ellice, Qu'Appelle Post, Touchwood Hills Post, Fort Pelly, Fort Carlton, Fort Pitt, Fort Edmonton and its satellites Rocky Mountain House and Jasper House. The total population of these posts, including Indian and country-born servants, did not exceed a few hundred, likely less. The territory was lawless and unprotected by arms. The Bay men were traders and laborers, not lawkeepers or soldiers, and the Company's regulations and effectiveness existed little farther than the post's palisades.

Travelers like Jones were facing an awesome, frightening, beautiful, wonderful wilderness, and a freedom that would never again exist. Out there on the plains were an abundance of game—antelope, elk, and buffalo still teeming in untold millions; more grasses and wildflowers, shrubs and herbs than they could know or count; and the nomads, the cossacks of the plains, the Sioux, Cree, Blackfeet, Blood, Assiniboines, and Peigans. Across the rivers, beyond the horizon, over the barrier of the Rocky Mountains lay the goldfields of Fraser's River in British Columbia.

The crossing from Fort Garry to Fort Ellice took the group the usual two weeks, with no notable problems or incidents. The weather was fine and the trail was good, with only a few muddy sections. The Little Saskatchewan, or Rapid, River had to be swum with a line and then crossed by a buffalo-hide boat holding all their provisions. Although it was a first, they managed well and kept up their usual twenty-five miles per day. At this crossing they found a blaze with the initials P.P. inscribed. Pierre Pambrun was still ahead of them.

Saturday, September 4, found them at the Assiniboine River, opposite Fort Ellice. On the west side of the cold, muddy water lay the flatboat ferry. Each man being reluctant to voluntarily swim the river, straws were drawn, the lot falling to Jim Smith. Three crossings later all the goods were ferried. At this juncture three halfbreeds came riding down the trail with the intention of taking the boat across for the travelers. Smith wished they had arrived sooner.

The high plateau above the confluence of the Qu'Appelle River and the southward-draining Assiniboine had been the site of fur posts of various companies since 1787. It was a strategic point along the northwest trails and important for trade and the gathering of pemmican. The present decaying fort had been built by the HBC in 1834 and named in honor of Edward Ellice Sr.[20]

Situated at the hub of plains trails, Fort Ellice was a frequent rendezvous and place of rest for prairie travelers. Explorers such as Hind and Palliser; plainsmen and mountain men from Rupert's Land and the Missouri headwaters; freetraders, hunters, and touring parties all stopped here, making it a kind of mail and message drop. When Jones arrived he found the two from Mankato had passed through August 31 and been duly noted in the post's daily journal. And here they caught up to Pambrun and an English hunter by the name of Louch.[21]

Pambrun's father had been with the HBC and for a time Pambrun Jr. was employed as a clerk, at one hundred pounds per year, but he resigned to become a freetrader headquartered at Lac la Biche, two hundred miles north of Fort Edmonton. When Jones met him at Fort Ellice, Pambrun was heading for Lac la Biche with ten carts and three half-breeds.[22]

Mr. Louch was an "English gentleman" on a hunting tour and typical of many English gentry who came to North America to escape the massive boredom then creeping through England. Louch had been traveling with Captain Brisco, late of the 11th Hussars, and William R. Mitchell, also in search of adventure and hunting. They found Louch insufferable and left him at Fort Garry while they went on, eventually joining the Palliser expedition. Louch was on his way to Fort Carlton or Pitt, hoping to hunt all winter and return to England in the spring.[23]

In hurried transactions that took less than a day Jones sold a cart for ten dollars and bought a buffalo hide and marrow fat from trader William McKay. The Faribault men joined Pambrun for the next leg of the journey to Forts Carlton and Pitt, as did Louch the English hunter who was thankful for the protection.[24]

A few miles north of Fort Ellice the Qu'Appelle was crossed to the north side, a difficult ford complicated by a steep descent from the high plateau to the valley. Carts and wagons had to be skidded down the muddy slope, a drop of several hundred feet in less than a mile. Oxen, pushed by heavily laden carts, sometimes lost their footing, or broke into a run in a vain attempt to keep ahead of the weight bound to them. Wheels were locked with ropes or spiked with timber to stop them from turning and to slow their momentum, and in some cases logs were trailed for additional friction. A final effort could be made by hitching men or oxen at the rear of the cart to slow the descent.

Once in the valley bottom there was the actual river crossing. Prairie streams, unlike their mountain counterparts, do not have gradual sloping banks worn down by spring floods. Instead they form deep trenches cut into the soft soil. The precipitous banks, several feet high, are impossible to descend with a cart. At a ford the banks would be worn down from constant crossing, but this August the river was high and the ford deep. Another had to be found. Pambrun found a new shallow ford and then the men set to work laboriously excavating a grade to water level, and another out the other side. Ahead was the ascent out of the valley, similar to the treacherous descent and accomplished by teaming the oxen two to a cart for the slippery plodding up the valley side. Two days out of Fort Ellice they finally regained the prairie plateau.

The track they now traveled was becoming known as the Carlton Trail, linking Fort Garry and Fort Edmonton through Fort Carlton with other prairie posts. In 1858 it was an unofficial route, traveled mainly by freetraders, buffalo hunters, mail carriers, adventurers, and now gold-seekers. As the HBC switched its provisioning from York boats at York Factory on Hudson Bay to cart trains from St. Paul on the Mississippi, this trail would become a prairie lifeline. A century later the Yellowhead Highway would retrace much of its route.

Cart trains, whether small like Pambrun's or large and long like those of the HBC, evolved a method of hitching and traveling that spread the load on the soft prairie soil. Each man was responsible for several carts. He drove one and hitched each successive cart at a corner of the preceding cart. To the lead cart he hitched one cart to the left rear corner, and one to the right, so that the ox pulling the right cart walked in the wheel rut of the first. Depending on the number of carts he was responsible for, the units spread out across the trail in a V with as many as sixteen wheel ruts instead of two. At narrow crossings, through groves of trees, down steep descents, or at fords, the area became a quagmire, crossed only with a good deal of effort and cursing.

Each day of the prairie journey began before the yellow light of a watercolor dawn washed over the grassland, stretching long shadows from carts and animals across the campground. The morning's fire was built with wood patiently gathered from each wooded island passed. Its smoke curled lazily into the air until, caught by a transient air current, it was whisked away. As the sun rose the wind came, gentle but freshening, so constant that when it died a silence was felt, a void that signaled all was not right.

The sounds of the cook clattering pans, breaking firewood, and opening provision bags roused the sleepers and one by one they stumbled from their blankets laid beneath the carts. This early in the journey breakfast might actually be different from the other two meals of the day. Bacon, beans, and bread were quickly and easily prepared while late sleepers had their blankets pulled off and were unceremoniously roused. In the silence that prevailed over early morning camps, the oxen were hitched while blankets, food, pots, kettles, and any unburned wood were reloaded. The air was still chilled when the men moved their carts onto the trail and continued the journey.

The weather alternated clear and rainy, but for Jones the trail was in good condition, passing between shallow lakes and sloughs. From the bulrushes, cattails, and sedges that bordered the ponds, canvasback and teal rose in flight, whistling overhead to the next undisturbed slough. They were a source of frequent fowl dinners for the travelers. The breeze carried the bouquet of prairie flowers, including the scent of fields of wild roses that somehow reminded those from Faribault of the life and loves they had left behind. Prairie sounds were drowned by the squeaking of oak axles and wheel hubs, ungreased because of prairie dust and mud that would too quickly wear the wooden shafts. Dust from the wheels ahead coated men and beasts alike, matting hair, filling noses, and, during dry sections, choking the air that they breathed.

The "nooning" was a welcome rest. The practice of a long noon break came from the use of oxen. Prairie guidebooks such as Capt. Randolph Marcy's *The Prairie Traveller* suggested that while oxen were recommended for long marches over a rough, sandy, or muddy road, certain precautions had to be taken. Oxen had to be kept at a walk and not made to rush or gallop. An early cool start was best with a long rest near grass and water where they would improve their condition in just a couple of hours. In this fashion they could easily do sixteen or eighteen miles a day. Often though this stop was made without shade from the broiling plains sun. The temperature might be "one hundred in the shade," but it meant little for there was none, save the shadow side of a cart or a hastily rigged tarpaulin. The men took this nooning as an opportunity to rest, cook a hot meal, keep up their journal, or repair gear. Then, as the sun began to descend from its apex, the oxen were hitched and the plodding began anew for several more hours. Should they be in the country "infested by hostiles," Marcy explained, the evening drive should be prolonged until an hour or two after dark, turning off the trail at a point where the ground is hard and going on a half mile or so to a camp without fires. Fortunately in these northern latitudes where days were long this was not often considered necessary, although at times prudent plainsmen would hide their trail and camp unobtrusively.

Most evenings camps were made before dark and a cooking fire built by the kitchen detail. The rest unloaded carts, unyoked oxen, and unsaddled horses. The beds were fixed beneath the wagons. After a supper of pemmican, or perhaps a roast duck, they sat around the fire, smoking pipes and telling stories of home or other lands they had seen. Above them was the unending prairie sky, brilliant with stars and planets. During this month the Great Comet, Donati's Comet, sped across the heavens near the Great Bear. To the halfbreeds it portended some great calamity and night after night they viewed it with fear and awe, always awaiting the stroke of doom. To those of Cree ancestry the Milky Way was the Chief's Road, Ursa Major the Tail of Stars, and the North or Polar Star was the Stationary Star. From the movements of the constellations they could tell the watches of the night. The clear air brought the heavens close and the stars told a story as clearly as any book or map. The evening ended with the men crawling beneath the carts and closing their eyes in weary rest.

On the eighth day out of Fort Ellice the ennui of the flat plains was broken by rolling ground, the harbinger of blue hills seen on the horizon. Trees appeared and the men knew they were approaching the Touchwood Hills, named for the easily lit wood growing there. Taylor of the HBC had built a small post here in 1852 and on the afternoon of Monday, September 13, he welcomed them to his home.[25]

Camped around the post was a large band of Cree Indians, recently returned from a buffalo hunt where they had killed 357 animals. Jones noticed that the Cree wore fewer white men's clothes and beads than any other Indians he had seen. "No brass or silver rings hung on their ears, or glass beads around their necks, but eagle's claws, and beads made from mussel shell were put in requisition, the buffalo robe, fantastically painted with red and yellow ... the bow and quiver of arrows, instead of the gun."

Marrow fat and service or Saskatoon berries were traded with the Cree; and Pambrun, after impressing them by shooting a goose on the wing, obtained a horse in trade for rum, tobacco, and clothing. At noon on their second day they left, taking care to stock up on firewood for the crossing of the treeless, waterless Quill Plains. Early travelers seldom referred to this expanse by name. Hind was told it was the Carry Wood Plain; Palliser called it the Buffalo Cart Plain on his map; while others dubbed it the Great Salt Plains for the number of alkaline lakes that dotted the area, though this gives a misleading idea of the extent of the saline, nonarable land. The name Quill came from the lakes to the northeast, where for many years Indians collected goose and whooping crane quills for trade at the Touchwood Hills Post, whence they were shipped to England for use as pens.[26]

Pambrun was worried about this crossing, fearful that the Cree camped in the Touchwoods might decide to follow the party and steal horses. Dropping out of the Touchwoods past Heart Hill he decided to use the old plainsman's ruse of "blinding a trail" to throw off anyone following. After stopping for supper near the last running stream he ordered the men to put out their fires and scatter the ashes. He then instructed one group of carts to take a course oblique to the trail, while a smaller party stayed on the trail. The latter was to proceed to a certain point and then turn off, meeting the first group at a predetermined location. A careful watch was to be kept on their rear. Camp was made some miles distant, on a small piece of prairie surrounded by willows. The carts were formed into a corral, a particularly good barricade when wheels were blocked, animals were picketed, and no fires were built. Noise was kept to a minimum and watches carefully posted. These precautions were second nature to experienced travelers, and usually had the desired effect. The party experienced no disturbance or alarm, but continued to post watches for the remainder of the journey to Fort Carlton, which, with the exception of the Qu'Appelle Plains crossing, was very similar in nature to the area south of the Touchwood Hills.

Pambrun aided the Faribault party on numerous occasions, offering them fresh meat, butter, and help with various chores and problems, such as looking for lost oxen and crossing sloughs. He passed on knowledge of plains travel learned over his past thirty-five years with the HBC, and told stories of his life with old "Here Before Christ," and more recently as a freetrader. The Faribault men told him stories of Fraser River gold. While Pambrun no doubt knew of the California and Oregon strikes this was likely the first he had heard of the rich finds in British North America. The talk infected him with gold fever, though it would not manifest itself for another two years.

After several days they reached another range of low hills which Jones called the "Big Hills," also known as the Lumpy Hills, Big or Lumpy Hills of the Woods, and Minitchenass Hills. The trail here was rough, passing over hard ground covered in boulders. The carts lurched and bumped, making them too uncomfortable to ride and awkward to guide in a unit.

On the far side of the Big Hills they once again found a good trail passing through a prairie dotted with lakes and groves of aspen and poplar. The flat plain ended, and camp could be made in the shelter of a small valley. On September 19 they camped at Lac au Chains and on the twentieth reached the South Saskatchewan River. Cree came to camp that night having tracked them from their last night's stopping point, indicating the wisdom of "blinding" a trail when not wanting to be found. In this case the Cree caused no problems.

The South Saskatchewan crossing was made by weaving a willow frame and covering it with two buffalo skins sewn together, making a bull boat capable of holding twelve hundred pounds. The carts were floated over tied one behind the other, a difficult day-long task with the fast current of the river. By nine o'clock most of the men were in camp, anxious to dig into the roast goose and elk steaks the cook had prepared. Hind brought on the wrath of his mess by wanting to eat without waiting for those still absent. He was forced to wait. Jones wrote, "We are beginning to feel as though we didn't care how soon he left us. As we are heartily tired of his laziness, overbearing manner and gluttonous habits." The rift was beginning to widen.

The ascent from the river was difficult and troublesome as usual. The oxen plodded along like the proverbial tortoise, but the horses baulked. An old Red River trick was used. The carts were unhitched and a rope taken from the cart to the horse's tail, "an infallible remedy to make them pull," Jones wrote. The camp that night was at Duck Lake, and Jones, who was reading a newspaper as he went, took another shot at the British and Sir George Simpson.

Reading Sir George Simpson's report of this country in the St. Paul Pioneer and Democrat, stating that this part of the country resembled very much the parks in England, this, we pronounce unqualifiedly false in every particular, bearing no more resemblance than the garden of Eden does to a sandy desert. It is destitute of its majestic oak, beech, and maple, that he boasts of. On the river a few birch may be found, but the rest of the timber and especially in this vicinity, to which he refers to, is composed of small growth poplar, balm of Gilead and willow. When Mr. Simpson wrote that report, I think he must have been considerably under the influence of Hudson's Bay Rum. . . . Some of our party, three—are English born, and have traveled extensively in England, and they all agree to the falsity of the report.

The region Jones and Simpson disputed was around Fort Carlton, or Carlton House as it was often called. The HBC had built three posts by that name but this particular one was on a level bench on the east bank of the North Saskatchewan River. Built in 1819 it was now gaining importance as the halfway house for cart trains between Fort Garry and Fort Edmonton. Though small in comparison with those forts, Fort Carlton was built in time-honored fashion with palisade walls and a guard walk around the interior perimeter. At each corner was a log bastion with cannons and inside, several buildings for quarters and warehouses. Three or four hundred yards west lay the river and east, a small garden and a house. Scattered outside the walls were varying numbers of Indian or Métis lodges or teepees with Red River carts and horses nearby.

At Fort Carlton, on September 23, the North Saskatchewan River had to be crossed. This time a Company York boat could be used, for a fee of 7s. sterling ($1.50 U.S.). While preparing to cross, the Faribault party turned their oxen loose to graze. When they could not be found an Indian was hired for a plug of tobacco to help Palmer find the beasts. Soon the Indian stopped and demanded another payment. Palmer refused and told the Indian, via sign language, that he was not to be trifled with. Trying another trick, the Indian continued looking but tried to lose Palmer. The wily little Englishman, however, stuck close and soon they found the oxen. Palmer then gave the tracker a pipe as further payment.

The crossing took the better part of a day, and again teams were doubled for the long pull out of the valley. Though some areas were called wooded, such as the Lumpy Hills of the Woods, they were in fact bare, only being termed Woody from a previous era. Frequent fires had denuded the country of trees, so wood still had to be carried. After a couple of days' travel, however, they came to the Thickwood Hills, named for the thickets that still covered the rough ground.

Several trails linked Fort Carlton and the next major post on the North Saskatchewan, Fort Pitt. All of them cut across the southerly bending elbow of the north branch, passing either north or south of the Thickwood Hills. Jones and Pambrun were taking the most northerly trail, past Mus-qua-lahepah-mah-ta-kat Lake, anglicized to "the lake the bear waded through" (today known unpoetically as Bear Lakes), then past Scent Grass Lakes and Jackfish Lake. Jones calls Jackfish by its alternate name of Pike Lake, the same fish, and remarks that in the distance they could see "Fort Pike, now abandoned." "Fort" is hardly the appropriate term—it was only a rude trading hut.[27]

Beyond here they passed three large balm of Gileads that rose high above the level plain, a landmark known as the "three brothers," and then English Creek and Frenchman's Butte or French Knoll, a large hill that rises above the prairie just east of Fort Pitt, a hill that would become a national landmark in the Riel Rebellion of 1885.

On Saturday, October 2, Jones was busy folding a wild rose into his diary and writing of how it brought back memories "of home, the garlands we were wont to weave to crown our Queen of Love and Beauty," when a band of forty Cree, painted and mounted, rode into camp. The alarmed men reached toward their rifles and pistols, but the Indians' outstretched hands indicated peace, and no shots were fired. The band escorted the cart train for the two- or three-hour ride to Fort Pitt.

This fort was situated in a location similar to Fort Carlton, on a river bench, but it was built on the north side of the river as a deterrent to southern Indian attack. Named for one of England's great prime ministers, it was built in 1829 as a trading post to cover the area between the two major posts of Carlton and Edmonton. Whether by plan or fortune, it was located directly across the river from a major buffalo trail and just a few hundred yards upstream from their fording point.

The buffalo trail had attracted a large band of Indians, of over two hundred lodges, the main camp of the small party escorting Pambrun and Jones. On the river's far shore another large group waited to cross in the Company's boat. Impatient tribesmen made a raft of their lodge poles and after they had loaded everything onto it, tied it to a horse and drove him in. The Indian family all clung to the raft, while the dogs were left to swim.

The breeze from the river curled the smoke of many cooking fires around the fort and carried the cries and shouts of children running around teepees chasing barking dogs and raising a dust that added flavor to the food cooking on tripods and another layer to enshroud any passerby. Behind the fort rose a low hill, dotted with hundreds of grazing horses.

The appearance of the cart train and the mounted warriors drew the whole camp's attention. Hundreds of dogs began a chorus of howling and barking, the children ran across the fields to escort the party, the men wandered over to see who the trader was, and the squaws kept busy about the camp. Pambrun met his cousin here and they lost little time in opening their wagons, rolling out the casks of rum, knocking out the bungs, and beginning to dispense and trade rum for furs. Freetrader Pambrun was a "whiskey trader."

Filling his tin pint cup, an Indian would then head for his lodge, take a drink, and pass it around. Others did the same and before long the entire camp was drunk. "Greasy old squaws and younger ones too, put their arms around our necks in a most affectionate manner, and saluting us as brothers—decrepit old cusses, would go through the same performance, and then drop down in maudlin insensibility," Jones wrote.

Part of the Faribault company was detailed to get the boat the Indians were using for crossing, while the rest sold Pambrun a cat and visited the fort briefly. Jones, finding that James Simpson, a country-born son of Governor Simpson, was in charge of Fort Pitt, took aim at the Britisher in his journal. "The fort is under the command of Mr. Simpson a young man of decidedly 'ain't I some,' and one of the mementoes that Governor Simpson, or Sir George, as he is better known, left behind him. A baron is his father, whether legal or illegal, it makes no difference to him."[28]

In siring illegitimate country-born children and using halfbreed and native women to his own purposes, Governor Simpson, himself illegitimate, had indeed been one of the worst examples of British male chauvinism. It was through his example that the racism and sexism of Victorian England took hold. It had not always been so. The fur traders first came to the new land without women but with no intention of celibacy. A trader needed someone to help make utensils, cook, repair moccasins, make camp, and keep his bed warm. Indian women were numerous and marriages, like those amongst European royalty, had the advantage of forming alliances. One sure way to capture a chief's trade was to "marry" his daughter.

The HBC banned these marriages *à la façon du pays*, in the custom of the country, but with little success. The Nor'Westers did not. Some Nor'Westers even pimped, stealing Indian women in payment for the debts of an Indian father or husband and then selling them to their own servants for great profits. Often the native relatives were in too weak a position to argue. Gradually country marriages and country-born or half-breed children became part of the natural order of things.

This attitude changed in the nineteenth century when men such as George Simpson began to use women with no thought of a long relationship. He kept young Betsey Sinclair, a young mixed-blood girl, "at bed and board" in Athabasca during his first year in the country and she gave birth to his first of several illegitimate children. He wrote of Betsey to a friend saying, "If you can dispose of the Lady it will be satisfactory as she is an unnecessary and expensive appendage, I see no fun in keeping a Woman without enjoying her charms ... if she is unmarketable I have no wish that she be a general accommodation shop to all the young bucks at the Factory and in addition to her own chastity a padlock may be useful."

Simpson had other mistresses. He left his last recorded consort pregnant when he returned to England to marry Frances and bring her to Fort Garry. Simpson's views were extreme, but they began to affect the whole of the fur-trade society. Where once it had been common, if not customary, for fur traders to have two families, one in the North West and another at home in the East or England, Simpson's move brought white wives into fur-trade society. Fur traders were thinking of themselves as Gentlemen, hence the workers were servants, and a white wife became a status symbol. Women had come full circle. Where first Indian wives had been the vogue, then country-born halfbreeds, now white was the standard. These women were spoken of as exotic plants. James Douglas wrote that "now we have the lovely tender exotic torn from its parent bed, to pine and languish in the desert." And pine away they did. They could not, it seems, adapt from the role of Victorian ladies. The standards of Victorian England supplanted the customs of the country that had made life tolerable in the early years, and began a rift of racism that would last for generations. John Jones, a racist himself, easily recognized this in others and in his hatred of the British found it an easy target. Despite his sensitivity he could not step back into objectivity of his own views.[29]

Jones never let his personal views of someone get in the way of striking a bargain, or seeking help, though. He noticed potatoes being grown at the fort and bought a bushel from Simpson for a shilling, about twenty-two cents, a price he thought very reasonable as he wrote, "Money is so scarce in this country, that when they get a sight of a shilling, they are willing to part with almost anything to gain possession of it." Shouldering their potatoes, Jones and company headed for camp on the far side of the river. They now lost the numerical advantages of traveling with Pambrun and his three men, but on October 3 young Joe Gibson of Woodville, Minnesota, and Brewster of Mankato, Minnesota, joined them for protection—the two gold-seekers who had been just ahead of them since Fort Garry.

The south side trail to Fort Edmonton ran due west from the crossing, but was indistinct and frequently lost in the creeks, swamps, and trees that lay in the travelers' path. Their compass was often resorted to. Feeling insecure without Pambrun's guidance they found the trail demoralizing. A cold, disagreeable night that dumped six inches of snow further soured their dispositions. How much better it would have been, they thought, to stay at home, working on the farm, in the store, or in the land office. Think of what their friends were doing now; how they were warm by a fireplace or stove. And that girl in whose hair the delicate rose blossoms had been twined, where was she? Not in this godforsaken country, that was certain! Tempers were squally, nights longer, days colder. Had any one of the men looked out beyond the light of the fire he would have seen an immense shape lurking in the night shadows and felt a cold wind pass when it moved, smelt the dust raised, for the Elephant was pawing its feet.

Despondency lasted for several days, until on the seventh they saw large herds of buffalo. Their drooping spirits soared in the excitement of the buffalo hunt and the satisfaction of fresh meat. The weather warmed —snow and rain stopped. Nights were spent beneath the carts, for they had never replaced the tents they had cut for saddle blankets, though they had plenty of buffalo robes for covers.

More buffalo were seen, tempting them to chase and hunt again, but Emihiser killed an elk and the steaks helped push the thoughts of buffalo meat from their minds. Around a rousing fire they found they were indeed once again enjoying plains life and wished only that they could locate the elusive trail.

Finally a week later they found a well-trodden westerly trail they assumed to be the cart trail to Fort Edmonton. The following day an Indian and his wife confirmed this and indicated the fort was another four sleeps away. On October 17 a train of twelve carts on its way to the plains for buffalo meat was met, and then a smaller train of four carts, heading for Fort Pitt, which they expected to reach in three days. Jones and company had been on the trail nine days, an indication that they had indeed been somewhat confused.

For another fifteen miles they drove their oxen and horses westward, across small streams, skirting groves of winter-stripped poplars. The animals were goaded to a faster pace; the cart trains had said it was only a short distance to the river, just a few pipes farther. Cries and curses seasoned with switches of willow and leather urged the train forward. The lead rider hollered something back and the driver at the head of the line whacked the haunch of his ox once more as he gesticulated to those behind. The horses were spurred to a gallop and their riders left the oxen to plod along and raced to the edge of the bluff where the first horseman had reined in. With unaccustomed levity they whooped and hollered, firing pistols and rifles in a blackpowder celebration of arrival. There, stretched before them, framed between the few late yellow and red leaves of willows, poplar, and aspen, lay the waters of the North Saskatchewan. High on the northern river bench stood the imposing post of Edmonton, center of the Saskatchewan district of Rupert's Land, springboard to the Rockies. In their exuberance even miserable, domineering Hind and cocky Palmer slapped each other in congratulation for the long journey and the many miles they had covered. Fifteen hundred miles lay behind them; a similar distance lay ahead.

*This sketch by Manton Marbles of the Nobles expedition shows Fort Garry in 1860 and the ferry across the Red River. (PAM, from Harper's Weekly, 1860)*

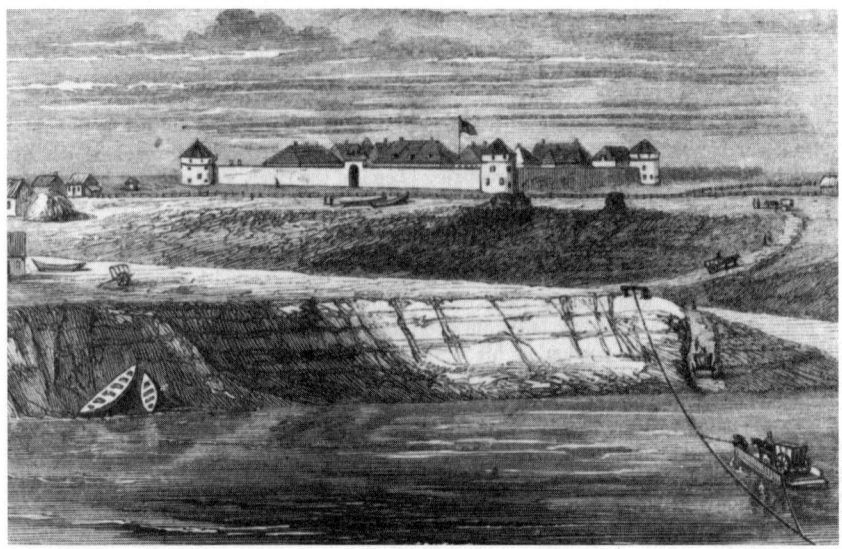

*A view of Fort Ellice after 1862. As a rule, miners and immigrants were not welcomed at the HBC posts; they bought up supplies and sowed seeds of discontent amongst the Company workers. (Geological Survey of Canada, 355)*

*Fort Pitt on the North Saskatchewan, one of the HBC posts where overlanders spent the winter working for their keep, and the site of the 1859 Hastings party gunfight. The trail to Fort Edmonton crossed to the south side of the river here. (Geological Survey of Canada, 781)*

*Fort Carlton in 1871. This fort was the halfway house for cart trains traveling between Fort Ellice and Fort Edmonton. (PAC 9171)*

*Fort Edmonton on the north bank of the North Saskatchewan. Most of the overlanders passed through this fort on their way west. They reported it was dirty and habitually short of supplies. (PAC, 9148)*

*This canoe party on the Canadian Shield is similar to the one Jessop traveled with in 1859. (PAC PA-45620)*

*Frenchman's Creek, Saskatchewan. Many overlanders crossed inhospitable country where no white man had ever set foot. The border country in this photograph was traveled by the Man from Brechin and other southern parties. (PAM 235)*

*Overlanders often had to be on their guard against Indian attack; however, in the majority of cases natives were the overlanders' salvation, and they never would have completed their journeys without native people's help. This photo, taken in 1871, shows a Cree camp south of Vermilion, Alberta. (PAC C-5181)*

*Bridge building was a time-consuming but necessary task for any Overlander. This photo shows a North American Boundary Commission party in June 1874, at the First Crossing of the Souris River. (PAC, PA-74644)*

Ox carts or Red River Carts, were the main means of transportation for the overlanders from Fort Garry to Fort Edmonton. These carts are using a later model wheel with a more refined hub. (PAC PA-42057)

The HBC's Fort Colville, Washington Territory, U.S.A., in 1860, on the route of many early overlanders, including John Jessop who arrived here in rags in 1859. (PAC C-77560)

# Chapter Three

## "Pampered Bastards of English Barons"

John Jones was impatient. Ever since his Faribault party had arrived here at Fort Edmonton four days ago Jones had been trying to see Chief Trader William Christie. This morning clerk Gabriel Crowe had said that the trader was busy in his office.

"He will be at his leisure and able to deal with you in half an hour."

Half an hour had long since passed. The clerk was at his desk tallying supplies that had arrived with the Saskatchewan brigade's four York boats three days ago. Since then two men had been fired for disobedience, insolence and drinking. Busy with Company records, Crowe had made no mention of the miners' arrival, even though they were the first to reach the fort.[1]

Outside the cold log building supplies were still being packed into the warehouses and the men's shouts could be heard over the barking of hundreds of dogs. Horses and cattle were in a corral nearby and the cold air carried their sounds to the second floor of the big house where Jones sat waiting for Christie. The clerk's quill scratched at the page, an irritating sound that piqued Jones's impatience.

After one and a half hours of waiting Jones stormed in, demanding that their business be concluded without further delay. Time was precious and if Christie did not wish to trade it was immaterial to Jones—there were freemen outside the fort waiting to trade. Incensed at the impetuous intruder, Christie rose from his desk with a passion. Looking Jones up and down he barked, "Well, come on. I'm tired of dancing attendance on you."

"Mr. Christie, I presume you call yourself a gentleman?"

"Of course I do. I am!"

"Mr. Christie, I demanded this trade in a gentlemanly manner, carefully avoiding in giving offence," Jones said, referring to his dislike of all Englishmen. "I want you to talk like a gentleman, as you are talking to an American and not any of your hirelings, for we Americans are not in the habit of listening to any braggadacio. Goodbye." With that Jones turned on his heel and stalked out of the room. "I'll be damned," he thought, "if I'll let a pompous Englishman upset our plans any further."

Jones first met Christie when they arrived on Monday morning, October 18. "His manner during our interview did not favorably impress us," Jones wrote. "He looked and acted as though he was the biggest toad in the puddle." Jones indicated that the men would like to exchange their carts and oxen for horses. Christie, needing both, agreed to attend to the matter the following day. That was four days ago and it was time, long past time, when they should be making their way into the mountains. Even now they had been warned that the season was too far advanced for safe travel.[2]

Christie had arrived to assume his new duties only two weeks before and since then had seen the arrival of the brigade, the Palliser expedition, the Faribault mining party, and a large band of trading Blackfeet. He did not like miners and certainly did not want to encourage them to hang about the post or find gold in the vicinity. It would only disrupt the fur trade. He had agreed to trade with Jones with some reluctance.

As Jones turned his back on Christie and stalked out of the office, he was called back. Christie apologized for his hastiness and led the way to the "kraal" to begin the trading.

Jones's party of thirteen, including Brewster and Gibson from Fort Pitt, had arrived on the far side of the river late on October 17. Their arrival celebrations of gunfire, shouts, and hollers had attracted the fort's attention and before long a small band of Indians, some freemen, HBC servants, and Fraser River–bound miners Hall and Hodgson from Mankato, Minnesota, had crossed to visit. Jones was of the opinion that the Indians had come with an eye to plundering, so a watch was posted.

The following morning some of the party descended to the North Saskatchewan and crossed to the fort—the commercial, religious, and social center of the entire Saskatchewan district. The establishment was impressive and by 1858 had developed limited suburbs of freemen.

Fort Edmonton had been relocated four times, bouncing upstream and down since the first fort was built in 1795. It had finally settled on this high bench in 1830. This was John Rowand's fort, the throne of the ham-fisted ruler of the Saskatchewan district and under his guidance the post became the most important and profitable on the western prairie. The Big House, called Rowand's Folly by his critics, was typical of his approach. Rowand knew how this mansion would impress the Indians, and whites, and built it in style. The building was roughly thirty by eighty feet, three stories high with a basement. Galleries or porches ran the full length of the front and back, greatly adding to its imposing appearance. For natives the most impressive feature was the multitude of windows, formed of small panes of glass seven by eight inches, the first in the West. Even George Simpson was impressed. He wrote:

> It is surrounded by high pickets and bastions, which with the battlemented gateways, the flagstaffs, etc., give it a good deal of a martial appearance; and it occupies a commanding situation, crowning an almost perpendicular part of the bank of about two hundred feet in height. . . . This fort, both inside and outside, is decorated with painting and devices to suit the taste of the savages that frequent it. Over the gateway are a most fanciful variety of vanes; but the hall, of which both the ceiling and the walls present the grandest colors and the most fantastic sculpture, absolutely rivets the astonished natives to the spot with wonder and admiration. The buildings are smeared with a red earth, found in the neighborhood, which, when mixed with oil, produces a durable brown.[3]

The decoration and grandeur had faded when Jones arrived but it was nevertheless impressive. Forty to 50 men were employed, which with families gave the fort a population of about 150. It took two buffalo per day to feed the post and eight hundred cords of wood per winter to heat. Food was often in such short supply that cattle had to be slaughtered or the men given time off to hunt for their own provisions. Employment was chiefly building York boats for the Saskatchewan River brigades, cutting timber ninety miles upstream and rafting it down, trading and keeping the post in shape. Without exception, native or halfbreed women were employed in making moccasins and clothing for the men and pounding dried meat into pemmican.[4]

As well as the dominating Big House, the fort enclosed warehouses, a bakery, kitchen and dining room, trade store, numerous servants' quarters, a blacksmith's shop, stables, a boatbuilding yard and shed, powder magazine, and several other outbuildings. On a hill behind was a windmill, but the stones were made from granite split nearby and were not very serviceable. Only during a gale could flour be ground, so nine-tenths of that used came via Red River Cart from Fort Garry.[5]

Fort Edmonton was commanded by William Christie, the country-born son of Alexander Christie, former governor of Red River and Assiniboia. Born in 1825 William went to Aberdeen, Scotland, for his education, returning in 1841. He began HBC service as clerk and in 1854 was appointed chief trader of the Swan River District. He assumed command of the Saskatchewan district, headquartered at Edmonton, in 1858, determined to see the post maintain its importance as a fur-trade center.

While waiting on Christie to trade, Jones and company witnessed the flag of St. George being hoisted over the fort to the accompaniment of cannon firing. "Meeting an intelligent looking half-breed," Jones asked what the celebration was and found that a large band of Blackfoot Indians had come to trade.

> Quite a number of the Indians were wearing the detested scarlet uniform of the British, and with which they seemed to be proud. The chief also wore a scarlet coat, but extensively fringed with gold embroidery, this being the distinction. He also flourished a dress sword, considerably rusty from exposure. No Marshal was ever more elated upon receiving his baton than this red nigger was with carrying his antique pattern sword.

The announcement being received by the Indians that the Master of the Fort was now ready to receive them, they formed themselves into an irregular line with the Chief at their head leading a horse as a present to the Chief Trader. At the gates of the Fort the Indians were received in due form by the Hudson Bay officials. The Indian Chief after a brief address, presented the horse, and received in return a Military coat after the same pattern he wore, as also an invitation to dine with him (the chief only) which is considered a great honor. Not understanding the proceedings we had recourse to our interpreter. He informed us that the chief was to be the recipient of the periodical entertainment given to all the Chiefs, when they called at the Fort. . . . Our informant stated that while at the table the Chief is plied pretty freely with rum, and if in consequence he becomes somewhat obstreperous and obstinate, they dose the rum enough with ladunum to put him to sleep, and in this insensible and maudlin state he is turned out, and given over to his followers. The gates are now closed, and the portholes are opened, there is just room enough to pass your hand through. The furs are now rapidly passed through the aperture by the thirsty Indians and the rum is distributed in the same manner with equal rapidity, and then follows a scene of drunken revelry that beggars description. Braves, squaws and children are all huddled indiscriminately, virtue and decency finds no resting place while in their Baccanarian orgie. Such a sickening and disgusting sight I never wish to behold again. And this is the way that giant monopoly has accrued its present enormous wealth. This is British philanthropy with a vengeance. Sleep was banished from our eyes during the night. Bedlam had let loose, and was on a "bender."

It was the following day when a tired and cranky John Jones went to the Big House for the fourth time and finally cajoled Christie into a trade. Jones traded four carts and one ox for two horses. The balance of the company followed suit. Jim Smith traded his navy pistol for a horse, and from their stores found two bottles of pickles and twenty pounds of dried apples, which were traded for flour and potatoes.

During their wait on Christie, the Faribault party had made the acquaintance of the British exploration team under Capt. John Palliser. Palliser, Dr. Hector, and Captain Blakiston had arrived at the fort shortly before Jones and all three endeavored to convince the men from Faribault that to go farther at this season was dangerous—sheer folly. "Three cowards," as Jones called them. Ed Hind and John Sandford of Faribault, and Brewster of Mankato, elected to stop and "winter at Devils Lake Settlement about forty-five miles distant from Edmonton. As far as Hind was concerned, nothing could have pleased us better."

The settlement, later known as Lac Ste. Anne, was established as a mission for the Métis and halfbreed freemen of the Edmonton area, a growing population who no longer worked for the HBC in the capacity of servants. A discussion of the settlement gave Jones cause once again to tear a strip off his favorite target. In his journal he wrote:

We found quite a camp of "freemen" on the west end of the Fort. "Freemen" is a term applied to all whites and half-breeds who are not in the employ of the Hudson Bay Company. The salary of a Master of a Fort for the first three years is £75 per annum and his rations; after three years £100, and rations; the remainder of the employees only receive from £17 to £25 during their term of service, which is three years and out of this, if they want any flour, tea, or sugar, tobacco, etc., it is deducted out of their wages, so that at the end of the year there is nothing coming to them. Their ration is only three pounds of pemmican and seven pounds of green or fresh meat per Day. These poor unfortunate devils are picked up in the north of Scotland and in Canada, and are induced to come to this wilderness with flattering offers. When once they have got them on the Saskatchewan River, they stand a poor show to run away from the tyranny to which they are subjected by those pampered bastards of English barons who are in power. At the end of three years the company are bound to take them and pay their passage to where he came from. We had several applications from these employees to take them, but we could not, nor did we dare to do so, for if caught the merciless [the HBC] would put the Indians upon our track, and "wipe us out," as the trappers say. Quite a number of them had made threats to run away upon the first opportunity, but I am afraid that opportunity will never present itself.

With some difficulty Jones and party managed to find a guide, a halfbreed named Rossette. They had now decided to use the Kootenay Pass rather than Sinclair's (Kananaskis). The guide would be paid ten pounds down and a further thirty pounds at the Hudson Bay post west of the Rockies. They had been told that although it would be dangerous they had either to cross now or wait until next August. Gold was waiting, so they pressed on.[6]

The open, warm weather of Indian summer lulled them into easy travel, in harmony with the surroundings. Rabbits bounded from every thicket of Saskatoon berry or wild rose. The streams and potholes were filled with waterfowl rising on approach. The travelers themselves were fit and rested, their mounts in fine shape. In all, the party found themselves in a state of mind that did not portend the difficulty of the journey that lay ahead, one that would test them to the limits of their strength.

## A Winter's Journey in the Rocky Mountains

Departure from Fort Edmonton having been delayed by trading with Christie, and later freemen, the Faribault men only managed to cross the North Saskatchewan into Blackfoot territory and travel two miles across the high prairie before night overtook them, on October 20.

The following afternoon they met a party of halfbreeds and Blackfeet bound for the fort who brought disturbing news. They had just crossed via Kootenay Pass—in four feet of snow. Worse, the Americans and Blackfeet were at war. It was not only the late season that made this route dangerous, but the Blackfeet. There was good reason for Fort Edmonton being on the Saskatchewan's north bank—it was safer—the river forming a barrier, like the moat of an ancient Scots stronghold. Southern posts had been abandoned because of the Blackfeet's warlike demeanor and the "port-hole trading" that Jones had witnessed at Fort Edmonton was in response to previous troubles. If the Blackfeet were indeed being stirred up by American soldiers south of the border they would retreat to the Saskatchewan plains, anxious to retaliate.

This "altered the complexion of things," Jones wrote. They decided to abandon the Kootenay Trail and head for the more northerly Sinclair or Kananaskis Pass. The guide appeared willing. Two days and fifty miles farther south guide Rossette announced that Blackfeet were ahead. Jones doubted him, the mist and fog being thick and visibility limited. Nevertheless when the guide fired his rifle in the air and told them to do the same they did. Rossette cautioned them to keep their guns loaded and their powder dry. In the distance a return volley was heard. Shortly, two Indians rode toward them. Rossette told the Indians that this was one of Captain Palliser's parties, "King George's men." The braves were satisfied with this and Jones, despite his dislike of Britishers, refrained from claiming American citizenship. According to Rossette, the Indians were two noted chiefs, "Bear's Hip-bone" and "Bull's Head." They led the men to a camp of about one hundred Blackfeet, where the American leaders that Rossette pointed out were shown "King George's medals and greeted with a kiss on the cheek."

This camp was a group of Sarcees, loosely part of the Blackfoot confederation. The Reverend Rundle met the band south on the High Wood River in May 1847 at which time this same Bull's Head was the principal chief. A tough, resilient warrior who had lost his right eye, he would remain principal chief through the signing of the 1877 treaty until his death in 1911.[7]

The Sarcees wanted to trade and as the Minnesotans could see the Indians had better horses than their own they agreed. In spite of Jones's protestation of the HBC's rum trading he found himself doing the same. For three worn-out horses, a blanket, a yard or two of cloth, and a half gallon of rum, they obtained three good Indian horses. Trading completed they left the camp, alarmed with the news they might meet a band of five hundred warriors during the next day or two.

Once out of sight the ten men scattered, each taking a different trail yet keeping in sight of each other. They traveled this way for several hours, often circling around groves of trees or small lakes in an attempt to blind their trail. Rossette feared that now they had good horses the Blackfeet would attempt to steal them back. Toward evening they formed a single line and rode hard for the main trail and made camp near a small lake.

The track they were following was known as the Wolf's Trail or Track, linking Fort Edmonton with the Bow River. It curved in a slight south-southwesterly direction, crossing Battle River, Blindman's River, Red Deer Creek, and Red Deer River, until they came into sight of the Rocky Mountains, covered in snow and still a great distance off. By the evening of October 26 they had a better view of the mountains and agreed that indeed the Rockies presented a formidable-looking barrier.

In camp that night Rossette recounted dismal tales of Indians and hunters being lost in the passes during winter months. Now that they had, so it seemed, escaped the Blackfoot danger, he assured them that they would in all probability lose their lives if they persisted in the rash undertaking of a winter crossing. "All this," Jones wrote, "fell on deaf ears." Their motto had been "Onward!" and it would remain so. They noticed, however, that the guide was packing his gear a little more carefully than usual.

Shortly after leaving camp next morning Rossette suggested that the Minnesotans keep to the trail while he went cross-country to hunt for game. It was thought that he was deserting. As he rode off several rifles were leveled on him. "If he's going to quit let it be with a few extra ounces of lead in his back," one of the men said. On second thought the rifles were dropped and an air of despair swept over the men. They were two hundred miles from the nearest white men without even the assurance that they were on the right track, and winter coming fast.

Before leaving, Rossette had pointed to a nine-thousand foot mountain to the west that bore a rude resemblance to an upturned face, a dome shape called by the Indians *Wy-teek-coo-stk-wan*, the Devil's head. It had been a landmark since before the time of Peter Fidler and they decided to use it as a beacon. By evening they had made thirty miles. As darkness closed around them they saw a campfire about five miles off. Fearful that it was the band of Blackfoot warriors they had been told of, they extinguished their fire and kept a vigilant watch all night. Nothing came of the sighting and they were left wondering who it might have been.

Three days later Jones and Amesbury, Jim Smith and Emihiser formed two hunting parties. Although the country was "literally alive with game," they had no success and Jones reported hearing "the unwelcome growling of the bears on either hand, and seemingly quite close—fears of ferocious grizzlies took possession of me, and I must honestly confess that I felt considerable trepidation, so much that I fancied that I was laboring under the 'Curse of the swamp'. . . . We made rapid tracks till we got out of hearing."

Jones and Amesbury became lost attempting to return to camp. They could see a hill ahead where they might get a view of the trail or the other men. On the way they ran into Jim Smith, separated from Ira Emihiser, as lost as he had been on the Red River over two months earlier. No obvious route was seen from the mountain, and rifle fire brought no response. Night came and with it a drop in temperature. The men had no blankets or food, having figured on killing game and returning before dark. They lit two fires, and also set standing dead trees ablaze as signal fires. Then, to the south, they saw what they thought to be a star, but it was not moving. They concluded that it was the other party's fire. Smith wanted to head for it immediately. However they waited for morning, a judicious decision for when they did leave they found an area of deadfall that had to be crossed—difficult in daylight, impossible at night.

All morning the three overlanders followed the sound of shots from the other camp and finally at noon stumbled onto the trail, having received a soaking while crossing a frozen river. Emihiser arrived at the same time. Wisely the others had stopped when it was realized that the four might be lost, and seeing the trees ablaze had set alight the return signal fire. Wind had confused the sound of shots being fired. After a hearty meal the men still managed to get in ten miles' travel.

The following day, November 1, the group stopped for their noon meal in a small prairie near the mountains. During the camp three Assiniboine or Stoney Indians came in, and finding them friendly the Minnesotans offered some provisions. By sign language it was explained that the gold-seekers required a guide—the Indians promised to provide one. That evening Hall accompanied them to their camp.

At the Stoney encampment, Hall found himself the subject of much curiosity. The Indians wanted to examine everything of American manufacture. His revolver drew particular interest and they asked to be shown how it worked. Grasping the opportunity to demonstrate the party's strength he set up a board and rapidly and accurately fired six shots through it. The Stonies were suitably impressed, and more so when Hall explained that each of the ten men carried a similar revolver and should any Blackfeet bother them there would be sixty dead as quick as they could fire. The Stonies were hereditary enemies of the Blackfeet and thought this was a great idea. They hoped, they told Hall, that the Americans would run into a war party so that they could reduce the Blackfoot numbers.

The Stoney bands were related to the plains-dwelling Assiniboine. Once part of the Sioux nation they had begun a westward movement some centuries earlier, settling mainly in the Red River region. One branch moved up the North Saskatchewan River and by 1800 were occupying the region around its headwaters. They reportedly annihilated the Snare Indians of the Jasper area. The name Assiniboine meant "people who cook with stones," and this group took the English translation, "Stoney."[8]

As promised, the band of Stonies provided a guide, "the whitest Indian I had ever seen, and in fact whiter than many half-breeds I had seen." Hall and the Indian joined the men at their next night's camp at the mouth of Dead Man's River and its junction with the Bow. The river came from the north side of Dead Man's Hill, where legend had it a great battle was fought, and that in the wood on the top of the hill was a grave where all the slain were buried.[9]

Traveling a trail skirting the mountain they reached the ruins of Old Bow Fort, high on a bank above the Bow River, on November 2. Sometimes referred to as Peigan Post it was a familiar stopping point for prairie travelers. It was established in 1832 but existed for only two precarious years before J. E. Harriott abandoned it in favor of Rocky Mountain House. The failure was due in part to its exposed position, and to the Blood's preventing the Peigans from trading and threatening to destroy it several times. Before many years passed all timbers had been burnt for firewood, leaving only some mud and clay chimneys standing. On a smooth board Jones wrote the party's name and a few comments, and placed it near the chimneys where it might be seen by passersby.[10]

The following day they came to the ford, a shallow but swift stretch of the Bow about 150 yards wide where several Red River carts had been abandoned by earlier travelers.[11]

Their Stoney guide led them up a clear stream of considerable size, the valley choked with windfall and forest fire debris that they had to cross and re-cross several times. An antelope was shot in the evening, providing fresh meat for the pot. It was obvious to all that they were now in the mountains. For some it was an awe-inspiring occurrence. To others the mountains were overwhelming, casting an aura of gloom and danger. Lord Southesk, an English sportsman who came down the Bow River in 1859, was one who felt relief in leaving the mountains. In his diary and narrative he wrote:

> There is something appalling in the gloom of the deep mountain valleys . . . confined within tremendous barriers of unmitigated rock, a gloom most horrible when storms and mists prevail. . . .
> Words cannot describe the desolation of the cold grey dawn in these rock-bound valleys, when heavy frost grapples the whole face of the earth, and nothing stirs with a full and energetic vitality except invisible creeping chills. The very mass and vastness of the mountains depress and daunt the soul. . . . You feel yourself imprisoned under some mighty ogre's sway; the unassailable, prodigious potencies that beset you all around crush out your courage. . . . In leaving the mountains, we seemed, to me to resemble the band of travellers in The Pilgrim's Progress, making their glad escape from Doubting Castle, the stronghold of that evil tyrant Giant Despair.[12]

The Kananaskis Valley lay broad and wide before them, the river winding its way through the forests of pine, spruce, and hemlock, bordered and framed with mountain peaks crowding out the sky, blocking the end of the corridor with a semicircular snow-covered redoubt. The heavy forest and windfall made progress difficult and slow. Palliser had traveled this route in August, three months previous to Jones, and he too had spent a good deal of time cutting through deadfall. Jones makes no mention of finding Palliser's track nor any evidence of previous passage. Palliser had named the pass, and river, for a legendary Indian who had an amazing recovery from a stunning ax blow.

On November 6, near the junction of Pocaterra Creek and the Kananaskis River, Jones's guide, who was not entirely familiar with the route, led them up a high ridge on the left, or east, of the valley. They camped after dark in a place where there was feed for their horses, not discovering until morning's light that they were on the edge of a forty-foot precipice. Their guide may have been attempting a route that would lead them through Elk Pass to Elk River, and then to the Kootenay River. Failing this he was either totally confused or deliberately misleading them. There was a route that followed the route of the present highway, up Pocaterra Creek, through Storm Creek to the Highwood River, and then the Bow River.[13]

Jones and his friends wandered through alpine meadows for the better part of two days, admiring bluebells, which Jones plucked and placed in his diary, and feeding on a flock of ptarmigan. The "white Grouse" were Jones's November 7 birthday dinner. They tried hunting Rocky Mountain bighorn sheep but without success, and soon after found a creek flowing in the opposite direction.

On Wednesday, November 10, after ten days in the mountains, they reached what they supposed to be the Tobacco Plains or the floor of some westward valley. What disturbed them was the sight of buffalo. Which side were they on? The west side, the guide assured them, so that evening they had a celebration, "a jolification to honor our release from the Mountains." Over a half gallon of rum and a bottle of brandy, they sang songs, told tales and lies, shared dreams for the future, and talked of the loved ones left behind. The Indian guide joined with his own songs, beating time with a stick on a packsaddle.

Next morning the Stoney left, as per their agreement, pointing out the trail and assuring them that they would reach the mountain fort of the Kutenais within three days. Through six inches of fresh snow the ten men plodded south. They were more than a little surprised when the following day the guide returned, intimating that he wished to continue. His reasons for returning remain unexplained, but it might be supposed that he discovered they were on the wrong side of the mountains and returned to correct his error.

For nine days and what Jones estimated to be 150 miles they continued south, always in sight of the mountains, now convinced by the sight of buffalo that they were on the east side of the Rockies. The weather turned cold during this week but thankfully game, in the form of rabbits, deer, elk, and buffalo, was plentiful, and on one stream the Stoney caught a fine mess of black-speckled and red-speckled trout. Rivers such as the Oldman and Crowsnest were forded, as well as numerous creeks. The guide led them too far south for a day, then turned and headed back to the Carbondale River where on the south bank of the river they again struck the Kootenay Trail.

The Kootenay Trail was named for the Kutenai Indians of the Columbia, Kootenay, and Flathead valleys, who used this pass and trail to hunt plains buffalo. They had once, perhaps a century before, lived on the eastern side of the Rockies, a plains tribe with the Blackfeet and Snakes as neighbors. By the mid-1700s the Snakes and Kutenais had been driven far back into the mountains by the aggressive Blackfeet. They retained the living habits and style of the plains, using teepees and the plains dress, and each fall traveled east via the North and South Kootenay passes for their annual hunting foray on the buffalo plains.[14]

Ironically the pass they were now approaching had been the original choice of Jones's party, but they had changed their mind due to Blackfoot danger. This was also the pass James Taylor had recommended in St. Paul, the pass known to Jamey Jock Bird as Medicine Rock Pass. The Jones party missed by just a couple of months being the first recorded white men to cross the North Kootenay Pass, being beaten by Blakiston of the Palliser expedition.

Blakiston crossed August 20, 1858, traveling east to west, and was followed two weeks later by Palliser, who crossed west to east. Palliser remarked that the pass "is not encumbered by fallen timber; the track is well defined and kept clear from obstructions by the Kutenai Indians, who constantly travel that way to hunt buffalo on the eastern plains." Blakiston did not claim discovery as many other explorers did, but rather noted that he was the first "Whiteman." Discovery is a subjective act. As an old mountain man said, "The deer made the first trails, the elk followed the deer, the buffalo the elk, and the Indians the buffalo; after the Indians came the trapper, then an army officer came along and discovered a pass." What the old-timer didn't add was that usually this army officer was being guided by an Indian.[15]

Now, on November 2, it was John Jones, nine Minnesotans, and one Stoney Indian guide who were on the height of the land, the great Continental Divide between waters flowing to the Arctic or Atlantic Ocean and those draining into the Pacific. Unlike Blakiston and Palliser, who crossed in the warmth and clear skies of summer, their previous night's camp had been in snow fifteen feet deep. The "well-defined and clear track" was buried beneath ice and snow. Buried to their waists in freezing snow and ice, shoveling the horses through drifts, the men were in no mood to fire their guns and proclaim a victorious crossing. Jim Smith found "the cold was intense. We had to keep guard over the animals all night, to prevent them from going back again to the valley we had left, which was dreadful work. We could only stand for about a quarter of an hour at a time. Morning, however came at last and with the earliest glimpse of daylight we started. The wind was blowing tremendously, and the drifting snow nearly blinded us."[16]

Jones continued: "We had very hard work in shovelling out a path for the horses, through a tremendous snow drift, the Indian all the time gazing in amazement. After we got through the snow drift the danger was not over—through the gorge we had to pass ... and it presented the appearance of a glacier. The balance of the way was steep and rocky and covered with ice, and it was with great difficulty that man and horse could keep their feet. The wind blew fearfully cold through the gap and if [it] had not been for the amount of labor we had done and were doing we would have frozen to death in a short time. Finally with great exertion we gained the gap, and made our descent rapidly to the valley below, which we finally reached in the afternoon and camped, where there was scarcely any snow."

The Minnesotans' trials were not over. On the North Kootenay Pass there are two heights of land, the main barrier of the Rockies and the MacDonald Range, which divides the Flathead Valley, which Jones had now reached, from the Elk drainage system. For two days they bribed the guide to stay while they wandered up a creek through fallen timber searching for the trail. On the third day he left, heading back for the valley of the Bow. Schaeffter lost his horse and blamed the Indian for stealing it. Although they wondered why he had returned to their assistance two weeks ago, none now thought to give thanks that he had brought them to the pass or wondered how they would have survived without him. Instead they condemned him as a "treacherous hound."

Ahead lay a mountain. The men ascended it in search of a pass. Now they began to see blaze marks and scarred areas on the trees where horses might have rubbed packsaddles. By four in the afternoon they were within a quarter of a mile of the summit. Smith, Houck, and Amesbury went ahead to see what the prospects were. Jim Smith describes what lay before them at the summit:

Never shall I forget the mingled sensations I experienced as the magnificent, but to us heart sickening prospect, burst upon our view. We stood upon the edge of a perpendicular precipice, hundreds of feet in depth, the snow on which we stood being so deep, that good sized pine trees resembled brush, only their tops being visible; while in every direction, far as the eye could reach, nothing was to be seen but snow capped mountains, with their interesting vallies running in every direction. The only thing that seemed to hold out the slightest hope was a river in a valley far, far below. This we agreed must run out of the mountains on the western side, and it was possible might lead us out at a camp of Indians, but how to get down to it was the question. Night was fast approaching, and it was equally impossible to descend at this point or to pass the night upon the summit without freezing to death.

Disheartened and scared, they retreated down the ridge, then taking a new angle, pushed and struggled their way onto the crest again, the sun's rays longer now. Again, a precipice dropped from the ridge and again they withdrew, traversed along its base, and staggered to the top, just in time to see the sun set behind the far hills. Here there was a chance. The cliff was steep but not perpendicular. It was bad, dangerous, and frightening, but not utterly impossible. For four or five hundred feet the face was so steep that neither horse nor man would be able to stay standing, but beyond that a controlled descent might be possible.

The disappearance of the sun intensified the cold. Despite the darkness they had to move. A decision had to be made. Jim Smith quickly ran over the options. If they stayed here at the summit it was likely that some of them, perhaps all, would die during the night. It was hardly worth consideration. An alternative was to abandon their horses and race in retreat down the ridge to the shelter of trees where fires could be built, then endeavor to reach the plains where there was a possibility of wintering, living off the abundant game. Or, they could push boldly on, hoping that the river below led to the west, that there were no further passes to cross, and that they might reach Kootenay Fort. The latter involved considerable risk.

They had only six days' provisions left. If the valley below had no trail they would be unable to retrace their steps. This would mean starvation and death from exposure, already beginning to creep into their bodies. Jones for one had begun to feel drowsy and stagger as his will to push on waned and his body temperature dropped. These were their choices. Now they must vote.

"We have come this far, let's keep going," they all voiced. "Onward!"

Without further hesitation they unsaddled and unpacked their horses, led them to the edge of the cliff, and pushed them over. Screaming, neighing, eyes rolling in fright the animals careened down the slopes, legs and hooves frantically trying to grab ground to stop their plunge. A leg would catch and a body catapult, somersaulting around and over rocks, bouncing off trees. As the initial screams of fright faded the men heard falling bodies smacking into trees and being ripped on rocks—then all was quiet save for the frantic braying of Jones's horse, wedged between two trees. Throwing the packs after the horses the men slid to Jones's horse and began to chop away one tree. In a mighty panicked lunge the horse broke free, continued his fall, and landed on a broad "comparatively level" ledge.

The descent killed two horses, surprisingly light punishment considering the fall. None of the men had been seriously hurt, so, gathering everything together, they continued their descent another few hundred feet, alternately sliding, falling, and walking. They came to another vertical drop and finding some wood decided to try to spend the night here.

The fire, fed with great effort, brought new cheer and warmth to the camp, and agony to a few of the men. Jim Smith found the heat was thawing spots that had gone numb. One foot was frostbitten. Some of the others had lesser frozen areas, but young Joe Gibson was in real trouble. Both his feet were badly frostbitten and the warmth of the fire and subsequent thawing brought an almost unbearable pain.

After an interminable night came morning. The horses had not moved and resignedly accepted the loads of the two dead mounts. Their descent continued, accompanied with bruising, bone-jarring falls, until at two o'clock they reached the valley floor and a broad, open trail. Jim Smith wrote, "Though not loud, heartfelt and earnest was the prayer of thanksgiving that ascended from more than one breast."

Their descent brought them to the headwaters of Lodgepole Creek. Following that stream led to the Wigwam River, past the magnificent ramparts of China Wall, out onto Wigwam Flats to the Elk River. Traveling south they crossed the Tobacco Plains east of the Kootenay River and on the third day, December 1, reached the long-sought Kootenay Fort, a collection of three squalid shacks under the care of trader John Linklater. It was not quite what they had been expecting after visiting the prairie forts, but it was a vestige of civilization at least, an oasis in a mountain wilderness.

The autumn trail from Fort Edmonton had taken them forty days. They had been on the road west for four and one half months. Although they had initially expected to reach the Fraser goldfields weeks earlier, they nevertheless felt a certain elation at crossing the formidable barrier of the Rocky Mountains. The prospect of gold began to fade in the face of harsh reality. Forward movement became not a search for riches but a means of survival. At Fort Edmonton they had been told that settlement and a wintering place were only three weeks southwest of Fort Kootenay. Surely then their trials and tribulations must be nearly over now that the fort was in sight. One wonders how they would have reacted had they known that another four and a half months of struggle and starvation lay down the trail to the Colville Valley.

## Washington Territory

The trading post Jones and his party arrived at in December 1858 was never one that could rightfully bear the title of "fort." Not only were the unfortified buildings little more than shacks, but the location changed at the whim of the current trader. Kootenay Post, also known as "Tobacco House," an outpost of Fort Colville, was now under the care of John Linklater and after several moves up and across the river was back in its original location on the east side of the Kootenay River five miles south of the border.[17]

Linklater was an Orkneyman, a small Scot called Scotty by his friends and Little White Man by the Kutenais. He had served with the Company for some years and had been in charge of this post since 1852. He had not married, preferring to wait for his retirement in Scotland, now just a few years off. When Jones's party arrived, "Little White Man" was nursing a sore thigh, the reminder of an Indian fight that summer.

Two mountain men, traders MacKay and Hamilton, had crossed the mountains with Kutenais and tangled with Blackfeet over stolen horses, killing three. As the Kutenais and traders withdrew westward the Blackfeet followed until finally at the Kootenay River they laid seige. Hamilton rode for help and brought back Linklater and enough provisions, Scotty said, "for a feast." The Blackfeet were driven back, but Scotty took an arrow in the thigh. Indian women brought him to his post on a travois.[18]

Kootenay Post was operated only during the winter. Linklater arrived here in early October with trade goods and returned down the Kootenay on horseback in March or April, before the spring floods washed out the trail. The furs generally amounted to about two hundred black bears, six hundred marten, and three hundred beaver, two thousand muskrats, dressed moose, elk and buffalo skins. The profit, Linklater said, was over 90 percent.[19]

Jones noted that the Indians had built a "chapel," as prepossessing as the "fort." The building measured just over ten feet square, had no fireplace or chimney, and had to be entered through a hole in the wall that served as a door. It had been erected the year before when the Roman Catholic priest had visited.[20]

These Indians had first come into contact with the Roman Catholic religion at the 1840 fur-trade rendezvous in Pierre's Hole, when they met Father De Smet, a missionary with the Society of Jesus. De Smet visited here the following year and "sang high mass, thus taking spiritual possession of this land."[21]

Jones and party visited various teepees, eating with the families and trading worn-out shirts, salt, soap, and anything else they could spare for provisions. About nine o'clock a cow bell tolled and the head man of each family led his family in prayers. "They appear," Jones wrote, "to be very zealous and devout in the performance of their rites, they are strictly honest, and you can lay anything down and leave it without any fears of it being stolen."

On the third day, December 3, the overlanders struck the southward trail. Linklater had given them a chart of the route. "In seventeen days," he said, "you should reach the Colville settlement. But watch out for the Spokanes, Pend d'Oreilles, Nez Percé and Colville Indians, they've been at war with the army all summer."

Having run the Blackfoot gauntlet east of the mountains, the Minnesotans figured they could accept similar risks on this side. Now they were nine. Young Joe Gibson's feet were so badly frozen that he had to stay with Linklater, a decision that resulted in him spending the most comfortable winter of all.

In his six winters at this post these gold-seekers were the first party of whitemen Linklater had seen. He watched them ride down the river with some reluctance, but remembered young Joe. Now he would have a winter partner, someone to listen to his stories of the Company and the Indian fights he had seen. "Just last summer me and Hamilton . . ."[22]

Had the overlanders known what lay ahead they would have chosen to winter on the Tobacco Plains. Now they headed down the Kootenay River, into the U.S.A., the river David Thompson had discovered in June 1807, and called the Flatbow, later the McGillivray.

At the mouth of Fisher Creek, the first crossing of the Kootenay, Jones met a band of Kutenais. In the intervening five days one mule had died, a victim of some internal injury suffered in the long slide and fall in Kootenay Pass. A camp was made while they waited for the ice to freeze, and again they traded for provisions with the Indians. Jones was beginning to discover, but was reluctant to admit, that the Indians were of more help than hindrance. No matter what the reality, nineteenth-century prejudices were hard to overcome. The Indians were a source of food, horses, and guides, and not once had the small, vulnerable party been harassed in any way. They were still "red niggers" to Jones.

By morning the river had two and a half inches of ice, a good covering but not enough for a bridge. The men went to work and piled snow across the river, then poured water on it and waited for it to freeze, thus providing themselves, much to the astonishment of the Indians, with a safe ice bridge.

The Kootenay River trail was a rough, rocky road in a narrow, confined valley. Though well marked through years of use by the HBC, it was the most difficult horse trail in the country and many were lost in the yearly brigades. Amesbury's horse died along this stretch, another victim of the long fall and rough road. They passed Yahk River, the spectacular Moyie River Falls, and the Kootenay Falls or Rapids, where shelves and ledges of bedrock and midstream rocky islets caused a series of drops, cascades, holes, and turbulent currents. The trail along the north side of the Kootenay River was slower than expected. Time was lost to strayed horses, and rest stops were made wherever sufficient grazing could be found. The second crossing of the Kootenay at Ducks or Paddlers Lake, where Walla Walla businessman Edwin Bonner would later build a ferry, was reached on December 16.

As had David Thompson and most other travelers, they found an encampment of Lower Kutenais in about a dozen rush lodges here, a place called Chalemptta. The Kootenay River broadened, slowing to a meander from one side of its well-defined trench to the other, creating different channels, sloughs, and oxbow lakes where waterfowl paused in migration. The ice was thawing, and the once continuous snow had stopped. Snow geese passed overhead. They rested for a day and traded for fresh mounts, dried fish, and a quart of wheat. Jones remarked that for the first time since Fort Garry he slept under cover, having accepted the hospitality of the chief's lodge.

Crossing the river they struck south again, traveling up the dark, dismal cedar canyon of Deep Creek. The farther they advanced the deeper the snow became and the worse the trail. They ate the last buffalo meat in the cedar bottom, surrounded by towering giants eight feet in diameter, looming over the weary and footsore party, blocking out what little light the winter sky offered. In the gloom the "Giant Despair" stalked them.

On their third day they held a conference. The snow was averaging a depth of three feet; provisions were low; the stock could not continue. They must either abandon their stock or decide to winter at Ducks Lake. Their night of decision was a terrifying one as a terrific wind howled through the fir and cedar, blowing snow through their blankets, with the frequent sound of crashing forest giants tearing the air in their death fall. The darkness was appalling. The nine men lay huddled in their blankets "in mute resignation, almost wishing that some friendly tree would fall and end our sufferings."

This night ended their goldfield dreams. The elephant of fear that crashed through the timber in the long hours of morning had been met, but their forward momentum was lost. The party would have to split. Amesbury, Emihiser, and the two Mankato men who had joined at Fort Edmonton, Hall and Hodgson, would take all the remaining provisions and push south in an attempt to reach the Colville Valley. Jones, Houck, Jim Smith, Palmer, and John Schaeffter would take the stock but no provisions and return to Ducks Lake, hoping to depend once again on the Indians for a livelihood, and if need be to eat the livestock.

"We bid a sad farewell to the boys," Jones wrote, "and started with heavy hearts. Little did we expect on that eventful morning that we should ever see each other again."

The Colville-bound party had drawn the long straw. They stayed in camp for two days, making snowshoes, and then followed old blazes south to Pend Oreille Lake. Soon after they came into the camp of "Old Paul," who pointed the direction to them and traded some provisions. Following a ridge they struck a trail and wandered into the camp of Spokane Garry on the Spokane River. They had been without food for three days, but this was New Year's Eve and they were welcomed into the celebrations.

Spokane Garry, a chief of these Spokanes, had gone to Red River in

1825 at the request of Governor Simpson to receive an education. He spoke and wrote good English and French. The men were treated well, but Jones, when he later recounted Amesbury's story in his journal, adds that "he is reputed to be very treacherous." The Spokanes had been at war the year previously, but after a couple of battles in which they had been beaten, and after 750 of their horses had been rounded up and shot and their lodges burnt, they submitted. One wonders why they helped the small party of overlanders. Nevertheless, they rested here for four days and then moved on to Colville Valley where residents offered them employment and board. Only two weeks had passed since the gloomy Deep Creek parting.

At Ducks Lake Jones and the four men who had remained with him busied themselves building small log shanties, accepting the hospitality of the chief to stay in his lodge while the work was completed. The chief's rude cabin measured eight by twelve feet, with a pine bough roof, pine bough floor, and chinking of "the same material." A piece of canvas covered the small door.

On December 24 the five wintering partners were surprised to be invited to a Christmas Eve celebration. The tribe kept track of dates on a crude calendar the priests had given them, perforating a hole for each day. They had also recorded the day the Minnesotans first arrived with a perforation for each man, and had also noted the day the five returned to winter.

The evening's celebrations began with a brave of "ciceronian style" dashing frantically from a lodge in a seminude state and there "spiriting in earnest," haranguing an unseen audience until the cold drove him back to the lodge fire. Once rewarmed he again rushed into the freezing night and in unintelligible eloquence repeated his performance. This continued for hours, and the somewhat ill-at-ease whitemen followed the example of the rest of the tribe, ensconcing themselves in a warm out-of-the-way corner and passing the time smoking the weed.

About eight o'clock the familiar ring of the cow bell called everyone to a service in the chief's lodge, where prayers and hymns were sung in a mixture of French, Latin, Kutenais, and English. The people all left for their own lodges, but in a few minutes, Jones wrote, "the squaws came in, in single file, and deposited their contributions of smoked venison and misas-gui-tom-i-ca, or service berries, at the foot of the altar. The altar was formed out of a square box made from cedar bark, the box was covered with a mat of rushes, and at the foot was also a mat. Catholic pictures were pinned to the side of the lodge over the altar. Each squaw upon depositing her contribution would cross herself in a pious manner before the altar and receive a benediction from the chief, who is acting priest for the band." The donations were then placed in large kettles and the cooking begun for the feast to follow on the morrow.

Dawn of Christmas Day, 1858, was tolled in "by that villainous cowbell," a reminder that prayer was at hand. After prayer and hymns a primitive communion was offered.

The priest's attendant filling a cup with the liquor of the berries, and a small piece of venison, giving it to the acting priest, who pronounced a blessing and having partook passed it to the attendant, who in turn passed to each one present, that had arrived at the age of discretion. After the Sacrament was administered the squaws and children who had been dressed in the best style, took their departure, the males remaining and seating themselves in a circle. Each one now armed himself with a large pan, kettle, or basket capable of containing fluid, and we were told to do likewise. An Indian now stepped forward and distributed the venison and berries, reserving for the priest and ourselves, the largest and choicest portions.

The feasting continued as the party went from one teepee to another, by which time the overlanders were not only full but had a kettle full of stew that would last for three days. It was a Christmas Day they would not soon forget. By the time the stew was getting low in the kettle they had moved into their new abode and New Year's Day and a similar celebration were at hand. Feasting, guns fired through the teepee smoke hole, and a receiving line that included the youngest babe at breast, brought the year of 1858 to a close.

The great quest of '58 that the overlanders had thought would see them digging for Fraser River riches was ending in a primitive Indian village along the Kootenay River. Three others were at Fort Edmonton, young Joe Gibson was at Kootenay Post with frozen feet, and of the four who had struck off for Colville they could hope to hear nothing until spring. The great Kutenai New Year's Festival was at once a thanksgiving for lives spared thus far, a celebration of survival, and a wake for the dreams of fortunes in gold.

## Winter This Side of the Mountains

While the ten Faribault men had been steadily making their way across the plains and through the mountains to the wintering point of Ducks Lake, other 1858 parties of British Columbia–bound overlanders were having less success.

### Hastings Party

From the town of Hastings, on the banks of the Mississippi thirty miles south of St. Paul, a group of eleven, some of whom would be connected with overland journeys for the next five years had set out in late July of 1858.[23]

Like the Faribault men they sent a small party down the Red River and regrouped at Fort Garry. On the way the land party had a run in with a group of Métis cart drivers and passed with fear the place where Métis John Beads and Louis Bosquet had recently been killed by Sioux. Traveling via St. Joseph they reached Fort Garry in thirty-two days.

The party left Fort Garry September 10 and reached Fort Ellice in eleven days. At the Touchwood Hills they were delayed three days by snow, an indication they were traveling dangerously late in the season. Four days out of the hills, on the Quill Plains, snow that "indicated the rapid approach of a northern winter" forced them to turn back.

Before reaching the relative safety and comfort of Fort Ellice, they met a cart train of one hundred wagons with halfbreeds from the Selkirk settlement, including John Dease. They joined the train and turned west again, arriving in twelve days at Moose Woods on the South Saskatchewan River. Here, on good land, there grew ash, elm, and aspen suitable for building and firewood and the halfbreeds moved into shanties as they did most winters, waiting to begin trading with Indians.

The Hastings party had never been cohesive and at the wintering place the two messes shifted. Most decided to winter here as the weather was now very severe, while others went on about six days. Buffalo were plentiful and the men set about gathering their winter meat supply and settled in beneath the drifting snow, huddled before the wind to wait for warmer traveling weather.

**St. Paul Party**

Meanwhile the St. Paul–sponsored party of George Burnham, Charles Goodrich, and W. Ellis Smith, which had traveled with John Jones's Faribault company to Pembina, lost five precious weeks awaiting supplies promised by Joseph Rolette. Not until September 14 could they leave the settlement.

They arrived in Fort Garry September 16 and three days later left in company with a halfbreed trader. Following the cart trail past Fort Ellice to the Touchwood Hills, where they met Henry Youle Hind of the Assiniboine and Saskatchewan Exploring Expedition, then in company with halfbreed traders they turned west to Moose Woods where they overtook the wintering Hastings party. Smith reported that they intended joining forces in the spring but Goodrich wrote: "We left them, however, because it was evident from their conduct that they would quarrel with the Indians," a rather prophetic judgment.[24]

Smith, Goodrich, and Burnham continued north, crossed the South Saskatchewan in a skin boat and with the odometer clicking went on to Fort Pitt, where they were offered a wintering house and provisions in exchange for work. Smith had been doing quite well for provisions. He had brought with him several bottles of "Pain Killer," a medicine "high in alcohol content," and at every trading post he had been able to trade one bottle for twenty pounds of pemmican. He recommended that liquor, tea, sugar, and Pain Killer were the best trade items to carry.[25]

James Simpson, in charge of Fort Pitt, had made several trips across the mountains. He figured they could make it there from Fort Pitt in twenty-five or thirty days, or a total of eighty from St. Paul.

Goodrich wrote to Nobles: "We intend crossing the country from here to the mountains, and not go by way of Edmonton. This course would have saved us 200 miles travel; but owing to a war between the Crees and Blackfeet Indians, which makes the route ... very dangerous, we will be obliged to go farther north, and cross the mountains north of the Kootenay Pass. We will probably go via Jasper House, leave our animals at that place, and take boats from there. ... We expect to [leave in May] and get across the mountains in sixty days."[26]

So the three men sponsored by St. Paul merchants, on whom rested the hopes of a trade route west, settled in at Fort Pitt to await the coming of spring.

The Red River settlement was the furthermost outpost of the Mississippi–Red River frontier. To overlanders it was the final provisioning point, the final harbor before launching onto the westward rolling sea of grass. News of the Fraser gold had not reached many communities until late in the spring of 1858. As prairie travel was only practical until perhaps October, there was little time for the organization and provisioning of companies and many got a late start. Some, like the Faribault men, pushed through the cold while others, such as the Hastings men and the St. Paul threesome, chose to winter where the snows caught them. The more judicious chose the relative comfort of the Red River settlement, early, for winter came quickly here.

One resident laughed at the surprise of easterners and said, "Hell yes it comes fast. Why one year I forgot to go outside one day and missed fall altogether. We have two seasons here; too hot and too cold." A snug wintering refuge awaiting spring green-up made a strong start possible.

**Holmes Party**

Tom Holmes, a frontiersman of the same cut as Daniel Boone and Simon Kenton and now a land developer, was looking for greener, or at least different, pastures at age fifty-four. With his latest town of Shakopee on its way to being well established he formed a party of fourteen to search for Fraser gold. They pulled out of St. Paul on July 25, 1858, bound for Fort Garry. It was the first of four overland journeys Holmes would lead.[27]

Holmes was as aware of the coming winter and travel difficulties as any plainsman and he and his Shakopee men holed up near the fort. During the latter part of the summer others had arrived, singly, in pairs, and in larger organized parties.

**The Moores**

The Moore brothers arrived with a mixed cavalcade. At the first hint of gold news in early spring they left their father's home in Grey County, Canada West, and started west. Short of money they stopped in Illinois to cut hay and arrived in St. Paul in June. There they became acquainted with a halfbreed who was guiding fourteen Sisters of Charity to St. Boniface in the Red River settlement. Three of these, Sisters Emery, Alphonse, and Lamy were bound for Father Lacombe's new mission at Lac Ste. Anne.[28]

By late July they had arrived in Red River. The three Grey nuns bound for Fort Edmonton met thirty-four-year-old Father Remas, sent by Lacombe as a guide, and began their long walk into privation. In later years, their mission would be visited by other overlanders. The Grey nuns went to their convent while the Moores scouted around for winter employment.[29]

## The New Brunswickers

While the Moores explored the Red River settlement a large party were camped near the corner of Pine and 2nd streets in St. Anthony, building wagons and rigging equipment. The company of twenty-one led by Albert Henshaw, mostly lumbermen from New Brunswick, had been here for weeks building thirteen wagons similar to Red River carts, "but much better made" to which single oxen would be hitched. With provisions for nine months and well armed they planned to go two hundred miles beyond Red River and winter on the "hunting grounds of the Hudson's Bay Company." A resident grandly remarked, "It must require some pluck to cross the borders of civilization and penetrate a pathless region at this season of the year in search of gold."

A New Brunswicker paused in his work, "Not half as much as to stay in St. Anthony all winter with nothing to do."

They rolled north on August 31 and plodded into the Red River settlement in November. Snow was flying so they postponed their westward journey and billeted with Kildonan district settlers. Merchants Andrew McDermott and John Inkster each grub-staked a group, including the Moore brothers, and took them up the Assiniboine River to cut stands of oak for their mills. In spring the timber would be rafted down to the settlement.[30]

Of the eighty-six overlanders who had begun the journey toward the Fraser River in 1858, none had reached their destination. Only the Faribault party of ten had managed, with great difficulty, to cross the Rockies. Poised on the edge of the grassland and scattered throughout the Saskatchewan country in the posts of the HBC, these parties would form the foundation for the companies that would cross in the following years.

# The Faribault Party

Winter was long for the five Minnesotan overlanders wintering at Ducks Lake in the Washington Territories. The festivities of Christmas and New Year's faded into the monotony of day-to-day existence. By January 9 their provisions were gone and their diet became minnows and lichen. The clever native traders would not allow them to fish, but traded them a few at a time. January 24 was a highlight—they scraped their flour sacks and found enough to make one "slapjack," split four ways. The five gradually weakened, developed stomach pains, and voided blood. Despondent, they spoke continually of home, fantasizing restaurant orders. Houck would call for a good mess of pork and beans; Jim Smith's palate was more sophisticated and he wanted mallard, lobster sauce, and a bottle of "Cabinet." Palmer, the miserable little Englishman, of course wanted a roast beef and plum pudding. Dutch John Schaeffter—cornbeef, sauerkraut, and "Sweitzer kase, and several gallons of lager." Jones had a hankering for "a huge loaf of homemade bread and enough golden syrup to devour it with, and to wash it down sundry bottles of Edinburgh Ale."

In early February two Indians from Kootenay Post passed on their way to Colville with HBC mail. The five wrote to Amesbury, who they hoped had made it to Colville, asking for tobacco, knowing that the two couriers could not bring back enough food to help. Two horses died and while the coyotes and wolves howled over the remains the Minnesotans shared the entrails and hide with their Indian benefactors, of which only three lodges remained.

Valentine's Day brought "to our minds the Valentines we left behind us, and we conversed freely and unreservedly of the past and our prospects for the future." Jones's journal, usually expressive and full of comment, became a dispirited record of the passing days.

February 16th Wednesday—Clear and cold during day and night.
17th Thursday—Mild and snowing throughout day and night.
18th Friday—No change in the weather.
19th Saturday—No change.
20th Sunday—No change—anxiously awaiting the arrival of the couriers, as they are overdue.
21st Monday—No change.

By February 23 the couriers still had not returned. It was evident that all five could not survive on the remaining horses and lichen, so again they split. Jones, Houck, and Palmer struck off for the Colville Valley, while Schaeffter and Jim Smith stayed at the Ducks Lake shanty.

Jones, Palmer, and Houck's departure on February 24 was somewhat sentimental. While they were readying to leave three squaws came in with a supply of moss and when they found the three men were about to leave they knelt down and offered prayers for their safety. "Upon rising," Jones wrote, "they shook our hands, kissed us and cried, at such a burst of warm-hearted feeling, which I never once dreamed they possessed, I came near blubbering myself. They again knelt as we started, though not understanding their language we knew sufficient enough that they implored the Great Spirit to guide us through in safety, and to shield us from all harm."

On this journey Jones's dream ability, his psychic powers, seemed to pull the group through. When near the Deep Creek–Pack River divide the trail was lost Houck and Palmer wanted to turn back, but Jones dreamed that the next day they would find a snowshoe trail and convinced them to carry on. By mid-afternoon, with feet bleeding from the snowshoe thongs, they found the trail. The next night Jones had a premonition that Pend Oreille Lake would be found, and late in the afternoon, to an accompanying flight of migrating swans, geese, and ducks, they arrived at an open section of the lake.

Jones, now dubbed "The Dreamer," continued with his prophecies. They would find food—and shortly stumbled on an Indian camp. They would meet an Indian and his squaw on the opposite side of the river, a portent of good news—and sure enough, some hours later there was the Indian and his squaw with the news that Amesbury and Hall's December party had made it this far. Here at Old Paul's encampment they hired an old Indian to paddle them down the Pend Oreille River to the founding Jesuit mission of St. Ignatius, opened in 1846.

The canoe journey took two days, a brief respite for Jones's feet. But on March 7 he once again began snowshoeing on the trail over the Selkirk Mountains to Colville. On the eighth the climb to the summit began. Jones's moccasins were red with blood, his strength and determination dissolved. He collapsed in the snow and told Palmer and Houck to take the guide and push on; he would follow if and when he could. Palmer went on; Houck refused. Coaxing and cajoling he finally got Jones on his feet and with force kept him moving, one foot at a time, one more step forward, until finally they crested the summit. Within hours they were off the mountains and into the Colville Valley. At the cabin of "Butcher Brown" they rested and ate. The next day Hall arrived with the HBC Walla Walla mail train and news of the remainder of the party.

Amesbury was staying with a "Frenchman," Mr. Perroway, a few miles down the road; Emihiser was further down the road with Thomas Brown, who had crossed the mountains with Sinclair in 1854; and Hodgeson had gone on to the Willamette Valley.

Jones stayed with Thomas Brown until the middle of April, allowing his feet to heal; Palmer went to work for the HBC; Houck found a job building a house; and Emihiser found work with Brown. These latter three stayed in Colville when Jones and Amesbury left on April 13 for the Dalles, arriving April 29. On the way they met several large parties heading north for the Fraser River, via the interior route, ready for the mining season of 1859. They were not tempted to join.

The journey was for all intents over, each man choosing his own route. The party was dissolving, not with a resounding round of cheers and backslapping, but silently and sadly. Most would never see each other again. They were moving on, though, while Dutch John Schaeffter and Jim Smith still lingered reluctantly at Ducks Lake. It was after the final split, Smith later wrote, "that our hard times commenced in earnest."

The "half-smelt size fish" stopped running; the Indians left; the remaining horses died and were eaten by wolves. For two months they lived on lichen and a little rotten meat the Indians periodically brought them. On April 29 Linklater arrived with Gibson, on his way to Fort Colville with his winter furs. Once more Smith and Schaeffter were on their way, and, always optimists, rejoiced in their deliverance. Their rejoicing was premature.

The trail up Deep Creek to the low height of land and then down Pack River to Pend Oreille Lake was a distance of about thirty miles. With the snow five to eight feet deep it took an incredible eighteen days. The brigade ran out of provisions and the lake's high water obliterated the trail, necessitating cutting a new trail along the shore. They spent twenty-three days on a journey that should have taken three.

At Pend Oreille River, Linklater and his horse train headed north for Fort Colville while the three overlanders continued toward Antoine Plante's Spokane River ferry, eighty miles south. Plante, a halfbreed, had a dislike of whitemen, at least these whitemen, and of supplying food. Finally, by paying very liberally, they obtained as much as they could eat and three pounds of flour. With these meagre provisions they struck for Fort Walla Walla, 175 miles away.

Jim Smith's feet were in bad shape. His moccasins were worn out and there was no way to replace them. Every morning he had to take his knife and cut open his feet in six or seven places, draining out a cupful of pus before he could walk a step. In such condition, living on roots begged from Indians, they made it to the fort on May 31. They arrived "with as good an appetite for pork and potatoes as people commonly experience," Jim Smith wrote. "This may be said to have brought our adventures to a close."

Jim Smith's final report to the *New York Commercial Advertiser* summed up the frustration, anger, and deprivation of their westward search for riches.

> This country has been sadly overrated. It is throughout its length and breadth, (and the same remarks apply equally to Washington territory) a barren desert, incapable of cultivation.... Most especially does this remark apply to the valley of the Columbia. The Fraser River mines are an unmitigated humbug, and have been the cause of more misery than will be generally known.[31]

Of the ten confident men who left Fort Edmonton in October 1858 not one reached his Fraser River destination. Yet in a perverse way their success (for they had crossed the Rockies in winter and survived) and their letters to eastern papers, spurred other men to try the journey. The knowledge these Faribault men had gained through incredible hardship was passed back to those who followed. They were the trailblazers—the first overlanders.

# Chapter Four

## The Man from Brechin

October 6, 1858, Victoria, Vancouver's Island. The streets were crowded with miners in uniforms of blue or red wool shirts; trousers (pants they were now being called) tucked into high boots; waist strapped with a revolver and bowie knife; and head crowned with a felt hat. Those arriving on the crowded wharves that lined the waterfront wore packs that contained "articles indispensible to the emigrant" suggested by the various guide books being rushed into print.

Indispensible were the beaverteen jacket, waistcoat, and trousers; duck trousers; drill jacket, waistcoat, and trousers; pilot overcoat, waterproof coat; two serge shirts or Jersey frocks; one felt hat; one Brazil straw hat; six bluestriped cotton shirts; one pair boots; one pair shoes; four handkerchiefs; four pairs worsted hose; two pairs cotton hose; one pair braces; four towels; and razor, shaving brush, and a glass. Many did without the latter three items.

In anxious hands and tied atop packs were the mining tools advised, the mandatory shovel and pan, pick and various pots, bedding, and cutlery. Those leaving traveled much lighter. With few exceptions they had little more than the worn clothes on their backs and the fare to a comfortable wintering ground or wherever they called home.[1]

"Hear ye, hear ye! All those bound for San Francisco. The good bark *Glimpse* sails tomorrow under the able direction of Captain Cove. Coaches available to the gangplank. Tickets still available for a few cold southbound miners. San Francisco. Hear ye . . ."

"The *Eliza Anderson* steams her way across the straits to the metropolis of New Westminster tomorrow. Those passengers wishing . . ."

"Capt. Taylor of the sloop *J. C. Caswell* invites passengers aboard bound for Port Townsend. The finest table, the softest berths, the lowest fares await. Gentlemen take heed, we sail on the morrow's tide."

"Tea from Asia, coffee, preserves and the finest silks are arriving on the bark *Sea Nymph*, just now docking from Hong Kong . . ."

" . . . the bark *Jeanette* . . ."

" . . . the *Jonathan* . . ."

Criers stalked the streets announcing ships coming and going, pointing the way to the docks for returning miners anxious to leave. On street corners stood stolid groups of dirty, blanketed Indians—though not much dirtier than many of the miners—watching this bustle and business so recently descended upon the quiet island trading post. Those natives who had moved onto the new Songhee lands near the fort were becoming corrupted. The men drank and begged, the women drank and prostituted themselves, offering their bodies to hungry miners.

On corners not occupied by Indians, auctioneers sold at exorbitant rates goods as useless to miners as the proverbial teats on a boar, yet eagerly purchased as reminders of home. Dress suits, wardrobe cases, walking sticks, and home furnishings went under the gavel. Passersby were delighting in telling one northbound miner the folly of his ways for he had just successfully bid on a heavy iron washstand. He now had no idea how he would transport it the three or four hundred miles to the goldfields. The auctioneer had left.

Over the hustlers' cries came the sounds of street traffic: the wagons and horses, the blasphemous goading of teamsters, wheels crunching in gravel and sucking in mud, boots echoing on boardwalks. On every street the sounds of progress reverberated, saws cutting lumber and hammers driving cut nails for an eclectic merging of architecture and businesses needed to support the thousands of gravel diggers.[2]

Through this cacophony of sound and milieu of miners walked a solitary man, a Scot, unknown by any name but that of his hometown, Brechin, Scotland. This Man from Brechin was singular—while those around him had arrived aboard one of the tall-masted or paddlewheel ships in the harbor, or perhaps by trail from Oregon, he alone had come west across the plains of British North America. Not only had he begun his journey with the Fraser River as his destination, he had completed the journey and would soon see the gold-bearing bars. His journey was also singularly tragic.

His story begins in Brechin, a small village in Angus, Scotland, located east of the South East Highlands on the banks of the South Esk River a few miles from the North Sea. In the late 1850s a man there was growing restless, dissatisfied. He might have been young or old, a blacksmith or a doctor, a big man or a small man. We know only that he came from Brechin and was strong in body and mind.

Leaving family and friends he sailed for North America as displaced crofters a generation before him had, seeking his fortune along the banks of a river that bore gold. By August 1858 he had reached the Mississippi frontier and joined with other adventurers ready to leave St. Paul for the new gold rush on Fraser's River.[3]

Fifteen of us left St. Paul's Minnesota, on the 16th of August, 1858, for Fraser's River, with a horse each. The first twenty days we got along pretty good, but after that our trouble started.

In 1858 routes to the Pacific northwest were ill-defined. The British Palliser expedition and Canadian H. Y. Hind Saskatchewan explorations were not yet complete and information was scarce. There were, however, certain recognized routes, not defined trails. One was the Stevens route, proposed in 1853 by the governor of Washington Territory, Isaac I. Stevens, as suitable for a western railway.

Travelers heading west from St. Paul tried to avoid two obstacles: the Coteau des Prairies and the larger Coteau du Missouri, a glacier-roughened plateau fifteen to twenty-five miles wide lying east of the Missouri River and west of the James River, extending from south of St. Paul, north across the international border almost to the Qu'Appelle River. In addition to avoiding the rough climbs, travelers, particularly those with wagons, were anxious to detour around the difficult crossings of the James, Sheyenne, Missouri, and Yellowstone rivers.

The Stevens route skirted the northerly end of the Coteau to Fort Union near the confluence of the Missouri and Yellowstone rivers. From there the Missouri and Milk river valleys led to Fort Benton in Montana Territory. The route presented certain problems, not the least of which was the difficulty in following it. There were no sign posts and few landmarks, the Coteau country appearing much the same mile after mile. By following the natural landforms overlanders often missed Fort Union, continuing across the prairies of Rupert's Land. In this case they might find the Hudson's Bay Company's Fort Ellice at the confluence of the Qu'Appelle and Assiniboine but more likely both forts would be missed and they would lose all chance of protection or provisions until they struck Fort Edmonton far to the north, Fort Benton in the south, or crossed the Rockies to Fort Kootenay.

A second difficulty was that the Stevens route passed through prime buffalo range, the hunting grounds of Sioux, Cree, Assiniboine, and the Blackfoot Confederacy. Eighteen-fifty-eight was a year of unrest—not a good year to be trespassing. The Oglalla Sioux in particular harbored much animosity toward whites. Treaty food and supplies were late and young braves were demanding action from old chiefs, calling them women, cowards, for not standing up to the whitemen who stole their land.

Cart trains and halfbreed settlements were being harassed by large bands of roving Sioux, forcing the families to travel armed and the cart trains to await reinforcement from other riders—a situation that would result in several deaths later that fall.

Into this unrest rode the Man from Brechin, his thirteen companions, and guide John Fletch. They had been warned of Indian trouble but probably felt that this size of party would assure safety. Indians very seldom molested a party of equal size, preferring to attack only when superior numbers assured success. Twenty days' travel placed them near the second crossing of the Sheyenne River, south of Devils Lake, the heart of Oglalla Sioux country. In a classic understatement the Scots overlander wrote: "After that our trouble commenced."

The South Indians came on us in the night, and took our horses and provisions, tied us hand and foot, and commenced dancing around us with their knives. One of our party [John Fletch] could understand a little of their language; he got them to understand we did not want to harm them—that we only wanted to travel through their country, and that we were going to pay them for it, but they would not listen to him. They said that some white men had killed some of their tribe, and their friends were to be revenged. By the time daylight began to appear they got up and loosened our feet and made us walk to where their camp was, and they put us in a wigwam, and left two Indians to guard us. The second night came, but it fetched an awful sight. They came and took us out to the woods, and tied each of us to a tree, and stripped our clothes off. They told us that the chief was going to burn us.

One can only imagine their terror. Whether the Brechin man and his party knew it or not, burning was not an uncommon death for Indian captives and Sioux cruelty has been well documented. H. Y. Hind for instance tells of men being bound naked and staked near a marsh, left to the ravages of insects and thirst, a lingering death that might take days.[4]

Both the Sioux and Blackfeet were known to release captives naked, hands bound and far from camp. Hind records one incident where naked Cree captives of a Blackfoot band had their hands bound behind their backs. A hole was then bored through their wrists and a stick jammed through so tightly that it could not be removed. The three captives were then released singly. The surprising fact was not that two of the three died, but that somehow one survived.[5]

Brechin and his party waited, unbelieving perhaps, hoping for some extraordinary event that would alter their situation. The chief arrived.

"After the chief came he ordered them to build a fire round a tree that John Fletch was tied to. They burned him to death and killed two more," the Scot wrote. The sentence continues, covering what must have been an incredible time and experience in eighteen words, "... and the rest of us got away with our lives after they had kept us about three weeks."

What happened in those three weeks? Slavery was reserved for women and children taken in raids. The men must have been kept more for "revenge" and "entertainment." Also, one would suppose that on escaping the men would run for St. Paul for it was now about September 26, a late date to begin a journey without provisions. Possibly they reached an agreement with the Sioux allowing them to retain some provisions and continue on. Somehow they continued, heading north and west, out of Sioux territory into the land of the Cree and Blackfeet.

When the twelve survivors left the Sioux camp they were riding horses and entering the extreme eastern edge of the range of the Blackfeet, where wealth was measured in horses. A raiding party's main purpose was to gather more horses, more wealth. Many trekkers took this into account and used less attractive oxen to pull wagons or carts. With their guide dead they had no way of knowing that the country they were riding toward was some of the most dangerous in North America, certainly the most deadly north of the 49th parallel. They were now south of the South Saskatchewan River and its forks with the Red Deer, where the former elbows north. In an arc to the south lay what British explorer Palliser had named the Thunder Breeding Hills, stretching west to Cypress Hills. From the Saskatchewan Elbow west was a land as yet unexplored.

When Palliser reached this point the year before he had been forced north by his men's fear of the Blackfeet. Eighteen men were not enough they said. Only two parties had crossed this plain. In 1800 the three fur companies of the day, the HBC, the North West Company, and the old XY Company, built Chesterfield House five miles below the forks of the Red Deer on the South Saskatchewan River. In 1802 Peter Fidler, in charge of the HBC post, sent a party of men south to the Cypress Hills to collect resin. They were the first. Two decades later the Bow River Expedition of 1822–24 sent a party eighty strong south to try to reach the Missouri River. They were turned back by the Blackfeet, and in the 1820s Chesterfield House had to close because of harassment.[6]

Into this arid land where the hills formed a faint blue line on the southern horizon, where the buffalo blackened the plains in thousands, and where the Blackfeet camped in the coulees, into this country the Brechin man and his party of twelve traveled—the first whitemen in over a half century.

> We travelled on for forty days, and a party of Blackfoot Indians came on us, and wanted to take our horses, but we would not give them, for we could not get along without them, so they went off in a rage.

This was likely a small scouting mission. It was common for these scouts to harass white travelers and to cajole or frighten them into giving gifts, trading horses, guns, and provisions for inferior goods, or simply to attempt to run off with pack animals. Many prairie travelers had similar experiences. A display of firmness and sometimes force would usually result in an end to the problem, as it appeared to have done on this occasion.

The Indians used many ploys to disarm and draw the fire of white parties. Knowing that most men were carrying only single-shot rifles that would take several seconds to reload even for the most skilled rifleman, the braves would dash in singly, hoping to draw fire so that the reserves could rush in before the defenders could reload. The best defense was to pick the Indian leader and draw a bead on him, keeping him in the rifle sights but not firing. He knew that should there be trouble he was going to die first. Larger parties would take extra care to organize and have only a few rifles fire at a time.

It was necessary to maintain a tight camp, a good watch, and a firm hand with the nomads of the plains. The skills and diplomacy needed to deal with them was usually in the hands of the Métis, or country-born buffalo hunters or traders, the guides. Without their knowledge any crossing was made more as a result of good luck than good management.

The Brechin man's party succeeded in dissuading the first scouting party but the Blackfeet carried their rage back to camp. They returned with reinforcements and engaged in a running battle.

We did not see any more of them [the scouting party] for three days, but on the fourth about 40 of them came down on us and fired at us, killing two and wounding three of us. We fired on them and killed four of them, and then threw part of our provisions away to lighten our horses, as we could trust to our guns for meat. There is no danger of a man starving on the plains if he has a good gun and can use it. We travelled for 15 days, at about 50 miles a day, and thought we had got clear of the Blackfoot Indians, but they followed us till we came to a large river, [probably the Bow River] and when we were crossing it they fired at us from behind trees. They did not hurt any of us then, but next day they attacked us in a thicket, and killed four of our party, and wounded one, that was myself—I got a ball through my thigh. There were now only six of us left, who got off from them once more, and we had no more trouble of them till we got to the Rocky Mountains. Having got everything ready for crossing the mountains, we saw some Indians coming down, and we made into the woods. It was too late, however, they had seen us, but they happened to be Coutine [Kutenai] Indians coming to kill their winter provisions. They were friendly to us, and gave us several small things. They gave me some stuff for my thigh, and it got better very soon.

A few days later, somewhat recuperated, the Brechin man and his five remaining companions escaped into the mountains, over a pass shown them by the Kutenais (likely the North or South Kootenay Pass).

We started into the mountains and travelled four days, and then about 20 Blood Indians came on us and killed three of our number and wounded the rest, so that we were not able to walk. They took us for Indians, as we were dressed something like them—for all our clothing had worn out. They took care of us as well as they could, and we got better again.

From the remainder of the account it appears that they began to travel as soon as their wounds could permit.

When they saw we wanted to go on they sent for our horses, and guided us through the mountains, and then returned back. As we came on, one man died, and that reduced our number to two, out of 15. We got on slowly, for we were poorly of our wounds; and we have now got into a civilised country once more, thank God.

Once west of the Rockies they still had over five hundred miles to travel to reasonable habitation. Weeks and months passed. Finally, they arrived at the Colville Valley, took a well-earned rest, and ate large amounts of food. Why them, they wondered, why them out of fifteen men? Back there in the mountains and scattered across the plains lay thirteen of their companions.[7]

From Washington Territory the man made his way down the Columbia River then up the coast to Vancouver Island and the old HBC Fort Victoria. It was now October 1859. It had taken him thirteen months to reach here. From a hotel in the town bursting around the bastions he wrote a letter to his home-town newspaper in Brechin, Scotland, and explained in brief detail the adventures he had experienced on his journey west. "I have commenced to work a little," he closed the letter, "as much as keeps me in life until I get well, and then I am thinking of going to the gold-mines on Fraser River."

His sheet of paper frugally filled with words, the Scot from Brechin folded it into an envelope, put on his jacket, and walked from his rooming house onto turbulent Yates Street in the eighteen-month-old town. He turned westward, away from the waterfront, heading up a slight incline toward the center of town.

He stayed on the boardwalk, walking with a slight limp—actually more a favoring of one leg—and sometimes rubbed his thigh where a scar marked a bullet's entry. He passed Moore and Company's clothing store, where architect John Wright had his upstairs office, and glanced at a commotion across the street in front of the Albion Saloon. So many people, he thought, as he dodged Chinese, skirted Indians, and avoided miners—so different from the plains east of the mountains.

Crossing Langley Street from the Langley drugstore, the Scot climbed onto the boardwalk in front of the Bank of North America. Across the street was the Oriental Hotel and next to it Phelan's grocery store. Last night a destitute miner had tried to break in to steal a sack full of groceries. When he pushed the door open he was disturbed and ran up the street. A block away he ran into Broad Street and in charging across the unlit street in hasty flight tripped over a stray pig, sprawled in the mud, and dropped his sack, but he managed to escape.

At the intersection of Government Street the Man from Brechin turned right a few doors. Dr. Kennedy's office was on the far side next to the Colonial Hotel. The doctor specialized in midwifery but also kept a good stock of patent medicines that helped to ease the pain of broken limbs, arthritis, or old bullet wounds. Next to the custom's office was the post office, his destination this morning. Luckily it wasn't mail day for then men would line up for hours waiting for their names to be called. Often they waited until ten at night, and then were disappointed. For a dollar, a day's wage, you could buy a place near the head of the line. Few had the money to spare.

He made his way to the post office wicket, paid his thirty-four cents for half an ounce to Britain and deposited his letter. The postmaster took the letter and thumped it soundly with his long steel-shafted date stamp —Cancelled. The postmaster glanced at the Scot from beneath his visor, watching him close the office door and step onto the boardwalk, where he disappeared into the throngs of pedestrians in gold-rush Victoria.

L to R, William Joseph Christie, Chief Factor, HBC, Fort Edmonton, who discouraged miners at Fort Edmonton. (PAM)  John Jessop, organizer of 1859 party across the Canadian Shield, an all-British route. (BCARS 69770). Dr. Augustus Thibodo, a Canadian member of Colonel Noble's 1859 expedition. (Northwest archives, Whitman College)

An early party of travelers near the Elbow of the South Saskatchewan River with Red River carts and a tipi. (PAC 9170)

*Miners leaving Fort Garry. Red River carts were used because they were made entirely of wood and were easily repaired on the trail. Oxen had more stamina than horses and were less likely to attract Indians, who prized horses and frequently stole travelers' mounts. (Watercolor by W.G.R. Hind, PAC C-9583)*

*Upsets were common at the outset of the journey as greenhorns had yet to become seasoned travelers. Oxen were not always cooperative, and the carts sometimes gave way. (Watercolor by W.G.R. Hind, Public Archives Canada, C-33757)*

Many streams had to be forded, or provisions and livestock floated across. Despite overlanders' fears of Indian attacks, death from drowning was a more immediate danger. At Fort Ellice, travelers had to cross the Assiniboine (shown here) and the Qu'Appelle. Both crossings were made with the help of HBC bateaux. (W.G.R. Hind, PAC, C-22710)

Overlanders were at the mercy of the weather. The combination of raging storms and river crossings often meant they were wet for days on end. (W.G.R. Hind, PAC C-28259.)

*"Crossing the South Saskatchewan by boat – July 14, 1862, South Branch."* This sketch by Hind shows the Saskatchewan Gold Expedition using a bateau to cross the river. (PAC 9587)

*Travelers' camp at dusk on the prairies, a time for relaxation, writing, repairing clothes and harness and perhaps some music.* (Major George Seton, PAC C-1068)

For overlanders there was nothing like the thrill of the chase and for parties that took routes south of the Carlton Trail, buffalo provided not only sport but a also a welcome supply of food. As some would discover, however, a diet restricted to meat often brought on scurvy. (Major George Seton, PAC C-1059.)

"Cutting up Buffalo," another sketch by journalist Hind, was a task often left to more experienced hands. On one occasion young Richard Alexander only took the tongue, not knowing where to begin butchering. (PAC C-33713)

# Chapter Five

## The British Imperialist

In the new colony of British Columbia the pace of progress following the 1858 rush was second only to that of miners heading up the Fraser River from gravel bar to creek mouth. There had been a momentary lull after the initial 1858 spring rush. Miners and merchants had been at odds and the location of a suitable jumping-off point had taken some time to settle on Fort Victoria, Vancouver Island, but a lack of supplies and transportation meant many would-be miners never left the coast. Merchants in the U.S.A. promoted the Whatcom Trail bypassing the lower Fraser; others tried to inflate the price of flour but were unable to reap expected profits when the HBC refused to follow suit. Those who did go up the canyons were amazed at the tenfold increase in the Fraser's water during spring flood. Bars were drowned under twenty, thirty, forty feet of thick, brown water. Miners headed back for the coast. The mines were a humbug they complained. Gold finds were exaggerated others grumbled. And by the time the corrected news was out many hundreds had reembarked on steamers and sailed south.[1]

By spring of 1859 the news was promising again. There was now regular communication between the West Coast and Canada, though still depending on the lengthy Panama route. Newspapers like the Victoria *Colonist* had begun and there was beginning to be a sense of community and civilization on the rugged West Coast. In the Canadas and throughout the eastern and midwest United States the Fraser gold brought new interest. Those who had waited for confirmation of gold now formed parties of fortune hunters. While most embarked on steamers for the long trip via the Panama there were a handful of British imperialists who saw an all-British overland route as being of particular importance in binding Canada and the fledgling west coast colonies into a nation.

One such individual was John Jessop, a twenty-nine-year-old school teacher and sometime correspondent of the *Oshawa Vindicator* from Whitby, Canada West. The *Vindicator* editorialized about the need for an all-Canadian route west and consistently ran laudatory reports of Fraser River wealth. In correspondent Jessop the editor found a bored, restless, poorly paid school teacher anxiously awaiting the adventure an overland journey offered. Jessop became an agent for imperialism, "intending to go to British Columbia through British Territory, and by keeping a daily journal contribute something towards the opening up of a route on British soil, between the eastern and western colonies of the empire."[2]

John Jessop was born June 29, 1829, in the cloth manufacturing town of Norwich, Norfolk, England. He was the son of John Jessop and Mary Phillips. In 1846, when John was seventeen years old, the family immigrated to Canada, part of one of the greatest migrations of time as the poor, the starving, the jobless, the destitute, and the persecuted peoples of Britain escaped their individual oppressions. They made their exodus as ballast, crammed in the holds of decrepit timber ships that would otherwise return empty to the resource-rich colonies.[3]

The journey of deliverance was not one to be envied. Young Jessop and his family were crammed into the stinking, sloppy hold of a leaking ship with sanitation facilities that seldom exceeded an open bucket, and only enough water for drinking. Their food was ship's biscuits and barley meal. The fortunate few who had the money and foresight to bring cheese, bread, or potatoes to stretch the meager rations could be found huddled in dark corners, gnawing in seclusion, jealously guarding each bite from the hundreds of hungry souls who came unprepared.

The grim below-deck world of the ocean immigrant was thirty-three inches of rough, plank bunk, a confined existence described as a floating cellar. In warm weather the fetid holds were aired as the sweating cargo was allowed on deck for a few brief hours of fresh air and sunshine, and in cold, wet weather they remained below, taking consolation in the heat of other bodies. Within two or three weeks the deaths began. Typhus and cholera stalked the holds and each day bodies were tossed over the sides. Those with money were wrapped in canvas and weighted; the others went over in the rags they wore, any good clothes having been scavenged. In the hundreds of ships that crossed in 1847 the average loss to fever was one person in three. Passengers could only hope that their voyage would be over in a few weeks and not stretch to a punishing three months.[4]

The ship the Jessop family sailed on had completed half its voyage across the Atlantic when a storm struck, lashing the ship with rain, salt spray, and sail-tearing winds. Waves crashed over the gunwales filling the scuppers and raining sea water into the holds. Barrels and luggage bounced and careened between bunks and deck supports, ricocheting off passengers, leaving them bruised and broken. Topside spars snapped, bulwarks splintered, railings tore out, and sails were ripped from the mast. A mast crashed into the deckhouse and waves swept it into the sea. Sea water began to fill the holds and the ship wallowed in the troughs between swells and waves, sinking lower and lower. While the wind and surf battered the ship the captain began jettisoning cargo in a desperate effort to keep her afloat.

The captain's efforts succeeded and the Boston-bound vessel made it to Halifax harbor. The Jessops went on to New York, then via the Hudson River to Watertown, across Lake Ontario to Kingston, and south to Toronto, their new home. John Jessop, by now a firm, strong man implanted with a hardiness and determination he later found wanting in some of his companions, found work in the bush of Canada West. Like many newcomers he worked wherever a job could be found, caring not whether the life was hard and dangerous. For the Jessops this was the beginning of a new life.[5]

Over the next few years John Jessop learned the printing trade, wrote for a few newspapers, and then in 1853 enrolled as one of the first students in Ryerson's Normal School in Toronto, a school begun by Egerton Ryerson, "The Pope of Methodism." A Methodist since the age of twenty, Jessop took to the profession of teaching well and in 1855 graduated with a First Class certificate, unusual, but not particularly prestigious.[6]

For four restless years Jessop taught school in the Oshawa area. It was in Whitby that the gold rush sparked the tinder of adventure that lay in Jessop's soul and made him look west to the opportunities on the far side of the plains. He announced his intention of traveling west by an all-British route, as suggested by the reports of Hind and Dawson, in the path of generations of fur company voyageurs across the Canadian Shield, and he was joined by six more westbound overlanders.[7]

Jessop's primary companion on this cross-continent trip, and the only other one to complete the journey, was Elijah Duff. "The man from Belleville," Jessop called him. While Jessop's reasons for taking the journey are obscured by time, Duff's are clear.

Elijah Duff was born in Quebec, August 15, 1823, the son of Captain R. M. Duff, an army officer who had served with some distinction in the Crimean War and the 1858 Sepoy rebellion in India. Following a family tradition Elijah Duff accepted a commission in the British Army. Soon though he fell in love and became engaged. Marriage plans were made, complete with a military escort in full dress uniform, many fellow officers and their wives, and family from both sides preparing for "the happy moment." Duff's dreams and plans were shattered a few days before the wedding by the tragic death of his fiancée. Lost in the agony of her death, disfunctioning, asking that eternal "Why?" Duff sought his catharsis in a westward expedition, to find new scenes and a new life, to continue living while retaining his love and memories. He resigned his army commission and joined Jessop's westward odyssey.[8]

In the early spring of 1859 an adventurer passed over the partly ballasted Northern Railroad, from Toronto to Collingwood, with knapsack, bowie-knife and revolver, and took passage for Fort William on board a small iron steamer called the *Rescue*, on her first trip to the head of Lake Superior.[9]

Thus, in his own words, the epic eight-month journey to the "golden sands and almost fabulous wealth on the banks of the Fraser River," began for John Jessop. His party's journey was to be unique in the story of overlanders for he and his companions were the only recorded travelers who, in trying to maintain an all-British route, made their way through the lakes and rivers of the Canadian Shield, the glacier-scoured rock wasteland that separated Canada from the HBC-controlled Rupert's Land.[10]

Jessop had three choices of routes: by steamer down the east coast, across the Panama, and up the West Coast; second, to approach Rupert's Land from St. Paul; and third, one frequently traveled by fur traders and explorers, the old canoe routes of the Canadian Shield to Fort Garry. From there he could continue west, via some route as yet unknown to him, to British Columbia. The first route was too expensive for a school teacher earning three hundred dollars per year; the second meant traveling through American territory. For Jessop the third was the only acceptable choice.

Jessop saw himself as an explorer forging a pathway west in the manner of La Vérendrye who, with his sons, was the first to walk out of the hardwood forests and rocky lake shores onto the inland sea of grass. Now, 123 years after the death of the intrepid Frenchman, John Jessop embarked on a similar quest: the search for a British route that others might follow.

## Haute de Terre

Jessop left Oshawa April 25, 1859, in company with six young men, "two or three from Kingston, one from Belleville and one from Paris." Boarding coaches of the recently completed Northern Railway, they traveled north to Collingwood on Georgian Bay in Lake Huron and embarked on the small iron steamer *Rescue* on her first trip after breakup.[11]

The little ship steamed north, across the leaden-colored waters, through swirling banks of fog, keeping to the warmer waters of the lake center, then skirted Manitoulin Island and continued west into the north channel of Lake Huron. As they approached the shoreline near the harbor of Bruce Mines ice formed a barrier two feet thick that had to be broken by repeated plowing before the ship could land provisions for the "half-starved populations."

From Lake Huron the steamer sailed through two locks of the Sault Ste. Marie canal, built in 1855, ascending into Lake Superior. As early as 1797–98 the North West Company had built locks here just large enough for their Montreal canoes, to ease the problem of portaging the strong inter-lake current.

This portion of Jessop and Duff's journey was far from being an exploratory one. The route to Fort William was well traveled, with 443 vessels passing through the locks in 1858. The *Rescue* was the first of 847 in 1859. The canal marked the halfway point. There were still 260 miles of lake to cross.[12]

A passenger wrote: "They who have never seen Superior get an inadequate, an inaccurate idea, by hearing it spoken of as a 'lake,' and to those who have sailed over its vast extent the word sounds positively ludicrous. Though its waters are fresh and crystal, Superior is a sea. It breeds storms, and rain and fogs, like the sea. It is cold in mid-summer as the Atlantic. It is wild, masterful, and dreaded as the Black Sea.[13]

Jessop's April journey was cold. The temperature hovered around freezing and if the cold damp fog did not penetrate the men's wool clothing the wind that rose certainly did. Their route was along the north shore, with careful attention paid to charts and landmarks for compasses had a propensity for strange swings on the Shield. The voyage took six to seven days, though time could be lost to ice blockages or slow travel in fog. On May 9 the western shores of Lake Superior were sighted and an anxiety rose amongst the gold-seekers to begin their adventure. Arrival was delayed, but adventure began prematurely.

Sheets of emerald ice blocked the entrance to Thunder Bay. Along the shore floes stood jammed and jagged, scouring the rocks and banks as they had for centuries, carving the granite rock lower with each passing winter. The passengers were disembarked off Thunder Cape, a 1350-foot peninsula rising boldly on the north side of the bay. Loaded with provisions and baggage they skidded across five miles of ice, guided by the smoke rising from the palisaded walls of Fort William.

The bustling pubescent settlement at the mouth of the Kaministikwia had been born of the French fur trade 140 years earlier. It was known as Kaministikwia in its infancy and became a North West Company post after the conquest of Canada by the British. In 1807 it was renamed Fort William, in honor of William McGillivray (the same gentleman for whom David Thompson would name the McGillivray River). It became the most important, and largest establishment in the North West Company's territory with upwards of fifteen hundred men and here the annual conference of wintering partners and Montreal partners met to plot and plan the next year's activities. For two decades the post flourished, until the North West and Hudson's Bay companies' 1821 amalgamation when supplies were shipped via the Athabasca route from Hudson's Bay. The fort's importance declined until now, in 1859, it was blossoming into a small town independent of the fur trade. The old fur post was changing, becoming part of a more complex economic Canada that would see this lakehead port become one of the continent's major shipping centers.[14]

Jessop, Duff, and party purchased a large birchbark canoe, not the thirty-six-foot *canot de maître*, the Montreal canoe used between here and Montreal, but the smaller *canot du nord* or North canoe that was used west of the lakehead. It was twenty five feet long, about four feet in beam, weighed about three hundred pounds, and was usually paddled by six men and portaged by two. They also engaged a halfbreed guide and an Indian steersman. Ahead lay six hundred and fifty miles of paddling with approximately sixty-two portages, depending on how many rapids the guide decided to run.[15]

The route was not the more familiar Grand Portage route but one discovered by explorer de Noyan in 1688 and brought back into use in the early 1800s when Americans proposed levying duties at Grand Portage. This Kam-Dog route had been used since.[16]

The overlanders had so far traveled with relative ease, but at the Kaministikwia River their personal adventure began with the most difficult section on the Canadian Shield route. The first thirty miles of the Kam are through swift water with one *décharge*, a place where goods were carried but the canoes lined. At mile thirty, Kakabeka (Cleft Rock) Falls were reached, and a long, arduous three-quarter mile portage, with a climb of 120 feet. Mountain Portage the voyageurs called it.

Above, the river gradient reached nearly ten feet per mile with nine portages, a stretch that required "hard paddling, portaging and tracking," the latter work in the ice cold and booming Kaministikwia. The carries were usually short but each time the canoe had to be unloaded, the baggage carried the few hundred yards, the canoe carried, then carefully inspected for damage, and reloaded. Tracking upstream meant wading in knee- and waist-deep water, tugging and pulling on ropes fastened to the canoe while the steersman pried and levered the fragile bark craft around threatening rocks. Blackflies and mosquitoes had to be ignored as lines were heaved and the canoe laboriously towed upstream. For those of the party like Jessop, who had come from the soft life of office work, the initial travel produced strained, aching muscles. Evening camps were a welcome relief, despite the influx of biting insects that descended. Ten days of such travel brought the party to Dog Lake, across a portage bypassing bad rapids on a trail one and a half miles in length and 347 feet in elevation.[17]

At the lake Jessop's party hired an Indian to guide them over the next section of trail. Travel eased for a while until Prairie Portage, three miles in length; de Milieu Portage, a half-mile; and Savanne Portage had to be crossed, so difficult that the North West Company had to pay hardy voyageurs a bonus to travel this way. Henry Youle Hind described the Great Savanne Portage in 1858:

> This common dread of the voyageurs is one mile and forty-one chains in length; it descends 31½ feet to Savanne River, and consists of a wet tamarack swamp, in which moss grows everywhere to the depth of one foot or eighteen inches; the moss is supported by a retentative buff clay, which is exposed at the western extremity of the portage. The remains of an old road formed of the split trunks of trees, probably constructed in the time of the North-West Company, passed through it; it is now in a thorough condition of decay. The same may be said of all the swampy portages along this line or route ... a false step from a rotten or half floating log, precipitates the voyageur into eighteen inches of moss, mud and water.[18]

Jessop refers to this section of trail in a letter, writing in the typical, impersonal Victorian third person:

A few days more comparatively easy going carried them over the divide between Lake Superior and Winnipeg, and what was a very serious matter in those days, to the end, or nearly so, of the Fort William stock of bacon and flour. Shortly afterwards, in making one of the numerous portages between Lac Des Mille Lac and Rainy Lake, a bag of peas was picked up which had evidently grown too heavy for some of the H.B.C. brigade that had gone ahead. This find proved a veritable godsend, and so long as bacon lasted, made a by no means dispeciable bill of fare. Afterwards, pea soup, straight, twice a day—a third meal could not be afforded—was a cuisine that can hardly be recommended as a permancy.

Across the divide the overlanders canoed along Pickerel, Doré, and Sturgeon lakes to Maligne River, continuing the routine of paddling and portaging, sustained only by pea soup. Jessop continues his account:

After passing two or three small portages and lakes, we made Pikeral River, and shortly afterwards the lake of that name. Here the aspect of the country is very much improved. Vegetation was further advanced, and the scenery generally much more interesting. The hills in this region are covered with strawberry vines, raspberry and hazelnut bushes, cherry and plum. Pines, both white and red, are more frequent, and increasing in size. On Pine Portage, especially between Bruce and Dore Lakes there are some quite large. I also noticed here and there a maple, and a little further on, while crossing Deux Rivieres portage, I observed a butternut and some elms.[19]

Pine Portage was also known as Portage des Mortes, commemorating a voyageur who, while carrying the bow of a North canoe, slipped. The canoe, water soaked after many days' paddling, weighed close to four hundred pounds and crushed the man as he fell. He died within a few hours and was buried on the portage. Such deaths and injuries were not uncommon in the fur trade and more than one remote portage bore a cross or two as a reminder.

Deux Rivières Portage's difficulty lies in the terrain. Swampy, muddy trails in one place, where each foot had to be placed on a narrow log runner or pulled from tenacious, sucking mud, and in another, steep hills forming a ravine that threw the weight of a canoe onto the lead man going downhill and the stern man when climbing. A partner's slip meant an effort to retain balance and not drop and damage the thin skin of the canoe. If Jessop's party were fortunate they only had such gear as could be transported in one carry. More frequently, two trips were necessary. With lungs ready to burst, knees about to collapse, and back and shoulders crying for relief the portagers struggled forward.[20]

Then the path would widen and the shadows of the pine forest recede. Ahead through a tunnel of trees, beneath the black mass of the bow, the lead man would see a patch of blue water. "There it is!" he shouted to encourage the stern man, whose view usually consisted of little more than the back of his companion and the trail at his feet. The pace quickened slightly on the final approach. The two men walked into the water up to their knees, careful not to scrape the birchbark, lowered the canoe, and began loading. In a place like Doré Lake they paddled only a mile and a half before the whole weary process began again.

At the southwest end of Deux Rivières Portage Jessop's party entered the Sturgeon Lake system, which flowed south to Lac la Croix and the United States border. Jessop continues:

There is a great similarity in all the lakes forming between the chain Lac des Mille Lac and Rainy Lake. The country is generally rocky, very wild and romantic, with occasionally a small tract that might be made serviceable for agricultural purposes ... At the outlet of the lake into Sturgeon River, or the Maligne, as it is sometimes called, there are some formidable rapids. These our guides examined, and determined on running, much to my own gratification, although some of the party were a little alarmed at the idea of passing through such a succession of breakers.

Running rapids requires great skill in order to avoid the masses of rock over which the water is tumbling with headlong impetuosity. It is really surprising to witness experienced voyageurs guiding their fragile craft among the sunken boulders, sometimes on one side of the river, again on the other, all the while dashing along at a furious rate. Persons of strong nerve, however, feel perfectly safe in the hands of those Indians and half breeds. They are intimately acquainted with every fragment of rock; every move is made precisely at the right time and in the right place, thus they steer through the raging torrents and boiling eddies with unerring precision and safety. Sturgeon river, or rather channel, something over 17 miles in length, is full of them, some of which have to be portaged.

Jessop's "gratification" at being able to run the rapids and his subsequent wet and thrilling passage through the breakers was an experience enjoyed by many canoeists, and was no doubt one of the reasons voyageurs continued to persevere over portages and across windswept lakes, anticipating the next stretch of whitewater.

On May 29, 1859, Jessop and his party reached Lac la Croix, the junction of the Kam-Dog with the Grand Portage route. As Jessop mentions, the Grand Portage or Pigeon River route traveled by La Vérendrye, was "much superior to the one we passed. It is however, objectionable on account of being chiefly in American territory." Jessop's party's route had passed twenty-nine portages, and though there were the same number on the Grand Portage, the latter was eighty miles shorter—150 miles instead of 230.

From Lac la Croix they paddled down the Namakan River and Lake, meeting on the way an Ojibway Indian and his son, who accompanied them for a few miles. At the old Indian's camp they left the Indian guide whom they had hired a few days before at Lac des Milles Lacs and managed to purchase a few sturgeon to supplement their diet of peas. They camped that night at Nu portage, between Namakan Lake and Rainy Lake, arriving wet from a heavy rain storm they had tried to outrun.

Their camps were simple affairs. The men disembarked while the canoe was still supported in a few inches of water, quickly unloading all the equipment before lifting it ashore. The guide and steersman then carefully inspected the canoe for leaks or abrasions, which were patched with boiled spruce or pine gum and birch bark cut from a nearby tree. At the same time others looked after the firewood and began preparing the evening meal, which was the same as last night's supper, and tomorrow's breakfast. The remainder unpacked whatever equipment was needed, prepared bedrolls, and hung wet clothes to dry. Soon after the sun disappeared into the lakes the men were in bed and asleep.

Too soon the morning light broke through the pines and bounced off the rocks. The guide would wake and sit up in bed, often stiff despite his bed of ferns and conifer boughs. He threw some dry branches on the fire, blowing to kindle the cooling embers. The coughing and clearing his throat of morning fuzz would stir another sleeper (one of the reasons for clearing his throat). The two men would mumble a few words to those still asleep, who would roll over, rub their eyes, and rise. The morning sun had not yet taken the chill off the air but packing soon warmed everyone and if that did not, then paddling would. Being short of food they traveled as the voyageurs, stopping for breakfast after paddling a couple of hours rather than waste the time in camp.

Entering Rainy Lake on May 30, the party had the canoeist's rare luck, the wind at their back. Hoisting a tent as a sail they sped effortlessly on their way, the canoe nosing into waves, splashing water over the bow. Forty miles later at five in the afternoon they arrived at Fort Frances, "glad indeed at the prospect of enjoying a little rest after fifteen days of hard toil."

The area around Fort Frances at Chaudière or Rainy Falls had been the site of trading posts since the French had established Fort Tekamanigan in 1717 and had been continually inhabited by Europeans for close to a century and a half.[21]

Jessop and his party expected to reprovision here but found supplies extremely low. In a letter to the *Oshawa Vindicator* he described the area:

> Fort Frances is beautifully situated on the portage ground opposite Rainy Falls, some three or four miles from the Lake, and nearly midway between Forts William and Garry. It is in a somewhat dilapidated condition. The company appear to be neglecting most of the frontier forts as though they expected them at no distant day to pass out of their hands. On the day previous to our arrival, four of their boats manned by some fifty or more of the company's servants, started with the winter's stock of furs for York Factory, taking with them all the supplies and men to be found in the place thus giving the ruinous buildings the appearance of being deserted, while the few Indians and people left had only potatoes and fish to subsist on until after next harvest. There is a fine farm connected with the Fort, which, in the flourishing times of the North West Company, was much larger. During our stay at the Fort, and run down the river, it rained almost without intermission, fully demonstrating that the river and lake are rightly named.
> 
> Upon entering Rainy River the country again assumes a new aspect. The granite rock gives place to the fine alluvial soil of great fertility, while every variety of natural fruit trees in full blossom bedecks the banks.... The river is about one fourth of a mile in width below the falls, but gradually widens as it receives the waters of several tributaries.... Here and there are seen patches of prairie land, level or gently undulating, looking like cultivated fields, formed by voyageurs' camp fires repeatedly burned there, and chiefly on the British side of the river.

Jessop's later reminiscenses of the trip down Rainy River were less of the river and more of their hunger. He wrote: "Not a pound of fish or flour, potatoes, or anything else edible, could be obtained. Down Rainy River, therefore, the party had to go, with an elongated visage and an 'aching void' about their *stomachic* region of each anatomy. Half-way down to Lake of the Woods, a supply of sturgeon was purchased at an Indian encampment; [Manitou rapids] but it was soon voted unanimously that pea soup straight, was far and away preferable to Rainy River sturgeon, with no etceteras."

The westward journey down the Rainy River marked a momentary detour from the Canadian Shield's granite and pine trees into an alluvial valley formed by ten-thousand-year-old Lake Agassiz. As well as marking a geological boundary the river also delineated the old Sioux and Ojibway lands, and marked the border between the British Territories and the United States.

As the river neared Lake of the Woods it flowed through swamps and reeds, past Oak Point and the HBC's Rainy River post established about 1794, referred to as Hungry Hall for its habitual lack of provisions. It was not a stockaded fort like Fort Frances, but a few buildings and a large Indian village. Travelers were sometimes warned not to camp here as the Indians would "steal the socks off us."[23]

At Lake of the Woods the route swung north through seventy-two miles of confusing mazelike islands and into the Winnipeg River, where Jessop stopped at the Rat Portage post in the hopes of more provisions, but again, "nothing more toothsome could be procured at Rat Portage for either love or money."[24]

Jessop and party commenced their paddle down the barren "rock bound Winnipeg" on May 4. Ahead lay twenty-six portages. At the Church of England's Islington Mission forty miles down the river the land changed briefly, allowing a small settlement and gardens, attractively situated on a low hill near the river which, as Jessop wrote, "present a most cheering appearance from the river." He continued:

> For many miles below Islington, the appearance of the country remains unchanged, being quite rocky, yet in some places a sufficient depth of rich soil ... is found to warrant the assumption that farming is practical. The river itself is full of dangerous rapids, some of which are passed by canoes and boats, while others are portages.
>
> About forty miles from its mouth, there are seven falls and an equal number of portages ... in the space of three or four miles. The whole volume of the Winnipeg rushing over those precipices, together with the dreary solitude of the locality, form a grand and imposing sight. After passing those falls, the aspect of the country is very similar to that already described on Rainy River.

Two miles below Fort Alexander, where Jessop was finally able to obtain a little flour to add to their scanty stock of food, the Winnipeg River empties into Lake Winnipeg, and it was an elated Jessop who paddled into the lake's waters as this was the last leg of their journey to Fort Garry. Only a day or two's paddling remained. From the mouth of the Winnipeg River they paddled the Grand Traverse, the long thirty-mile paddle to the mouth of the Red River. They began their journey in the early morning calm, but this time the winds were against them.

We had a tedious time of it in crossing Lake Winnipeg, in consequence of the wind being adverse and rather stormy. The southern shores of this lake are very low and marshy, while the water for some distance from them is quite shallow. We were obliged to keep close to the shore, which made the distance much longer than directly across.

At last, however, we hailed with joy and satisfaction the mouth of the Red River of the North and entered it about noon on Saturday. . . . We were proposing to run up to Fort Garry during the afternoon and evening but the stormy headwind and rapid current prevented us from making such progress, and we were glad to camp on the first convenient spot. In the evening we were joined by the Rev. R. McDonald, from Islington Mission, who next morning favoured us with a short service in Indian and English before starting. . . . We proceeded to the Stone Fort, at the lower end of the white settlement.

After a night's rest at the Stone Fort, Lower Fort Garry, the small party of hungry, tired voyageurs-cum-gold-seekers continued their upstream paddle to Fort Garry, twelve miles south. Upstream paddling is never easy but this morning they were buoyed by the sight of hundreds of people crowding the riverbanks and an extra effort was put into each stroke. Paddles were raised in answer to cheers from shore, though not so often as to lose momentum. They could be forgiven for thinking this was a welcoming committee for overlanders, but while the excitement was appreciated, it was in response to a more important visitor. From behind riverbank oaks a plume of smoke and steam rose, the signal flare of a new craft rounding the bend.

Ahead of them was the little SS *Anson Northrup*, pretentiously steaming her way downstream on an excursion and introductory tour to the Stone Fort. She was not an attractive boat, in fact the opposite, a "small, shabby stern-wheel boat, mean and insignificant."[25]

Caught up in the community's excitement, the party rose and "gave her a salute of eight guns, which was all we had loaded, and they in turn gave us a shrill blast from their whistle and passed on." It was the beginning of a new era on the Red River.

Captain Anson Northrup had no grandiose plans for his miserable little boat. He stated clearly that he had made the trip only for the two-thousand-dollar bonus offered by St. Paul merchants. After reaching Lake Winnipeg he turned around, steamed upriver past Fort Garry, Pembina, and Georgetown to McCauleyville, where he tied up and deserted her.

For Jessop it was an exciting climax to the first part of his journey. Now, on Saturday, June 13, 1859, after a "most tedious and fatiguing" journey of twenty-eight days, they had arrived at Fort Garry, the jumping-off point for the plains expedition.

John Jessop, Elijah Duff, and the other five Canadians were witnesses to the dying days of the Canadian Shield fur trade. The forts were collapsing along with the monopoly of the HBC, the economy changing, and though it would be many years, decades, before a transcontinental route etched its way over the rock shield, this group played their part in flagging the way for those who were to follow. The significance was lost on the exhausted young men, however, for, as Jessop wrote, "at Fort Garry Fraser River seemed infinitely further off than at the mouth of the Kaministikwia, and, with one exception, all the party called a permanent halt."

Jessop was left with the prospect of continuing alone, a prospect not to be taken lightly and one too impractical to be given serious consideration. However, at the Red River settlement he heard of another party planning a similar journey. While Jessop had been planning a journey suitable for an agent of British imperialism that would "contribute something towards the opening up of a route on British soil," the American Nobles expedition had been organizing in Minnesota to establish a route linking Minnesota and the North West in such a permanent commercial fashion as to make U.S. absorption of the Red River settlement inevitable, and, for them, profitable. Somewhat ironically it was this group that Jessop proposed waiting for at Fort Garry.

*"Camp at Saskatchewan – July 13."* In this camp scene Hind identifies two Handcocks (presumably in the tent), Carpenter, Flett, Jos [?] and Redgrave. The two pans in the foreground form a Dutch oven for baking. (W.G.R. Hind, PAC 9586)

# Chapter Six

## The Northwestern Exploring Expedition

The scene was chaos and confusion. On the hill overlooking the "apostolic capital of Minnesota" twenty men with twice as many horses and oxen milled about the wagons, carts, buggies, and tents that formed the first camp of the Northwestern Exploring Expedition. Men shouted, oxen bellowed, horses neighed and farted. Scattered about the field were sacks of flour, sugar, and beans; barrels of pork; bags of dried beef; bags of dried apples; sacks of coffee and long tin cannisters of tea; wooden kegs of powder, bags of shot, and chunks of lead; rifles, shotguns, revolvers, and bowie knives; red, blue, and green blankets; fishing rods, packsaddles; ox yokes; tin kettles and plates; iron saucepans; carpet bags, valises; boxes of soap; axes; shovels; buffalo robes, butcher knives; spy glasses and clothing. To add to the disorder, it was raining.

Around the perimeter of the turmoil St. Paul citizens crowded, curious and enthusiastic. This was the first major expedition to outfit here. If the men now sorting and packing provisions were successful in locating a new route west, everyone in the city would benefit.[1]

By mid-afternoon the confusion reached its finale and wheels began to turn. Oxen were goaded, mules flogged, horses spurred, and with shouts and cries the expedition rolled into motion. "Ho! for the Rockies. . . . Ho! for Fraser's River." "My compliments to the Saskatchewan!" "Write me from the gold mines!" "Send back the biggest nugget you find!" "Let me buy you a pass over the Rocky Mountains!" "Good bye and Good luck!"

Colonel William Nobles's Northwestern Exploring Expedition was born of impatience, a factious party with as many goals as participants. Its conception was the 1858 meetings that spawned the Goodrich, Smith, and Burnham party that for all intents had failed. The three men were still somewhere on the Saskatchewan plains instead of at the goldfields sending back route information. There was now no doubt of the richness of the Fraser River mines. The "humbug" rumors, a result of the spring's high water flooding the gold-bearing bars, had been dispelled.

The ice had no sooner gone from the Mississippi in the spring of 1859 than the St. Paul city council determined to try again, with military leaders whose discipline would see the project completed on time. At their regular council meeting of April 19 a tabled resolution was brought forward.

Whereas, the exploration of the immense and fertile district Northwest of Minnesota, is an object of paramount importance to this City and State, and a general interest prevails in the Northwest for the speedy organization of a party for that purpose, therefore,

Resolved, That Col. Wm. H. Nobles, of St. Paul and Gen. S. B. Olmstead, of Fort Ripley are hereby requested ... to organize and lead a party of exploration from Minnesota to British Columbia, during the spring and summer of 1859.

The resolution was adopted unanimously and the next day, with a speed indicating prior consideration, Nobles and Olmstead accepted their roles as expedition leaders. Olmstead was a farmer living near Belle Prairie and had served as president of the territorial council in 1854, presumably with some military background. He and Nobles proposed a route "From St. Paul to the head of navigation of the Red River of the North; thence northwestwardly to the Elbow of the South Saskatchewan; thence westwardly to the sources of that river, in the Kootonais Pass of the Rocky Mountains." This was the route followed by the Man from Brechin. Other parties had taken a more northerly route.[2]

Lest one should think this party of annexationists were intent only on finding gold and a route to the Pacific, they proposed to explore the eastern base of the Rockies, "carefully prospecting for gold in the mountain streams, and obtaining full particulars of soil, water, timber and mineral resources, as far north as Edmonton on the North Saskatchewan ... we are led to believe that the vicinity of the Rocky Mountains between their summits and the limits of navigation on the Saskatchewan rivers ... will be found more desirable for settlement of a populous and prosperous community than even the well known valley of the Red River of the North."

From Edmonton they would follow the HBC Athabasca Pass route to the Thompson River country, "only a few days travel from Edmonton." Here they would divide, depending on the interests of the members. Some may wish to go to the mines; Olmstead wanted to see the Pacific coast; and Nobles planned to explore the Columbia River country, returning to Minnesota by the elusive Marias Pass, the Missouri River, and Fort Ridgley. Nobles expected to be back in St. Paul by November 15.

The presumptuous proposal made no mention of Captain Palliser's British Exploring Expedition, nor Henry Youle Hind's Canadian government-sponsored Red River and Assiniboine and Saskatchewan Exploring Expedition, both now traversing the plains, nor the fact that the

Nobles-Olmstead expedition would be an American party exploring British territory.

Volunteers "not exceeding one hundred" would be accepted on payment of three hundred dollars for their share of equipment and provisions. In addition each man was to bring "1 coat, 3 pairs pants, 6 flannel shirts, 4 undershirts, 3 pairs drawers, 6 pairs socks, 1 pair boots; all of coarse and strong material."

Norman Kittson was to act as financial agent, though he would not take part. James W. Taylor, resident secretary and "historiographer of the Expedition," accepted his position with another lengthy epistle, quoting letters from George Burnham of the 1858 party, Jamey Jock Bird the old plainsman, and Father De Smet, who had approached the upper Columbia in 1845 and published glowing accounts of its potential.[3]

Anticipating an important journey of discovery, eastern papers such as the Toronto *Leader* and *The Globe* and the Detroit *Free Press* picked up news of the expedition and assigned correspondents. The New York *Evening Post* and *Harper's Weekly* sent Manton Marble, the New York *Tribune* sent John W. Hamilton, and the *Globe* referred to an unnamed correspondent who would be forwarding reports. The St. Paul *Pioneer and Democrat* assigned Joseph Wheelock. The Smithsonian Institute appointed Dr. C. L. Anderson of Minneapolis as naturalist and geologist. Nobles and Olmstead promised Dr. J. D. Gooderich would bring along a "good chest of medicines."[4]

By May 17 the expedition was beginning to come together, though volunteers were not as numerous as had been expected. Taylor wrote to the *Pioneer and Democrat* for the benefit of those requesting information reminding potential members that they must pay their own way, and suggesting, "There is no better point to obtain what is needed than in this city." Taylor further suggested that Olmstead was hoping to have a steamship on the Red River by June, in which case the expedition would try to force its way through the Saskatchewan River rapids to the foot of the mountains.[5]

The group that assembled at Nobles's house for outfit inspection on June 4 included the seven correspondents, scientific and medical personnel, and a number of St. Paul greenhorns in their twenties who were headed for the gold of Fraser River: William N. Caldwell; Nelson Harris, a barkeeper; James Cheever; George McCullough; George N. Reed and Thomas Lynch, both clerks; John Young from Kentucky and W. W. Thompson, both real-estate men; Henry Smith; Joseph Mondieu, wagon master; John Pat Dignan, the proprietor of a billiard saloon; Duncan P. Kennedy, described as a northwest trader; and John B. Sandont of Rivière du Loup, Canada East. Taylor would join a few days later. A total of twenty men.[6]

While the "Fraser River gold hunting and Saskatchewan exploring expedition," was readying, a young medical doctor from Canada was checking into Davis's American House in St. Paul, hoping to join the journey west.

Dr. Augustus J. Thibodo, twenty-four, was a resident of Kingston,

Canada West. He had completed his bachelor's degree in 1851, at age seventeen, and his master's in 1854, both from Queens College, Kingston. In 1854 he also completed his M.B., at that time sufficient to practice medicine, at Trinity College, Toronto, Canada West, the first graduate of medicine. While at Trinity Thibodo no doubt met H. Y. Hind, professor of geology and chemistry, who led the Assiniboine and Saskatchewan Exploring Expedition of 1857 and 1858.

After graduation Thibodo went to California and returned two years later with a good deal of money, which his father made him share with his brothers. He went to the Crimean War and later practiced at Guy's Hospital in London, England, becoming a Fellow of the Royal College of Surgeons. Thibodo returned to Canada from Liverpool in March 1858, and a year later left home on hearing of the Nobles expedition. He was a young man used to cramming a good deal into a short time.[7]

By steamship and rail Thibodo, and his horse, Old Charlie, made a fast journey through Canada West and across the Great Lakes to Milwaukee, where Thibodo caught the train for Prairie du Chien. The final lap was up the Mississippi on the steamer *Milwaukee*, which docked at St. Paul June 7 at 10:00 P.M.[8]

The expedition was to have begun this day, but Nobles was delayed by his father being near death, and despite the expected "military discipline" General Olmstead found his personal business pressing and resigned. Already fragments of the group's mosaic were beginning to come apart.[9]

Thibodo went into partnership with Kentuckian John Young, possessing between them "two white mules and old Charlie," and on June 10 the Northwestern Exploring Expedition lumbered to a halting start. The next day was almost Thibodo's last for his horse reared, threw him from the saddle, and tumbled on top of him. Though he remarked that it nearly killed him he fortunately suffered only bruises.[10]

The expedition was ill-fated before it had really begun. In seven days they progressed only seventy-five miles up the Metropolitan Trail to the St. Cloud Mississippi ferry. The slow beginning was part of Nobles's plan, the idea being to give the stock and men a chance to break in easily. They could not afford the time. Two weeks had been wasted in provisioning in St. Paul. Prairie travel required being on the trail at first green-up to ensure good forage. Ideally they should have been in Fort Garry by June 1. Manton Marble wrote that the journey had to "be begun *adagio*, and then *crescendo*. A *sforzando* movement at the start would have knocked them up in a week." However, in an age when an average pace was twenty-five to thirty miles per day their pace of ten was more a *largo* than the *adagio* the composer called for.[11]

The slow pace was in part due to the wagons and stock carrying tons of provisions from St. Paul that could have been purchased in Fort Garry (a thought incompatible with the interests of St. Paul merchants), or shipped via the Burbanks' new freight route, saving the stock for the plains and allowing faster travel.

Secondly, Nobles was setting a unusually inefficient daily schedule.

The train would not get underway until 8:00 or 9:00 A.M. A half-hour break was made for lunch and then they would continue until supper time when camp would be made. His feeling was that the stock should rest while dew was on the grass. While this may have been an easy pace for the men it was not consistent with the advice and practice of most ox drivers. Usually an early start would be made, between two and four in the morning, with a stop for breakfast later and then a long nooning when stock could rest and a hot meal be cooked. Travel then continued until late in the evening when camp was pitched. This travel regimen had evolved from decades of prairie travel and resulted in rested stock capable of traveling many miles per day. Nobles's decision not to follow suit resulted in days and then weeks being lost, placing the expedition in danger of failure.

Following in the tracks of Nobles's inappropriate horse-drawn sulky was a small party plodding steadily forward, referred to as the Bovine party for their choice of oxen and wagons. If Nobles was the hare, the Bovine party was the tortoise.

The Bovine party was organized by Joseph C. Moulton, who in May had annoyed Nobles by announcing an expedition challenging the colonel's choice of route and method. The newspapers, committed to the Nobles expedition, gave Moulton little attention other than to criticize his experience and plans. On May 24, 1859 the *St. Paul Daily Times* wrote sarcastically: "We regret to learn that Mr. J. C. Moulton, who we believe has graduated as an explorer after making a few trips across the plains to Red River, has taken it upon himself to get up a counter-expedition to the Pacific coast, and to do it by misrepresentation and deception."

Moulton announced that the trip could be made for less than Nobles's three hundred dollars per man and proposed to make the journey easier by following Nobles, taking advantage of any roadwork or bridging the advance party undertook.

Moulton retaliated. His expedition had been misrepresented and placed in a false light. He had been approached by people wishing to make a trip to Fraser River but who were not suited to or satisfied with Nobles's scheme. Nobles had decided to try to use the steamer *Anson Northrup* to go up the Saskatchewan River, and failing this to pack his animals and head straight west for the Rockies and there divide his party. Moulton chose to use the time-tested cart trails to Fort Garry and then the developing Carlton Trail to Fort Edmonton and the most feasible pass that could be found. He intended using oxen and wagons to Fort Garry and then oxen and Red River carts. Moulton maintained, "We do not hold out our company as an opposition to Col. Nobles, or to any other expedition to open out and explore the Northwest."

On June 13, 1859, three days behind Nobles, Moulton and his Bovine party of six or seven men, including W. E. "Billy" Bunker, Koffman, Clorine, and Reese, started up the northern trail behind Nobles, dogging the heels of the increasingly annoyed colonel.[12]

As Nobles's expedition neared St. Cloud differences in equipment, personalities, and expedition philosophy were causing difficulties. The men had worked out the problems of pitching tents, cooking, and partners; yet the group was not becoming a cohesive company. Idiosyncracies created tension. Marble, without identifying individuals, explained the makeup of the group.

It was a motley crowd. There was the man of monstrous egotism, who passed life on the contemplation and exposition of his own achievements and virtues, and men of no virtue at all; the enthusiast, and the man who ridiculed all enthusiasm; the man who believed nothing; men of good principle, men of bad principle, and men of no principle; scholars and ignoramuses; industrious men and lazy men; sick men, who could be harried with a rush, and well men that a bull would hesitate before trying to butt over; water drinkers and whiskey drinkers; men that were boys, and boys that were men; Nova Scotians and Indian half-breeds, Scotchmen and Canadians, English, American and Irish.[13]

Some, like W. W. Thompson, had flattered themselves into thinking they would be a second John C. Fremont, explorer, general, and politician. Most were simply anxious to reach the distant goldfields as soon as possible.

St. Cloud had been wilderness until recently. Three years before there had been only six houses. Now there were three thousand inhabitants, a fine hotel, three churches, a hospital run by the Sisters of Mercy, and a primitive newspaper. At the embryonic town someone suggested that the new stage road be taken instead of the old Middle Trail, and, always wanting to promote the good features of the new state, the twenty men set off up the Sauk River.

The founding state legislature of 1858 had authorized improved state roads as an encouragement to immigration and by June 1858 a trail had been surveyed linking potential townsites. The following spring the United States Army was called in to commence construction but they didn't get very far and it was left to the Burbanks' newly founded Minnesota Stage Company, which had acquired a mail contract to Fort Abercrombie and a lucrative forwarding arrangement with the HBC as added incentive, to see the road to completion. By June 1859, when the Northwestern Exploring Expedition turned west, it had still not been completed.[14]

The new stage road followed the divide between the headwaters of the Mississippi and Minnesota rivers. The normal "height of land" was, however, a concave divide filled with "a small-pox of lakes, bogs, ponds, sloughs and morasses." Wagon master Dignan's task was to ride ahead of the wagons and carts and locate a route through these sloughs, carefully guiding his horse from side to side, seeking high, firm ground. Despite his efforts the first animals would sink to their knees in mud, the obstinate mules sitting or lying down. Horses would make a few lunges and then quit. Only the Indian ponies and oxen carefully and steadily plodded their way across. Often the fastest method of crossing was to unload the wagon and carry goods by hand, then return and, grasping shafts and spokes, laboriously turn the capstanlike wheels through the quagmire while the driver berated the mule or horse with a variety of oaths and encouraged it with a whip popped over its head.[15]

The country was magnificent, but the trail took its toll. The shafts of one wagon broke, capsizing it. Lynch broke down with four spokes knocked out of one of his wheels, then three more times his wagon collapsed until it was left behind. A felloe shattered, another wheel lost spokes, the stock stampeded, and the packhorses ran off. Journals were filled with notations of equipment breakdowns. Nobles now changed his cart, specially built in St. Paul, for a more appropriate wagon and team of four horses. The delays and frustrations were only to become worse for the equipment breakdowns were the physical manifestation of a growing discontent, an anger about to erupt.

An occurrence at the Munich ferry exemplified the differences in the group. Here Wheelock was appalled at the "brutal conduct of some of the men in refusing to cross some Dutchmen and the narrow escape of one of them from drowning." For several days Kennedy and Nobles had been having increasingly frequent arguments. On Friday, June 24, Kennedy again refused to obey orders and Nobles insisted he leave the party, which he did, going over to join the Bovine party.

At Alexandria the exploring party caught up to two of the Burbanks' stages, handsome Concord coaches designed to carry passengers in cushioned comfort. The coaches were on their maiden run and had been here three days waiting for the "sappers and miners" of the stage company to complete bridges. The coach party was an auspicious one. Captain Blakely, one of the owners, was aboard, as was James Wickes Taylor, a Nobles supporter and guest of the stage line. Besides these two gentlemen there were Sir Francis Sykes and Messrs. Sheffield and Peters, three English sportsmen on their way to hunt buffalo with a costly variety of Purdy, Lancaster, and Wesley Richards rifles and shotguns, and two winsome Scotch lassies.

Wheelock asked his readers:

> What is this mysterious errand which sends these two young misses on their solitary journey six thousand miles away from the guardianship of the parental roof—and twenty-five hundred miles beyond the verge of civilization—over wild deserts where the buffalo ranges sole lord, and through strange tribes of savage men. What inspires the courage? What is the sought reward of the peril and privation? Doff your star-plumed beavers—bend low your airy knees, proud shades of departed chivalry and courtesy—for living men have ceased to know the grand old heroic love—which whetted the swords of men, when men were brave and women true . . . it is an errand of simple love that sends these bonny lassies . . . to fulfill the vows made three years ago in Scotland, and with her sister for a bridesmaid, to make a happy home for the man whose honest love beckons her to the frozen fastness of the north. The destined husband . . . is a factor in one of the most remote posts of the Hudson's Bay Company, on Lake Athabasca.[16]

Wheelock was a verbose, incurable romantic.

Nobles lingered a few days while his brother-in-law Lucius Parker finished bridging the streams for the stage company and enjoyed the company and sport of the English hunters by rambling after upland game birds and deer. Three days later they were on their way, but within two and a half miles two wagons collapsed again.

Beyond Alexandria the trail difficulties persisted, punctuated by encounters with other teamsters, pilgrims, overland parties, and travelers. On June 30, a day when broken wheels completely discouraged Thibodo, a large Red River cart brigade passed with Anson Northrup, "a middle-sized grey haired resolute looking man," returning to collect his two-thousand-dollar reward for taking the little steamship he had named for himself to Fort Garry.[17]

The following day another man, John Palmer, joined Thibodo's mess. He was to be clothed and fed in return for cooking. A touch of cold and rain embraced them for a few days, but the traveling improved slightly, allowing the appreciation of the beauty of hundreds of white pelicans rafting on Pelican Lake. "Between two islands," Wheelock wrote, "the eye rested on what seemed to be a long line of foam beaten up in some wind or storm upon the edge of a chafing reef. Suddenly the seething white mass arose alive and fell again in a spray like spray."[18]

By the third day they had reached the Ottertail River and the celebrated Dayton City, a log house and lean-to containing a few bunks and a cooking stove festooned with dried sturgeon and catfish.

Another southbound Red River brigade passed led by "young McKay," James McKay, the famous Red River guide, who warned the Minnesotans that two traders had been shot off their horses by Indians and that his own train had been in danger several times. They were joined by two other small Fraser River parties, each with three men, one with a cart and the others with a wagon, both drawn by oxen.

HBC Governor Simpson, dressed in a white capote, a fur-trade coat and hood of wool, trotted swiftly past in his buggy on July 5, St. Paul bound. There he would meet with the Burbank brothers, and propose and consummate a covert arrangement whereby the HBC would help the Minnesota Stage Company buy and operate the steamer *Anson Northrup*. HBC involvement was to remain secret but would insure received freight rates far below other customers. The SS *Anson Northrup* would become the SS *Pioneer*.[19]

Taylor's earlier suggestion that the whole journey would be made with the ease of steamboat travel sponsored by Olmstead had by now been proven unworkable. The mountains would be reached only by those willing to walk or ride horseback. Not all the participants were as keen as they had been two months earlier.

Soon after Simpson passed, the exploratory party reached the Red River of the North and Fort Abercrombie, established late the previous summer. Named for its founder, Lt. Col. John J. Abercrombie, the fort was a link in a chain of military posts from Minnesota to Idaho, intended to protect emigrants traveling the northern routes. The fort, still undergoing periodic fits of construction, consisted of the commander's quarters, canvas storehouses, and log shanties that nestled in the shade of tall, broad trees. The shanties served as barracks for the officers and enlisted men. Fort Abercrombie was to play an important role in the protection of settlers during the Sioux uprising of 1862, even now beginning to foment.[20]

In crossing to the Red River Trail the party passed from Minnesota to the Dakota Territory, named for the Dahcotas, as the Sioux called themselves. This trail was safer than the plains trail a few miles east but still sentries were increased and each man traveled with his revolver loaded, capped, and at half cock. One foolhardy watchman stood his time around a blazing fire; the rest carefully smothered the fires to remain hidden in darkness.

They suffered not from the Sioux but from mosquitoes and mud holes. Nightly smudges helped a little, as did "taking the veil," riding like ghostly apparitions with pieces of cheesecloth draped over their heads.

Nothing excited an overlander like the sight of buffalo. It need not be a herd of thousands. A solitary outcast bull or cow would bring an adrenalin-intensified image of adventure into his mind and destroy all semblance of trail discipline. To kill a buffalo, the symbol of plains wilderness, was a signal of accomplishment for an overlander. On July 9, northwest of the Elm River two buffalo were spotted and the tedium of travel broken when Caldwell, Lynch, Marble, and Wheelock started the chase. Three miles later Wheelock headed them off, the other three pursuing and firing into them. With help from camp one animal finally slacked its pace, stood still, fell, and rolled over dead. The other was shot later that day. As the next day was a Sunday a rest was made and the buffalo meat jerked, the hide made into a lariat, and the horn saved by Thibodo for a drinking cup. The expedition was blooded.

On Tuesday, July 12, the Moulton Bovine party split off near Goose River, taking a western trail leading more directly to St. Joseph and Fort Ellice.[21]

Successive pancakes, each day being another, flipped off the immense griddle of the horizon, smoking hot from the fiery heat of the sun. That was how Wheelock visualized this land. On this hotplate Taylor became lost. Near Park River the party had stumbled on a field of blueberries and strawberries and when the train stopped Taylor wandered on alone, casually picking berries, lost in delusions of grandeur about the great North West. While bending to pluck berries the nearsighted philosopher lost his glasses and not knowing east from west was soon totally confused. Wisely he walked to a slight rise to wait for his rescue.

When they realized "the savant" was lost, Wheelock remembered seeing him like "Great Orion, sloping slowly to the west." Then someone remembered seeing a black object on a hill. Wheelock and Henry, a Cree halfbreed, saddled up and rode off, and found that sure enough the black object was Taylor, who greeted them casually as though keeping an appointment.[22]

A few days later, July 17, the last mile of the 460-mile journey to Pembina was walked, and the fragmented, disjointed, tardy Northwestern Exploring Expedition arrived at Joseph Rolette's trading post. They had averaged only twelve miles per day, half the usual, and should have been well onto the plains by this time.

Pembina, the border town founded on smuggling, was the beginning of the end. Many, particularly those bound for the goldfields and less interested in scientific and commercial pursuits, had become disenchanted with the "military leadership" of Nobles. Disillusionment opened a rift and this breach, coupled with Gooderich becoming ill and Nobles himself losing enthusiasm, resulted in a party upheaval.

In all accounts save one the catalyst of the split is left unstated. Wheelock, the correspondent for the St. Paul *Pioneer and Democrat*, had sent back regular reports. In a dispatch written at St. Cloud on June 18 and published on June 23 under the subhead "Beauty's tribute to the brave," he described a midnight visit of women to the camp.

When we were encamped at Coon Creek on Monday night last, this affectionate Civilization suddenly made its appearance in two carriages, at midnight, in the midst of a howling storm of wind and rain—in the person of young ladies— neither maids nor wives ... this created a profound sensation in the camp, particularly among some of the boys who had the honor of being intimate acquaintances of our fair visitors.

Had it not been for Caldwell's reaction and the fact that the event was ignored by most of the diarists, the incident could be passed off as nothing more than a flirtatious visit. However, for weeks since the paper had caught up to the expedition Caldwell and a few others had been fuming over Wheelock's indiscretion. Now, sitting in his tent at Pembina, Wheelock remarked that the incident at Coon Creek was a despicable affair.

"You're a damned liar," Caldwell roared. "Sheriff Turnbull did not bring the girls into camp."

"He did," Wheelock said. "I saw him myself, driving them away in the carriage. If you deny that then you're a damned liar, and something else besides."

Caldwell jumped for Wheelock, pushing him down with his hands on Wheelock's throat. The other men pulled them apart.

"I'm warning you, Wheelock, you shut your God-damned mouth or I'll thrash you. You'll be a lucky man to reach the Rocky mountains alive."

Wheelock kept talking and Caldwell momentarily backed off, but over the next few days he and the others involved in the Coon Creek incident became angrier and told Rolette that if Wheelock continued he would be dead before they had traveled 150 miles. According to Wheelock this irritant exploded other causes of disaffection.[23]

Marble wrote that after being three days at Pembina "the expedition's boil came to a head and expelled its rotten core—a tent full of scapegraces, who from this point took their own way to Fraser River." Those who left for Fort Garry and the Carlton Trail were William Caldwell, Pat Dignan, George Reid, Nelson Harris, George McCullough, and Jim Cheever. They left on July 22. Thibodo wrote, "I do not suppose we will ever see them again."

Dr. Gooderich was going to return to St. Paul with customs inspector Jim McFitridge and soon after Caldwell's party rode off Taylor decided that he too would go to Fort Garry, then south to St. Paul. This made two "go-backs" so far.

The company lingered in Pembina more than a week, a cathartic, interesting, and restful layover with opportunity for trading. Thibodo got a porcupine quill collar for his hunting shirt, six new pairs of moccasins, and had three pairs of his own soled with rawhide. The highlight was a dance at the settlement of St. Vincent's across the Red River. Marble described it to *Harper's* readers:

> Jigs, reels and quadrilles were danced in rapid succession to the sound of that 'dem'd horrid grind,' fresh dancers taking the place of those on the floor every two or three moments. The men were stripped to shirt, trowsers [sic], belt, and moccasins; and the women wore gowns which had no hoops. A vigourous shuffle from some thick-lipped young dancer, with his legs in flour-sacks, or a lively movement of some wrinkled hag, trying to renew the pleasures and activity of her youth, would call out a loud chorus of admiring "Ho! ho! ho!" and, fired by contagious enthusiasm, a black-eyed beauty in blue calico, and a strapping *bois brule*, would jump up from the floor and outdo their predecessors in vigour and velocity—the lights and shadows chasing each other faster and faster over the rafters; the flame, too, swaying wildly hither and thither; and above the thumps of the dancers' heels, and the frequent "ho's!" and the loud laughter of the ring of squatter sovereigns, rose the monomaniac fiddle-shrieks, forced out of the trembling strings as if a devil was at the bow.[24]

A similar dance was held at Joe Rolette's the following night for the aristocracy of Pembina. The enthusiasm was similar and the fiddle of better quality, but the dancing was more decorous with "less license."

With the dance shadowing their mind the greatly reduced party rolled west toward St. Joseph on the twenty-fourth, arriving the following evening. This village was settled by Métis after the severe 1852 Red River flooding. As the Métis moved so did the American Fur Company post and Father George-Antoine Bellecourt's Catholic mission. The town was laid out in long river-fronted lots, similar to those of the Red River settlement, insuring that each landholder had waterfront, a wood lot, and agricultural land. The settlement now consisted of one hundred houses. Kittson's fur company post was enclosed in a high stockade and the "nunnery" and church were larger than average to serve the predominantly Catholic population. Father Bellecourt had also built a lumber mill attached to the church.[25]

Thibodo visited the convent and was told that since Bellecourt's arrival he had performed upwards of five hundred marriages. But here Bellecourt was a humble priest, not the activist who had once fought the control of the HBC so strenuously that he had been recalled by the archbishop of Quebec. At St. Joseph, Bellecourt was, like so many before and after him, trying to convert nomads to agriculture, a sedentary life that held little appeal to wandering buffalo hunters.[26]

St. Joseph was shuttered. Most residents were off on their semiannual buffalo hunt, hundreds of carts and people moving across the plains in search of their year's supply of meat, hides, and leather. Those who remained spoke of constant harassment by Sioux: in eight years over four hundred horses had been stolen, most of them buffalo-runners worth from one hundred to three hundred dollars each and often the families' sole means of support; many cattle were stolen; shots fired through windows; and at night lone individuals were attacked. For weeks at a time the townspeople would only travel in groups, even when as close as a mile to their homes. The summer and fall buffalo hunts were often the scene of battles between halfbreeds and the Sioux, and it was usually the Métis who came out ahead.

The hunts were rolling villages, unequaled anywhere in North America. For the 1858 summer hunt for example one brigade consisted of four hundred armed men, eight hundred women and children, eight hundred horses, five hundred oxen, one thousand carts, two hundred train-dogs, and numerous mongrel curs. Discipline was strict. Anyone disobeying the elected leader had his harness slashed. A raised flag indicated a halt, and at nightfall a corral was formed with all the shafts pointing into the center of the circle where lodges and tents were raised and cooking fires built.

The hunt itself was unlike the later methods that resulted in the virtual extinction of the buffalo. Where buffalo hunters of the 1870s used heavy-caliber Sharps rifles and shot from a stationary stand, the Métis' was an exciting, highly mobile hunt. When the herd was spotted the men mounted their favorite buffalo-runners and galloped in hot pursuit of the herd, which was by now stampeding. As a hunter caught up to the buffalo cow he had selected his rifle was discharged from a range of inches.

> As fast as one fires he draws the plug of his powder-horn with his teeth, pours in a hasty charge, takes one from his mouthful of wet bullets and drops it without wadding or rammer upon the powder, settles it with a blow against the saddle, keeps the muzzle lifted till he is close to his game, then lowers and fires in the same instant without an aim, the muzzle of the gun often grazing the shaggy monster's side; then leading off, his horse wheels away and loading as he rides, he spurs on in chase of another, and another and another.[27]

Soon the plains were dotted with carcasses and wagons, and Métis busily cutting up meat. Fresh hump and tongue would be eaten that night and the remainder made into jerky and pemmican. Stories of hunts, Indian fights, and trails through the Rockies were told around the fires at night and one who parlayed this into a job was Michael Klyne of St. Joseph, hired as guide to Fort Ellice. Close to fifty, "Old" Klyne was still active, a skilled mountainman and plainsman who never missed picking up the tracks of buffalo or human, who saw the faintest whisp of smoke on the horizon, and who always knew where game could be found.[28]

The descriptions of the trail taken from St. Joseph on July 27 are vague. Left to his own devices Klyne would have led the party along a trail similar to that traveled by Palliser in 1857, but Nobles was determined to use his scientific equipment, described by Thompson as "odometers, muleometers, hogometers, a mammoth compass (with variation to the east—a peculiar kind of compass, only known to renowned explorers like Col. N.)." Nobles kept contradicting Klyne, who was using only the sun on clear days and compass-weed on cloudy days to follow his track.[29]

For two days they traveled north along the east side of Pembina Mountain, a low 210-foot ridge that from the level plain appeared to rise high above the trail, the shoreline of ancient Lake Agassiz. Westward the plains maintained that elevation, until another shoreline was met at the Coteau des Prairies. Their first camp was Allard River, so-called the guide explained for a Frenchman who made maple sugar here. Others called this Allard's Point, another ocean name given to a grove of oaks that formed a recognizable feature in the sea of grass. Their track led them south of the Assiniboine River and Spruce Woods and north of Turtle Mountain to a ford of Souris or Mouse River. Marble described the scene:

> There was every variety of color in the beautiful landscape which met our eyes; brilliant prairie flowers in the foreground, or growing in the debris tumbled down from the bluff on which we sat. The trees, down upon whose tops we looked—as flying birds see forests—the rushes and ranker grass near the river's margin, the exquisite cool grays of the sandy beach defined in such graceful curves by the brilliant blue reflected from the water, the thick verdurous underbrush, here and there sentineled by stately trees, which covered the plain beyond the river; the lighter green upon the long level meadow seen at the right of the river with troops of shadows chasing each other over its surface; and far beyond—miles away—the dark brown of the opposite cliffs, and the faint, hazy blue of hill in the extremest distance.

Thibodo, likewise impressed with the valley of the Souris, wrote in his diary: "Wednesday 3rd August 1859.... It would form a magnificent picture for a painter or photographist.... Little wood to be seen and where found only stunted oak and poplar, roads excellent, arrow grass very annoying, it works its way everywhere. Sleep every night with my rifle inside my blankets and my revolver under the pillow!!! on guard for Indians. On the last watch tonight. Very cold and foggy. Walked 20 miles on foot last Monday. Tuesday about 15 miles, Wednesday about 8 miles. Pretty good foot work for new beginners."[30]

All the party but one were now walking. Thibodo's Old Charlie had been left near St. Joseph with a sore back and their only stock was needed to pull the wagons.

The days were "red hot," but the party still began their journey at 8:00 A.M., sunrise and cool temperature hours past, and stopped about 5:00 P.M. as the sun's rays began to lengthen and cool. "Animals suffer from the heat," Thibodo wrote, "but no effort was made to alter the schedule." Yet the days were good ones, "full of enjoyment," Marble wrote. "Each one rewarding our labour of travel with some new beauty of landscape or of sky, some hidden beauty under our feet." Ducks, whooping cranes, and sandhill cranes rose from every pond, usually just as one of the men crept within rifle range.

Sunday came, a day of rest, and Thibodo wrote: "Read a couple of chapters in the Bible, mended shoes, mocassins [sic] etc. etc. Will write to my Mother today and to J.B. [John Brown, editor] of the Globe."

Thibodo's letter to the *Globe* was printed October 20, 1859 headed "GOLD HUNTERS' EXPEDITION" and dated "In camp 41 miles from Fort Ellice, Hudson's Bay Territory, August 7th, 1859." After detailing the route from St. Paul he remarked on what he thought would be the best route west from Canada.

... were I starting from Canada, I should never come this way—it is far out of the direct course, and the roads are very bad. The way which I would recommend would be from Toronto to Fort William on Lake Superior, and thence to Fort Garry; from there to Fort Ellice—distance 300 miles to Kootenais Pass of the Rocky Mountains. It is only six weeks travel from Fort Garry to the Rocky Mountains. Animals and provisions suitable for the journey can be procured cheaper at Selkirk settlement than anywhere else, and a traveller has the satisfaction of starting with fresh animals. Pembina [Red River] carts are the best to cross the country with. Since the steamer has been placed on the Red River, the St. Paul people will try no doubt, to persuade emigrants that the shortest and quickest route is *via* St. Paul to Fort Abercrombie and thence to Selkirk Settlement; but anyone who has come over that route (that is from St. Paul to Fort Abercrombie), and is unprejudiced will say that it would be next to impossible to find a worse road.

Thibodo was, interestingly, recommending the route recently traveled by the Jessop party. He finished the letter at Fort Ellice, noting their August 9 arrival. They would have arrived two days earlier but Nobles had insisted that they were heading too far north, and disregarding Klyne's direction veered west, passed the fort, and had to return east the next day.

At Fort Ellice they found that one branch of their party (they thought Caldwell but in fact it was Moulton) had passed a few days earlier.

To Marble and others it became clear at Fort Ellice that Nobles "could never justify the 'lofty and high sounding phrases of his manifesto,' and that it was even doubtful we should be able to get through the mountains before snow fall, to say nothing of returning overland." Nobles, who had been speaking of returning since Pembina, gave up the expedition here, much to the dismay and disgust of several members. Thompson was peeved. "Not one of our party would have left St. Paul had they not been told by him that he would guide us all the way through."[31]

The leadership passed to John Hamilton, the New York *Tribune* reporter. Nobles charged him "to lead the party on, to explore the tract of country lying to the northwest of Fort Ellice, and to report on the same." Nobles justified deserting responsibility by suggesting that from here the trail was well marked, and he must explore the country between Fort Ellice and Devil's Lake in Minnesota for possible routes. Who might have marked this westward trail Nobles did not say.[32]

Wheelock and Marble, the expedition's best journalists, and guide Klyne returned with Nobles. Their route took them from Fort Ellice to Turtle Mountain, Devil's Lake, St. Joseph, Pembina, Fort Garry, and then south via the Crow Wing Trail to St. Paul. Dr. Anderson hired a canoe and Indian guide and set off down the Assiniboine River for Fort Garry.

*The SS International, seen here on the Red River near Georgetown, made her maiden voyage with the first group of 1862 overlanders on board. (PAM)*

*The Red River cart was the main transportation for goods freighted from St. Paul to Fort Garry until the sternwheelers arrived in the early sixties. This group of Métis teamsters nooning in 1858 is typical of those met by overlanders. (PAM)*

*Jasper House was abandoned when overlanders passed by. Several houses were built in this area. Photographer Charles Horetsky identifies this building as Jasper House in January 1872. Note the flintlock rifle of the hunter (outdated even in 1872) and the young Bighorn sheep ram's head. Roche Ronde is seen to the northwest. (PAC 9173)*

*In a scene typical of overland journeys this Red River cart is fording the First Crossing of the Souris River. (PAC C-24382)*

*This photo shows the route of the precipitous Disaster Point trail, a climb of 1700 feet, described on page 209. (Jasper Yellowhead Historical Society)*

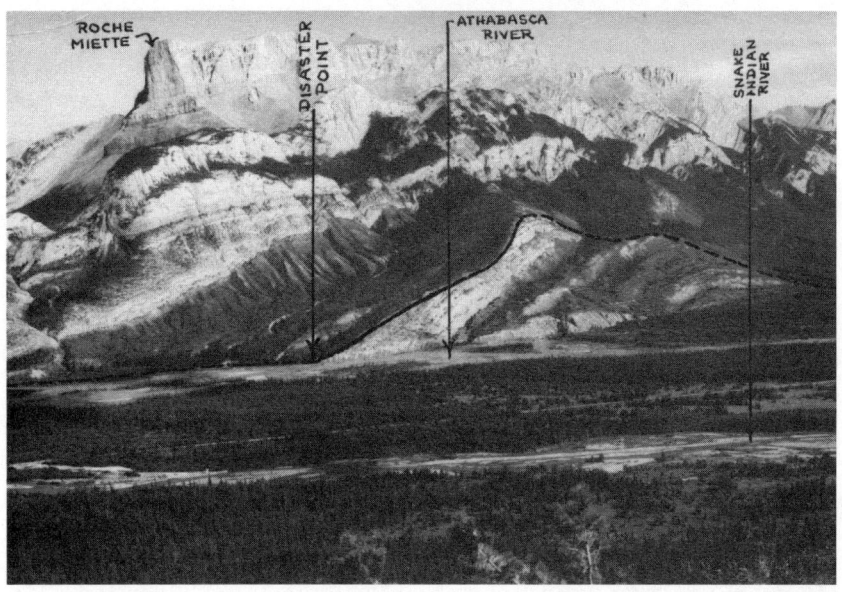

*When the 1862 overlanders reached the Cariboo the road was still under construction. Roadhouses such as this one at Clinton were about to spring up at various mileposts.*

*The heavy bush of the Jasper and North Thompson area made it tough going for pack animals. The site of Slaughter Camp looked very similar to this scene on the North Thompson River. (PAC 22605)*

*Fort Kamloops on the south bank of the Thompson River in 1865. The overlanders rafting the North Thompson came down the river at the top left and swept into the main stream. (C. Gentile, BCARS 95311)*

*The treacherous waters of the Fraser and North Thompson rivers claimed several overlanders' lives. Frank Penwarden and T. Strachan drowned on the Thompson. This later group is at Murchison Rapids on the Thompson. (Kamloops Museum 1469)*

# Chapter Seven

## Across the Rocky Mountains

The acrid smell of gunpowder wafted through the log house within the palisaded fort, pinching the nostrils of the dozen men huddling over the body on the rough plank floor, blood seeping into the wood grain, breath coming in bubbling gasps. A revolver lay on the floor. As the man's body was lifted to a rude bed another moved away, holding his own wrist in a tight grip to stem the flow of blood. Hammond found a rag and wrapped his bullet-shattered hand, thinking how this had all begun, how he should come to be here with a shot-up hand and his former friend Martin dying in this remote Saskatchewan country.

The trouble began months before, during the long winter at Moose Woods. They had left Hastings, Minnesota, in high spirits and if they had appeared arrogant and aggressive it was with the adventure and confidence of youth. Their journey to the goldfields of Fraser River was the opportunity to break away. Though warned of their late start they had expected to see the auriferous river bars by the year's end; instead they had only reached the halfbreed trading post at Moose Woods on the South Saskatchewan. And the winter had been a long one.

Snow and cold had confined Hammond and his eleven partners for days at a time, the temperature dropping to twenty and thirty degrees below zero for weeks. Snow tumbled from the leaden sky and the freezing wind screamed off the plateau, swirling down the river coulees and draws, filtered and broken only by the thin groves of aspen and poplar growing at the river ford. The cold, short six-hour days of midwinter meant interminably long nights lit only by tallow candles and smokey dishes of oil with cloth wicks. Collecting firewood to warm their drafty huts was a constant chore, though the plentiful buffalo allowed them to stock their larders well and the chase helped to alleviate winter boredom. The confinement exposed raw, frayed nerves, and as the days slowly lengthened men became increasingly quarrelsome.

Arguments, foolish and petty by most standards, became overwhelming in isolation. A man might sample a stewpot and be accused of stealing food; another left his bedroll in the way; a piece of equipment was borrowed and not returned; a fire was allowed to burn out; a horse wandered off while the man on watch slept; one man imagined he worked harder than the rest; any number of small incidents sparked disagreements. The tensions of expedition travel and winter confinement fomented jealousy and discord in the Hastings party, and Hammond and Martin were at the center.

They remained at Moose Woods until February 15 when they traded carts for dog sleds and set off northward for a twenty-five day journey to Fort Pitt where the party split, a few going on to Fort Edmonton.

Fort Pitt was not much of an oasis. The buffalo had not approached the fort that year and the Company had thus been left short of food. Also the three overlanders from St. Paul, Burnham, Gooderich, and Smith, had been living here all winter, consuming supplies while working for their board. The Hastings party put added pressure on limited resources, and crowding aggravated latent cabin fever.

The present situation, Hammond injured and Martin dying, had begun an hour ago, with an argument over provisions. With blasphemous oaths and threats of blows being tossed back and forth Martin drew his revolver and in a blur of anger fired at Hammond, the ball lodging in his hand. Hammond returned three shots, each hitting Martin's body, throwing his final two shots wild. Martin was dying on the floor of a servant's house in Fort Pitt, his quest for gold lost. He died within a few hours and was buried outside the fort by his overland companions.[1]

The HBC were not in the habit of providing room to travelers, preferring to keep any transients moving. In some cases though, the overlanders, Americans for the most part, could offer skills not usually available to the fur traders and therefore a bargain could be struck. While accommodation and supplies for wintering could not be purchased for cash they could be traded for employment. Under such an arrangement the St. Paul party stayed at Fort Pitt and likewise at Fort Edmonton Ned Hind, who had left the Faribault party with Brewster and Sanford, had found work as a saddler.[2]

By spring the overlanders were ready to move again. The various groups sought guides, formed new alliances, and traded for goods. This hustle of activity centered on Fort Edmonton, which most groups had to pass in search of mountain passes. By March, overlanders were being recorded in the post journal.[3]

With the fracturing of the Northwestern Exploring Expedition at Pembina and Fort Ellice, and the wintering 1858 groups no less than ten parties totaling 102 men were scattered across the broad Saskatchewan plains from Lac la Biche and Fort Edmonton in the north to Fort Ellice and Fort Benton in the south. These small leapfrogging, overlapping parties of young men probed the plains and mountains for paths and passes like the fingers of a hand.

### Tête Jaune Party

One overlander company crossed the Rockies via the northern Tête Jaune Pass in the summer of 1859. Evidence indicates it was led by Pierre C. Pambrun, the freetrader with whom Jones had traveled the previous summer, augmented by a few of the wintering fifty-eighters. These included Ned Hind, the ousted 1858 Faribault party leader who had wintered at Fort Edmonton; Brewster and Sanford of the Mankato and Jones party who wintered at Lac Ste. Anne; C. D. Loveland, an American employed on the chapel at the fort; E. W. W. Linton; and Alfred Perry.[4]

Two months later, July 19, the Fort Edmonton clerk noted: "Three of the Yankees who left this place with P. C. Pambrun for New Caledonia returned from Jaspers. They say I guess it's no go." One of these "turn-backs" was Hind.[5]

### Goodrich-Hastings Party

The Fort Pitt gunfight between Hammond and Martin precipitated the restructuring of the Hastings and St. Paul parties. Before the snow had melted small groups moved from Fort Pitt to Fort Edmonton.[6]

At Fort Pitt Hector, who had stayed to nurse the sick, remarked, "The time passed very pleasantly, as some of the Americans were very superior fellows, and had already traveled through most of the western states and California."[7]

Hector left the recuperating patients on April 26 and within a few days a second group of overlanders started for Fort Edmonton, arriving May 18 to find the post in its usual state of spring starvation; each man was responsible for his own foraging.

Charles Goodrich wrote to St. Paul, explaining that because of Indian troubles they would not bypass Edmonton as planned, but would layover and continue by a route north of the Kootenay Pass, possibly Jasper House.[8]

At Fort Edmonton the wintering overlanders blended into a variety of parties. Burnham joined the Palliser expedition under Hector. McLaurin, Williams, Maxwell, and Cook joined Palliser. Goodrich and Smith joined with the seven remaining Hastings men, including Hammond and a few others who had been around the fort, and struck south on June 9.[9]

This latter Goodrich-Hastings party met Hector at Windy Creek (probably Pipestone Creek) June 12. On the thirteenth he wrote: "A party of Americans, now only nine in number, the rest having engaged with Palliser, were camped here. I desired Peter Erasmus to continue our course by the Blackfoot track while I went with the Americans to put them on the trail for the Old Bow Fort, where they intended, without a guide, to cross the Rocky Mountains by the pass which Palliser laid down. Dined with them at noon, and, leaving with them a map of Kannanaskis Pass [sic], I struck off to the eastward."[10]

Goodrich and his companions followed the Wolf's track to Old Bow

Fort where on July 1 they met four Fraser River-bound overlanders who had wintered at Red River. They headed up the Kananaskis River. Hammond says travel "was very difficult and wearisome, the trail being covered with fallen timber, and numerous small streams being very high. Our provisions had given out soon after entering the Mountains and we suffered a great deal from hunger, our principal diet for more than twenty days being such berries and dried fish as we could obtain from the straggling Indians we met."

They arrived at the Tobacco Plains twenty-eight days later. Goodrich remarks that the Indians did not annoy them but on the contrary supplied them with fresh meat on several occasions.[11]

Linklater was not at his Kootenay post this early in the season, but Goodrich did meet another party of miners, the Tom Holmes-Shakopee party who had wintered at Red River.[12]

The Goodrich-Hastings overlanders hired a guide for two blankets, one hundred balls, and half a pint of powder. They followed the Kootenay Trail south, pausing at Paddlers Lake where Goodrich and W. Ellis Smith met the Indians with whom the Faribault men had wintered and signed their calendar-cum-guest-book. They arrived at Fort Colville August 10, 1859, having cooked and eaten their last provisions the day before.[13]

Goodrich, Smith, and Burnham were a disappointment to the merchants of St. Paul. Their proposed journey of a few months had taken well over a year and been unsuccessful in opening an effective route from Minnesota through the British Territories. The Fraser River was still many miles distant.[14]

## Palliser Expedition

As wintering American overlanders arrived at Fort Edmonton in the spring of 1859 they came in contact with the Palliser expedition, about to embark on the final season of their three-year exploration of the interior of Rupert's Land and New Caledonia. Rumors were again circulating about Indian troubles. There were reports of the U.S. Army and the Blackfeet engaging in battles and skirmishes, and the Cree and Blackfeet fighting on the southern plains. No one was anxious to be caught in the middle. There was safety in numbers. So when overlanders approached Palliser and requested permission to join his party, Palliser was pleased to have them along. He later wrote:

> Our party was now of a very motley description, comprising Scotch and French halfbreeds, Americans, Indians and squaws, one Dutchman and a negro. I had considerable difficulty in forming a party at all, in order to enter a country so very little known, and considered very dangerous.
>
> I should not have succeeded in traversing the country ... but for the large preponderance of the Anglo-Saxon element among our forces, which were thus constituted: ... Americans, Maxwell, McLauren, Cook and one colored man, Dan Williams. ... Although these men were not as effective voyageurs as the halfbreeds, yet I could perfectly depend on them in case of a panic and desire to

return among some of the men, who all more or less feared the country we were now attempting.[15]

Palliser and his variegated party headed south, in part to escape the starvation of Fort Edmonton where the food now included dead rats. Hector was left behind to await the expedition's mail and orders coming from Red River with James Beads. While waiting Hector hired George Burnham, one of the St. Paul party who arrived June 6. Hector wrote of Burnham: "I engaged one of them, [the Americans from Fort Pitt] Burnham who had been a California miner, as I had found at Fort Pitt that he was very handy and thoroughly to be trusted."[16]

On the tenth Hector started after Palliser and on the nineteenth joined with the rest of the expedition at the Hand Hills. They rode southeast along the Red Deer River to the site of old Chesterfield House, then south following the Saskatchewan to the Cypress Hills. It was a circuitous route the would-be miners were taking. There were a few tense encounters with Indians who used the usual harassing tactics of stealing, threatening, and even kidnapping a guide but through the diplomacy and good sense of Palliser and the obvious strength of the well-armed party, they escaped without serious fighting.[17]

At the Cypress Hills, on August 4, Hector and Palliser divided. Palliser rode west to cross the Kootenay Pass and try to rendezvous with the Boundary Commission survey. Maxwell, Cook, and Williams went with Palliser. McLaurin and Burnham rode north with Hector to follow a pass he had discovered the previous year and try to locate a route to the Fraser suitable for horses.

From Old Bow Fort Hector went to the headwaters of the North Saskatchewan then swung west through Howse Pass, last traveled by Joseph Howse in 1810. Prospecting as they went they descended into the Columbia valley on September 17, one month out of Old Bow Fort.

Short of food and his men exhausted, Hector had to abandon his plan. In defeat and retreat he turned his party south, up the Columbia. They crossed to the Kootenay drainage on October 2 and arrived at Kootenay Post on October 7.

Overlanders McLaurin and Burnham heard from Linklater the story of the Faribault men Burnham had traveled with from St. Paul to Fort Garry a year and a half earlier. Hector's dramatic, exaggerated version, with two of the party dead and more missing toes to freezing, no doubt convinced Burnham that he had been lucky in not attempting an 1858 crossing.[18]

Palliser in the meantime had traveled west through the North Kootenay Pass and arrived at the Tobacco Plains on August 18, weeks before Hector or Linklater. Palliser went on to Paddlers Lake where the party again split. While Palliser went via canoe, John William Sullivan, the expedition clerk and astronomer, was told to proceed via a land route to Fort Shepard in British Columbia. Sullivan and the diminished party of overlanders arrived at Colville on October 23 suffering from dysentery, the result of living on nothing but berries for several days. They were cared for by one of the Scotch settlers, Mr. McDougall, who with a little laudanum, brandy, and good wholesome food soon restored them all to good health.[19]

McLaurin and Burnham immediately started for the Similkameen gold mines, reported to be about five days' journey northwest. Burnham would not be heard of again, but McLaurin was destined to play a tragic role in luring more overlanders west.[20]

Palliser and Sullivan continued their explorations of the interior of British Columbia but they and the gold-hunters parted company here at Fort Colville. Where the overlanders went is again unknown, except that Dan Williams continued his search for gold, eventually making his way north to the Peace River.

### New Brunswick Party

When the New Brunswick party of twenty-one argonauts arrived at the Red River settlement in November 1858 they were joined by the Moore brothers and several others and went to work cutting timber for Andrew McDermott and John Inkster. Up river on the Assiniboine, in the parish of Baie St. Paul, there was a good stand of oak that these lumbermen cut and squared into timber. In the spring the timber was rafted down to the settlement. Never before had such quantities been available and the grub-staking merchants McDermott and Inkster reaped rich profits. Those less willing to gamble were annoyed at the merchant's profits. Mr. Barron, a French-Canadian settler of White Horse Plains, unsuccessfully petitioned the governor and council of Assiniboia for legislation prohibiting such logging and reserving it for residents.

The New Brunswickers introduced not only commercial logging to the Red River but the eastern broad ax, used for squaring timber. Before this the settlers had only been familiar with the chopping ax or the hatchet-shaped trade ax of the HBC. In exchange the easterners learned the ways of prairie travel and found a guide, James Whitford, a reliable and knowledgeable halfbreed.[21]

As well as the original twenty-one, the Moore brothers, and Whitford, they were joined by Irishman Charles Cooney, William Fairweather, William Edgar, and approximately twenty others, making a party about forty-five strong.[22]

They left Fort Garry in early June on the Carlton Trail. Unfortunately none kept a journal or wrote to newspapers. Their minds were intent on moving west, unconcerned about passing information back east or basking in editorial glory. Whitford guided them with skill and vigor and on July 26 in the midst of a thunderstorm they reached Fort Edmonton.

They camped across from the fort until August 3, trading as all overlanders did for provisions and horses. The Fort Edmonton clerk thought little of the party and made frequent references to their appearance and habits: "Of all travelers we have never seen such a miserable set. Theirs was a mixture of Yankees, Dutch, Scotch, Irish, English, Norwegians and Canadians. They looked to me as if they had just escaped from Doures Penitentiary or a worst place."

Overlanders were finding that the Company was not the only source of supplies, much to the chagrin and annoyance of the post managers.

The gold hunters traded some provisions for old shirts and other old articles ... they traded more provisions from the freeman, they are greater beggars than the Blackfeet.... Friday 29th. The fortune hunters are here still. They have a miserable set of horses.... Sunday 31st. The Yankees [the New Brunswick party] trying to trade Whiskey with the Blackfeet. I told the painted Gentry not to drink it, that they were trying to poison them, I also would not let the Yankees in the fort all day. The Blackfeet were not willing to trade the Whiskey. They told me that one drank a little and got sick at once.... August, Monday 1st ... the Yankees still here on account of the Blackfeet.... Tuesday ... traded five carts from the Yankees. They are making preparations to leave tomorrow. Wed. 3rd. Weather fine ... the Yankees left about mid-day.[23]

The New Brunswick party headed south toward the Kananaskis Pass, where their trail was crossed by Hector on August 16: "The night was very cold, and in the morning the water was frozen over, and the ground quite white with hoar-frost ... we reached old Bow Fort [approaching from the south]. Here we found that a party of Americans had started only the day before from this place to cross the mountains by Kananaskis Pass. Before starting they had broken up their carts and wagons, and we found the ground strewn with the fragments, some which we applied to repairing of our pack-saddles."[24]

Under the expert guidance of Whitford the party made excellent time and despite their ragtag appearance crossed the mountains without any problems, passing the Kootenay post before Linklater arrived for the winter. They arrived at Colville on September 13.

A few of the New Brunswick party stayed in Colville, like Charles Montgomery, while the remainder such as the Moore brothers and Cooney hurried on to British Columbia, attracted by news of gold strikes in the Similkameen country. Whitford wrote to Red River from British Columbia on September 17, announcing the safe arrival of the whole party.[25]

### Caldwell Party

"I do not suppose we will ever see them again," Dr. Augustus Thibodo wrote when the Caldwell party left Nobles's Northwestern Exploring Expedition at Pembina on July 22. With Caldwell were five other Fraser River–bound overlanders; Cheever, Harris, Reed, Dignan, and McCullough, all deciding to head north for Fort Garry and follow the Carlton Trail rather than the southern plains route.[26]

The small party left no record of their passing until Fort Carlton, where they met Ned Hind who had returned to Fort Edmonton in mid-July after attempting the Tête Jaune Pass with Pambrun.[27]

At Fort Carlton the peripatetic Hind met the Caldwell party, and again turned around.[28]

On the evening of September 14 a lookout on the walls of Fort Edmonton spotted a group of men moving on the southern bank of the river. Word was sent to the post clerk who rode out on a scouting party with eight well-armed men. By the time they had crossed the river and climbed to the plateau the mysterious men had disappeared.

The next day the mystery was solved when, in the midst of a heavy rain, the Caldwell company crossed and made camp two miles from the fort, remaining in the area a week, trading for carts and provisions and trying to find a guide. When no guide could be found they set off on their own September 20, toward the Kananaskis Pass.[29]

On October 4, Southesk was riding with his party northeast of Old Bow Fort, heading for Fort Edmonton after a hunting foray through the Rockies, when movement on the plain attracted his attention.

> Before we had gone many miles we observed a large party approaching us on the open plain. We supposed them to be Blackfeet, and as they were on bad terms with the Stonies, all of us loaded and prepared for a fight. The three Indians then rode forward with myself and two others to reconnoitre; . . .
>
> We soon made out the enemy to be nothing but a company of Americans, bound for Fraser's River. Mr. Hind, whom I had met on the 9th of August, was among the number, having fallen in with his present companions at Fort Carlton. Mr. Colville [Caldwell]—brother of Sheriff Colville of St. Paul, Mr. Dickman [Dignan], Mr. Reid and two or three others whose names I did not learn, made up the whole brigade. There were two very fine mules, of immense size, in their band, but having rather too few horses, they had already been twelve days on the road from Edmonton, which was poor travelling.
>
> It was an agreeable and useful meeting on both sides. They liberally supplied us with salt, flour, rice, dried apples, etc. . . . and we in return, gave them tobacco, fresh meat, a moose-skin, and a shoeing-hammer. Besides this, Matheson shod several of their horses. We also engaged one of the Stonies for them as guide over part of the mountains, an arrangement they could not have made for themselves, having no interpreter, and speaking no Indian language.
>
> We dined together, then parted with many kind wishes and farewells, and went on our ways rejoicing.[30]

The party crossed the mountains with their Stoney guide and arrived at Kootenay Post on October 30. Linklater's normally isolated post was being overrun and depleted of provisions by gold-seekers. For the overlanders, Linklater's post was an oasis and message center. Caldwell learned that the remainder of the Nobles expedition was just a few days ahead. A message was sent forward asking that the trail be blazed.

## Moulton-Jessop Party

The twenty-eight-day paddle across the Canadian Shield brought John Jessop, Elijah Duff, and their five companions to Fort Garry on June 13, "after a most tedious and fatiguing trip." Their plan was to wait for the "Noble and Olmstead Party" but the journey had jaded the young men and "Fraser River seemed infinitely further off than at the mouth of the Kaministikwia." All except Jessop decided to stay in the settlement and abandon Fraser River riches. Later, after sufficient rest allowed a renewed perspective thirty-six-year-old ex-army officer Duff decided to press on.

While waiting for the party of annexationists from the south, Jessop sent regular letters to the *Oshawa Vindicator* reporting on the route thus far, the agriculture of the settlement, and anything else he felt important. In a July 13 letter imperialist Jessop railed against the Hudson's Bay Company and those who would join Assiniboia with Minnesota.

The one thing needful for this colony, is the overthrow of the Hudson's Bay Company, which ... will usher in a new and more fortunate era. ... Whatever future Government it may have, whether it be Canadian annexation or an independant Crown Colony, must be infinitely better than the state of things existing under the iron rule of the Company. In consequent of the weak, vacillating supineness of the Canadian government, it certainly behoves the mother country to take prompt and judicious measures ... a great probability of this important outpost, this powerful bulwark against American aggression, being lost to Great Britain forever. There is at present a strong party, especially among the halfbreed population, whose tendencies are in the direction of American annexation. This is not to be wondered at, when we consider that they are living not over 70 miles from a territory where no monopoly exists, and where they would have the privileges of enjoying all the benefits accruing from free and enlightened laws and an unshackled commerce. Surely the Imperial as well as Canadian Government, bad as it is, will waken up to the important fact that the connection of this most magnificent country with them and with Britain hangs trembling in the balance.[31]

As laudatory as Jessop was about the potential of the Red River settlement he was still anxious to continue west to more immediate potential. He told *Nor'-Wester* editor James Ross, "If gold is not to be found I'll begin a newspaper."

When six weeks passed with no sign of Nobles, Jessop and Duff grew impatient. Disregarding trouble with the Sioux and ignoring "the foolhardiness of this undertaking" they purchased a well-used Indian pony and Red River cart and headed west, without a guide, on July 23 (one day after the Caldwell party split from the Nobles expedition at Pembina). In ten days the two lone overlanders reached Fort Ellice. Here they fortuitously met a Nobles splinter group, the Moulton or Bovine party.[32]

Moulton's group had planned to follow Steven's route, as had the Man from Brechin, aiming for the Yellowstone River and Fort Benton. They too swung north and ended up at Fort Ellice. Jessop and Duff abandoned their Carlton Trail route and joined Moulton to strike directly west toward either the Boundary or South Kootenay Pass. The party of eight men with six carts left Fort Ellice August 2. It now included Moulton, W. E. Bunker, Koffman, Clorine, Reese, Jessop, Duff, and two others.

Six days later they crossed the Qu'Appelle River and on August 24 reached the Elbow or "great bend" of the South Saskatchewan. Unlike others who later took this route, the Moulton-Jessop party kept their Red River carts beyond the Qu'Appelle and made the first cart tracks across the southern Saskatchewan plains.[33]

For a few weeks they "lived literally and figuratively on the fat of the land." They marched west at a steady fifteen to thirty miles a day through vast herds of buffalo. "Not a clear day passed without seeing from ten or a dozen to as many thousands or more," Jessop wrote. They walked through a time and wilderness that was never to be seen again, an enviable era for adventurers. There was beauty and there was grandeur, yet often these were lost in the struggle of the moment. Their Sharps rifles provided them with tender heifers and there were ducks from the potholes, prairie chickens from the grasslands, deer, badger, foxes, an occasional bear, and the "vicious looking prairie wolves."

The consistent meat diet brought on sore gums and lymph glands, the early symptoms of scurvy. The most serious problem was a lack of fodder for their stock for a few weeks earlier a raging prairie fire had swept across hundreds of miles of prairie, burning all but the soil and evaporating many small creeks. The fires were often started by Indians to drive buffalo or hamper white parties but this year's fires were particularly widespread. The horses weakened and died. Water was scarce and often too alkaline to drink. Rain water became important for drinking, yet soaked the buffalo chips that provided fuel on the treeless plains.[34]

There were other problems. One party member narrowly escaped being trampled by an enraged buffalo bull by leaping a wide gulch in a spectacular broad jump. Death came close for Billy Bunker, "a stalwart Missourian," when he carelessly took hold of his rifle's muzzle while arranging his cart's baggage. The rifle discharged, the ball tearing away the flesh and muscle on the inside of his right thumb then passing through his neck near the jugular vein and exiting near his collarbone. His companions were certain he was dead—at best only a few hours from the grave—but the neck wound proved to be of less consequence than his wounded thumb. For three days Bunker was delirious, suffering from lack of water and having to ride in the springless cart over rough buffalo tracks. Walking, even in pain, was far better than such an ambulance so within three days he was on his feet. His neck healed quickly but his hand was weakened for life.

Past the South Saskatchewan the party lost sense of where they were. Was the river they followed the Bow or the Belly? How far to the mountains? Would the remaining stock last? Jessop felt a growing urgency to be farther along.

They watched and hoped for a view of the Rockies but rain and mist, necessitating compass travel, blocked any distant views. Then, on September 15 six weeks out of Fort Ellice with the cold winds of autumn sweeping in, the clouds parted and "with a bright sunrise such a view as lasts a lifetime met the gaze. For an immense distance the great continental backbone was plainly visible. The loftier peaks were obscured by fleecy clouds; but the entire range almost down to the foothills presented an aspect of dazzling white."

The mountains were only a day's march away, they thought. In fact it took ten days of wading through numbing streams and hindering ravines to reach the foothills. At a camp near the "Old Man Mountain" or Chief Mountain, the Kootenay Pass landmark, the impenetrable wall of rock loomed above them.

The company had no idea where to locate the pass, no idea between which peaks, up which river or creek lay the western route. Somehow they had expected the pass to be more obvious, but there were no signposts, just the grass behind and the mountains in front.

Four scouts were sent to reconnoiter. One swam the river near camp and headed for the mountains. Suddenly he was surprised by a party of mounted Blackfeet. Quickly summarizing his party's position—three horses left and winter setting in—he decided not to fight or elude them but went with them and indicated that more whites were nearby. Mounted behind a Blackfoot brave, the man was brought back to his camp. During the day several more Blackfeet rode in with their women and children and made camp. Surprisingly a Kutenai Indian was with them, evidently unconcerned about riding with hereditary enemies. The Kutenai was returning to the Tobacco Plains. Jessop, writing in his usual third person, noted:

> This most providential event no doubt saved the lives of that small party of whites, as they would have got into the mountains with no possible chance of getting through them before winter and starvation would have confronted them. A present of blankets, clothing, ammunition, a rifle, some tobacco and other etcs. secured the services of this Indian as guide through the Rockies.

Red River carts became packsaddles in a recycling of transportation and the overlanders rode off with their Indian companions. "This cavalcade of tattered and dilapidated whites, and well-dressed, splendidly mounted and stalwart Blackfeet went in a northwest direction and at the end of the day's march met a much larger band with their winter's supply of buffalo meat, consisting in all of some 14 or 15 lodges."

While the Moulton-Jessop party enjoyed the Blackfoot hospitality and the guiding of the Kutenai, both events more common than harassment or shootings, they also experienced the common scam. When the whites were about to leave the next morning it was discovered that their horses had strayed. Several hours later they still could not be found. As an incentive to lagging interest a reward of clothing and other items was offered, goods of value to the Indians in the coming winter. In short order several young braves rode the "lost" horses into camp. The next day the Blackfeet and the overlanders parted, the Blackfeet heading south and overlanders west.

Following up a "large sized millstream," the Waterton River, they found the mountain freshness, green grass, and sparkling water gave their dejected spirits a lift. Their new-found exuberance was spiced with the relief of having a guide and knowing their location for the first time in months. Zigzagging up Blakiston Creek they crossed over a ridge beneath cloud-covered peaks and in falling snow crossed the South Kootenay Pass into the Pacific watershed. Their guide was honorable, and six days later, October 8, led them out of mountains to Linklater's Kootenay River post. "The canny Scotchman here greeted the travellers with hearty good will and negotiated a purchase of grizzly bear meat and berries, which were all that could be obtained at the H.B.Co. log cabin trading post."

They rested for a week, trading with the Kutenais who had gathered here for the Jesuit priest's annual visit. To Jessop's dismay the party found themselves in the U.S.A. and they would have to remain so for the rest of the journey. A journey westward through British Columbia was not possible from the post.

They followed the Kootenay River south. At each campsite Billy Bunker carved his "notes of passage," his name and date: Oct. 15, just south of the post: Oct. 19, the first crossing of the Kootenay. The weather was fine for traveling, without snow or debilitating cold, and in good time they again crossed the Kootenay River at Ducks Lake and arrived at the Pend Oreille River. Here the party split. Four men, including Jessop and Duff, crossed toward the Spokane River. The other four followed the Pend Oreille River north to Fort Shepard in British Columbia. Jessop wrote that these latter "poor fellows, after five or six weeks fearful hardships, suffering and privation, managed to get through by the aid of friendly Indians, but in a terribly exhausted conditions." Beyond, their fate is unknown.[35]

Jessop, Duff, and two others continued south to the Spokane River crossing, striking the new military road to Colville. Jessop turned north and found a settler's house (likely that of Antoine Plante). The settler told him a pack train was preparing to leave Fort Colville for the Similkameen mines. Jessop saw this as his chance to reach Victoria via Kamloops and the Fraser and so set off on a long, fast walk to try to rendezvous with the packers.

Arriving at the garrison town he found himself "the observed of all observers. One of the 'boys in blue' wanted to know who the overlander's hatter was, for nothing was left but the rim of what was a decent piece of head gear six months previously. Another was anxious to ascertain where his boots were made, as his only pedal protections were rawhide moccasins of his own manufacture. A third was interested in the garment that had once been a pair of tweed pantaloons, but of which nothing was left below the knee, and indeed not very much above. A couple of shirts then doing duty (all his stock) were minus sleeves. The front and back of a vest were fastened together with buffalo thong. Coat wanting, having been long since traded off to an Indian for something to eat. An old Scotch plaid over all did yeoman's service as a protection against almost zero weather. Thus clothed, or partially so, the overlander reached Fort Colville that Guy Fawkes Day, '59."

Severe cold winter weather set in and the pack train was unable to proceed so Jessop rested in Colville for a couple of weeks then headed to the Dalles in company with W. H. Barron, just down from Quesnel River. Duff stayed in Colville splitting shakes for sixty dollars a month and board.[36]

On December 1 Jessop met Dr. Thibodo at the Snake River ferry, from where he continued to the Dalles along the route taken by the Oregon-bound wagon trains in the 1840s and then, as the river was still frozen over, kept walking to Vancouver, Washington. Here he caught a coastal steamer to Victoria, arriving on Friday, January 6, 1860.

Jessop was one of the first overlanders to reach Victoria or Fraser River via an overland route, but while successful in reaching his destination he was unsuccessful in meeting his goal of following an all-British route, having had to dip into the U.S.A. from Fort Kootenay to Vancouver, Washington Territory.

From the comfort of editors' chairs in Canada the editorialists of the *Oshawa Vindicator* criticized him, and despite their imperialist views suggested that in future gold-seekers should get an earlier start by proceeding via Minnesota. They crabbed at his wasting time at Red River, ignoring the fact that had he left earlier he would have traveled alone.

While supportive of his effort, the *Vindicator* summed up Jessop's journey by remarking that his attempt had failed because, "by sticking to British soil in the first portion of his route, he was obliged to abandon it in the latter portion." Such is the value of hindsight. The fact remains that of all the overlanders who had started out with specific destinations Jessop was one of the few to complete the journey.

In eight months he had traveled over three thousand miles, most of them on foot, through a vast, sometimes hostile, wilderness. He was a tempered man, now, and though the grandest adventure of his life was over there were many challenges to come.

## "A Summer's Jaunt"

For the young men of the Northwestern Exploring Expedition adventure lay west through a country which, despite Taylor's assurances, was unmarked wilderness. Only two overlander parties crossed this border country in preference to the Carlton Trail. The first had been the group traveling with the Man from Brechin in 1858; the second was the Moulton-Jessop party, now traveling a similar route one week ahead of Thibodo and his seven friends.

Thibodo left Fort Ellice August 13 after spending three days dividing expedition equipment, trading horses, and buying supplies. Young, Palmer, and Thibodo formed one mess, with two mules, three horses, and five hundred pounds of provisions in two carts. Thibodo weighed himself while loading and found he had increased from 137 to 155 pounds. For his riding saddle Thibodo got an Indian saddle, a packsaddle, and a buffalo robe. For a couple of pocket handkerchiefs he got three long rawhide cords and some sinew; for his pipe he got a buffalo blanket. Finally in desperation the day before they were to leave he gave an Indian his spyglass, overcoat, black pants, vest, and sash for a useless-looking horse. Trade goods had a certain fluidity on the overland trail often changing hands several times. When Thibodo treated William MacKay's ill brother-in-law he was paid with a fine knife that had been given to MacKay a few months previously by Lord Southesk.

Pierre Nomm'e, a renowned halfbreed Assiniboine guide, was on his way to Fort Qu'Appelle having resigned from Southesk's hunting party in a contract dispute. Southesk described the fifty-three-year-old Nomm'e as a "quaint-looking oldish man, with a dark, bony French Indian face, and long black hair. He wears leather trowsers [sic], which have become like varnished mahogany from stains and hard usage, a blue cotton shirt, and a dark-blue woolen, mushroom-topped, lowland Scotch bonnet, such as I remember common in Forfarshire in boyhood, but it has red and white chequers round the headpiece, and Pierre has added a glazed leather peak. His eyes are weak, so he wears huge goggles made of wire and glass, which have a strange effect, throwing a dash of the pedantic into his rough and hunter-like appearance. He seems a good-natured fellow, and is said to bear a high character."[37]

Pierre agreed to guide the overlanders to Qu'Appelle so with Nomm'e's family and belongings piled into two carts the adventurers continued west. Wheelock joined them for a few miles, he reluctant to see friends leave and they were sorry to lose his enjoyable company.

They reached Qu'Appelle Post on the fifth day, after an uneventful march, except for Thibodo having to pull two teeth for Boney (John Palmer) and one for Sandont. At Qu'Appelle they exchanged Red River carts for packhorses, and once again went through the laborious trading process. This time it was more expensive. Thibodo's mess traded two revolvers, eight pounds of powder, one tobacco bag, two carts and harness, a suit of clothes, some handkerchiefs, buckshot, percussion caps, and some odds and ends for one handsome bay mare, said to be the region's best buffalo-runner. Hamilton, Young, and Henry Smith also traded for horses. In reloading they gave Pierre a pile of excess provisions—150 pounds of sugar and pemmican, a tent, and numerous other items. In return he gave them a map as far as the Elbow.

Watches were doubled, two men standing guard per two-hour shift. The necessity of the added precautions was driven home as they rode down into the valley of the Qu'Appelle River at Fishing Lakes. The short-lived Qu'Appelle Mission lay in charred ruins, a desolate contrast to the beauty of the surrounding landscape. The year-old mission was established by cathechist Charles Pratt, a halfbreed hoping to convert the Cree. The ruins were a monument to his failure. The overlanders rode with apprehension as an unwelcome partner.[38]

The river's name, "Who Calls?" or Calling River, was from "the Natives who imagine a Spirit is constantly going up and down the River, and its voice they say they often hear, but it resembles the cry of a human being."[39]

The valley of the Qu'Appelle lies east and west, a gently curving depression two to three hundred feet deep, up to two miles in width, and three hundred miles long. Along the valley bottom lies a string of jewel-like lakes connected by a muddy serpentine cord of river that rises just east of the Saskatchewan and flows slowly to the Assiniboine River at Fort Ellice.

The party followed the valley of the Qu'Appelle. For one week most of the pond water was bad, alkaline and unfit to drink, and as they wandered away from the river without sufficient kegs to collect water dry camps were made. Sometimes a well was dug at camp and seepage gave men and stock some moisture. Wood was scarce but buffalo chips plentiful, providing a fire rich with the incense of herbs and flowers. Hamilton's mule died, writhing in agony. Its death was caused by congestion and inflammation of the intestines. They saw an Indian encampment of forty-two lodges, but somehow managed to pass unseen.

By leaving their carts at Fort Qu'Appelle they had decided to rely on game for food. But while the Moulton-Jessop party described living off the fat of the land Thibodo complained that they never seemed to have enough food. Unlike the more experienced Moulton-Jessop men Thibodo's young men lacked the necessary skill. They were greenhorns, and paid the price of inexperience. On August 31, Thibodo wrote:

High rolling prairie, very tiresome climbing and descending the steep hills. Shot a fox on the run with a rifle ball. Lynch shot 2 badgers, had a shot at a buffalo and at a deer. Saw a great many deer. Buffalo too numerous to mention. They seem to number thousands. As far as the eye can reach the prairie is dotted with them. Travelled hard all day made about 25 miles. The boys ran some of the buffalo, killed one brought some meat into camp. . . . Camped at six p.m. without wood or water, very thirsty. Suffered a good deal. Grass very bad. Toasted some of the buffalo steaks on my iron horse picket and eat it almost raw, so very hungry, had walked nearly all day . . . it is very hard to walk all day and then watch for 2 hours every night. The weather very cold like our Canadian November weather, no water. Hard frost at night, ice on the dipper in the water pail.

Sept. 1: I nearly froze on watch last night, a never to be forgotten day. I never suffered so much in my life from want of water and food. No water for 24 hours. Horrible sensations walking all day on the burning prairie without one drop of water.

Their agony of thirst was quenched that afternoon at the South Saskatchewan Elbow. "Water never tasted so sweet," Thibodo wrote. Here, where the South Saskatchewan made a ninety-degree turn north, they reached the westernmost point of exploration.

The Elbow offered everything: wood, water, and meat. Since time began the plains people had traveled here, building fires along the banks of the River-That-Turns and sheltering below the high banks of the Saskatchewan. It was a spectacular area of breathtaking beauty, with a horizon broken only by soft hills that rolled across the broad land. Where countless native hunting parties had camped in times past the men lit their evening fire, and the poplar- and willow-scented smoke drifted on the river breeze.

They were surrounded by the Great Plains sea. Settlement was 550 miles back at Fort Garry. Qu'Appelle Post lay 150 miles east as the crow was supposed to fly; Fort Carlton 150 miles north; Fort Edmonton 350 miles northwest; Fort Benton on the Missouri, 300 miles southwest; and the outpost Fort Kootenay, their destination, lay 450 miles west, across a pass in the Rockies. With only uncharted rivers to follow they had to strike a narrow valley and trail that would lead to a pass. Averaging fifteen to twenty miles a day, the nearest post was ten days distant—if the trails were good—if they could be found—if they could travel as straight as the crow flew. In an area of over thirty thousand square miles they and the Moulton-Jessop party were the only whitemen. They could expect no further assistance. It was a time of gaining maturity, of acting on initiative.

The westward trek was reflected in Thibodo's journal as a similarity of days, the magic and excitement of the journey lost in a struggle with hunger and discomfort.

Saturday, 3rd Sept. The scenery on this river is very strange, wild looking, an appearance peculiar to this Western country. Made about 25 miles today, walked all day, mocassins [sic] wore out and stockings, feet full of thistles. Suffered a great deal of pain ... could not sleep from the cold.

Monday 5th Sept. Wind blowing hard ... suffered from thirst. ... Disolved [sic] partnership with John Young. He could not agree.

Tuesday 6th Sept. Camped late on the Saskatchewan. ... First night since St. Paul that we had no watch. I shot an antelope today, excellent eating. Henry shot a badger and this evening we all had a great hunt after a porcupine. ... I wounded two large bears today, strange grey coloured."

In this minor notation Thibodo indicates the wilderness he had entered. The two bears were plains grizzly, as dangerous and doomed as the free-roaming Blackfeet. American explorers Lewis and Clark wrote that they would rather face six hostile Indians than a grizzly. Their scientific name spoke at once of their disposition and men's fear—*Ursus horribilis horribilis*—the horrible, horrible bear.[40]

"Thursday 8th Sept. ... raining now and horribly disagreeable. ... It rained fearfully hard during the night. Wet through, got all our stuff wet ... slept in the water.

9th Sept. ... Lynch's white mule Paddy died this morning. ... We all suffered fearfully today. Nothing to eat from last night until 1/2 past 5. ... Last night and today we have suffered more than any day since we left St. Paul. Wolves very numerous."

After a three-day layover at the September 9 camp, in sheltering timber, resting and drying clothes, they continued, dispositions slightly improved. It was the practice for each man to be completely responsible for himself and his equipment. They worked as a team but did not expect others to support them. Thus on the thirteenth Thibodo made arrangements for Sandont to carry his provisions and equipment across the Rocky Mountains, in exchange for his stud Billy and mule Jennie. Both were giving out and there was no other way to complete the crossing. Sandont agreed to let Thibodo ride Jennie until the crossing was made.[41]

The surrounding country had changed from a flat plain to high hills. The Great Sand Hills that lie to the southeast of the Saskatchewan–Red Deer confluence were often mistaken for the foothills of the Rockies, only adding to discouragement as the passing hours proved explorers wrong.

Lynch spotted a log house on the far bank of the river on the sixteenth, the remains of Chesterfield House at the Red Deer and South Saskatchewan confluence.

Having found a comfortable camp, the men took the seventeenth as a day of rest. Hamilton inexplicably resigned as group captain. Sandont was elected in his place. Many overlander parties were informal traveling associations but these men chose to have bylaws delineating responsibilities and liabilities. A new agreement was drawn up, each man signing and receiving a copy.

For another warm and weary month they continued along the Saskatchewan (or Belly as Thibodo called it) toward the Bow and Belly confluence, then southwest along the Belly toward the Rockies. The days were hot, but beginning to cool as autumn approached, with frequent rain storms, one of which kept them in camp for four days.

In spite of the abundance of game the men were usually short of food, often hungry. The game they shot was insufficient to feed eight men who walked many hours a day. Two deer that Lynch shot dressed out at 150 pounds only lasted five days; a buffalo heifer, bittern and a rabbit another two, until they once again found themselves dining on soup with one chunk of meat and a cup of unsweetened tea.

19th Sept. Had a severe attack of diarrhea for the last 4 days caused probably by eating so much fresh meat. . . .

30th Sept. This morning's breakfast was composed for each man, 3 table spoonsful of Minute pudding [flour and water] and one small biscuit, which had to serve also for lunch. That is hard fare for traveling. We begin to suffer from want of food. I do not know where this is going to lead us to. . . . My teeth are all very sore and a swelling of the Lymphatic glands of the throat.

Scurvy again. The unknown antidote grew all around them in the form of rose hips. A handful a day would provide enough vitamin C to alleviate the malady. As their diet decreased, desperation increased.

1st Oct. . . . too sick and sore to walk. . . .

2nd Oct. . . . Boys have no idea where we are and have all got the blues very badly. I hardly know what will become of us if we do not strike the pass soon.

3rd Oct. Lynch dug out and slept in a badger hole. Nearly froze.

5th Oct. . . . Clear cold morning, almost frozen. Wind from S. very cold, but clear. I pray the Lord it may remain clear till we find the pass or a river. We are in a very dangerous strait, the mountains are all covered with snow. . . . Boys suffering and talking about chances of starvation, finding Indians or going to Fort Edmonton.

As morale dropped arguments became more frequent and at one point another split in the party was threatened. Then, as the food was at its lowest and depression at its highest, a hunt was successful. Lynch shot one goose, Henry Smith two, and John Smith a badger. Three geese, a biscuit, and coffee for breakfast started the day off right. Then Henry Smith shot a four-hundred-pound doe elk for a splendid supper.

This party was moving through a wilderness of over half a million square miles, tracing a narrow corridor through the southern portion of this tract. This day evidence showed that geography, the lay of the land, determined the paths of man. An uncrossable river, a creek fordable at one place more easily than another, a sand dune to avoid, a hill to traverse, these and the ancient trails of game and natives drew wanderers along an ill-defined yet distinct path. Here, incredibly, in the midst of this vastness they stumbled on the tracks of a cart, and close beside it a fresh boot print, a sign of the Moulton-Jessop party's passing.

On the tenth the remains of an Indian camp were found, with fresh horse dung and recently cut poles, likely the camp that Jessop stopped at. Closer to the mountains a vermillion box, some clothing remnants, and the tracks of whites were found, an encouraging sign that they were heading in the right direction. They followed a river south (likely the Waterton) into the mountains. Snow began to blow around their feet, swirling under the horses and then changing to a chilling rain and hail. A small grove of spruce beckoned them and for a day they camped in the protective thicket. Almost imperceptibly fortunes and humors were improving. The twelfth was a day of shelter and rest spent huddled around a fire playing whist and euchre as yarns and tales mingled with pipe smoke.

Thibodo took time to carve his and Hamilton's name and the date on a tree, then turned in the cold to tackle the mountains once more. This morning lady luck was with them. Soon after starting they met a Kutenai halfbreed with his two squaws and four horses. This was a hunting ground, he told them, not the route to the pass, but as he was heading back to the Tobacco Plains on the west side, he would lead them. The overlanders' foothill wandering was over. Once again, a native came to the rescue.

Unlike many other overlanders, such as Jones, Thibodo recognized their good fortune. "The boys are all cheerful now, we seem to have a pretty sure thing of getting across the mountains. . . . Gave the Indians some Medicine . . . he says, or motions, that in 9 nights we will be with English people, or turned up noses. . . . We never could have got thro' here without the Indians' assistance, the trail is almost entirely covered with snow. . . . It was a merciful dispensation of Providence that we met this Indian for I do not know what would have become of us."

The mountain crossing was unexceptional. As game was scarce, so was food, but with persuasion the Kutenai guide shared provisions, and with the little left in their packs they managed. It rained as often as it snowed, saving them from the freezing temperatures that had frostbitten young Gibson and others of the 1858 Jones party.

On the eighteenth they camped on the Flathead River in the Pacific drainage and four days later crossed the final ridge to Linklater's primitive HBC post on the Kootenay River.

Linklater had good news. A group of the fragmented Northwestern Exploring Expedition, Moulton, Jessop, et al., had passed two weeks previously with the help of Indians and had proceeded to Colville Valley. Linklater explained that Thibodo had come in on the east side by a pass known only to the Indians, and had then gone by way of the Boundary or South Kootenay Pass into "Uncle Sam's Territory." The small Scot also told them the story of the Jones party of 1858, a tale that lost nothing in the telling.[42]

Linklater told them he had only seen three other white parties here, those of Jones, Hector, and Moulton-Jessop, which shows how untraveled the area was.

Six lazy days were spent on the broad plain. The nights were clear, the days warm and hazy in the mellowness of an Indian summer. Here on the banks of the Kootenay River, fringed with willows and cedars, they were wrapped in a blanket of green, shaded in the morning shadow of towering, ice-crusted peaks; the opposite of the pancake griddle described during their June Dakota Territory trek.

The days were spent resting, readying gear for the next leg, visiting with the Indians, and trading. The softness of Sunday morning was broken and disturbed by the tolling of a bell calling the pious to morning mass in the crude log chapel. Father Joseph Menetry, a black-robed Jesuit, arrived to carry on the work and keep the promises of Father De Smet. Menetry advised the Thibodo party not to go to the Colville mines, but to proceed to the Dalles. The mines, he said, were a humbug, costs were high, no work was available, and many had starved.[43]

Trading was important—the Kutenais had fine horses and the overlanders needed fresh mounts. Thibodo, for one, was walking now, having traded his mule and horse to Sandont. Unfortunately prices were high. Previous parties had traded for 150 horses, and prices were rising.

Linklater too was trading and Thibodo watched the action with interest. Three bear skins or twelve marten bought a three-point blanket; one grizzly hide equaled twenty charges of powder and ball; one muskrat skin—one charge of powder and ball; a beaver skin equaled a file or knife; a buffalo robe bought forty charges; a five-dollar musket and blanket equaled one horse. By Friday they had seven fresh horses, three hundred pounds of meat, and an Indian guide named Consum Claro who for one blanket per man was to guide them to Colville. Payment would be on completion. Bidding farewell and thanks to Linklater they headed down the Kootenay Trail.

It was common practice for overlanders to leave notes of passage along the trails. Those of a previous decade had inscribed names, dates, destination, deaths, and trail information on sandstone bluffs, cattle and horse skulls, and even on occasion, human skulls. Placed at trail junctions, river crossings, and campsites, these messages were a method of keeping in touch, of recording their passing and perhaps meeting friends.

Thibodo's party found several messages carved in trees. The first was at the crossing of the Kootenay River: "N. E. Bunker & Co. crossed here Oct. 19th, 1859." The others were only twelve days ahead of them. Thompson followed suit and carved their names and date at the same crossing. An Indian caught up to them in a canoe with a message from Hamilton, who had remained at the post; the Caldwell party of eight had arrived two days after Thibodo left. They wanted them to blaze the trail so Caldwell could follow. Thibodo hoped they could find the trail, let alone blaze it. Their guide had deserted and, despite their intentions not to pay him until the journey's end, he had left with two blankets, some ammunition, and a Sharps rifle.

On November 3, a few miles downriver they passed another tree with names carved in it. This one read "McLaurier and D. C. Loveland, Sept. 25, 1859." How these two overlanders came to be here on September 25 is a puzzle. McLaurin was reportedly with Palliser and Loveland had taken the Tête Jaune Pass, yet here was record of their passing, an inexplicable frontier archive.

On November 9 at the Ducks Lake Thibodo, like every other overlander and explorer who passed here, found Indians who would trade food and bargain for passage across the river. The Indians showed Thibodo their "visitor's book"—some papers on which travelers had autographed their names. Captain Palliser had passed on August 29. "Ellhi Smith," presumably James Elnathan Smith; "Goodrich," who with Smith and Burnham had made up the first exploring expedition from Minnesota; and "the Selkirk," who may have been one of the Red River or Selkirk settlers who came across the Sinclair in 1841 and 1854, had all signed.

A short halt was made waiting for the river to freeze over and they found the shanty where the Faribault men had wintered the year before. On the afternoon of the twelfth the Caldwell party rode in, looking "very hard and rather hard up for provisions." Caldwell, Dignan, Reid, Hind, Harris, McCullough, and Cheever made up this well-worn band. The two groups of overlanders had last seen each other at Pembina on July 22 when Thibodo had imagined that they would never meet again. Old hostilities were washed away in the excitement of meeting.

The combined party now totaled sixteen men, with yet another Indian guide, this time being paid a Sharps rifle, a suit of old clothes, and a horse. Their crossing to the lake was similar to Jones's trek the previous year, though shorter. They left the crossing on November 14 and found traveling hard. There was little or no feed for the horses, their own provisions were scant, and the trail passed through downed timber. Creek crossings kept the men wet from the bottom up and rain kept them wet from the top down. By the time they reached Pend Oreille Lake all were weak from diarrhea. Somehow they kept going, past the mountain-ringed lake to the ancient Pend Oreille River crossing at *Seneacquoteen*, a Kalispell Indian word meaning crossing.

The two groups had been traveling together, though sometimes separated by hours on the trail. Caldwell's group was heading for the Dalles, Thibodo's for Colville. Somewhere along here Thibodo's company changed their minds and decided to take Father Menetry's advice and head south for the Dalles, so on November 23 the sixteen (their guide having deserted again) headed south for "The Frenchman's," Antoine Plante's small farm north of the Spokane River. At Plante's, on November 25, they met Samuel More from New Jersey and Dr. Fiat, "a French physician of considerable note, formerly of California, but more recently engaged in packing to Fort Alexander" on the Fraser River. He suggested that the mines at Walla Walla were worth investigation.[44]

Where a few days before they had been starving they were now ill from overindulging on hospitality. Bacon, coffee, and bread never tasted better. Civilization, such as it was, had once again been reached—the remainder of the journey would be anticlimactic.

The group split. Thibodo continued south with Fiat, More, Plante's son François, and Indian chief Spokane Garry and his two sons. Within a few days they struck the new Mullan Road military route from Fort Benton to Walla Walla built by Lieutenant Mullan that year. Along the way Thibodo met John Jessop, who having left the rest of his party was traveling with W. H. Barron, a Montrealer who was just down from his Quesnel River ranch. Barron was a forty-niner and he and Thibodo spent many an hour reminiscing about Kingston, Montreal, and old California times.

Walla Walla, December 3. Here the Northwestern Exploring Expedition ended, small groups of men going off in various directions: to seek gold, head down the Columbia, or winter wherever there was work. Dr. Augustus Thibodo, now 171 pounds, a 34-pound increase over what he reckoned to be a 2119-mile journey, hung out his shingle at the McAulif and Co. store; Young and Lynch hired out to a sawmill for thirty dollars a month and board; Hamilton and Thompson headed for the Dalles in a boat; Jessop kept on toward Victoria; Canadian John Sandont stayed in Walla Walla, waiting for spring and a chance to try gold mining. Of the remainder nothing is known, except that they intended to try for British Columbia gold in the spring of 1860.

The expedition's end was confirmed in St. Paul by letters printed in the spring of 1860. Thibodo wrote from Walla Walla giving an account of the journey to Taylor and generally being encouraging about life on the Pacific slope.[45]

Sandont reported from Fort Walla Walla that the entire party had crossed safely. " 'The mines,' Mr. S. says, 'are very good,' and most of the party will go there in the spring."[46]

It was an anonymous writer, likely W. W. Thompson, who voiced the majority feeling in a letter dated Portland, Oregon, February 4, 1860:

> Ho! The last sad remains of the 'North Western Exploring Expedition,' brought up on this coast, about two months ago. The first point of civilization we struck was Walla Walla, a little sort of a mining town, about 300 miles above here on the upper Columbia. And when we struck that town, old boy, we didn't hurt it very much.... Our supply of dog meat and horse meat gave out some days before, and we were sadly in need of grub when we got among the Walla-Wallawers....
> 
> We had a hard old time of it. The 'beautiful valley of the Saskatchewan,' along the banks of which J. W. Taylor envied us our summer's jaunt, is a humbug—a gross, unmitigated, damned humbug! I am sorry that so good a man as J.W.T. should throw himself away upon so poor a subject. He should have accompanied us.... We all got flattered into the idea that we would become a sort of a second John C. Fremont—that we would eat dog meat, run for President and all that sort of thing. We have already realized the dog meat part of the programme; the rest is in the future....
> 
> The news from the mines is go. Parties are starting every day from here; but it is rather too early to go up yet. A good mining outfit from here will cost about

*At Seneacquoteen (the crossing) on the Pend d'Oreille River natives had for many years had a semi-permanent camp. Southern groups of overlanders passed here. (See page 127). Note the distinctive Sturgeon nose of the Kootenay canoe and the woven-reed tipis.*
This shows a camp of the North American Boundary Commission in 1860. (PAC C78978)

# Chapter Eight

## 1860

In the colony of British Columbia, 1860 was a year of exploring and prospecting. Since the discovery of gold in 1858 virtually every bar of the Fraser River had been prospected, named, and sluiced of its fortunes. Murderer's Bar, Mormon Bar, Foster Bar, French Bar, Hill's Bar, Boston Bar, Big Bar, Crow's Bar, and more were staked and raped. As claims were recorded and gold finds dwindled miners panned and rocked their way up the many tributaries of the tawny flood. In 1859 prospector Peter Dunleavy discovered gold on the Horsefly River and later that year Benjamin MacDonald panned some gold from the Quesnel River and printer's ink spilled the news of the new strike across the continent.[1]

With the Quesnel discoveries hundreds of miners moved from the semiarid Fraser-Chilcotin grasslands into the wet forests of fir, cedar hemlock, and cedar; east toward the sources of the Quesnel and Horsefly rivers, closer to the area soon to be discovered and called "Cariboo."

The prospectors working the banks and bars of the Fraser and Quesnel rivers in 1860 were distilled from the first rush of thirty thousand fortune seekers in the summer of 1858. They were a heterogeneous group, a blend of teenagers and grandfathers; Poles, Italians, Scots, Mexicans, Welshmen, Californians, Yankees, Métis, French-Canadians, and Englishmen; strong men and weak men, a diversity fused with the commonality of gold fever and restlessness.

Scattered on the timbered banks of the Quesnel River amongst this rabble were five men who would form a partnership for further exploration in search of the mother lode, one of whom would have a greater influence on the mass overland emigration two years hence than any other single person.

His name was Timoleon M. Love, a gunsmith by apprenticeship, a house carpenter by trade, gold-seeker by profession, and adventurer by nature. Timoleon Love was born in Kentucky on October 1, 1827, the son of Granville N. Love and Clemintina D. R. Mershon, a second-generation Kentuckian of Slavic descent. Like many young eastern men he felt the West beckoning and in 1845 he headed for the Missouri country. In 1848 he joined the United States Army in the Mexican-American War, being discharged a few short months before the California gold strike of 1849. Timoleon had grown into a handsome man, five feet nine inches tall with blond hair, blue eyes, and a fair complexion.[2]

Gold became young Timoleon's first love and for the next decade he panned his way through California and Oregon, even north to the short-lived Queen Charlotte Islands' strike, gaining an expertise and confidence that others often mistook for arrogance, prevarication, and fabrication. His reward was in seeking, not finding, riches. Prospecting for gold was his excuse for the exploration of unwalked trails and unpaddled rivers.

When gold was found on the Fraser, Love was one of those who rushed and by the second season of mining on the Quesnel River he was at Quesnel Forks where, on June 20, 1860, he obtained a license to build a toll ferry. His interest was speculative for he did not install a ferry and on August 15 sold his interest for six hundred dollars. Love was feeling an urge to move on. At the Forks he met four other miners, Alfred Perry and D. F. McLaurin, who were overlanders, and Gilbert Parker and Thomas Clover. They formed an eastbound prospecting party, traveling up the Fraser River through the Yellowhead Pass to Jasper House.[3]

Post clerk Henry Moberly had only recently arrived. Jasper House had been abandoned for many years but in 1858 Moberly had convinced William Christie that it should be reopened, and so had opened the trail, slashing and cutting his way through three hundred miles of muskeg and spruce forest, a track that drew travelers toward the Yellowhead Pass as surely as buffalo drew hunters.[4]

At Jasper House Love's party of five split, intending to explore as much of the country as possible for signs of gold. McLaurin and Clover headed for Fort Edmonton via the Athabasca River and Fort Assiniboine and Love, Perry, and Parker chose to follow Moberly's route. Perry and Parker soon turned back, intending to winter at Jasper House or make their way along the foothills to Rocky Mountain House on the North Saskatchewan River. Love arrived at Fort Edmonton on the evening of October 23, just a few days behind McLaurin and Clover.[5]

The three miners found they had two choices: work for the HBC or walk east toward winter and the Red River settlement. Horses were not for sale and Chief Factor Christie let it be known that he was not in the business of selling supplies to miners, particularly when he could use help and knew Love was a carpenter. So the three settled in to winter at the fort.[6]

Parker and Perry returned to Jasper House where they prospected, hunted, and rustled for a living. On November 28, Parker went hunting, hoping to find some game to fill their pot. Like snow melted by a warm Chinook wind the man from Tennessee vanished. His disappearance could only be explained, Moberly reported to the Fort Edmonton clerk, by his trying to cross a lake on weak ice and falling through.[7]

# 1861

Spring comes late on the prairie. If a man doesn't watch it will be gone before he knows, a brief blooming that rushes from the snowdrifts of winter to the parched grass of summer, a time of reawakening from cold hibernation and long nights. The gray sky warms and snow piled deep on branches softens and slips to the ground. A branch snaps back in a pendulum motion that triggers another branch, and then another until the tree is bare.

In the pines and spruce between Jasper and Edmonton the snow lingers, but on the grasslands toward Fort Pitt and the Bow it disappears suddenly, absorbed into the soil made porous by gophers and ground squirrels. The thaw melts the river that for months has blocked canoe travel. The ice cracks and shifts forming great angular piles on the bends and frozen dams at narrow gorges. The swollen waters flush winter debris down to lakes and the ocean. A warm wind speeds the thaw and brings geese and ducks to the potholes, carrying the shrill cry of the killdeer plover that replaces the scurrying silence of the snow bunting.

It is a restless time for men. Spring brings a stirring in the soul, the mind, the loins. It is time to move, to shift away from the fire's warmth, the evening pipe, and the static workbench, to find a woman to lie with, to make new beginnings. Soon the grass will be greening in the mountain passes and at the end of the trail there could be gold—if gold really matters. It is the looking that counts, a man's freedom to think his own thoughts. Somewhere out there in the thaw is the Elephant, and he must be sought.

The Elephant called Thomas Clover early in the spring of 1861. While snow still covered the ground and with only the promise of spring in the air he packed his gear. At age fifty-two, having already outlived some of his friends and cohorts, he was anxious to get started prospecting again, always with the hope of being able to set himself up in better circumstances, always attracted by the next day.

He made his way up the ice-bound North Saskatchewan to Rocky Mountain House, arriving just as the fort was being closed for the last time. After a few weeks there and some prospecting of the Clearwater River he began to work his way back down the North Saskatchewan, panning a few gravel bars and even building a rocker at one point to retrieve seven dollars in dust. From Fort Edmonton he wrote to his partner Timoleon Love, who had gone to Red River with McLaurin for supplies, to report on his prospects:

I left the Rocky Mountain House in early April for the head of the main Saskatchewan, which was much too early, to prospect to much satisfaction; but will state that what prospecting I did do, and the general appearance of them as gold-bearing, is satisfaction enough in my own mind that it will pay—which is all that is necessary to say to one of your experience.[8]

While Thomas Clover waddled along the Saskatchewan's frozen banks on "misery slippers," Timoleon Love and D. F. McLaurin were working out their engagement at Fort Edmonton. On April 22 they quit work and readied themselves for a trip east. Christie was glad to see them leave. Their work had been useful but he had no room for mining activists. "They have done more harm than good by being here amongst our men, putting all sorts of nonsense into their head," the clerk wrote. At least three men had left the service of the Company to prospect.[9,10]

Christie was aghast at the cheek of these servants.

"Have you not bound yourself to the Company for four years?" he roared at them. "I've never heard of such a thing in all my time."

Gunn, retiring servant, shot back, "Well then, it's high time that it *should* be heard of. I want my back pay."[11]

At Jasper House Henry Moberly gave notice of resignation and headed west to prospect in British Columbia where his brother Walter was road builder and surveyor.[12]

Perry also felt the stirrings of spring and decided to return west. By the first of June he was in New Westminster promoting the idea of a road from the plains to the goldfields. He told John Robson, *British Columbian* editor, "The country [is] most favorable for a road; and at a comparatively small outlay a road could be made which would divert the present travel via the Isthmus."[13]

## Dr. Reid and Red River

Fear and apprehension were as contagious as smallpox along the banks of the Red River in the spring of 1861. Timid settlers packed their homesteads and drove their livestock west across the shallow basin of ancient Lake Agassiz toward a low rise dignified with the name Stoney Mountain. The Red River was on the rise and day by day it became more obvious that this was to be another disastrous spring flood.

During the week of April 16 the Red invaded like an incoming tide, thick with silt, branches, timber, firewood, and occasionally livestock. By the beginning of May 1861 the Red had formed a lake twelve miles wide. From sunrise to sundown the river rose as much as a foot. Bridges were swept away and houses disappeared. Andrew McDermott's new mill floated off. The mill dam gave way, as did Angus Matheson's dam down in the Scotch settlement. Fields of corn drowned, and Robert Sandison's mill looked for a time as if he had chosen to construct it in the middle of the river.[14]

For two weeks the water stayed high, then as it gradually receded the people returned. Behind the flood waters the fields, houses, stores, and trails were covered in a thick layer of silt. Trade goods were watersoaked, lost, or buried in mud. The trading season would be a disaster. As they had after each of the three previous major floods the settlers considered moving.

The floors of homes were still wet when Dr. Alexander P. Reid of London, Canada West, arrived in the settlement with the intention of buying supplies for a trip to the Fraser River mines. A large number of men with him had the same idea. Now they would have to wait for the steamer *Pioneer* from Georgetown, which had been delayed when twenty feet of flood water had floated her into the trees.

While awaiting the arrival of supplies, the adventurers learned of the renewed hostilities of plains Indians toward intruders on their buffalo range. The *Nor'-Wester* editor recommended that parties should have guides not only to find trails on the sea of grass but in case they met Indians; the Reverend Thomas Woolsey wrote cautioning that the Indians "have of late caused much alarm to all persons who have had any particular regard for their own scalps."[15]

The result of these reports was that most of the intrepid adventurers turned back. However, not all were deterred. Reid and four others—William Jones, George Leith, F. Contu, and one unnamed man—continued on for Fraser's River. On June 13, two days after the *Pioneer* unloaded, Reid's party snapped their bull whips and with a cry of "Westward Ho!" began plodding west. Accompanied by a guide, they numbered six and for at least part of the journey traveled with an HBC train of seventy Red River carts bound for Fort Carlton.[16]

Their exuberant departure and buoyant outlook were soon swamped by the Assiniboine's water. The trail, usually well marked, had disappeared in the lakes and swamps formed in the wake of the flood. Streams usually forded had to be ferried. The Reid party built a craft that they referred to as a rectangular canoe. It was made from two buffalo hides sewn together end to end and then wetted to become pliable. The hides were wrapped and lashed to a frame nine feet long, three feet wide, and eighteen inches deep.[17]

The water overlying the trail meant locating a new road that often took the men out of their way and twice resulted in the party becoming lost en route to Fort Ellice. The swamps were terrible. Day after endless day they were forced to wade beside the carts ready to apply muscle power and shoulder the carts through the tenacious mud, the driver urging the horses and oxen on with cajoling, cursing, threats, sweet talk, and the crack of a whip above their ears.

Initially a splattering of mud annoyed Reid, but that minor annoyance soon passed as they found themselves completely coated with a thick black mask, a suit of armor that left them unable to recognize each other. A turbulent stream might present a difficult crossing, but also a cleansing immersion. In places the prairie flooding was so deep and continuous that staging had to be built atop the carts to keep the supplies dry. Even then clothing and blankets were soaked and provisions damaged in water that as often reached their necks as their ankles.

"The mosquitoes," Reid wrote, "tormented us almost to madness; no rest did they give us night or day." The trail was always beset by biting insects but in 1861 the extensive shallow lakes and swamps provided a habitat conducive to an even greater hatch than normal. Every step in the long grass stirred a torment of mosquitoes, every foot of wading in the marshes brought forth a renewed attack by squadrons of the long-nosed devils. Lung-filling smudges gave meager respite and even a strong wind did little to waft away the madness. The mud coating acted as a shield against the needled proboscises but aided little against the torment of the ever-present, whining, buzzing cloud.[18]

Cart trains from Fort Garry usually took six to ten days to travel the 230 miles to Fort Ellice. Reid's party took thirty. They rested two days, rid themselves of the worthless guide, then moved up the Carlton Trail on July 16.

The river valleys were verdant green, lush with oak, aspen, cottonwood, and willow; scented with the sweet smell of cool green vegetation; shaded and alive with the sounds of birds and animals. The land that marched to the far horizon was by comparison a barren table land. There were no limits to the eyes' vision. Wood was nonexistent, for no islands of protective trees broke the skyline, so buffalo chips, patiently gathered on the weary day-long treks, provided fuel for the cooking of meals. They were a surprisingly efficient substitute, though it took some three bushels to cook a dinner for the party. And always there was the wind—sometimes hard and strong, whipping the oilcloth covers of the carts and driving sand into the men's eyes, clogging their nostrils, matting hair and beards and sandblasting their exposed skin; and sometimes so soft and subtle that it barely moved the leaves and petals of the wild roses that sprang up wherever they could gain a root-hold.

Ahead the skyline was broken by rolling land that grew as they approached. They crossed the Little Touchwood Hills, passing into the Touchwood Hills, so named for the trees that made such good fuel for firestarting. The Touchwood's respite from flat lands was short. Beyond lay the treeless, virtually waterless Quill or Great Salt Plains, a desolate stretch of alkaline ponds and flat table lands broken only by a few eskers. Water and firewood had to be carried but no matter how much water was stored it was never enough. Eventually the men were forced to sip the brackish, mineralized pond water, so bitter that it was almost undrinkable. It acted "rather actively on the intestinal canal."[19]

They crossed the South Saskatchewan on August 29 and reached Fort Carlton the next day. Here they were kindly received by Arthur Purden, the clerk in charge, but were unable to obtain fresh horses. The Indians were in no condition to trade anything. The HBC could not be considered whiskey traders, but they did supply Indians with enough spirits to keep them interested in gathering fur and food for the posts. Not being materialistically minded, the Indians were satisfied with whatever goods would see them through the year. Once these necessities had been bartered for it was difficult for them to decide what to do with any remaining credit and they usually opted to trade for baubles and booze.[20]

Having completed their fall trading, the Fort Carlton Cree were "communicating freely" and not anxious to trade with Reid and his party. They were told that it was madness to proceed, particularly to think of passing Fort Pitt and going on to Fort Edmonton. The Blackfeet had sworn to kill every whiteman that passed. Not to be deterred from their goal of reaching the goldfields in one season, they obtained what information they could about the trail, for no guide would accompany them, and forded their horses and carts across the North Saskatchewan. After nine confusing days on the ill-marked trail they reached Fort Pitt.

Their horses were "pretty well used up," so for a week horses and men rested. They finally exchanged horses with the post clerk, hired a young Cree Indian guide, and welcomed the addition of Louis St. Arneaux to their party, a Bay man who was to take two kegs of gunpowder to Fort Edmonton.[21]

As sure as Indians wore feathers there was danger on the next leg. The Blackfeet were troublesome at the best of times and such a small party could expect to receive the worst of any fight. On their first day out of Fort Pitt the party of seven men stopped in a small valley for lunch where, their guide said, not too long ago there had been an Indian battle. In October 1860 a band of twenty-two Cree were attacked by a large war party of Blackfeet. Four Blackfeet were killed in the melee but for the Cree it was virtually a massacre. Only two escaped scalping. One of these was Reid's guide. As he showed them his arrow wound there was a general commotion and the sound of whooping and yelling. History seemed about to repeat itself.[22]

Down the valley slope galloped a band of Indians. With a swiftness born of experience, the guide and Louis St. Arneaux formed the carts into the time-practiced rough circle of the Métis buffalo hunters. Rifles were charged: powder, ball, and percussion cap for the miners and an old flintlock for the Cree and St. Arneaux. The men waited, patiently as the Indians rode closer. Rifles were cocked. There were doubts now about having left the relative security of Fort Pitt. How good a shot was the next man? How good a shot were they themselves? There was a stimulating rush of adrenalin, an excitement at the prospect of fighting for their lives with hostile Indians. They had come for adventure and here it was galloping toward them.

"On they came," Reid wrote, "yelling and cutting up like—well, just like Indians, and they were Indians, too, but they turned out to be Crees. We had a talk and a smoke; they told us that we should meet a band of Blackfeet, 400 in number, in about five days."[23]

The excitement waned, but for the next five days they walked a knife edge, alert and wary. They arrived at Fort Edmonton in nine days without further incident. Behind were miles of experience; ahead, hundreds more.

## Fort Edmonton to Victoria

The arrival of Dr. Alexander Reid's party at Fort Edmonton was duly noted in the post's journal.

August Saturday 24th Weather fine Louis St. Arneaus [sic] arrived this morning with five Gold fevered Canadians. St. Arneaux [sic] delivered us two kegs of gun powder and one cart in good order. the five Gold diggers crossed and are trying to get a Guide to take them across to Fort Colville, it is very doubtful about their getting one as they have to pass thru the Blackfeet country."[24]

Hiring a guide was as difficult as finding a woman in a gold-rush camp—they were few in number, attached, expensive, or not interested in the job. They waited and traded and tried to purchase more provisions, a task as difficult finding a guide. HBC posts were not envisioned by the governors as existing to supply travelers, particularly miners. The post barely had food enough for residents. The Reid party obtained only a few pounds of dry meat and two small bags of tallow. They were given little information about routes or passes, choosing to rely on the guide they finally found, albeit at some expense. Baptiste Gabriel, described by Reid as an Assiniboine halfbreed, felt that if he was going to risk his scalp guiding these strangers through the lands of the Blackfeet then he was going to be well paid. In one account Baptiste's wages were given as twenty-five pounds sterling, a year's wages for a post laborer.[25]

The party of six left Fort Edmonton on September 2, 1861, carrying only thirty days' provisions, barely enough to see them to Fort Colville in good traveling weather without detours to avoid hostile Blackfeet. For six days Baptiste led Reid and his four companions on a circuitous route through the woods, away from the main prairie trails, avoiding confrontation with wandering bands of hostiles. On the sixth day of cautious travel the Rocky Mountains were sighted. On the eleventh, somewhere north of the Bow River in the foothills of the Rockies, Baptiste Gabriel's short-lived courage and devotion evaporated like dew on summer grass and, as had so many guides before, he deserted, taking additional payment in the form of two horses.

At a council the five men decided that it was impossible to go back. The decision: press forward hoping to strike a river recognizable as the Bow, find the pass, and then head south and west to Fort Colville, then on to Fraser River. When they did reach the Bow a few days later they could not find the ford toward the Kananaskis Pass trail. After following the river for some distance they sent three men fifteen miles upstream to locate a ford. No success. They were in the mountains now and as far as they could see the same wide river and deep mountain chasm stretched before them.

In a scene replayed throughout the overlander drama the Reid party was in the midst of pondering their situation when two Indians appeared, as if they had read the script. With signs and rudimentary vocabulary the overlanders indicated where they had come from and asked how to best cross the mountains. One of the Indians replied that they were now in the pass and, in return for a horse, blanket, buffalo robe, gun, powder, etc., he offered to act as their guide.

Travelers usually crossed here to head up the Kananaskis River. Reid's guide, however, continued up the Bow River for three days, past the uplifted Mount Rundle along the wide valley beneath the towering splendor of the Sawback Range and Cascade Mountain.[26]

On the third day they reached a large Stoney Indian camp near the massif Hector had named Castle Mountain. They were well received and exchanged several horses for clothing and ammunition. This was the same band that had helped Jones in 1858. The chief explained that near here were two passes (the Howse and Vermilion), but that the southern one was the best.[27]

They set off, reaching the "limits of perpetual snow" while crossing the height of land that afternoon. Reid later wrote: "He struck another stream—or rather headwaters—and followed down until, by successive additions, it became a large stream. We travelled along this, headwaters of the Kutenai branch of the Columbia [the Vermilion River where it runs through Kootenay National Park]." Now the party left the river, crossing the Brisco Range via the present-day Sinclair Pass or one of the more northerly passes like Luxor Pass.

They camped and "at 11 p.m. the guard woke us up saying that the guide had left." Reid's best horse, and his partner's, had been stolen. Pursuit was pointless—by first light the guide and horses would be beyond reach.

September 21. Again, retreating was as difficult as going forward so they advanced, but when on reaching the summit all they could see were snowclad rocky summits in all directions they wondered about their decision. At noon they found a small stream and stopped for breakfast, then began to follow a faint trail. They soon came in sight of "a very large valley stretching out in a NNW and SSE direction, with an immense sluggish stream winding its way NNW. We came upon a well beaten trail in the evening which followed this stream, which I afterwards found out to be one of the sources of the Columbia."

The five men had stumbled out of the Rockies into the Rocky Mountain trench through which the Columbia River flows, in the vicinity of present-day Radium, British Columbia. Dame fortune was with them again for at noon two more Indians wandered into their camp. Neither party knew the other's language so communication was painstakingly slow. Eventually Reid understood the signing. To reach white settlements in the direction they were going, north by northwest, would take sixty days and they would have to cross three ridges of mountains. The whitemen should turn south through the Columbia valley, following the river to the Lower and Upper Columbia Lakes, then across Canal Flats to the Kootenay River, and fording it continue south to a missionary settlement at Fort Kootenay.

The doctor's party had little left to barter with, their fortune with guides having been rather poor to say the least. However, they offered the hunters four horses if they would take them to any place where there were whites. The Indians refused. It would, they said, take twenty days to reach this place they spoke of. The men turned and began their southerly journey on a dreary and difficult road, their hopes somewhat renewed with the prospect of finally finding their fellow whitemen.

By October 4 they reached the lower end of both the Columbia lakes and the dog meat they were eating so "fasted for a few days, by way of a change." If nothing else was found they had determined to kill a two-year-old horse of Reid's but fortunately, for the horse at least, they found salmon in the shallow stream and speared seven. The salmon, a few woody tasting rose hips, and a boiled buffalo-hide rope lasted until October 14. Again reduced to a state of starvation, the men killed a worn-out pack horse, not Reid's, which before it had been wholly consumed "contained some fine specimens of maggots."

On October 15 they met another Indian hunter who told them that by dark they would reach a place where there were whites. In exchange for some oddments of clothes and ammunition he took them to the camp of two British Royal Engineer sappers engaged on the boundary line survey. These were the first whites the Reid party had seen since leaving Fort Edmonton on September 2 and they were more than grateful for the sappers' fine treatment. They were on the 49th parallel, the boundary between the British colony of British Columbia and Washington Territory in the U.S.A., approximately sixteen days' travel from Fort Colville. After forty-three days wandering in the wilderness, to find the surveyors' precise positioning was like emerging from a thick fog to see a lighthouse. Reid's party were almost giddy with relief.

From here they followed the Kootenay River, taking the same trail that Jones, Jessop, Thibodo, and so many others had before them, arriving at the Colville Valley on November 6, just over two months after leaving Edmonton.

In Colville Valley, Dr. Alexander Reid lingered for a few days accepting the hospitality of Thomas Brown, one of the Sinclair 1854 emigrants, who had boarded and hired some of the Faribault party in 1859. While resting Reid wrote a letter to his father in London, Canada West. The letter took months to reach its destination and in the meantime rumors of Reid's death circulated. A current report in Red River was that he and his companions had been stripped of all clothing and provisions and left to perish. Letters to that effect had been forwarded to his family, offering the usual condolences. Fortuitously a messenger from Victoria arrived just a few days before the letters edged in black, bringing word that Reid had crossed the mountains safely. Soon Reid's letter, dated Colville Valley, November 9, 1861, arrived, confirming the messenger's reports.[28]

Reid described Colville as a small mining town with a population comprised of miners, thieves, and gamblers. The town was dangerous even during daylight. One evening Reid was jumped by two men and while one held him by the throat the other robbed him of twenty-five dollars. Fortunately he had taken the precaution of placing the bulk of his money in security. Reid and his partner decided that this was not a good place to stay. They arrived in Walla Walla, a larger town than Colville but with a similarly composed group of residents, November 26. The population was usually about one thousand but would swell to four or five thousand with various influxes of miners.

The town of Walla Walla is dull, Dr. Alexander P. Reid thought. November 1861 was cold. Everyone was indoors or at the coast, and most miners were still in the gold camps. Reid's partner stayed in Walla Walla but Reid was stubbornly determined to continue. He boarded the Oregon Steam Navigation Company's last steamer of the season down the Columbia River to the Dalles, a distance of 210 miles. Rapids here necessitated a portage for passengers and another steamer was boarded for the 186-mile journey to Portland, Oregon. There Reid spent Christmas—"not very merry." For twenty dollars he purchased a ticket for the four-hundred-mile steamer trip to Victoria, Vancouver Island.

Arriving in Victoria early in the new year he found work as a carpenter at twelve shillings per day in summer, and sixteen shillings per day in winter. Board was twenty-four shillings per week.

On January 29, 1862, he wrote a prophetic letter to his brother which concluded: "I do not think I shall go to the mines this year. The Cariboo are the richest yet discovered, and are about 600 miles from Victoria, through a mountainous country. It is impossible to get in before the middle of June, as the snow is 15 to 20 feet. . . . There will be a frightful rush in the spring; provisions will be enormously dear, if obtainable at all. . . . Many will leave their bones there. Men who have iron constitutions to endure the hardships must make large fortunes. Hundreds will be disappointed. . . . If the present reports prove true, of which I have little doubt, I may possibly go to the gold regions next season."

Reid subsequent fortunes are unknown. His Victoria letter is his track before he becomes lost in the thousands of "Gold-fevered men" in British Columbia. Reid's letters, appearing in the Toronto *Globe*, the *Montreal Witness*, the *Norfolk Reformer* of Simcoe, the *Prototype* and *London News* in his hometown of London, Canada West, and in an 1862 handbook on *British Columbia and Vancouver's Island* by Duncan MacDonald, heightened the fever burning in the eastern townships.

*The coastal town of Victoria, the destination of many overlanders and the usual wintering place for Cariboo miners. This sketch shows a busy Yates Street looking west toward the harbour about 1860. (BCARS 22527)*

# Chapter Nine

### The 1862 Prelude

For many an eastern young man it had been hard to pass up the Fraser rush of 1858, but when it was called a "humbug" they felt vindicated. Then the papers started talking about a place called Cariboo and a river they called the "Canal." Headlines said men were picking up gold from the bottom of a creek named Antler, and washing seventy-five dollars a pan, three months' wages for those who were paid. They could wait no longer. They were heading west.

Since the first '58 gold rush to the Fraser, eastern papers had been printing reports from returned miners, overlanders, express company representatives, imperialists, and expansionists. Many were at odds with one another, newspapers tending to print reports supporting editorial opinion. There were two givens: gold was indeed being found in handsome amounts and young men were better off staying at home than searching for it.

James Fisk, who was leading U.S. wagon trains west cautioned, "None who have homes and a reasonable means of livelihood should be incited by big stories, however true they may be, to immigrate to far off territories after a phantom future."[1]

A letter from James W. Taylor was reprinted in the Toronto *Globe*, May 25, 1862: "Let me be understood. I dissuad altogether from goldseeking. Its prizes are dassling, but rare, four-fifths of its adventurers will be dissappointed."

It being assumed that men would go, despite the cautions, which route was best? Fact-gathering discussions were held in farmhouse kitchens, taverns, hotels, and fraternal halls in Canada East and West, in the Red River settlement, and in St. Peters, Minnesota. Little had changed since the first gold-seekers headed west. There were still only the three basic routes: a risky and expensive sea voyage; the uncompromising "all-British" route across the Canadian Shield; and the rail and sternwheeler route to St. Paul and then across the prairies and Rockies. This latter appeared the easiest and fastest but gave trade to the Americans.

The discovery of west coast gold had created a demand for a western road. As early as 1834 there had been talk of an "all-steam route west" and various pamphleteers and authors had hatched westbound schemes. When the eastern railroad orgy had laid hundreds of miles of new track talk swung to a railroad west. By the 1860s politicians and promoters were speaking of rails from sea to sea. Most westerners, and all who had walked west, realized the likelihood of such a route in the immediate future was as likely as no mosquitoes in spring.

The power of the press was an important factor in the choice of routes, particularly in this year of 1862. The *Montreal Witness* for instance stated: "Two lessons we think may be learned: that at present the overland route is not safe for travel; and that pending the result of further exploration, "Saskatchewan Gold" is more uncertain than tempting. Our desire in these remarks is not to discourage North-Western travel, but to prevent loss and disappointment to individuals." The *Montreal Witness's* position was consistently negative but the editors did advise taking a woman to the goldfields and settling. Then, on March 12, an item said the sea route via Panama was the way to go, and listed the "three most difficult things in gold mining: First, to find it. Second, to get it. Third, to keep it."[2]

The view of *Globe* editor George Brown was that the Canadian Shield route was best, particularly for travelers from eastern Canada. Route choice was also influenced by reports in the *Globe* via the *Nor'Wester* from adventurer Timoleon Love who, in partnership with Tom Clover and D. F. McLaurin (all ex-California and Cariboo miners), gave glowing accounts of gold discoveries on the North Saskatchewan near Fort Edmonton. Love actively promoted the Saskatchewan mines all winter, preparing to take advantage of any interest he could spark.

Love's support for the Saskatchewan mines was based on little prospecting of his own. He had now been at Red River for two winters and one summer, in which time he had only Clover's infrequent letters to go on but editors quoted Love, Clover, and the Reverend Mr. Woolsey of Fort Edmonton, who backed Love's gold findings, as confirmation that there was gold near Fort Edmonton—and Fort Edmonton was on the overland route west.

The editor of the *Nor'Wester* addressed the Red River settlers, who were holding their own meeting. Now it was proven that gold was there.

Who will take the lead, and who are to follow? We are such a staid plodding people, that we dislike such a novelty as gold digging. Mining is not in our way of thinking—it is an outlandish business, fit only for Yankees and other desperate speculators—a wild goose chase—a thing to be sternly frowned down by paterfamilias when thoughtless, ardent sons speak about it! Yes! this is the light in which nine-tenths of the people of Red Deer regard the gold business.

Mr. Love will, next month, at the latest, go through to St. Paul, to form a party for actual operations. Mr. George Flett, Mr. George Gunn and others will endeavour to organize a party of Red Riverites to anticipate Mr. Love. Very good so far. The rivalry is generous—carry it out, gentlemen, and the results will amply reward your efforts and benefit the country.

A letter from George Flett of Headingly proposed that a Red River party try for Rocky Mountain gold. Flett argued that Red River people, Métis, would have an easier time than American gold hunters for they could converse with the Indians and knew how to survive on the land. His plan was to form a group of twenty-five to thirty tough men, "half gents—bread and butter heros—who cannot toe the mark—will not do," and leave about May 20.[3]

The various congregations of easterners sorted all this information and by March decided on the overland route via St. Paul. The men took their savings, sold goods, or borrowed the necessary monies, and boarded the Grand Trunk Railway.

Why go? Why stay? The most many young men could hope for was to work for an older brother who inherited the family farm, or apprentice with never enough money to marry or move ahead of what their fathers had known. Some of the older men had less defined reasons. Stephen Redgrave, the organizer of a Toronto party, was such an example. Redgrave was thirty-one years old. Born in England, educated at Rugby, and well married, at eighteen years of age he moved his family to Australia following the 1852 gold strike. He mined at Ballarat, became a warden at the penal settlement, and then a Colonial Mounted Police inspector. Wounded several times in brushes with bush rangers he left Australia in 1859 under a gray cloud of censorship. South Africa was his next stop, then England, then Canada, all in the same year. In Toronto he joined the police force and was promoted to sergeant.

Redgrave was a big, overweight man. A heavy face with a small beard gave an appearance that amplified his blustery bombastic demeanor. He was a blowhard who seldom lived up to his word or his own self-aggrandizing image. He was also dissatisfied. Redgrave felt a need to prove something, if not to others then to himself. He carried a heavy burden—he had never attained the wealth or position that he felt he was destined for, or capable of. His only consolation was to tell himself he had done all he could, and then try again.

The journal of Stephen Redgrave, April 23, 1862.

Being determined to go to the Cariboo Gold Diggings I resigned the Police force just when my prospects of promotion was more certain, just half an hour before the train started. As for bidding anyone good by, I had no time, neither did any one believe I was going, as if there were such a great attraction in Toronto. As to Canada—I could not recommend a young man to stay there. It is the same in Canada as in the States, the almighty dollar is blessed above all things.[4]

Another example is Robert Harkness, twenty-nine years of age. In 1856 he married Sabrina Jane Wood, a woman he loved deeply as his goldfields' letters indicate. His father, though "stern and unsociable," set him up in business as a general merchant in Iroquois, Canada West. There he and Sabrina had three children, the last, Catherine, born just two weeks before his departure west. Harkness's catalyst seems to have been some indiscretion and harsh words spoken, which his subsequent affectionate love letters continually allude to and apologize for.[5]

The Phillip brothers went west on a whim. Both in their early twenties, William and Thomas had been born near Montreal to a wealthy family. Their father was a doctor who had inherited an estate in Ireland. William had traveled extensively throughout Europe and eastern North America. As he wrote in his journal, he "seemed to have lost the faculty of keeping still." The overland trip to the gold mines was ideally suited to a restless young man. He passed his enthusiasm to his brother Tom, and "had no difficulty in obtaining my father's sanction, with money enough for the trip." In a poetic mood William scratched in his journal:

> We are the voices of the wandering wind,
> which moan for rest,
> but rest can never find.
> So! as the wind is, so is mortal life,
> A Moan, a Sigh, a Sob, a Storm, a Strife—[6]

Young James C. Carpenter was called to the bar "of Practising Barristers" in January 1862 and had gone into partnership with John L. Proveaux in Toronto. His practice lasted only months, for in April Carpenter succumbed to gold fever.[7]

Peter McIntyre was later referred to as the "giant of the party." A farmer's son from Quebec, he was twenty-eight years old and well over six feet tall, with a build to match. He later explained:

We had heard stories of the wealth of Cariboo. The young fellows of our locality were all excited about it, but we saw no opportunity of getting to the goldfields, as the cost of making the trip by way of Panama and up the Pacific Coast was so high we could not even contemplate it.

Then came rumours that an overland expedition was to be formed to cross over the great waste lands, penetrate the Rocky Mountains where only fur traders and explorers had ventured. Our minds were excited, and half-a-dozen of us decided to join if we could raise the necessary amount to outfit ourselves. Money was scarce—very scarce—in Quebec in those days.

Finally a friend offered to loan me $200, the amount required. A tremendous sum, it seemed, but I accepted it, and my companions managed to secure some money as well.[8]

Alexander Fortune boarded the Grand Trunk Railway for yet another reason. Fortune, thirty-one years old, of St. Anicet, Canada East, was the son of a doctor and had studied for the ministry at Knox College. He had been advised on account of ill health to live more in the open, so he left his wife of seven months, Bathia Ross, and headed for the new colony of British Columbia. Fortune reminisced about the hopes and feelings of those who went west.

We had witnessed the reports of several who succeeded, but not about the failure of the majority, hence we thought we might be among the lucky ones who could go to Cariboo gold fields and be back in a few short years with a competency to live amongst our friends and have a comfortable home for the time of sickness or old age. Why not succeed as well as others? We were criticized for thinking of such a move; 'better to stay and work patiently in the east rather than go to uncertainties in the west', they said. But when have the young listened?⁹

They deserted kind mothers to escape cruel fathers; left civilization for wilderness. Their only hope was to leave, the only question had been to where? Now they knew—the golden Cariboo. They left because "there isn't any place as pretty as one one that lays ahead," and "jest to get where I ain't."¹⁰

In Shakespeare's *Taming of the Shrew* the question is asked: "And tell me now, sweet friend, what happy gale blows you . . . here?" The answer would have suited the overlanders: "Such wind as scatters young men through the world to seek their fortunes further than at home where small experience grows."

There were those to leave behind. Fathers, mothers, brothers, sisters and friends, and dear hearts with whom so many future plans had been made. California widows they had once been called. John Hunniford for instance left a wife and three children in St. Catherines. His terse diary, usually restricted to three laconic lines, expands only on September 7, when his raft hits a rock in the Fraser and he writes: "thought of my quiet home that I left. Regreted leaving my wife and children." Harkness remained homesick for Sabrina for four long years.

It was always their intention to return. Few meant to stay in British Columbia; fewer still in Cariboo. They were going to make a fortune and return as soon as possible. Two to five years they estimated. With hearts torn at the thought of not seeing a loved one for years they left. But the parting was only momentarily sad. A golden adventure waited.

## Canada West to St. Paul

In the small village of Huntingdon, Canada East, on the eastern bank of the St. Lawrence River the predawn darkness was broken by the yellow light escaping from the window of David Millne's Inn and the lamps carried by two hundred villagers. It was not yet 4:00 A.M. on this April 23 but already they gathered, horses and carriages tied outside, friends and relatives clustered around tables filled with bottles and glasses toasting the men about to venture west.¹¹

The young men such as John Bowron, his cousin Bill Schuyler, and schoolmate George Tunstall were buoyant in their enthusiasm and adventuresome anticipation and talked of the fortunes they would bring home.

In the inn's quiet shadows and outside in the damp other men stood quietly—James Sellar, his brother William nearby; twenty-five-year-old blacksmith Henry Blanchford—kicking the mud with their boot toes, shuffling uneasily as feelings of emptiness mixed with desperate hope. They were anxious to be done with goodbyes. Wives held back sobs or smiled through tears of farewell while arms enfolded young children. This was not parting for a day's work in the fields or a journey to Montreal, but a parting for years, in some cases forever. Perhaps Cariboo gold would make life easier and the years of loneliness worth the price.

At a table James Wattie stood with his younger brother William and told listeners of his mining in California. He had gone there in 1852, at age twenty-two, and returned three years later. Now he was leaving the family farm just up the road and taking William west to a new strike where his friend from California days, John Angus "Cariboo" Cameron, had claims that were soon to prove immensely rich.[12]

A young Englishman by the name of Merriat hovered uncertainly around the group's fringes. He was new, as green as grass, and nervously hummed a tune with the words, "By studying of economy we live like a Lord." Within days he would be nicknamed and known only as "the boy Economy."[13]

Soon they were all there, some twenty-five men, and though surrounded here in Huntingdon by French Canadians they were Protestants all—not a Roman amongst them.[14]

As the clock inched toward 5:00 A.M. the final affectionate farewells were made, the last "God Speed" spoken. They boarded the wagons that family and friends had brought, and headed down the muddy road to Chateaugay, New York, and the railway.

Delayed by poor road conditions they arrived just thirty minutes before the train pulled out at 10:00 A.M. The railroad took them to Ogdensburg, where they recrossed the border and St. Lawrence River to Prescott. Waiting for the Grand Trunk they strolled around town, racked up a few games of billiards, and had photographs taken to be sent home. Blanchford and James Sellar wrote letters to "our better-half's."

Before noon they again boarded the Grand Trunk and in two hours sighed into Toronto's Union Station. They were joined here, in a great commotion, by the Redgrave Toronto party, bringing the number of British Columbia-bound men on board to forty-eight. Redgrave's group, with only a couple of men over twenty-two years of age, was the least cohesive and most troubled of the 1862 parties west.[15]

William George Richardson Hind who "stalks like a ghostly figure through the pages of Canadian art history," climbed aboard with his sketch pad, ready to become the unofficial but only "expedition artist." Hind was born in Nottingham, England, in 1833 and about 1852 followed his brother, Henry Youle Hind, to Canada. Henry Youle was in charge of the Canadian Red River and Assiniboine and Saskatchewan Exploring Expedition of 1857 and 1858. While William did not accompany Henry on that excursion he did join the 1861 Labrador expedition as artist. The balding Hind appeared scholarly and sported a silky beard and eyeglasses, and was given to smoking a pipe and carrying a sketch book. It might be said he had an artist's temperament for he had trouble fitting into his overland group and was later described as having "grand and occasionally eccentric habits."[16]

The young barrister James Carpenter was here, along with Richard

Alexander, a pink-cheeked Scots lad of eighteen, a wheat merchant's clerk scratching boring notes in his small daily diary, and a dozen other young men. Robert Harkness had said goodbye to his wife earlier, in Iroquois. Already he missed her companionship and his children's laughter. The momentary melancholy was soon swept away by exuberant companions.

At Stratford three more Huntingdon men joined to shouts of greeting: Alexander Clyde, Robert Edgar, and David Dunsmour. Alexander Clyde was an exception. At twenty-eight years of age Clyde had a wife and three young children, his own blacksmith's shop worth $8000, and two apprentices, Thomas Clyde and George Reid, each being paid $7.50 per month to swing a hammer and pump a bellows, all members of the Evangelical Mission. Clyde watched Reid leave, balancing in his mind a hammer in one hand; a gold pan in the other. With Huntingdon village quiet, the men gone, he dropped the hammer, removed his stiff leather apron. "Thomas, mind the store. Watch Fanny and the young ones. I'm for Cariboo."

At Sarnia there was time to lift "Padies Eye-water" in a toast to Britain and all British subjects and give "three brave and hearty cheers for our homes, and for Canada, and Canada's Son's." All nationalistic bravado done with, they crossed to Port Huron and the United States of America.

While Harkness and the Huntingdon-Toronto party rolled through Detroit by rail, another large party was leaving St. Catharines and Queenston on the Niagara Peninsula under the leadership of Thomas McMicking. The McMicking brothers, Thomas "the Sixth," age thirty-three and Robert, eighteen, were of United Empire Loyalist stock, of Scots descent, born at the family farm in Stamford Township, Upper Canada, which Thomas McMicking "the Fourth" had established after fleeing from the Delaware River country about 1783 following the Revolutionary War.[17]

Thomas was educated at Stamford, a religious man, pious, and harsh in his opinions of those who did not live up to his Presbyterian ideals. Yet his education and the trust men felt in him made him emerge as a leader. His appearance verged on effeminate. Clean-shaven with deep, dark eyes and soft features he was atypical of the image of a wagon-train leader.

At twenty-five he married Laura Chubbuck and his fourth child was born after his departure to British Columbia. By 1862 he had worked his father's farm, taught school, gone into business as a general dealer, and been defeated in the Niagara election as the Clear Grit candidate. Like Redgrave, McMicking was not satisfied with his professional progress.

His young brother Robert had left school at age thirteen when his father died, a fact reflected in his poorly written journal. He became interested in things electrical and began work in a telegraph office. When Thomas invited him west he was living at home with his widowed mother and four older and three younger brothers and sisters.

"Our personal outfit," Thomas McMicking wrote, "consisted generally in one good strong suit, from three to six changes of under-clothing, a pair of knee boots and a pair of shoes, a rubber coat and a pair of blankets; and armed with a rifle, revolver and Bowie knife. Besides these every one was provided with a few drugs and patent medicines."[18]

Party treasurer John Bowland described the scene:

He started amidst the tears, prayers, and sorrows of wives, children and kind neighbours. An address was delivered in behalf of the citizens of Queenston by Arthur Shaw Esq. and responded to . . . by Thomas McMicking. . . . We left amid cheers while John Fannin played "Cheer, Boys, Cheer" on his cornet.[19]

At St. Catharines they boarded the Great Western Railway, and twelve hours later they arrived in Detroit. John Bowland found the second class accommodation "a rough ride all the way" for the seats were bare boards only eleven inches wide. George Pullman had not yet invented his well-sprung, comfortable coaches so passengers had to put up with the jarring of primitive pin couplings and crowded, often smelly, confinement.

From Detroit there was a choice of two routes. The Queenston party went north via the Detroit and Milwaukee Railway to Grand Haven and by the steamer *Detroit* across Lake Michigan to Milwaukee. The rough lake crossing was more uncomfortable than the train for some as they spent a good deal of the time bent at the rail watching the water pass by.

The other route, taken by the Huntingdon men, was via the Central Michigan Railway to Chicago, around Lake Michigan, and then north to Milwaukee. The Huntingdon boys had a spree in Chicago and were in fine shape for a trip that Sellar described as very pleasant, "over the prairies, so beautifully spotted with country Towns, the buildings are generally of a Gothic style & chiefly painted white, so that a small town at a distance has a beautiful appearance." This first week's journey was a nine-hundred-mile passage into wilderness. They moved from two hundred years of civilization, through farm lands recently wrested from the natives by men like Simon Kenton and Daniel Boone, to a frontier still untamed.

The Huntingdon and Queenston parties had both grown in size by the time they reached La Crosse on the Mississippi River. The Huntingdon group was first to reach the docks. Anxious, they found the Davidson Line dock and boarded the *Northern Belle*, lining the rail to watch the bales of goods being stacked on deck, the passengers walking the gangplank, the crew stacking cord wood for the boilers and, high in the pilot house, the overseeing captain. The overlanders tuned their ears to the bell, waiting for the signal, the surge that would pull them from shore. Departure time was to be 12:30 P.M., but the dock only faded from view in the light of the early dawn, and two hours later they unceremoniously nudged the left shore—broken down.

McMicking's men had reached La Crosse on April 26, a day behind but now their side-wheel packet, the *Frank Steele*, overtook the *Belle*. With great cheers and firing of guns the Cariboo-bound parties greeted each other. Rather than board the *Belle*, passengers waited for the *Keokuk* under Captain J. R. Hatcher, who had been sent to pick them up. Soon they steamed victoriously passed the *Frank Steele*, whistle blowing, bell ringing, and guns blazing skyward. They arrived in St. Paul at 1:00 P.M. the next day and made their way to the American House.[20]

Aboard the *Frank Steele* McMicking was irate. By arrangement with the railway his party had been sold first class tickets through to St. Paul but once aboard they were crowded together between decks with no room to lie down and refused provisions, although they offered to pay extra. John Bowland took a state room for his health's sake, but said the others "looked rather hard in the morning, but endured it like men." John Hunniford, who had left St. Catharines two days before the others, had joined and tersely wrote: "26 Saturday Passed the night on Deck very uncomfortable had nothing to eat. 27 Sunday On the Mississippi all day had nothing to eat arrived in St. Pauls at 8 o'clock."

Robert McMicking, tired and hungry, quickly jotted: "Got to the City Hotel got our supper and went to bed." It was to be their last mattress for several months.

## "Ho! for Cariboo"

For several months of the year St. Paul was a city isolated by winter. Red River carts from the north waited for green-up and steamers from the south waited for breakup. When the steamer *Keokuk* barged through "vast fields of accumulated ice" in the 1862 mid-April breakup a lone overlander was aboard. William R. Burgess was the precursor of several hundred overlanders to arrive in St. Paul this spring.[21]

A party from St. Thomas were the first to unload on the crowded St. Paul river-front docks and make their way up the hill along the muddy, melting streets and slush-laden plank sidewalks to the Merchants Hotel. The St. Paul merchants were waiting for them, directing their newspaper advertisements toward them.

> OUTFITS FOR GOLD MINERS! Parties going the overland route to Cariboo Gold Mines will find at CAMPELL's, Third St., Burnheimer Block, St. Paul, A COMPLETE OUTFIT! Rubber Blankets, Coats, Leggins, Caps; Tent Cloth; Grey Blue and Red Over Shirts; and everything in the Furnishing Line.

The St. Thomas party wasted little time loitering. The *St. Paul Press* reported on April 24 that the party had "procured considerable of their outfit from our merchants and mechanics" and were leaving that morning. Joseph Wheelock, journalist with Nobles in 1859, now editor of the *Press*, still believed in the Saskatchewan route and St. Paul's role and added, "This, it is true, is a small party, but as soon as the route is thoroughly known plenty of others will follow."[22]

As the St. Thomas men boarded the Burbanks' stagecoaches for Georgetown on the Red River, others were arriving, not only from Canada but also from small Minnesota towns. During the month from mid-April to mid-May hundreds of men passed through, most stopping to buy provisions and arrange transportation. James Sellar's list itemizes goods purchased from Bell & Brothers, St. Paul, a list that would be typical for most parties.

| | |
|---|---|
| Picks, 11, | $10.00 |
| Shovels, 12, | $12.00 |
| 3 sets cooking utensils, | $18.00 |
| ½ sheet of Iron, | $4.00 |
| nails, | $3.00 |
| sea Biscuit, | $4.00 |
| 300 lbs Ham, | $24.00 |
| 20 lbs Tea, | $18.00 |
| 30 lbs Coffee, | $6.00 |
| 2 lbs Ginger, | $0.50 |
| 2 lbs C. Tartar, | $1.00 |
| 2 Kegs Gun Powder, | $19.00 |
| 3 bags Shot, | $9.50 |
| 60 Yards Duck, | $19.80 |
| 10 lbs Baking Powder, | $1.00 |
| Gun Caps, | $2.00 |
| Prairie Matches, | $3.00 |
| L Matches, | $1.00 |
| Rope, | $2.00 |
| Baking Oven, | $1.75 |
| Twine & Needle, | $0.75 |
| 2 Axes | $2.50 |
| Sythe and snath, | $2.00 |
| Bushel Beans, | $1.50 |
| 25 lbs leads for bullets, | $2.55 |

These supplies, with sundries, came to a total of $195.80 for the Huntingdon company.

Their supplies purchased, the men settled down to hand sew four tents. Bowland described them as "all seated on the floor sowing away like good fellows; looked rather comical; we astonished the neighbours —they thought we belonged to the Government, as we were asked the question sundry times."

Here too the overlanders had to make decisions about forward travel. In 1859 a number of small companies including the Burbank brothers, Capt. Russell Blakely, and John L. Merriman had merged under the name of Minnesota Stage Company. It was their maiden journey that had leapfrogged the Nobles 1859 expedition. The Burbanks ran advertisements claiming "the roads are well stocked with First Class Horses, Concord Coaches; with careful and experienced drivers," and attracted the overlanders to their office just down the street from the American House. Departures for Georgetown, Pembina, and Fort Garry were on Mondays and Wednesdays at 4:00 A.M. and were to connect with the new SS *International*, a sternwheeler now being built at Georgetown, the height of navigation on the Red River of the North. The boat was to be ready by May 10 in time for the overlanders' departure.[23]

The Queenstown group organized to take advantage of the stages, which could only take ten passengers per trip. Transportation costs on the frontier were expensive. McMicking's fare from Queenston to St. Paul, 900 miles, was $16.65; from St. Paul to Fort Garry, 750 miles, it was to cost $25.00. McMicking appears to have been able to strike a bargain once again for a cheaper fare from the Burbanks. Sellar, of the Huntingdon party, wrote: "But as Burbank & Co. would not make any reduction off 32 dollars for fair; and 5 Dollars for freight, Our Huntingdon Company concluded that they would engage private conveyance, and accordingly at 4 P.M. we came to an arrangement with Mr. Webb of St. Paul who is a forwarder to take 16 of us through to Red River [Georgetown] for the sum of 150 dollars and take 3500 pounds of freight through free." The Huntingdon boys left on April 29 for the upriver staging town of St. Anthony.

While British Columbia's interior was being explored and opened by prospectors so were the areas of Washington, Oregon, Idaho, and Montana. Many of these strikes were as recent as those in Cariboo so in the spring of 1862 the merchants of St. Paul were outfitters for gold-seekers of diverse destinations. The American wagon-train expeditions to gold-fields south of the 49th parallel were led by two men, James Fisk and Thomas Holmes, who led a British Columbia–bound party in 1858. With the many destinations offered and the rumors that floated along the Mississippi and Red rivers that spring it was not unusual for a man or a whole party to change destination while en route, and thus Canadians joined Holmes and Fisk and Americans were drawn to the Canadian overlanders.

With all of this activity St. Paul was experiencing unprecedented opportunities for commerce. The town papers kept up a running score of who was arriving and leaving. From mid-April on there were parties of Canadian gold-seekers arriving and departing almost every day. The papers were filled with departure news and party lists in backslapping glee that perhaps at long last the merchants' dream was going to materialize.[24]

One arrival who was of particular interest to *Press* editor Wheelock was another journalist, George Wallace.

> We had the pleasure yesterday of a chat with the gentlemanly editor of the Toronto Globe, Mr. Wallace . . . he comes as an agent of a company which has in contemplation the establishment of a complete passenger and transportation route to the Cariboo country and is engaged in gathering such information as will determine the practicability of such a route. We learn there are two companies looking to the formation of different routes.

Wallace is an enigma. While his post-journey life is well known, documentation begins with the overland journey. His connection with the Toronto *Globe* is unclear, certainly he was not editor. Journalist? Correspondent? No bylined reports of his were published, though he did become a well-known editor and publisher in British Columbia, indicating a newspaper background. Was he connected with the British Overland Transit Company scheme? Was his "editorship" a ruse to ingratiate himself with organizers and editors? He remains a mystery. Likely he was a journalist, with a propensity toward promoting.[25]

On April 27 the Queenston, Huntingdon, and Redgrave parties arrived and daily more adventurers docked and climbed the hills of St. Paul. On the twenty-ninth a meeting of Canadian overlanders was held in the American House. The various hometown groups came together in a patchwork fashion, joined forces, and then divided into messes of ten men to facilitate stage and river travel. Not everything was as expected and Redgrave's men were disappointed by his lack of leadership. "Form yourselves into parties of five or six," he said, "and do the best you can." It was evident now that he knew no more about the route than any of them and many were annoyed at Redgrave and his cronies living high, "finishing plenty of brandy." William Hugill said he was "a regular humbug, entirely incompetent for the position he assumed."[26]

It was an unexpected enormity that faced them, the lurking Elephant, a metaphoric beast that drove some back. The presence of the unknown placed pressure on the leaders. Bombasity and self-aggrandizement mixed with brandy were a poor glue and as John Bowland put it in his *Christian Guardian* letter: "The 'big-bugs' and 'little-bugs' separated. Redgrave's party from Toronto fell apart, leaving him sullen, damning their ungratefulness. Harkness and Hugill were among those who once went over to the Queenston party."[27]

The St. Paul meeting and the Redgrave incident served to emphasize not only how many men from Canada were following the overland route west to Cariboo but also how fraught with danger the trip ahead would be. On the stage trip north to Georgetown, beyond St. Cloud, Alexander Fortune felt civilization slipping away.

> We seemed to be following the retreating footsteps of winter for the lands were wet and cold and the grass had not shown. ... Here was the near limit to settlement. The vanguard of the bold pioneers of the sturdy class who reclaimed the Eastern States and the Canadians from the primeval forest were overtaken by us near St. Cloud.
>
> The advantages of civilization; the centres of refinement; the books; the papers; the post offices, the railways, telegraphs; sidewalks; the streets and roads; the churches and schools; the homes; our dear homes where we left wives, mothers or sisters, fathers and brothers, all like a panamoric picture passed before our memory at this verge of the unsettled west.
>
> With some foreboding of want and hardship, with no little dread of the Indian scalper, and with positive proof of no servants, spring mattresses or silver spoons to sip our hairy pemmican, we left St. Cloud.

Bowland describes the stage journey: "The first day we travelled from 75 to 80 miles. Felt dizzy and sick at the stomach the first day, but felt better as we travelled. The company changed horses every 15 or 20 miles; four horses to a stage or wagon. It was a rough and tough ride and such a shaking no poor sinners, I think, ever got before, of 318 miles. But we sung, talked, and laughed as our heads bumped against the sides; and I am happy to say that not one hard word has been spoken, but all is laughter and good feeling since we started."[28]

In the four years that gold-seekers had been taking this route north it had evolved from a Red River cart trail to a wagon road. Now canvas-covered freight wagons and a steamship on the Red River replaced Red River carts and linked the two frontiers, a system developed with HBC money and contracts and the Burbanks' wagons. The Burbanks and their partners, however, were finding that this was not the door to expansion they had anticipated. The HBC still blocked immigration, mail, and trade that would open the interior. For Minnesota, the freight route had been the furrow where the seed of commerce could be planted and many small towns sprouted tenuously. Where once cabins and claim shanties had been built in lonely isolation there were now towns, if only on paper. Breckenridge, for instance, was one cabin and a hotel under construction, founded in 1857 with optimistic townsite speculation in mind. Poor in appearance it was, on the map, "a large city laid out with blocks, streets, avenues and parks."[29]

At this stage stop at the confluence of the Bois de Sioux River and the Otter Tail River (actually the head of the Red River), Fortune and his friends in the expanded Acton party met two men. John Nicols was aboard a southbound stage, coughing and spitting in what seemed to Fortune the final stages of tuberculosis and "not likely to live many days." By coincidence here too was Dr. William B. Simonton who had decided to head west. He advised Nicol not to go back to friends or doctors or he would surely die, but to travel the prairie where the air and outdoor life might restore his health. If not he and the Acton party would bury him, as would his friends if he stayed.

Simonton has long been a misunderstood overlander. We now know that William B. Simonton graduated from the medical department of Pennsylvania College in Philadelphia with an M.D. in the spring of 1851.[30]

After graduation his trail disappears until the American Civil War begins in April 1861. By July 19 he has arrived at Fort Abercrombie on the Red River as acting surgeon, 2nd Regiment of Minnesota Volunteers, U.S. Army. There are no records of his enlistment nor his discharge but his appearance here at Breckenridge only a few miles south of Fort Abercrombie and his subsequent reference to his military service preclude any possibility of his being a deserter, unlike a few other 1860's gold-seekers. In mid-May the troops at Fort Abercrombie had been payed to date and Acting Surgeon Simonton appears to have taken that as an appropriate time to sever his service. His national duty was behind him. Ho! for Cariboo.[31]

While most of the overlanders were bouncing along through fine weather in coaches filled with camaraderie, Sellar and his companions were hauling supplies on foot with the help of Mr. Webb. They set a blistering pace—thirty-five miles the first day—which prostrated several men with fatigue. They were developing a stamina and strength that would make them contemptuous of others' slow travel.

At the first major stopping point of St. Cloud they held a meeting and elected James Wattie, the California miner, captain and appointed him and three experienced members—Joseph Whyte and blacksmiths William B. Cameron and Harry Blanchford—to remain and buy cattle, wagons, harness, and feed for the rest of the journey. At Chapman and Miller's general store they made their largest expenditure: $534. The bulk of this went for a wagon at $75 and eight oxen for $249.50, the latter unusual low price no doubt the result of some hard bargaining.

By the fourth day of marching for twelve hours Sellar's feet were covered in penny-sized blisters. To save them he tried walking on tiptoe and sprained his instep so badly that he could not walk. By the next day he was at it again, his perservering nature coming through. The weather had been fine for the travelers so the mud holes and creek crossings were less trouble than they might have been. On May 6 they reached the Ottertail River, where they camped for the night and began ferrying their goods over at seven the next morning, a three-hour task. Seeing another party of thirteen they decided to wait, a mistake as it turned out. Now they had to scramble ahead to avoid being elbowed away from bunks and tables at the trail's hostelries by the "set of beasts."

Sellar and William Gage raced ahead to make reservations at Fort Abercrombie, arriving an hour ahead of the main party, soaking wet from a heavy thunder shower. The St. Paul stage arrived as the wagons did, and aboard were two whimsical wandering friends, the "Phillip's boys (Thomas & William) from Durham. And I can assure you that no person can imagine the amount of pleasure it affords a person, to meet with acquaintances from your own Country, in such a desolate land!"

Washington- and Montana-bound Americans braided their wagon tracks with Canadian overlanders as far as the turnoff for St. Joseph where they would follow Stevens route west, the route the Brechin man in 1858 and the Moulton party in 1859 had tried to follow. Their plan was to organize at Georgetown.[32]

Minnesotan Andrew Holes joined the St. Thomas party north of St. Cloud. Of an English family that had moved to New York—his grandfather was a soldier under Wellington at Waterloo—he arrived here after a stint as school teacher, and was now working in a lime kiln while proving up his land claim near Moorehead. Holes was well over six feet tall. He was impressive in appearance and mannerism and a solid party member.[33]

## In Camp at Georgetown

By the first week in May, as the riverbank oaks were beginning to show a wash of green and the waters of the Red River rose toward their trunks, the HBC post of Georgetown, Minnesota, was sprouting with tents. "It is a miserable hole of a place," young Richard Alexander thought. Here they had rushed for hundreds of miles to get a head start and now Burbank told them the steamer *International* would not be ready to sail on her maiden voyage for ten days.

The HBC established Georgetown in 1859 as a transfer point for goods carried south from Fort Garry by steamer and then on to St. Paul by the Burbanks' freight line. Robert McKenzie was the first man in charge. He went for supplies and froze to death. James Purden was next. The men mutinied under his ill treatment and he found it prudent to leave. Alexander Murray, the present incumbent, succeeded him. In 1862 about forty men were employed.[34]

No one was impressed with the landing. Sellar wrote: "Georgetown is one of the Sea Port towns of olden times. It is composed of one store, at which you can buy nothing [the HBC warehouse], one Hotel at which we could neither buy grog nor Victuals, one barracks and some three or four Indian wigwams and one dwelling house."[35]

The barracks and some tents were housing a company of thirty infantrymen as a safeguard against Sioux, Cree, and Chippewa Indians who were making noises about an incomplete treaty and demanding money for passage through their land. Last fall the Red Lake Indians had demanded three thousand dollars from the Company for wood cut by the woodhawks and at Pembina the captain had to assuage them with provisions before he could proceed. The Indian threat was common knowledge. Alexander wrote on May 10, "There are some Chippewa Indians down at present, rather awkward looking customers. They demand payment for the right of the steam[er] running on their river and it is not impossible that there may be a fuss." John Hunniford seems to have been little impressed with the Indian danger for he records, "Had good fun with a drunken Indian at night." The Indian alarm served to break the monotony of what had been becoming a camp of discontent. By mid-March there were over 150 Cariboo-bound miners camped here in twenty-five camps, plus American parties passing through, plus the soldiers and the HBC men.

The steamer they were waiting for was the SS *International*. When Anson Northrup abandoned the ugly little steamer *Anson Northrup* on the river bank and ran south to St. Paul to collect his two thousand dollar prize money he expected that the Red River trade was his for the asking. The HBC refused his rates and Northrup settled by selling his "pine basket" tub to the Burbanks, whose silent financial partner was the HBC. Though less than ideal as transportation, and while passengers often had to help her down the river shallows, the *Pioneer*, as she was newly christened, monopolized the Red River trade.

In an effort to capitalize on the expected rush of argonauts Burbank and company decided a larger sternwheeler was needed, and only just in time for the *Pioneer* was crushed by spring ice. Their solution to the problem of finding a boat on the other side of the Minnesota divide was to buy on sheriff's sale and exhume John Davidson's cadaver *Freighter*, which in his failing race with Northrup had been left in the swamps of the divide between the Minnesota River and the upper Red. Dragged to Georgetown and rebuilt, she was 137 feet long, triple decked, 26 feet in beam, with a draft of a mere 42 inches. Compared to the *Pioneer* she was magnificent, a river queen. But she was not yet finished.[36]

Georgetown had a temporary post office and in hopeful anticipation the men checked for mail. Robert Harkness was so eager to read his wife's letter that he hastily ripped it open as soon as he got outside and the ever-present wind caught and blew away the "sow leaves" she had enclosed. In his reply of May 9 Harkness spoke of the overwhelming trip ahead.

It is not yet decided which way we shall go ... but it may be some months that I cannot hear from you ... This seems to be the hardest of all. It is a great task to undertake the trip ... just think of having to walk 20 miles a day for two months. But I am strong and healthy and do not fear the task.

Many took the lull in activity as a time to write home and strangely at least three wrote on May 9: Harkness to Sabrina, Bowland to the *Christian Guardian,* and Hunniford to his wife Lettitia. Thomas Murphy wrote to the *Canadian Freeman* on May 1 and Richard Alexander to his friends the Dicksons on May 14.

In the evenings the men sat around the fires, some smoking and drinking, others like John Bowland singing hymns and offering prayers before bed. A concertina or fiddle would liven the dark and Fannin would dig out his cornet and soon a sing-song or dance was underway, though the partners were less attractive than they might have wished.

On a Sunday a foreboding accident occurred when a gun discharged in a tent, boring two holes in Robert McMicking's coat, which had been hung over the barrel, passing through another coat, then a towel, and exiting through the tent roof. Though passed off lightly the accidental discharge exemplified the inexperience of the men, some of whom were little more than teenagers.

Alexander and his mess often went out shooting and bagged duck, snipe, plover, and curlew on occasion, though generally the hunting was poor. The weather turned from "awfully hot" to "rained very hard" and "very cold." Every day men arrived by stage, by foot, and with wagons. On Monday, May 12, "a fine spring day," Alexander Grant Dallas arrived on his way to Fort Garry to assume his new position as governor of the HBC. His wife and ten-month-old daughter were traveling with him.

Dallas was received in fine style. Murray and McKay came with a spring cart and the infantry lieutenant and his company turned out to salute him. Later while Dallas was in residence the overlanders formed up in two ranks under McMicking and marched to the residence. The front rank fired a volley, then the rear rank, and if the marching had not attracted the attention of Dallas the salute certainly did. Thomas McMicking introduced himself and the company and Dallas, suitably impressed, thanked the men. He promised them all the help and protection he could offer and in return for their gunpowder salute introduced John McLellan, valet and piper, who played a couple of tunes. The company then gave three cheers for Dallas, three for the Queen, the president of the U.S.A., and the piper in turn and then for good measure three more for Dallas and three for his wife. They wheeled about and marched back to their camp singing "God Save the Queen."

Next day the governor came to the overlanders' camp to meet with the various party captains. Meantime McLellan inflated his bellows and played some jigs and reels while the gold-seekers danced. It was quite a time for the newly immigrated Scots in the group, dancing a jig in the shade of Minnesota oaks beside the Red River of the North, surrounded by the tents, fires, and smoke of two dozen camps.

Dallas would not wait for the completion of the *International* but started for Fort Garry on the fourteenth with James McKay and a couple of impatient overlanders. On the fifteenth nine overlanders left by canoe, eager to be away and irritated by the delays.

Tempers in the camp were souring with the passing of each boring day. The men had rested, trimmed their gear, written letters home, brought journals up to date, hunted, relaxed around the fire, eaten and drunk in the tavern—there was only boredom left. On the fifteenth when some men had been in camp for two weeks, the fair spring skies clouded and rain poured down. The hand-sewn tents leaked, the fires steamed, and the men's petulant patience dissolved. A meeting was held and a delegation stomped through the mud to see the steamer's captain.

They were faced with Captain Cornelius P. V. Lull, a former Minnesota sheriff now married into the Burbank family, described by Alexander as "the august individual who is Squire, Justice of Peace and 'head cook and bottle washer.' " Lull no doubt recognized that he had a growing problem here on the banks of the Red. The overlanders were not the only ones who were waiting. Dallas's wife; John Black, the newly appointed judge of the General Quarterly Court; and several Red River families were also getting impatient. To compound the problem Bishop Tache, an Oblate priest at Red River, was about to arrive with his entourage of three priests, several nuns, and "editor" George Wallace. Lull placated the delegation with promises and pemmican. The Company would provide food for the remainder of the detention. And in an effort to speed the work and alleviate boredom he suggested that some of the men might help with the work. By the following day overlanders were fitting pipes; however, the food provided was greasy, hair-ridden pemmican that tasted like candles.[37]

The "long and lonesome" days of discontent warmed and finally Captain Lull announced that the SS *International* would leave on her maiden voyage on Tuesday, May 20. The sternwheeler's motor would be *Germinaverunt speciosa deserti*, "The deserts have bloomed." The overlanders were perhaps unimpressed with the motto, but exceedingly thankful to be off.

When the steamer finally cast off her lines on Tuesday afternoon to the resounding echoes of a military salute James Sellar and a score of others were left standing in the rain. The *International* could not take everyone and had therefore refused to board the Huntingdon party's stock. Consequently Sellar, Blanchford, Stevenson, Reid, Cameron, and Hall, aided by a Dutch guide, crossed their cattle to Dakota Territory to follow the river trail to Fort Garry. Other overlanders settled in to wait, yet again, for the second voyage.

It was with some humor, then, that Sellar watched the steamer crash into the bank at the first bend of the river. After extricating herself she steamed another mile and ran ashore toppling both tall smoke stacks and crashing the wheelhouse. Captain Lull and his desert rose were off to a prickly start.

As earlier parties had discovered, the Red River was a serpentine stream, taking two steps sideways for each one forward. Piloting the 125-foot craft around some of the hairpin turns was difficult and with some frequency the boat grounded, hit trees, and broke parts. For hours on end they were disabled by accident or wind. Each night they tied up, for the river was far too difficult to run in the dark, and each night the overlanders sought out a piece of cabin floor or deck for a bed.

On the night of May 23 a committee made plans for celebrating the Queen's birthday on the following day. Captain Lull was approached and asked if the Union Jack (which had been carefully sewn in Georgetown by Alexander) could be flown. Permission was denied. Lull may have wondered at the lack of argument, until the next day.

On the morning of May 24, Mrs. John McLean, who was traveling to Red River with her husband to settle, was asked by a miner, "Have you noticed the kind of flag we're flying today?" Proudly waving from the top of the pole was the cook's dishcloth. When Captain Lull came storming out of his pilot house the pole was surrounded by Canadian miners. The dishcloth would not come down unless the Union Jack flew in its place. Not wishing to pass the approaching small settlement sailing under a rag the captain surrendered. On a journey threatening to become comic opera, on an American steamer, in American waters the Jack was raised to rousing cheers and a toast of river water to Her Majesty Queen Victoria. The afternoon was spent over a long social dinner with more toasts, speeches, and songs.[38]

On board the *International* the overlanders were, for all the stops and breakdowns, being carried northward in relative style. To the murmur of the panting engine and the thrashing of the paddlewheel they met new friends; to the sound of the steam whistle they saw new vistas.

Frank Penwarden wrote a letter while on board detailing some of his gold-rush companions. "The crowd is composed of many intelligent, respectable and good looking young men, while others of them are desperate looking characters. They have followed every conceivable avocation. Six of them are doctors, several of them lawyers, some merchants, others carpenters, wagon-makers, shoe-makers, tailors, farmers, laborers, etc."[39]

Alexander used the time to meet passengers who were not would-be miners. He spent a good deal of time "in conversation with Mrs. Dallas, a very pleasant lady, quite a rarity in these parts," whom Leonard Crysler described as a "healthy stout Scotch girl." Alexander was born in Edinburgh, Scotland, and had been intending to go to university but the death of his mother and his father's decision to return to Scotland forced him out of school into the work place, and now to undertake this journey. It was with some elation that he discovered two other Edinburgh

Scots on board, Mr. L. B. Gregg, a St. Paul commission merchant, and John Black, the newly appointed judge.[40]

While Alexander and his cohorts steamed along in relative style, Sellar and his party were plodding northward on the Red River Trail. The main Huntingdon party had been in Georgetown nine days, "some was working, some was sporting, and some was lounging about," Sellar wrote, before Captain Wattie came up with their new wagons, oxen, and feed just hours before the sternwheeler cast off. Wattie and some others boarded while Sellar took the wagons on.

Sellar found himself "introduced into the misteries of the Cooking business." The others, in good expedition tradition, managed to burn everything so Sellar became cook by default. This was a resolute, unfaltering party. When a morning's travel was slowed by wading through four to ten inches of water they pushed hard all afternoon to make up the time.

They rode now through a high, dry, level prairie where as far as they could see from horseback there was not a stick of wood to be seen. On Friday, May 23, they crossed the Goose River and in the early morning light rode through a scene that set their hair on end. Scattered on both sides of the trail for over a mile were wrecked Red River carts casting long westward shadows and dotted on the bald prairie face like smallpox were ninety-six graves. Their guide told them the story.

Some nine years ago the Red River Métis buffalo hunters were passing through and at daybreak set their stock out to graze. Breakfast over, they went to round them up but found instead some Sioux lurking about. With Red River carts for cover the Métis managed to hold off a war party of three hundred Sioux for four hours. The Sioux finally retreated, leaving behind ninety-six dead and several wounded. The Métis lost their stock, one man was killed, and three wounded. Since that time the Sioux had been sniping at the Métis, occasionally killing one (as with Beads in 1859), and stealing from the various Métis settlements.

The graves and wagons looked only days old to Sellar, an unsettling warning of the lurking Sioux danger. While gathering wood Sellar knelt down and picked up a small silver teaspoon, which he saved as a relic of the event.

At some point the guide had led them away from the Red River Trail on a branch that led toward St. Joseph rather than Pembina. The ride was through "as beautiful a country as ever man set eyes upon, . . . open Prairie as level as a floor, robed as it was with a mantle of green grass from 6 to 10 inches high gently waving in the wind." The road was good, the fords had firm gravel bottoms and gentle banks, and provisions were in good supply.

On the twenty-fourth they passed one of the few cart trains still competing with the Burbanks' steamer, a group of twenty-five carts that Sellar likened to the French-Canadian carts of his home county. On Sunday they were up as usual at an early hour and finished breakfast when Blanchford and Sellar brought up a sore topic: the impropriety of traveling on Sunday. It was often the custom of overlanders to take one day off per week to rest men and stock, make repairs, prepare food, cut hay, and write letters. Choosing Sunday also accommodated those wanting to observe the Lord's Day as a day of rest. A heated argument took place around the fire, one that would be repeated in the months to come, but as Sellar and Blanchford were in the minority they traveled on.

It may not have been a good idea. At 7:00 P.M. the guide indicated they were only two miles from St. Joseph so Sellar and Reid rode on to order supper. By midnight they were thoroughly bewildered, if not lost, on Pembina Mountain, and, being defenseless "save the weapon of Providence," were sure they were about to be attacked by howling wolves. Pressing on despite their fear they found the authors of the cacophony to be two hundred dogs of St. Joseph, on the other side of the Pembina River. The others did not arrive until 2:00 A.M. They too had been lost, and delayed when an ox ran off with a cart scattering the load and breaking an axle. The cart would have to be retrieved the next day. So much for Sunday travel.[41]

Over a rough road they passed St. Joseph and reached the Red River at its confluence with the Scratching River (now the Morris). They paid a settler fifty cents to be ferried over in a canoe then swam the cattle across. Now they were back on the main trail, crowded with traffic to and from Pembina and Fort Garry and the small farms along the Red. They arrived at Fort Garry three days behind the *International*.

The sternwheeler journey had become more exciting with each downstream bend. While for a time the continuous breakdowns added excitement, they soon became passé. They steamed toward Pembina, noticing a growing number of Indians along the bank. The natives would fire a few smoky test rounds into the air from their flintlock trade guns, and the overlanders would answer with a sky-rending volley from fifty-caliber Sharps and other percussion pieces. During the nightly riverbank stops watches were posted.

At Fort Pembina those who naively thought the firing was a welcome were rudely awakened. The demonstrations were decidedly aggressive with shouting, gesticulating, firing of guns, and an attempt by some drunken braves to board the *International*. The boarding party was repulsed only because there were 150 armed men aboard. Bishop Tache was scurrying from group to group, his overlarge head wagging on his stout frame, explaining to these men, as he would to so many, "The native is a man, for his is born amid weeping, he grows up amongst tears or dreams." His words had little effect.[42]

The native posturing was a preamble to the Sioux War, the autumn uprising that would see the *International* grounded for eight years and the Minnesota-Mississippi river country erupt in bloody battle. The fingers of fate were tightening their grip and the overlanders had squeezed through in the nick of time.

With visions of armed Indians in their minds the overlanders cruised downstream into the British Territories and late the next day arrived at the stone walls of Fort Garry. Greeted by settlement inhabitants in carriages, boats, and on foot in what was termed "a grand affair," they responded in usual fashion by firing yet another volley. Most of the men had probably not burned as much powder in their entire lives as they had in festive fusillades north of St. Paul. They can be excused the feeling that this welcome was for "The Overlanders," rather than for the maiden voyage of a grand, new steamer bringing a new era to this frontier outpost.

## The British Columbia Overland Transit Company

In grasping for the western wealth of overland routes entrepreneurs hatched transportation schemes both bizarre and ordinary. During the California rush there were "wind-wagons," which failed when the brakeless wagons sailed into an arroyo, and the visionary Rufus Porter "Air-Line," a one-thousand-foot-long propeller-driven balloon powered by two steam engines on one end and wagon trains on the other. Between there were "transportation companies" who proposed comfortable, cushioned service across the continent in a time rivaling that of the Pony Express and at fares far below those of steamships. While the Canadian experience did not spawn imaginative schemes like Porter's, there was one company that entered the transportation market at the height of interest.[43]

The British Columbia Overland Transit Company first appeared in the April 5 edition of the London *Times* with a prospectus that was the epitomy of selective editing, half-truths, and erroneous information. The scheme confused the story of "The Overlanders" for decades for it was erroneously theorized by many writers that the overlanders of 1862 began walking when their BCOTC transportation failed.[44]

The company's lengthy proposal stretched to a thousand words, detailing government subsidies, capital of £500,000, fifty thousand available shares, a prestigious board of directors, and giving in effect a brief history of the British Columbia gold rush. The land awaited British capital and capitalists, it announced.

The only drawback to the future greatness of the country is the distance by sea from Europe—five months via Cape Horn, and 40 to 50 days by steam via Panama. To obviate this and at once give an impetus to emigration to British Columbia, the overland route from Canada passing direct through British territory, has been organized by the promoters of the Overland Transit Company. Several surveys have resulted in tracing a direct road, which, with a perfect organization of land transport is at once available.

Over a "natural road" that connected the Red River settlement and Lytton on the Fraser River, easily traveled by carts, the BCOTC proposed:

... a perfect land transport train of horses and spring carts adapted for passenger and goods traffic, and erect log shanties for stabling and refreshment at stated intervals along the entire route. Cattle and provisions will be collected at these stations, and armed mounted escorts will be formed for convoy. ... there can be no question that the route will be placed in a perfect state, ready to meet the requirements of an enormous emigration traffic. ... the distance from Lake Superior to British Columbia will be performed in twelve days. Hence Europe could be reached from British Columbia in, say, 25 days.

On Saturday, the 31st May, the British Columbia Overland Transit Company will despatch from Glasgow, in the first-class and powerful screw steamship' United Kingdom ... a party of first and second class passengers for ... British Columbia. Time from England to British Columbia, about five weeks. More than one half the distance from Montreal, [to St. Paul] is by Railway.

FROM ENGLAND TO BRITISH COLUMBIA £42.
SALOON CABIN BERTHS, £5 EXTRA.
(Children under 12, half price.)
The State of Dietary will be First Class.
50 lb. of Baggage allowed to each Adult Passenger from St. Paul's.
Surgeons will accompany the Passengers the entire way from England to British Columbia.

JAMES HENSON, Secretary.
Offices—British Columbia Overland Transit, 6, Copthall Court, Throgmorton Street, E.C. London.[45]

When the lengthy prospectus appeared it met with responses ranging from eager acceptance to doubt, skepticism, and, in some cases, anger.

Eagerness showed in the faces of young men like Henry Isaac Collingwood, who just days after the announcement appeared at the BCOTC offices. Several clerks were busy and the secretary, Mr. James Henson, waited on him. Collingwood asked if he could book his passage from St. Paul as he wanted to travel to Canada on his own, but he was told only complete packages were available. On Saturday, April 26, he returned and paid a deposit of twenty-two pounds.

From publication until mid-May close to thirty young men paid their fares and accepted receipts. As the sailing date approached a flurry of fares were confirmed as John Martin, S. Thompson, A. Goodard, and Benjamin Moore signed aboard. Collingwood left London on the twenty-ninth for Glasgow where the screw-steamer *United Kingdom* was ready to sail.

In the meantime the prospectus had raised concern in a number of places, including the Colonial Land and Emigration Committee and the House of Commons. Bureaucratic wheels turned slowly. On May 17 the committee called the unadvertised principal of the company, a Colonel Sleigh, to its offices.

Burrows Willcocks Arthur Sleigh was born in Montreal in 1821, the son of Dr. William Willcocks Sleigh and Sarah Campbell. Sleigh was educated in England and Canada and at age twenty-one enrolled as ensign in the 2nd West India Regiment, where he purchased his lieutenancy and transferred to the 77th Foot. His army career was short. The regiment moved to Halifax, then Quebec, then England in 1848, when he sold his commission.

Sleigh bought 100,000 acres of land in Kings County, Prince Edward Island, and in about 1850 moved to Canada as an independent gentleman. He became a justice of the peace and a lieutenant-colonel in the militia of P.E.I., a rank he still used.[46]

In his first transportation venture he bought the steamer *Albatross* with the intent of establishing a steamer service from New York to Quebec. With government support offered the scheme had the prospects of success but the lack of navigational aids along the route made marine insurance too expensive. He abandoned the scheme, sold the *Albatross* and his P.E.I. estate, and returned to England.

He published a book of adventures in British North America, *Pine forests and hacmatac clearings,* and began the successful *British Army Dispatch,* which he sold for £900. With his brother William, a barrister, and two other partners who put up £1,500, he started the *Daily Telegraph,* a penny daily. He soon bought their shares for £450, sold his half, and gave the remainder in payment for machinery and paper debts.

According to one account Sleigh then went to Russia and received a large land grant from the Romanoff family. When he did not prosper there he returned to England.[47]

His next appearance was in bankruptcy court in 1857, where he admitted to living expenses of £1000 per year, assets of less than £50, and debts of £523. Sleigh is said to have had ideas that outran his income, but the scheme he hatched in the spring of 1862 was more fraud than energetic ambition. Her Majesty's emigration commission, however, satisfied themselves that Sleigh and the BCOTC had made the proper arrangements and had it in their power to carry the emigrants to British Columbia as advertised. To be cautious they notified the colonial secretary of some doubts, which he in turn passed to Governor Douglas on Vancouver Island.[48]

Douglas discovered, though it took months for the mail to reach him, the same discrepancies soon to be published in the *Times.* None of the Victoria merchants listed as directors, Edward Langley, Thomas Southgate, and S. Gambitz, had any knowledge of the company. In London, "directors" Frederick Mangles, N. J. Fenner, and Robert Green also denied involvement. Then a letter appeared from an anonymous "Canada West" who tore the scheme to pieces. Having recently returned from "America" he estimated the travel time from England to the diggings not at five weeks, but a more realistic ninety-one days. The emigrants might well have to winter on the plains, he pointed out, and if not would arrive too late in the year to start looking for gold. Crossing with four-horse spring wagons was impossible.

BCOTC Secretary Henson attributed the letters to "jealousy." Shipping interests did not want an overland route and were trying to undermine the scheme. Henson quoted sources varying from Douglas to Woolsey that proved, with creative editing, that his route was not only possible but practical. But "Canada West" was supported by Dr. H. Bauerman of the British Land Commission and then letters by Dr. Alexander Reid of 1861.

Sleigh, not content with one scheme, now hatched a second, the "British Columbia Postal and Steam Navigation Service." He advertised for staff, preferring retired calvary officers, to take charge of an express service based on the successful Pony Express of the U.S.A. Those applying for positions must be willing and able to become shareholders.[49]

The newsprint discussion raised questions and doubts, but by the time anyone thought to react the *United Kingdom* was sailing for Quebec with the thirty-one young hopefuls accompanied by "through agent" James Hayward, who had been hired by Sleigh on May 19 at a salary of ten pounds per month and one dollar per day for provisions from Montreal.[50]

They arrived in Quebec June 17 and boarded the Grand Trunk Railway for Toronto where they booked into the Rossin House on York and King streets, a massive Italian-style, five-story hotel. It was a favorite of English travelers. Lord Southesk, artist Paul Kane, and Dr. Rae the arctic explorer had all stayed there.[51]

The Toronto press were in attendance to interview them. They were the vanguard of five hundred, it was reported, and were all well equipped with guns and ammunition. Their fare did not include food past Montreal so they had purchased two months' of supplies in Toronto and were off to St. Paul the following day.

At the April meetings that were the beginnings of Redgrave's Toronto party a man had spoken up, loud in praise of the St. Paul route. H. L. Himes was then, or soon after, an agent of Sleigh, and the route was seen through the dollar signs in his eyes. In spite of his solicitor's advice to "have nothing to do with it, unless the money were in the bank," he became the advance man. On June 15 he arrived in St. Paul to make arrangements with the Burbanks for stage and steamer transportation to Fort Garry.[52]

In St. Paul the bubble was burst by a thumb and forefinger rubbed together. Until now travel had been financed by drafts on London accounts. Frontiersmen were not so trusting. The Burbanks wanted cash, not promises. No money, no travel. Hime expected Hayward to be bringing the money. Hayward expected Hime to have it. Actually, Sleigh had the money.

The St. Paul papers were sympathetic but it was plain the scheme had come to a dead halt. "Mr. Hime leaves this morning for Toronto, and Mr. Hayward for London, to investigate the causes of the miscarriage. . . . In the meantime the main party of gold-seekers will dispose of themselves as best they can. A portion will return to England, some will proceed to the Red River settlement and either go on . . . or if that is impracticable, await till next spring, while still another portion will probably remain in Minnesota." One of those returning to England was Henry Collingwood, who had been elected by the dupes to carry their fight to the courts.

The Burbank brothers wrote a letter that was printed in several newspapers indicating that "both Mr. Hime and Mr. Hayward seem to have done all in their power to carry out the arrangements made by the B.C.O.T.C. in London with said passengers had have failed to do so only for the want of money." A similar letter was written by the travelers on behalf of Hime and Hayward, neither of whom profited from their connection. Hime received nothing and Hayward only his first month's salary.[53]

The *Nor'-Wester* was equally indignant, but was more annoyed that those against the scheme had suggested that the area west of Fort Garry was *terra incognita*. They were not surprised though for the chief advisors were the HBC who would "like to create or keep up the impression that this is a howling wilderness. ... we must inform British statesmen that the large parties of emigrants, including women and children, have gone hence to British Columbia, and thought it was a mere pleasure trip."[54]

When Hayward reached London in late August he immediately went to the office and found it closed up. Sleigh's West End bank had folded and his house was empty. In the meantime Henry Collingwood had reached London, found Secretary Henson, and had him brought to court on charges of fraud. Subsequent evidence showed that Sleigh had packed his bags and money the day following the preliminary hearing and skipped for Paris, leaving Henson to shoulder responsibility.

After several day's trial, during which some returned passengers were heard as well as Henson, Hayward, and Hime's solicitor, it was still not clear whether Henson was in cahoots with Sleigh. Alderman Finnis, who was hearing the case, was inclined to think he was, but there was cause for considerable doubt.[55]

When Sleigh could not be found Henson was released on bail of one hundred pounds, on August 22. On August 29 the case was "allowed to stand over" while a warrant was issued for Sleigh. And there the case rested. The trial fizzled out and no further evidence or proceedings have come to light.

Nothing is known of the few passengers reported to have stayed in North America. None appears in the rosters of any of the American wagon trains and despite rumors of some reaching Cariboo no such evidence has been found. The only ones to find the BCOTC successful were the newspapers, which from April until December, from London to San Francisco, got yards of copy from the proposal and failure and had great sport with Colonel Sleigh, whom the San Francisco *Bulletin* referred to as "Colonel Sly."

Sleigh did return to England, but evidently laid low enough that he escaped debtors, irate victims, and the courts. He died in Chelsea, England, March 22, 1869, at age forty-seven. His *Colonist* obituary describes him as "a genial creature, very fast in his habits, excessively extravagant, and possessed a natural antipathy bordering upon contempt for men who paid their debts."[56]

# Chapter Ten

## Fort Garry—"Big Bugs and Little Bugs"

The unrelenting wind that had swept past previous overlanders and erased their tracks of passage still gusted around Fort Garry's stone walls in June 1862. Sweeping across the unbroken month-wide plain from the Rockies, the breeze blended scents: grass, rivers, buffalo, fire smoke, and then cattle and crops, the human smell of settlement. When on rare occasions it ceased, a feeling that something was amiss prevailed. In the winter and spring of 1862 the west wind carried more than smoke; now the scent of gold and the lure of adventure wafted through the settlement.

Timoleon Love's and George Flett's letters to the *Nor'-Wester* fanned coals of interest like blacksmiths' bellows. In March's last bleak weeks, at the time of the vernal equinox, three meetings were held regarding Saskatchewan gold: one at John Macdonald's house in St. Andrew's Parish, another in the Kildonan schoolhouse, and a third at Pascal Breland's place in the White Horse Plains district. The sense of things was that gold did exist on the Saskatchewan and if Red River men wanted their share they had better form up and move out. James Ross, *Nor'-Wester* editor, condemned the HBC efforts "to throw cold water on this gold business, in the face of indisputable facts." While mining might injure the fur trade the HBC would not be losers; they had the financial means to profit. Like the Minnesota expansionists Ross saw in the discoveries wealth and prosperity for the Red River settlement. Miners would help lift the HBC's suppression of settlement providing a market heretofore controlled by monopoly. Little wonder that the settlement was in favor of miners.

By May 14 the meetings had distilled into one party of nearly twenty men under George Flett, which planned to leave for the Saskatchewan gold diggings about June 10. Flett was taking lessons from American wagon masters and hauling over three hundred pounds' worth of goods to be traded in winter months when mining was closed.

When overlanders surged down the *International*'s gangplank in the shadow of Fort Garry's cold stone walls they were arriving in a community already inflamed with gold. They disembarked with urgency, having many tasks to complete. The leaders had to gather route information, oxen, carts, and provisions were to be purchased. Then, too, this was their last fleeting touch with known civilization, albeit a primitive and strange one.

Alexander Fortune: "Some of us might have been excused if we had retreated instead of going into the vast unknown and unsettled west.... But not so, did our brave boys. Good-bye for months, we wrote; good-bye it was forever in the case of some of our best young men. We can picture to ourselves the troubled hearts of mothers and fathers for the sons of their hope when they read those last letters.... How the wives of such as were married wept and pictured themselves the long years of separation with the sad dread of no reunion with their beloved."

Richard Alexander, the young Scot, and Harry Handcock, the young Irishman, went through the settlement like a social whirlwind, parlaying letters of introduction into a few free meals with editor James Ross and his charming wife, and William MacTavish, HBC factor and governor of Assiniboia.

Although they were not aware of it at the time, with more elbow room than ever before young men spent two weeks in a graduation party celebrating their passage from adolescence to adulthood. There would be no fledglings at journey's end. Some spent a lot of time drinking. Richard Alexander, the young Scot, recorded that he, Carpenter, and Hind "got jolly tight," and paid for it the next day when, Alexander said, he was "sick as a dog all forenoon." He bragged too that he and his Irish friend Harry Handcock had "chased some Indian girls through the bush and had some great fun." These young men had been brought up in the dark shadow of young Queen Victoria in an intolerant, restrictive, repressive society. Most who were unmarried were virgins. They arrived in a land where common-law marriages of convenience were the norm; where liquor, dancing, and pre-marital coupling were accepted. Some had quite a time.

They balanced this with going to church, just in case. Two services had been arranged for the overlanders. The Reverend Griffith Owen Corbett in the afternoon and the Reverend John Black at the Presbyterian church in the evening. The Reverend Mr. Corbett's text was taken from Matthew, chapter 17, verses 45 and 46. "Again the kingdom of heaven is like unto a merchant man, seeking goodly pearls: Who, when he had found one pearl of great price, went and sold all that he had, and bought it." Some missed the point of the message because the courthouse-*cum*-church was crowded and hot, and many left early.

The Reverend Mr. Corbett was something of a hypocrite. For the past year Corbett had been "having dealings" with his young Métis servant Maria Thomas, on buggy and sleigh rides and even in his home, making "connection" with her in the hayloft where he had carefully chiseled a hole to watch for Mrs. Corbett. The result, not surprisingly, was that Maria became pregnant. Corbett tried to arrange a marriage for Maria, but failed. As he preached to the overlanders he was, to say the least, worried. Two abortion attempts had failed, the first with a potion he concocted, then one by physical means. Even while he gripped the pulpit in evangelical passion he was trying to devise more effective schemes. He would try again in a few days, and twice more after that.

What Maria got for "praying with her knees up" was pregnant. What the Reverend Mr. Corbett got for having "carnal knowledge" and "attempting to procure the miscarriage" of Maria was six months. He was charged in December 1862 and disgraced, sentenced, and imprisoned in February 1863.[1]

The Reverend Mr. Corbett's indiscretions were only muffled rumors when the overlanders listened to his sermon, and Alexander Fortune was so impressed with the community's starched front that he wrote: "People with whom we spoke showed that reverence for God and His word that we felt, as tho his word had come with them and had been their rule of life. We were told that only one girl had been unfortunate in the whole forty years of their sojourn in the Selkirk Settlement." It was a blindered view; even Corbett himself said during his mid-winter trial "many children were being born without fathers."

Less concerned about the morals of the community and more concerned about a place to make a good living free from harassment were the Schuberts. Francis Augustus Schubert was born in Dresden, Germany. At age twenty-seven in 1854, he emigrated to New York City where he met a young Irish girl, one of many Irish immigrants fleeing poverty and famine to start a new life. Catherine O'Hare came from Rathfryland in County Down, Northern Ireland. She was born April 23, 1835, and with her family crossed the Atlantic by sailing ship in 1850.[2]

They were married in Springfield, Massachusetts, in 1856 and immediately moved to St. Paul in what was then still the Northwest Territory, Minnesota statehood being two years away. The Schuberts settled across the Mississippi a few miles upstream from St. Paul near the mouth of the St. Peters or Minnesota River, the site of massive, stone-towered Fort Snelling. There was a growing community around the military post and it was an ideal location for a tavern. Augustus and Catherine's livingroom beer parlor, a room as large as the rest of the house, was soon attracting a regular and socially acceptable clientele. Before their first Christmas a son was born, Augustus Junior on December 23, 1856. A daughter, Mary Jane, was next, in about August 1858, and another son, James, on March 7, 1860.[3]

One evening in 1860 after putting baby to bed Catherine went to attend to guests seated around the living room fireplace. Suddenly they were startled by a crash of glass from the rear of the house. Catherine ran to the bedroom, surprising a Sioux brave crawling up a plank into

James's bedroom, intent on kidnapping the child. She scooped up the baby and ran into the parlor, alerting the others. Augustus grabbed a fire poker and rushed out the door, catching the Sioux before he could escape. The iron poker made a fine cudgel and Augustus severely beat the retreating kidnapper.

The following night forty Sioux warriors rode to the tavern and demanded Schubert. The subsequent threats against him and his family's lives were taken seriously and Schubert decided they should leave. Two other families joined and two or three nights later the three families loaded what they could on packhorses and disappeared into the prairie darkness.

The small group of refugees arrived safely at the Red River settlement in late fall and within a few weeks Augustus and Catherine had opened a "grog-shop"-cum-roadhouse on the American or eastern side of the Red River, opposite Fort Garry. This hostelry was not one of the finest establishments in the settlement. In the *Nor'-Wester* of December 1, 1860, an item read: "On the morning of the 26th ultimo November, one Michael Sweeny was found dead in his bed at August Schubert's house. Sweeney had been much given to drink, and the fact of his sudden death at such a grog-shop as Schubert's leads to the opinion that drink was the direct or indirect cause of it."

The Schuberts and their three young children did not find life easy here. Only months after they arrived the 1861 flood swept through the settlement. Then in the stifling heat of summer Indians broke in and stole ten gallons of whiskey and all the crockery and dishes. Ironically on that day Augustus was fined five pounds in court.[4]

Augustus's indignant fury at being robbed without compensation and then fined was projected onto the settlement. He listened to the men at his tables talking of the West, and when Red River men convened to discuss gold Augustus was there. Catherine's feelings are unclear, myth and rhetoric having confused the facts. An initial reluctance to move again would be expected, but her subsequent determination could equally well reflect a strong belief in what the family was attempting. Whatever the case, the Schuberts joined.[5]

The Schubert family were exceptional for they were not miners but settlers gradually moving west: Germany, Ireland, St. Paul, Fort Garry, and now British Columbia. They emulated the Oregon families in the forties. They were the only family to join what became known as the McMicking party. Catherine was carrying her fourth child. Had she admitted to being pregnant, it is doubtful McMicking would have accepted them.

Other women joined the overlanders, despite popular belief to the contrary. The Saskatchewan Gold Expedition of George Flett was formed in the main of Red River people, with a few Toronto men, and included three women and two children. That country-born women should be part of such an expedition is not surprising. Men needed women as helpmates, as women needed men. A man's role was as provider and thus we find women accompanying their men on various forays, such as the buffalo hunts. To stay home was to be short of provisions. Should a woman not have a man she would often accompany a group, offering domestic services in return for food.[6]

Nor is Catherine Schubert's travel while pregnant particularly unusual, though much has been made of it. Women had been giving birth on prairie trails for decades. The only difference was that they were Indian or Métis halfbreeds, and Catherine was a white women of Anglo-Saxon descent. The original overlanders for instance, the Oregon-bound Selkirk settlers of Sinclair, had at least one child born en route; the second in 1854 and one son born to Mrs. Thomas Brown near Fort Pitt and another to Mrs. Robert Flett on the Bow River. These facts take nothing from Catherine, but if she is given heroine status for walking the plains while pregnant, the same status should be accorded many other Métis and Indian women.[7]

Regrettably but understandably, these women overlanders remain anonymous. In the journals of the white Anglo-Saxon protestant overlanders we see that Métis, or halfbreeds, were accepted, but in a lower social order. That year the *Nor'-Wester* had printed "Tschudi's Classification Of Human Hybrids," a detailed list of what each instance of mixed-blood should be called and there was still the feeling, even by some in Red River, that "mixed-blood was bad blood." Where fellow WASPs were often referred to as Mister, the Métis were given only a first name. Women, one step lower in the social order, were simply not referred to by name.[8]

Men of Victorian times admired other men, enjoyed being with men, perhaps as strongly as men did in Elizabethan times. It was a cultural bonding that resulted in a certain amount of homosexuality that was not "buggery." Men's quests likely had something to do with the imperial military fate, the fact that for centuries past men had been not only expected but demanded to serve in the military. Fortune hunting, as exemplified by the overlanders, and adventure, as with the hunting parties of military officers wandering the plains, were natural offshoots. Women in civilized areas lived more settled, domestic roles, but not only in the kitchen. While men were questing, these gold-rush widows became, by necessity, farmers, merchants, and businesswomen. Had overlander journeys continued likely more women would have joined. However, in 1862 there were only four.[9]

Hiring a guide or pathfinder was an important task. Southern U.S. immigrations had hired the "out-of-work" mountainmen such as Thomas Fitzpatrick, Stephen Meek, Andrew Sublette, and Moses "Black" Harris to pilot them across the featureless plains, to desert waterholes, and through snow-covered mountain passes. Later, the wagon-rutted trails were so obvious that once again the mountainmen were obsolete. The equivalent guides in British North America were Pierre Botineau, now working for the Holmes Party in Montana; Jamey Jock Bird, in his late sixties; the renowned James McKay; the Whitefords, and other Métis such as those hired by Palliser.

Trail finding was not the only reason for hiring a guide. Country-born men could also teach the overlanders trail savvy, how to deal with Indians, how to cross rivers, and, in the American experience at least, aid in establishing discipline. The Red River Métis, however, with the possible exception of those mentioned, never gained the guide stature of the American mountainmen.

The McMicking party charged Alexander Fortune, George Wallace, and Alexander Robertson with finding a guide. They crossed the Red River to the St. Boniface cathedral, now being rebuilt after the December 1860 fire had leveled it, to ask the advice of Bishop Tache. Alexandre Antonin Tache had been in the Red River country with the Oblates since 1845. He knew the local guides well and "recommended a certain man, who refused to go with us, considering himself too old for such a journey." A cathedral workman then suggested Charles Rochette, and the Bishop agreed.[10]

Back at the fort they were warned that Rochette (or Rossette, but more commonly, Racette) had guided before and deserted (the Jones party of 1858). He was also of a family that gained notoriety by close association with Indians and was a relative of George "Shaman" Racette, "a remarkable man, monstrous in size, strength and appearance, supplying the middle link between man and the gorilla, physically," and mentally. Charles was of hardy stock.[11]

Warnings aside, Rochette was hired on June 2 to guide the party to Lac Ste. Anne, a little north of Fort Edmonton, for the reasonable sum of one hundred dollars or twenty pounds sterling. Though Rochette was guide, the leaders conducted their own route research. Lengthy meetings were held with Governor Dallas, Assiniboia Governor MacTavish, Bishop Tache, Chief Factor Christie, who was on a visit from Fort Edmonton, Timoleon Love, and other guides such as John Whiteford and later Peter Erasmus. In this alien culture they found "few of the inhabitants speak the English language; and our attempts to gather information from them were frequently frustrated."[12]

*Globe* correspondent Wallace reported that "since arriving in Fort Garry we have been incessantly engaged in collecting reliable information about the route, and we find the Northern road by Carlton, Edmonton and the Jasper House pass is the one recommended by the most experienced travellers. The road to Edmonton is quite as easy as that from St. Paul to Georgetown, but we shall have much difficulty in getting from Edmonton to Jasper House pass, as the country is marshy and densely wooded. . . . The whole distance to the Cariboo mines, it is expected, will be got over in 60 or 65 days, or perhaps much less if the party get on well and meet with no formidable obstacles on the way."[13]

This route offered a good trail and a reasonable chance of finding buffalo, yet avoided the ranges of the most troublesome Indian tribes. It was doubly practical as HBC Governor Dallas had promised help. To the chagrin of Christie, who thought of miners as something lower than the belly of a buffalo, Dallas had sent a message to posts to aid the trekkers wherever possible.

While some negotiated for a guide, others scoured the settlement for frugal buys in provisions and equipment, employing the best Irish horse traders they had. There were other methods of choosing. Crysler wrote: "We have had some sport here buying horses and oxen. Most of the boys don't know much about horses but think they must try them and so gallop about without thinking whether they will draw a cart or not. We had a race yesterday between two half-breed horses, one an Indian's, the other a good sized black horse. The black was ridden by a cariboo fellow and the pony by a half breed. The pony won easily."

Carpenter detailed the overland outfit for a five-man mess: four carts, four horses, three oxen, four hundred pounds of pemmican, seven hundred pounds of flour, thirty pounds of tea, one large ax, one small ax, scythe and snath, one keg of powder, three bags of shot for ducks and geese, seventy pounds of lead for balls, any quantity of percussion caps, thirty-five pounds of tobacco, a tent, two water casks, a canteen each for water, two double lines for hauling carts etc. across the rivers, twenty fathoms of half-inch rope for tethering, one dressed hide for hobbling, four saddles and bridles, four long-handled spades, one draw knife, a one-inch augur, a large gimlet, two pickaxes, three miner's prospecting pans, three camp kettles of different sizes, coffee pot, plate, knife, and fork each, tin cup each, mosquito bar, sheet of iron for rockers, and a supply of light reading, wearing apparel, about twenty-five pounds of mercury, and a powerful magnet, and a well-financed group should have horse for each cart and a riding horse per man. Each man should have a strong valise and a strong box. Moccasins were best in Carpenter's opinion, "but unless a man can afford a pair a day at half a dollar, he had better bring all his old boots as well as new. Two good strong suits of clothes, and a change of flannels etc. are wanted. Each man should have a double shot-gun, a pair of good blankets, and an overcoat (a Mackintosh)."[14]

Prices were already inflated from pre-overlander travel. Where once there had been no market residents were now profitably selling surplus goods. Parties were paying eight to twelve cents per pound for flour, ten to twenty dollars for a cart, five for harness, and fifty to one hundred for a horse. McMicking struck unusual bargains for he records flour at three dollars per hundredweight (112 pounds), carts at eight, horses at forty, and oxen at thirty. More likely his flour price refers to goods purchased in St. Paul.

The *Nor'-Wester* reported that before the miners arrived flour "was selling at 14s to 16s per cwt; [a shilling equaled 25 cents] immediately on their arrival many raised it to 18s and 20s and some actually had the conscience to ask 25s. The real and effectual obstacle lay in the course of the Company, who virtually said to the miners—'Get flour from the settlers if you can, but if they ask more than 16s you can fall back on us.'" Alexander confirms that storekeepers expected a large profit but were prevented when the HBC guaranteed fixed prices, "which consequently protected us from being imposed upon." On one hand this move can be seen as an HBC attack in the years-old free enterprise versus monopoly trade war in Red River, and not as an aid to miners. On the other, as James Ross pointed out, "they would not have done this under Sir George Simpson. He would have haughtily kept them at their distance and rejoiced if for want of supplies they had been obliged to return to their native hearths."[15]

Times and attitudes had changed since John Jones and his cohorts had crossed Simpson's empire in 1858.

As details were finalized McMicking found his Queenston party was the nucleus of a larger company. Attracted by the efficiency and integrity of the leaders, men drifted from confusion to organization. McMicking now faced the likelihood of leading ten times the number of men he started with. While evident at Georgetown that the number of overlanders was growing with each arriving stage not until Fort Garry, with men arriving on each sailing of the *International* and by river trail, did organizers realize there were now 250 men moving west. While some were bonded by hometowns, many were simply joining groups along the way. Fort Garry, not St. Paul, St. Cloud, or Georgetown, was, finally, the jumping-off point for overlander travel. So here, on the edge of the plains, the companies shifted into new alliances based on religion, destination, and traveling style. Journal of Stephen Redgrave, Fort Garry, June 2nd, 1862:

An ox and cart was purchased and we had a little Whiskey over the bargain. Mr. Love was with us. We are going in his party to prospect for Gold on the Saskatchewan. I poisoned one brute of a Dog and at about 1 a.m. I shot two. They were thrown in the river.

June 3rd, Nearly all of the Gold Diggers are gone on to White Horse Plains where there is good grass for their cattle. I do not think we shall go before the 10th. The fact I have been treated so badly with them all ever since getting up the party makes me glad to get rid of their company. And not $1.00 would they pay me for my expenses.

In a fit of pique Redgrave adds, "I expect it will be pretty bad for some —there are many who will soon wish themselves back to Toronto."

When the "big bugs and little bugs" separated, Redgrave was left in the sieve as sort of odd man out, his prestige greatly diminished, his ego deflated. Bolstered by those who had stuck by him, he spurned the larger McMicking party and joined George Flett's Saskatchewan Gold Expedition, a small party where he could still feel important.

The result of the shifting and merging was that the 250 men formed into three major parties: the McMicking party, George Flett's Saskatchewan Gold Expedition, and a party of Americans. Thomas McMicking's party was the largest; the American party, the smallest. For the journey from Fort Garry to Fort Edmonton each of these parties would keep individual schedules and follow separate, though similar, routes.

Before the American St. Peter's party arrived at Fort Garry and while the Redgrave-Fleet-Whiteford-Love coalition dallied in drinking, the McMicking group quickly finished their tasks and rolled out of the settlement. McMicking recognized the need to get away from the post's attractions if they were to start on time.

It was therefore agreed that as each separate party were ready they should move slowly on in order to obtain good feed for their animals, that they should rendezvous at White Horse Plains, 25 miles from Garry, and there wait for the balance of the company and be prepared to start from that point on Thursday morning the 5th of June.[16]

James Sellar recorded the departure. "At 2 p.m. struck tents and pulled up our stakes & started up the Assiniboine River in a Westerly direction, which drew to a close our career in Fort Garry. All appeared to be in the best of spirits as we left the fort, but as we wound our way up the River there was many an eye filled with the tear that flowed from a full heart, as that was the last of civilization until we should cross the Mountains which was yet 1300 Miles before us."

## McMicking Party to Fort Ellice

The departure from White Horse Plains could not be considered spectacular. The overlanders did not gallop into the sunset or away from sunrise, yet there was a certain ponderous magnificence as over one hundred carts groaned into mobility, ungreased axles screeching, drivers shouting and cursing, oxen bellowing and stamping.

Teamsters like Wheeler Mickle must have reflected on those early days when bull-whacking up the Cariboo road. Perhaps it was Mickle who years later was cracking his bull whip over the heads of stubborn oxen, swearing at them, damning them to hell, and calling all the curses of both the Devil and God on their heads. A minister of the cloth was standing nearby and taking offense shook his fist at the driver and said, "Young man you'll go plumb to Hell talking like that."

"Hell, you say," the young man hollered back. "I'm going to Cariboo, Father, if these horns and arseholes will just take me there."

And that's where they were heading on that spring morning when they marched westward onto the plains.

By June 5 those who had decided to follow the Queenston group had gathered at Long Lake on the edge of White Horse Plains. Inexperienced plains travelers that they were they arrived in a dehydrated state, not having taken the precaution of filling water casks. They laid the blame on the guide. He likely had assumed anyone would have such sense.

This morning after breakfast a mass meeting was held "to try and get Organized into one body and have some regulation & order as to our manner of travelling." It was called to order at 10:00 A.M., Thomas McMicking in the chair, with a water cask handy, and George Wallace, the secretary-treasurer, seated on the ground, his paper on his knee. A roll call showed the following hometown parties and their leaders: Queenston, W. H. G. Thompson, 24 men; St. Thomas, B. H. Hutchinson, 21 men; Huntingdon, James Wattie, 19 men; Ottawa, Joseph Halpenny, 8 men; Toronto, George Wallace, 7 men; Montreal, William Morrow, 7 men; Ogdensburg, N.Y., Thomas Phillips, 7 men; Red River, Augustus

Schubert, 3 men, 3 children, 1 woman; Acton, Alexander Fortune, 6 men; Whitby, Donald Simpson, 6 men; Waterloo, Mr. Brocklebank, 6 men; Scarborough, Joseph Zephania Hough, 5 men; London, Adolphus Urlin, 5 men; Goderich, A. C. Robertson, 5 men; Chatham, 3 men; a total of 136. With parties who joined after Long Lake the group grew to approximately 160.

The first order of business was to unanimously elect Thomas McMicking as captain. Then bylaws were adopted:

First; that this body of men do organize themselves into one body.

Second; that Thomas McMicking be Captain of this Organization.

Third; that there be a committee formed of all the Captains of the different Companies.

Fourth; that this organization shall be governed by the Captain and guide assisted by the committee.

Fifth; that it shall be the duty of the committee to meet every day at noon and night and arrange the distance to travel and the time to start.

Sixth; that the committee shall draw out a form for watch at night, so that every man shall have an equal proportion to do.

Seventh; that every man pay the sum of one dollar to defray the expense of the guide.

Eighth; that every man comply with the rules, or be subject to such penalty as the captain and committee shall see fit to impose.

Ninth; that there shall be no trading carried on with the Indians, should we meet with any parties on our way for fear of disputes arising and getting into trouble.

Tenth; that any person who may offend an Indian or Indians, (and in case that his person be demanded as a satisfaction) he shall be handed over to their discretion, the Committee to be invested with power to withhold him if they see fit.

Eleventh; that the whole company shall start every morning at 5 a.m. except the Committee see fit to change the hour.

Twelfth; that each company shall take their turn at the head of the train, so that one will have no advantage over the other by always being first and getting the best camping ground and the best supply of wood, etc.

Thirteenth; that there shall be no liquor used amongst the Indians.

Fourteenth; form of watch. That the whole company be divided into battalions of 21 in number and that three shall watch every night out of each battalion as follows: one from 10 p.m. until 12 midnight; one from 12 until 2:30 a.m. and one from 2:30 until 5 a.m.[17]

Such organization and bylaws had been standard procedure for California-bound companies, and California miners Wattie and Putnam no doubt had major input into the formation of the 1862 bylaws.[18]

Californians often formed hometown joint-stock companies to meet the costs of travel and mining. Though no records survive to confirm Canadian men formed such companies, the Huntingdon company, likely because of Wattie, had a similar agreement. Group purchases were made in St. Paul and St. Cloud; they elected Wattie as captain and remained a tight group until journey's end, one of the few overland parties to do so.[19]

With the shimmering noonday sun directly overhead the meeting was adjourned, the horses saddled, the oxen harnessed, and with groans and squeals, like a string of plodding ants drawn by honey, the train wheeled into motion. The majesty of the westward cart train was not lost on James Sellar. In the heat of the day, his buttocks and back wet with sweat, his face shielded by a broad-brimmed hat and his long-gun slung across the saddle horn, he rode off to one side and paused to look over the line of 150 men and 120 carts, each loaded with eight hundred pounds of food and equipment. They were passing to

> a destination in the far North West, where the Red men of the forest goes prowling about at all hours, waiting for an opportunity, when an innocent white may fall into their power, in order to shed his blood & feast upon his flesh. When those things were taken into consideration, well might the waysiders say! raving & mad, were those who had undertaken & set out upon such a perilous expedition. But when we thought of the motives that had caused us to leave our homes & friends we felt proud to know that we were the first on the way, to open up a communication with the gold fields of the Saskatchewan, if successful, & if not to push our way over the Mountains to the far famed gold region called Cariboo.

It was the most exciting moment of his life.

It would be easy to dismiss Sellar's fears of Indians as the rantings of a greenhorn. Not so. At one time there had been a European-native equality, and acceptance, but in the last several decades that equality had been challenged. The natives of the plains and Rocky Mountain foothills were beginning to realize that if they were to hold land for themselves it would have to be soon. The growing numbers of westward-bound miners and settlers were putting the squeeze on, while adventurers out for sport were decimating the buffalo herds. As evidenced by the Sioux and Chippewa along the Red River the fuse of the powder keg was lit. When it exploded the Indian Wars shock wave would last for thirty years. The 1860s were the initiation, not the cessation, of plains warfare.[20]

James Sellar's pessimistic view of Indians was balanced by McMicking's cautious optimism. "All parties acquainted with the country, ... were unanimous in recommending us to use the greatest caution, both upon our march during the day and especially while camped at night, in order to guard against the Indians who are continually roaming over these plains. We were informed that should they make any demonstrations it would be more likely for the purpose of stealing our animals than with any design against our person." McMicking's final statement gives the opinion, backed by previous overlanders, that the natives were horse thieves not murderers—usually. The Man from Brechin found otherwise. It was often a matter of knowing the game's moves. The plains' changing temper gave reason to be wary.[21]

And what of this James Sellar who writes of Indians and leaving home? What is his mettle? Of the pre-1862 overlanders we know little of their interior; little of their exterior for that matter. We have initials, a surname, a hometown, perhaps an age, but the man himself remains locked in a coffin of mystery. Not so the 1862 overlanders. These men, for reasons still foggy, became heroes, and thus were given a heroes' space in records and documents. So we know Redgrave, the self-righteous prig; Harkness, the love-lorn; stiff Thomas McMicking; laconic John Hunniford; and the young rake Richard Alexander.

James Sellar, then, as an example. Surname Sellar; Christian name James; initial M.; younger brother of William, also an overlander, and Fred, who stayed home. They were sons of Joseph Sellar, an Englishman, and Lettitia, an Irishwoman, and were born in or near the village of Huntingdon, Canada East. James was born August 22, we learn from his journal, and when the census enumerator knocked on his door in the summer of 1861 he was twenty-six years old; an apprentice, perhaps to the tanner and currier listed above him; recently married to nineteen-year-old Mary Jane. He keeps a daily journal, 7½ by 4¾ inches, leather bound, written in ink, each page frugally filled edge to gutter and top to bottom. From the pages a portrait emerges.

On religion: Sellar was a protestant, small p, and a Protestant. While he lived in what was to become the province of Quebec, he was not French-Canadian, nor Catholic. In fact, as we shall see, he was rabidly anti-Catholic.[22]

His mind was arithmetic and he sought detail and order. He meticulously records expenses; times are precise, 2:30 P.M., 8:20, 4:45; rivers are given a width, cliffs an elevation. Fort Garry is stone, "wall's are 12 feet high & 4 feet thick and encloses 4 acres of ground & six houses." Down the trail Fort Carlton is square timber, mortised, timbers on end, "teneted into the Cills & plates," square tower, 50 acres under cultivation.

Sellar had an impatience born of determination. The Huntingdon party had broken in their bodies early, walked on despite blistered feet, stiff, aching muscles, wet clothes, and other discomforts and so were disparaging and perhaps peevish to a fault of those unable to keep up. He was a farm boy, as were most of his party, and could not abide being delayed by "certain parties who knew nothing about carts & cattle or anything else save standing & looking at others working or getting behind a counter, neither of which will be of any benefit to a man when his ox and cart is stuck fast in a mud hole."

Beneath a surface of irascibility there lay a man confident enough to share feelings, an unusual characteristic for the time. Sellar spoke of "a full heart" or "tears in the eye" without destroying his ego. His writing shows a subtle, almost perverse, sense of humor. While accused of laughing at others' misfortunes, on closer inspection he is laughing at inconvenience. Sellar picked up the pieces and carried on.

The Huntingdon party were hustlers and Sellar was usually the edge of their wedge, up early, out in front with an ax clearing trail, the first volunteer to swim a river. On an expedition one wishes as a companion someone determined, confident, who can laugh at adversity and be willing to pick up tools. Sellar was such a man.[23]

The vastness of the plains elicited different responses. John Dodd saw the open lands as being as magnificent as the sea, offering many thousands of acres fit for the plough, a likely sentiment for a farmer. His perception was one that saw the plains as boundless, free, with nothing to block your vision. He thought they had as much potential as the goldfields—yet he didn't stay. Many others felt lost and helpless in the overwhelming emptiness. There was the feeling that these engulfing plains were an ocean of liquid grass, not a scape of solid earth. The illusion caused a sickness the early fur traders called *"le mal de prairie."*

In the first couple of days they passed Portage la Prairie, where La Vérendrye had wintered 124 years previously, and the last of the Garry oak, taking the precaution of loading up with wood for spare cart parts. When they came to a long wooded section, very low and wet, Sellar wrote that the "water was over two feet deep, & mud to the wheel hubs. This was the first of muck and mire for the Counter-hoppers & fun it was for the clod hoppers."

The day's routine was regulated to favor stock, not men. Men were wakened by the last watch at 3:00 A.M. in the cool, no-color of predawn. Breakfast was cooked, gear loaded, oxen and horses fed and watered. By 5:00 they were on the trail. At least that was the plan. In the first few days starts were a little slow as clerks became cowboys and teachers, teamsters. As they became proficient the start was moved to 4:00 A.M., with a drive till 7:00, feed till 9:00, drive till 12:00, feed till 2:00, and then drive again till 6:00 when they would make camp.

It soon became evident that despite rules and regulations first up and first away meant first in line, a decided advantage when it came to crossing mud holes, churned into impassable quagmires for the following carts, and in the choice of campsites and what wood was available. Alexander Fortune had early on in the trip been appointed to remonstrate with the guide, informing him that he was to obey only the instructions of the captain, not go ahead with one party at others' expense. At one point the Acton men threatened to shoot the ox of any false starters.

The Huntingdon men made it a matter of pride to be first. Sellar describes morning starts which "caused many a good laugh to see a whole Battalion running with Cups of Tea, & Pan Cakes in their hands, Eating as they went along, & often set the whole company in such a fit of Laughter that half lost their places, & then came a general consternation, Some running with a Tent some with pail full of dishes & some with various things belonging to the Tent department."

Fortune excused the "ambitious and pushing spirit" with mention of the short Cariboo season and the likelihood of a long, jobless winter.

> Men laboured hard, laboured late and early and intelligently, and lost patience with those who had been detaining them in making a start. Their patience was somewhat tried. In a large crowd of men we can nearly always find some who cannot do much for themselves, who are so helpless when thrown on their own resources that they would as soon starve and die, as get out of the old ruts of life and habit.... They needed brothers or sisters to get their food prepared, they were looking around for servants to attend them.... Much time was spent over their toilet. They had great self esteem; but did not make the friends they most needed. They were a burden and a drag to our company on the start. He had

some Christian Samaritans in our company who helped them betimes and they soon learned the few routines of travelling duty and necessity and sought to please and make themselves useful.[24]

This early portion of the journey crossed the ancient bed of Lake Agassiz, a potholed, mottled flatland that from a bird's eye view presented a paisley pattern of land, water, marsh, and grass, mirrored by islands of clouds. A seven-week drought had dried many streams and swamps so, unlike Dr. Reid of the previous year, they did not have to wade continuously through several feet of water, nor were they attacked by hordes of mosquitoes. There were still mudholes and streams to be crossed though. The more delicate members carefully removed shoes and socks, rolled up their pants, then crossed and redressed. They soon realized that if they were to progress there was no use being "too fastidious about the matter," and then waded right in, becoming muddy in one place and bathed in another.[25]

Their first Sunday, June 7, found them 112 miles from Fort Garry. Sunday was a day of rest, part of the day devoted to simple religious services and the remainder to writing, washing, repairing, and resting. And for Sellar, "introducing ourselves into the mistries of that part of the domestic life, which the fair sex charge with having destroyed their sweet and lovely tempers i.e. washing."

West of the ancient portage from Lake Manitoba to the Assiniboine River, the Carlton Trail began a gradual ascent from the ancient lake bottom to the second prairie steppe, climbing from eight hundred to eighteen hundred feet where the Little Saskatchewan River (now Minnedosa) cut the plain. Cutting a straight line west past Salt Lake they came to the Shoal Lake narrows and climbed a small bluff to make one of their most memorable camps. The site afforded a view northward up the mile-long lake filled with "all kinds of fresh water fish" and surrounded by some of the finest waterfowl shooting.[26]

After supper some fished, others went shooting, and the musicians entertained. Tom Jones was on concertina, George Ballie on violin, John Fannin on cornet, and circled around were thirty others, "playing on different kinds of Brass instruments, claanetts, flutes, violin and a concertina and others would gather in a group Singing over a few favorite pieces of Vocal Music," like "Castle in the Air," "The Old Oaken Bucket," or "The Yellow Rose of Texas," whiling "away the hours of evening until bed time as merrily and pleasant as though in some grand concert hall of the first fashion in an eastern city."[27]

There was a harmony to their voyage. As Oregon settlers had sailed west in their Conestoga prairie schooners so the overlanders skulled the prairie in their leather and oak dories, from fort to fort, harbor to harbor, the scouts and watchmen keeping an eye on the limitless horizon for storms and landmarks. West of Shoal Lake McMicking said they sailed a surface "as beautiful as any that I ever laid eyes upon . . . as smooth as any Carpet that ever was stepped upon, while the uplands were thickly covered with wild Roses & wild Peas just in full bloom. In short it seemed like the home & birth place of the choisest of nature's beauties."

They guided the oxen down a side gully into the five-hundred-foot deep ravine of Bird's Tail Creek, crossed the creek, and climbed again and a short distance later came to the valley of the Assiniboine. On the far side, like a derelict coastal castle, was the squat edifice of Fort Ellice. They descended, lowering the carts with ropes to the Assiniboine rivermoat, and crossed with the aid of a bateau drawbridge-ferry. They had arrived at their first anchorage.

## McMicking Party—Fort Ellice to Fort Edmonton

River crossings, more than any other events, brought danger to overlanders. While they scratched anxious journal jottings about Indians who they imagined were just over each day's horizon with bows drawn, they skidded down hills and swam prairie rivers of more immediate danger. On this Monday morning, June 16, they were poised above the Qu'Appelle River, the rain pouring down, the ground slippery and stock nervous.

The crossing to Fort Ellice had gone with relative ease. The HBC had decided that if travelers were going to insist on using the Carlton Trail, the Company was going to profit. In a move indicating their changing attitude, they set the ferry fee at fifty cents per cart, half a day's wages. In the tedious, laborious five-hour crossing the Company made sixty dollars, the equivalent of a servant's wages for a month. Their new policy gave tacit approval to plains travel.

The overlanders struggled up Beaver Creek to the flat table land and the fort. The buildings were being rebuilt, again. The first time servants had run out of firewood and had relocated. Now the old fort was crumbling around trader McKay and so two miles south he was building a new post, still unoccupied. They continued on to the old palisades, where they settled in for Sunday's rest and a sermon by the Reverend James Settee, a Swampy Cree native ordained in the Church of England in 1853 and stationed at Fort Pelly.[28]

The weather turned foul. A driving rain swept in from the southwest so Monday morning was spent repairing carts and harness. When the bad weather persisted, they packed up and turned northwest toward the Qu'Appelle crossing.

Bill Morrow, a Montreal merchant, was at the top of the hill with his ox and cart while Dodson Prest held the spokes of the five-foot wheel, ready to use it like a capstan to slow their descent. The ox lurched into unexpected motion, dragged Morrow down the hill, and threw him across the track. He was unable to gain a foothold and Prest was incapable of slowing the cart. As he scrambled to clear himself, Morrow's head slipped beneath the wheel, like the head of a Krishna devotee crushed beneath the juggernaut's wheel. Prest abandoned the cart and ran for Dr. Edward Stevenson.

Stevenson found Morrow unconscious, his ear almost torn off, but alive, saved by his head being pressed into the same mud that had caused the accident. Stevenson bound him up and placed him in a Red River cart ambulance for a few days' rest and recuperation. The ostreperous ox meanwhile took a fit and ran over the ferry, dumping the cart load and losing all but one bag of flour and one trunk. What was perhaps surprising was that so few accidents of a similar nature occurred to these novices. Their ox-tending needed a little refining.

Sellar did not hear about the accident until the next day. As usual the Huntingdon company were in the vanguard. They paused only briefly at Fort Ellice and crossed the Qu'Appelle on the Saturday evening, took the usual day of rest, and uncharacteristically dallied during Monday morning's rain. Then with guide Rochette and thirty other carts they climbed out of the Qu'Appelle valley toward Cut Arm Creek, where the party regrouped.

On the morning of June 18 a half inch of ice covered the water buckets. Despite the cold by 5:00 A.M. they were on their way through country broken by ravines, gullies, and clumps of aspens and willow. It was hard traveling for the cattle so at their nooning the committee met to consider the afternoon affairs. It was discovered that Rochette the guide was missing. Someone remembered him borrowing a double-barreled gun, a shot-pouch, and powder flask that morning on the pretense of hunting for dinner. They waited, hoping Rochette would show up. Some blamed Bishop Tache; perhaps he and Rochette were in cahoots together. Sellar remembered newspaper accounts of guides deserting earlier overlander parties and was sure this was the man he had read of last summer. In fact, Rochette had deserted Jones in 1858, but Dr. Reid, of whom Sellar was thinking, had been deserted by Baptiste Gabriel west of Fort Edmonton.

Finally, what to do? Turn back, or proceed? The majority felt the road was well enough marked to allow them to proceed. They were confident that what in '49 had been called "the emigrants's trinity of good things" —wood, water, and grass—would be easy enough to find. "We got into order," Sellar wrote, "and started with full determination to push our way through without a guide."

Apprehensively, they rolled on. Greater uneasiness came that afternoon when two mounted Indians and several on foot were spotted. Without a guide for translation they did not attempt to make contact but rode with tense trigger fingers. The night watch was doubled and the committee charged each man to be on his toes for infiltrating Indians. As the realization that their guide had deserted became firm, their self-confidence increased. They would have to rely on their own skills. McMicking saw this band of strangers become cemented with the bond of hardship.

Beyond the Qu'Appelle, Captain Wattie convened another meeting of the Huntingdon company to better divide up the daily chores. The result was:

1st    four to take charge & do the cooking.

2nd   three to attend to the cattle & mules to see that they got water three times a day regular & drive them up when ready to start.
3rd   three to cut, & carry the wood.
4th   two to attend to the carts & do all repairing.
5th   two to grease the carts at least once a day.
6th   three to carry water at every camping place, for all cooking purposes & for all hands to wash with.
7th   that those who were at leisure first at night should pitch the Tents.[29]

Where James Sellar's journal is expository, John Hunniford's is concentrated and sparse. He writes not less than three and not more than five completely unpunctuated lines per day. In measured diary lines he makes his way from one camp to the next.

June 21 Saturday Broke up camp at 3 oclock stopped for Breakfast traveled 20 miles roads bad weather hot Beautiful Rolling Pararie with clumps of popalar and small lakes of good water was very tired at night health good.

June 22 Sunday was in camp all day beside a number of small salt water Lakes on a Beautiful open pararie Day fine and I enjoyed the rest preaching in the evening health good slept the most of the Day.

June 23 Monday Broke up camp at 3 oclock stopped for Breakfast and dinner Traveled over a Beautiful country with stragaling Lakes and clumps of Popalars coming close to the Touchwood hils Traveled 20 miles Day fine health good.

Hunniford's writing continues, functional and dependable, day after day, from spring in St. Catharines to winter in Victoria.

The hills he makes reference to on June 23 were a gentle swelling of the prairie's tedious, eroded plain. The column passed between the Beaver Hills to the north and the File Hills to the south before entering a shallow pass between the southern Little Touchwoods and the northern Touchwoods. Thomas McMicking remarked on the beauty of the hill region in true protestant, Anglo-Saxon, pioneer style: "It seems a pity [they] should have remained so long wasted and desolate." McMicking could not be expected to appreciate the variety of life that swirled around this oasis in the form of native tribes, Métis, traders, and animals.

Touchwood Hills House, where John Jones had met trader Taylor in 1858, was abandoned. Even assessor Sellar gives no description or detail, noting only that they gathered what wood they could for the treeless plains ahead and moved quickly on.[30]

The old post was at a crossroads. Due east was Fort Pelly, southeast Fort Ellice, west the wintering area of Moose Woods (now Saskatoon), and north by northwest Fort Carlton. It was the latter trail the overlanders followed.[31]

The trail now led out onto the treeless Quill Plains "as level as a floor as far as the eye could see." Sellar's party traveled along a ridge between two long, narrow lakes, an esker left by the retreating glaciers. Despite the sandhill and whooping cranes that frequented the pothole water basins this was a desolate crossing. There was, however, a certain vividness, a simplicity that keened perception. Robert Harkness described walking "under a burning sun & over a vast prairie without a tree in sight as large as your finger." On this Wednesday, June 25, his mind was focused on Sabrina. This was their wedding anniversary. "My thoughts wandered eastward & as I knew they met yours coming westward I derived no little pleasure from the consciousness that we were thinking of each other & of that dear and ever-to-be-remembered day that made us one."

The far side of the plain was reached in two days but still the terrain provided little shade from the sun's cast-iron heat. One evening Sellar deadpanned, "It was found to be necessary to tie our mosquitoes nets fast around our necks so as to keep the mosquitoes from flying away with them as they were about the size of humming birds in Canada, & as numerous as midges on a sand bar." A chuckle comes off the page as he concludes, "Some of the delicate youths had to suffer."

Again, friend Sellar provides details of an incident on June 28 near Wakaw Lake. Their location had been reckoned by Captain Wattie pacing off the day's travel. A dispute arose at dinner time about the distance traveled that day. Some felt that Wattie was inaccurate. It was decided to have Wattie walk ahead and count his paces while others chained the distance. Off Wattie went. "Mile one," he called. Only eight feet short the survey crew admitted. Mile two—fourteen yards long. Mile three—four yards short. And so it went for fourteen miles. Wattie, the pedometer, was vindicated. End of dispute.

The area beyond the Quill Plains had a luxuriant growth of grasses crisscrossed in all directions by old buffalo trails. It was a favorite pasture "of the immense herds," McMicking wrote, "as their bones were thickly scattered over the whole country."

McMicking was pleased now with the military precision, order, and discipline of the company. Fifteen minutes after the order "Every man to his ox," baggage was packed and the train in motion. But precision did not lessen fatigue. The animals were tiring and the poor men's dispositions led to disagreements and disputes. Bill Thompson changed his mess group; John Hunniford and Tom Murphy had a quarrel that broke into a fist fight. It was the Sabbath rest that kept the group together. McMicking knew that without this opportunity for restoring energy and soothing ascerbity the whole group would collapse like a cart wheel with a broken hub. It was sufficient evidence that "the law of the Sabbath is of physical as well as of moral obligation, and that its precepts cannot be violated with impunity."

At various times during the journey everyone realized danger. Human nature being what it is, they imagined that accidents and death would happen to someone else; as individuals they felt immune. For the most part any thought of danger was lost in the day-to-day struggle and any lingering doubts were overwhelmed by the sense of adventure. This was the greatest experience of their lives—most would not trade it for anything. Never had such freedom been experienced, never had bodies been stronger, and never had men been more confident. In this mood they arrived at the South Saskatchewan River.

Here they had to ferry provisions and supplies in the HBC bateau or flatboat and then drive the cattle over separately. James Kelso, a twenty-eight-year-old Scot lately of Acton, rode in amongst them, herding forward the reluctant swimmers. It was a cold day and he had put on his macintosh. Lost in the excitement of the crossing he hardly noticed his misstep and fall into the stream until he tried to breathe and found only water wrapped around him. He swam for a few moments, turned on his back to rest, turned again, and sank with a call for help, pulled down by his watersoaked macintosh. He might have panicked at the realization he was drowning but rather he felt annoyed that he would not see the other side of the river or the end of the journey. What a foolish way to die. Ah shit! He had something much more dramatic in mind, like fighting Indians, or dying to save a friend, not drowning while herding some dumb cattle-beast. He rose, and sank again, gasped for air, and took in water.[32]

Sellar's party was on a bluff above the river and not for several moments did they hear the commotion. Most of the men were non-swimmers but blacksmith George Reed, Thomas Phillips, and William Strachan rushed down the bank to the river. The journal of Alexander Fortune: "He was given up as lost, when a good friend, George Reid, stripped off his clothes, plunged into the river and dove after our drowning comrade. He came up like a hero with the helpless body of Kelso. He found a spark of life and kindled that spark into a flame and after a long labour got him to breath."

At this crossing, where Kelso almost drowned, there would soon be a ferry, operated by Xavier Letendre, a trader whom the Indians called Batoche. The ferry became the center of a Métis community and in 1885 this place called Batoche was thwacked into Canadian history like a bullet into a church wall—the place where the Métis made a final, desperate, futile stand in their battle for recognition as a distinct and separate people.[33]

Fort Carlton was the pivotal point for the Carlton Trail and lay on the North Saskatchewan River, a little less than twenty miles beyond the South Saskatchewan crossing. While prairie fur-trade posts could not be considered as provisioning or recreational way stations, there was a degree of both at these timbered fortresses. McMicking purchased fresh buffalo meat that hunters had just brought in, a meat that "resembles beef, but is a little coarser in the grain, and more juicy," and certainly a welcome change from the dry, greasy pemmican that had been their staple diet. It was a short stay. One night and they were off.

The crossing of July 1 was again made in the Company bateau, this time at only 12.5 cents per cart. There were no accidents until late evening when three of the London and Montreal parties' cattle were swept downstream and lost.[34]

At 11:30 that night, as everyone except the watch was comfortably bedded down, a raging thunderstorm swept in from the prairie. Lightning stabbed through the darkness. Rain, driven into pine-needle icicles by the wind, darted out of the shadow to pierce the men. While they struggled to hold their tents erect the hammer of Thor crashed around them. Canvas snapped and flapped, ropes flailed, stock reared and, strangely, above all the tumult could be heard the sound of men laughing. What else was there to do? Roused from sleep, soaked to the skin, relief came only from humor. Their start up out of the valley of the North Saskatchewan was late and slow the next morning, but there was a pervasive feeling that another milestone had been marked.

On the far side of the North Saskatchewan they noticed a change in the terrain. At Fort Garry they had journeyed through the short-grass prairie, then into the mixed-grasslands. Now they moved into the aspen parkland, rolling hills, groves of aspens, willow bottoms, giving the appearance as the name implies of a park. The water was from running streams not from ponds of stagnant, alkaline soup, and the weather was cooler. At one spot they even passed through immense fields of wild strawberries and feasted on dessert of freshly picked fruit and freshly squeezed cream.

The days were filled with activity that brought new strength to their bodies. Sick men like John Nicols became well; fat men lost weight and became strong. Like a Toledo sword they were heated and hammered, condensed, then plunged into the legendary dragon's blood and tempered. They were emerging sharp, tough, resilient, and flexible.

The trail took them along the fringe of the parklands, past Blaine Lakes, north of Redberry Lake, and then on a long curve toward the north end of Jackfish or Pike Lake. Most travelers camped at the south end of the lake but according to Robert McMicking the overlanders took a swing north, crossed Jackfish Creek through the cattails and marsh grass, and climbed the small hill that brings one to the bluff overlooking the lake. Here, at one of the most attractive sites since Shoal Lake, they spent their Sunday day of rest, July 6. They had been on the trail from Fort Garry for just over a month.

Sellar's party, ever the precursors, were thirty miles ahead, spending their Sunday on the banks of the English River. Where they lunged ahead is unclear. Likely it was a culmination of fast starts and long days after the crossing of the Saskatchewan. A number of other carts had been traveling with them and as they neared Fort Pitt the Huntingdon men decided they would be first to the next river crossing. Sellar consulted a map and decided they had twenty to thirty miles to go, not the two or three expected. They plotted therefore not to have breakfast before inspanning and to push right through to the fort with no break. They were almost foiled. At 2:00 A.M. the other companies crept out of camp. An hour later the Huntingdon company were out of their blankets and racing after them. They crossed Moberly Creek, passed Frenchman Butte, and touched the curve of the North Saskatchewan, where they found the others camped for breakfast. They roared past, figuratively speaking, and arrived at Fort Pitt at 11:10 (again Sellar's preciseness), "One hour in advance of the other parties." The main group with Captain McMicking were still a day behind.

Sellar put his arithmetic pen to paper:

There was a field of Potatoes about 2 acres in size on one side of the Fort and about 15 acres of Wheat on the other side. These were the only signs of cultivation to be seen in the neighbourhood. The river is about 250 Yds wide & runs at the speed of 4 miles pr hour.

(9th) He slept late & got Breakfast at 9 a.m. when the cooks Baked bread to carry along & the remainder done up all repairs.

At 9 p.m. held a general meeting to make some new traveling Laws as we were just about to enter the country where the Blackfeet and Cree Indians were fighting and where they had striped a party of whites but a few days previous and sent them back naked. The following were the resolutions:

1st that all Guns be cleaned and kept in first order & ready for action at short notice.
2nd that Capt. McMicking should be colonel of the Expedition.
3rd that A. C. Robinson [Robertson] [be] Captain.
4th that the Company should be divided into 4 companies for traveling convenience.
5th that the whole company should travel in close order, to prevent the Indians from attacking the center of the train and dividing it.
6th that the services of a guide be procured to guide us to Edmonton.

There is no doubt that the overlanders were entering a battlefield. The Cree and Blackfeet had been at war for some time and resented any intrusion into hunting grounds that were becoming depleted of game. Precautions were taken in response to warnings by the HBC trader. The fort had been located near an ancient buffalo crossing as a convenience, but it was on the north side of the river to decrease the likelihood of a surprise attack. Mitchelle, the Iroquois guide, suggested they take the shorter south trail. Alexander Fortune described Mitchelle as "true, faithful, efficient and agreeable, and most useful in finding the easiest route and the most acceptable camping places."

Two new obstructions now arose: rain and fog. The fog caused the Huntingdon company to wander off the trail and end up one and a half miles south. Luckily, it lasted only a short time. Not so the rain. It rained continuously. Where previous travel had been relatively dry and pleasant because of a drought, this present portion of trail was more like the Great Flood of Noah. And wetness is one price humans hate to pay no matter what the goal.

John Hunniford: "July 11, wet to the skin felt very uncomfortable. July 16 was wet and very uncomfortable all day waded swamps to the middle. July 18 forded one up to my chin my feet sore from constant exposure to water."

James Sellar: "July 15 Crossed a very bad slough . . . just imagine yourself standing . . . on a marsh from an acre to a mile wide & covered with water from 15 to 24 inches deep & the earth beneath your feet so soft and boggy that it sinks 12 or 15 inches more. July 17 . . . came to another bad slough about ½ a mile wide with one of those creeks running through the center, which will likely never be forgotten by any who had to cross it. It was about 10 feet wide & 4 feet deep of water, but how deep with muck at the bottom of that I cannot tell, but I know we could not get an Ox over . . . till we filled the creek with carts & then built a bridge of cart boxes on top, as there was no timber."

Question: "Captain McMicking, is this really the "over*land* route?"

Answer, from John Fannin: "It's at least three feet *over*land where I just tried it."³⁵

Thomas McMicking: "To such an extent had the water risen that between the 18th and 21st we built eight bridges, averaging forty to one hundred feet in length, besides wading without much ceremony through everything not more than four feet in depth. Upon one occasion ... a stream was spread to a great distance over the adjoining plains and ... we had waded for at least half a mile up to our waists."

A bridging episode on Sunday, July 20, divided the camp. Alexander Fortune and some of his friends decided that absolutely no work was to be done on the Sabbath. They therefore would not help to bridge the stream, disregarding the threat of rising water and the possibility of the bridge being swept out. "We will trust the God of the Sabbath, who also rules the floods," Fortune said. To their relief the bridge was still intact on Monday morning. Although Fortune felt that the bridge-building Sabbath-breakers did not resent their use of the crossing, he obviously did not talk to James Sellar. "By partaking of the benefits of the bridge they put themselves on a par with the receiver of stolen goods." Some did not even wait until the Monday morning but drove across as soon as the bridge was complete.

After crossing a particularly difficult ravine in the afternoon Sellar rode ahead, scouting for a camping ground. He rode into a small clearing, the land fell away, and Sellar found himself upon the table land hanging over the valley of the North Saskatchewan directly across from the "long looked for Fort." He wheeled his horse about, dug in his heels, and galloped back to find his company setting up camp. "Fort Edmonton," he cried. "The fort is just ahead."

No time was lost in repacking and setting off at a quickened pace. There rose from the ranks "a hearty and tumultuous cheer," McMicking remembered, "which was repeated again and again as the different parties came up, until the surrounding forests re-echoed with the sound." And Hunniford? "Arrived at the river opposite Fort Edmonton at 7 p.m."

It was a sodden, tattered, jaded, and weary band of men that camped that evening of July 21 high above the river. But the prairie sky cleared in welcome and the bright sun and sight of the fort brought back confidence—they would reach El Dorado.

## St. Peters Party to Fort Edmonton

On June 7, 1862, the second major party left Fort Garry bound for Fort Edmonton and the Cariboo. Known later as the Symington party, the nine men had been dubbed the "Cariboo Party" when they set out from their hometown of St. Peters on the Minnesota River near the end of April.

On the last Saturday in March several prominent townsmen met in the law office of Davis and Hanscome, convening what was to be known as the "Cariboo meeting." The *St. Peters Tribune* explained that "Cariboo" was a gold region where according to accounts the "precious ore is bedded in the earth, distributed in the crevices of rocks and by some great convulsion of nature thrown into the branches of trees, and is now tempting like that apple which Mother Eve toothed with unfortunate results." The editor hoped that the gentlemen meeting would find it "inexpedient to leave their comfortable homes," but if they did decide to go wished for them "the most ample compensation for the toil and hardship endured."[36]

They arrived in St. Paul on the *Favorite* May 10 and then Captain Davison of the La Crosse & St. Paul Packet Company "generously carried the party from St. Anthony to St. Cloud free of charge, only stiplulating that payment might be made on the return trip if the venture proved successful."[37]

Traveling with four mule-drawn wagons they rolled north to Fort Garry, arriving around the beginning of June. Several more men joined here. Dr. Simonton was one. He had arrived on the maiden voyage of the SS *International* as had Alonzo Miner and D. Miner, both St. Peters men who had signed on with the Holmes train then deserted. Up to eleven more joined, for the party that left Fort Garry was, according to Copeland and Davis, twenty-three strong. The Fort Edmonton journal reports twenty arriving. They left Fort Garry June 7, five days behind McMicking, while the members of the Saskatchewan Gold Expedition were still drinking and writing letters home. Only one report and one newspaper item survive to explain their westbound journey.[38]

*St. Peters Tribune*, August 6, 1862:

> The Cariboo Party. Yesterday the families of our Cariboo Party were rejoiced by the arrivals of letters from the travellers. They have thus far enjoyed excellent health, and the trip has been free of all accidents to man, beast or equipage. The roads travelled over on the route are pronounced good, and but little difficulty has been encountered in crossing streams or sloughs. When last heard from, they were 240 miles west of Fort Garry. 25 miles is the average travelled each day.

The letters received in St. Peters had been mailed from Fort Ellice, 250 miles west of Fort Garry about June 18.

The St. Peters party likely took the Carlton Trail to Fort Edmonton, for the mules and wagons would restrict them to the best road. It is indeed unfortunate that a more complete account of their journey does not exist for theirs was evidently the first overland party in history to cross the prairies with mules and wagons.

Under a clear summer sky the St. Peters men arrived at Fort Edmonton on Thursday, July 31. The post clerk's quill scratched out their arrival notice in the thick post journal: "An other party of twenty miners arrived with wagons and they have no oxen they are to follow the others no intelligence of Mr. Love or Flett." Their mule and wagon journey had taken them sixty-one days, five days longer than McMicking, who just the day previously had abandoned Red River carts and pushed on to St. Albert.[39]

## Saskatchewan Gold Expedition to Fort Edmonton

Fifteen days' walk west of Fort Garry, beyond Portage la Prairie, the Little Saskatchewan River, and Shoal Lake, a deep angled cut cleaves the prairie. This Bird's Tail Creek is only twenty-five feet in width, but it has cut a trough eighty feet deep and one mile broad at the Carlton Trail crossing. Could we travel back to Wednesday, June 25, 1862, about 7:30 in the morning, we would see two men hunkered over gold pans in the shady bottom of this cleft, one young, his face having felt the stroke of a straight razor but few times; the other whose beard, had he let it grow, would be tickling his navel. Richard Alexander and Timoleon Love.

When Love and McLaurin returned from St. Paul in the autumn of 1861 they had hatched a new gold scheme. McLaurin did not live to see it come to fruition for he died in the muck of a swamp while out duck hunting one evening, the victim of a stroke. His death slowed Love's quest, but not for long. Love knew that those who had made the most reliable money in California and British Columbia were the entrepreneurs: the merchants who brought in and sold at enormous profits such basic items such as shovels, picks, gold pans, pants, and boots, all of which wore out quickly. With the money from the gold he and McLaurin had forwarded to the United States mint he set out to become an outfitter and merchant.

In Red River two men aided Love's scheme. Edmund Lorenzo Barber was an American who, on behalf of his cousin George Brott, had brought goods to the Selkirk settlement to open a retail store. In February 1861 Brott requested he close the store and return the goods to Breckenridge. Instead he opened a store near Fort Garry. Love became a minority partner.

The gold sent to the mint did not bring as much cash as expected, so with contacts supplied by his friend Robert Tait, Love went to old Jamey Jock Bird and arranged for additional financial backing, using Bird's savings deposited with the HBC. The Burbank brothers accepted Bird's drafts, adding that "the trade for the Gold districts must be large & you who are prepared for it will make money. We understand the immigration from Canada to those districts via Fort Garry will be large this season."

So Love had supplanted his gold lust with friends, promoting gold, and potential profiteering. Now, with miles passing beneath his feet again and his ears filled with the rattle of water over gravel he turns to his pan, his touchstone. He marks his passage with swirls of water and gleans from the creased bottom a flake, just one, light enough to be picked up with spit on a finger. It is enough, this speck of fly dung, to give this day meaning, this journey reason.

In Red River, in early June, the seat of Love's baggy pants were set aflame by his own passionate fanning of gold news. In the final audit, he was a prospector and by nature had to keep moving. He could not stay in Red River and see so many men head west to his gold strike. The overlanders had sought him out. Here was TIMOLEON LOVE. This man had been there. "We have found Mr. T. Love," Leonard Crysler wrote, "but I can't tell what to think of him."[40]

Some did not know what to think of Love but they sought his counsel. "Love says we can go in fifty-four days to the mines," Thompson wrote. And they asked him to lead a party. Love waffled. "I would need at least $500 to guide you to Fort Edmonton," he told James Carpenter.[41]

Love. What must he have thought of these young easterners? Love, who for the better part of two decades had been chasing either Mexicans or gold. A conversation between Timoleon Love and Robbie Tait, Kentuckian and Red River born: "My God, Robbie but they're green—don't know if they're punched or bored. They've come here by railroad and steamboat, and now they're to walk west, in old boots and dress suits some of them. Store keepers and teachers; and that copper-nosed, fat-arsed cop who bitches all the time.... I've waded more rivers and walked more passes than those pissers know exist. What do I want with them?"

"What you want with them is a large enough group to move through those miserable heathen Blackfeet and Cree and still keep your clothes; men to help you hunt, and men, or boys, to help you dig that damned North Saskatchewan gravel. That and your guide money. Throw your traps in with Flett. By the time you get to Edmonton those school boys will be licking milk from your fingers and you'll have your crew."

Love cogitated. Love pondered. Love waited, not to make a decision for that had been made long before, but waiting rather for acceptance. Not until June 11 did he take a piece of paper and scratch on it: "This is to certify that I have this day sold all my right and title to the goods held under the firm of E. L. Barber and Co. with the provision that the said Barber will settle the amount here in stated, Thirteen pounds 15 shillings."

For thirteen pounds, sixty-five dollars, thirty-five-year-old Love was hitting the trail again. The party he joined was a coalition of the original Red River party formed by George Flett, those who had stuck by Redgrave, more who had chosen Love as leader, and a few others who for various reasons had split from the McMicking party or arrived in Red River on their own. Most of them planned to stay at Fort Edmonton to test Love's theory of Saskatchewan gold. According to George Flett, the Saskatchewan Gold Expedition comprised 64 men, 3 women, 1 boy, 1 girl, 43 oxen, 23 horses, 4 cows, and 1 calf.

Apart from Flett and Love, the Red River men who were part of this group were John Whitford, a "reliable Red River Métis," a cousin of Flett's on his mother's side; George Gunn, a second generation Red River farmer; Hector McBeath, son of Robert McBeath, a councillor of Assiniboia; Donald Matheson, a "jolly, handsome young Scotsman" of Sutherlandshire descent who had ridden with Captain Blakiston of the Palliser expedition and the Earl of Southesk in 1859-60; and George or Geordie Sutherland and John Atkinson, Red River settlers.[42]

Where the McMicking party was formed along military lines with regulations, bylaws, and watches the Saskatchewan Gold Expedition (SGE) was a loose-knit, informal association based more on the Métis buffalo hunters' experience. Guidelines were set and Love and Whitford emerged as leaders.

"The Bugle is sounded every morning at 3 o'clock and when we get underway, the British Flag waves bravely on the foremost cart. Mr. Love leads the van one day with the Flag cart, and we [Whitford-Gunn] do it the next—time about all the way. Our parties are very agreeable," George Flett wrote to his Red River friends. Redgrave added, "The Bugle to wake us and the Flag to warn us to be ready."

Like previous parties they were on the road by 5:00 A.M., took regular breaks for the stock, and used Sunday as a day of reflection and for repairs.

The final party consolidation took place at Portage la Prairie on Saturday, June 15. "Found a number here waiting our arrival and among them Harry Hamilton, so we will from this day travel together," Alexander tells us. They waited a day to attend the Sunday public worship of "venerable clergyman Archdeacon Cochrane" whose impressive discourse "addressed the miners very pointedly." His sermon: "My sins are ever before me." Cochrane must have heard rumors of the gold-rush towns.

Lest there be an impression that an overland journey was all drudgery, consider this of Redgrave, Wednesday, June 18:

> 4:40 a.m. travelled first 15 miles through beautiful Woods appeared like a fairy ground, here all sorts of flowers were in full blossom the Wild Geranium, Ladys Slippers, Woodbine Roses Wild Mint & other sorts of different descriptions—also indeed the morning was so fine, the Sun just rising the perfume of the Wild flowers, the birds singing their cheerful notes that it was quite charming beautiful lakes here and there—with beautiful Water Lillys in and around them—Wild Gooseberry & Current also Cherry were in abundance (but not yet ripe) all of which tended to remind one of their home of childhood dreams.

One week later they spent their first "Sunday in the wilderness," and listened to a discourse on the origins of Christianity by Eugene Francis O'Beirne, one of the most grasping, exasperating hitchhikers history ever inflicted on travelers.

O'Beirne enters the Canadian stage in the geographical center: Red River. He arrives on the steamer *Pioneer* on September 15, 1861, an inauspicious entrance. On October 15 the *Nor'-Wester* reports:

> A gentleman recently arrived in the Settlement, proposes establishing an Academy in which a first class education will be imparted. He is a graduate of the University of Cambridge—which is a good guarantee of this qualifications. We have seen documents and certificates which speak in the highest terms of his

fitness and we hope Red River will afford sufficient encouragement to induce him to devote his valuable experience and great attainments to the interests and education of the Settlement.

Now, less than a year later, O'Beirne stands before a scrubwood fire, leaning on his walking stick, giving a lecture from Paley's *Evidences of Christianity* to a bunch of teenage adventurers and misfit fortune hunters. The Academy of Red River?

Eugene Francis O'Beirne was a fraud. Born between 1809 and 1811 on the family farm in Cloone, County Longford, Ireland, he was educated at St. Patrick's College, a Roman Catholic College at Maynooth, but was expelled in June 1830. In retaliation he spent most of his time writing pamphlets and lecturing on "The Internal Economy and Discipline at Maynooth College," trying to bring its principals down. He became an apostate and gave fervent anti-Catholic lectures all over England but "layed it on too thick," the *Birmingham Journal* wrote. After a few months at St. John's College, Cambridge, in 1842-43 he disappears for seventeen years.[43]

His story surfaces again in the pages of *Cheadle's Journal* and *North-West Passage by Land*. Briefly, Cheadle notes: "Invited by prosperous friend to come to Louisiana. Did well there until prosperous friend failed. Engaged by Planter at Salary of $2,000 per annum [an extremely large amount in the 1860s]. Comfortable and happy until Civil War broke out. Appointed Captain of Home Guard. Honor too great for him; fled North. Appointed Classical Professor at Jackson College, Columbia, Tennessee, through good offices of the Bishop of New York."

There is no record of him at Jackson College but he continued north to inflict himself on British North America.

> There, he became quite a temporary celebrity and was known as the "Irish Schoolmaster", it being believed that the University of Oxford his place of education.... He did not seem over fifty years of age and knew all about the personalities of leading English public men. In default of employment, he borrowed money from different citizens under the pretence that, if he could raise sufficient to go through a course of theological training his ordination at the hands of Bishop Anderson [Bishop of Ruperts Land] was certain. When his hotel bill got in arrears, he commenced a round of visits to hospitably minded Red River citizens, reserving the bulk of his partronage for the clergymen of the Colony. By the Spring of 1862, Mr. O'B had so worn out his welcome that he was urged to take passage with a party of Canadian immigrants on their way to the gold fields of the Cariboo.

The overlanders did not take the time the Red River folks did to reach a concensus about O'Beirne. Every expedition needs someone to play the goat, to be the butt of jokes. Redgrave explains, July 8:

> There is an old man who knows John well—a half preacher (but old sot) he is going across to Cariboo—he was always interfering with everyones business so they were determined to have a trick with him—he always walks ahead nearly a mile of the carts so in going thru the wood one of Love's men got a Red blanket & pack kerchief on his head and with his gun rode around and rushed out of the

Bush giving the Indian War Whoop—& fired twice above him—if you had seen him run & shout you would have thought he was mad.

"What's the matter Mr. O'Beirne?"

"Indians, Indians!"

Of course we would not believe him & he gets in a fearful rage.

So every day now it's, "How about the Indians Mr. O'Beirne?"

Redgrave added fuel by saying, "Mr. O'Beirne, that white cap cover you wear—to the Indians that means you're our Chief. It marks you." The cap cover disappeared. At every bush the old con man runs behind the carts. "I'll mind your ox," he says, "and you take my gun and shoot them."

Redgrave asks, "What's the matter there, do you feel okay?"

"I am so nervous I don't know what to do but something will happen, I know."[44]

O'Beirne was on the mark. Something did happen—just a few days down the road.

The first weeks of westward travel were, as Redgrave indicated, a pleasant prairie walk. There were sore feet, blisters, and aching muscles but these were salved by the low-key adventure and prairie beauty. There was one aggravation: mosquitoes. The overland parties of the half decade from 1858 to 1862 were bound together by one thing: the pestering, biting, sucking, long-nosed curse of the swamps. Redgrave even turned to doggerel verse in retaliation.

... again those mosquitoes worse than ever—we had to smoke them out of our Tent, but I cannot help giving them my passing opinion—

> Those Mosquitoes bold if Tales could tell
> Of their torments to many how they've eaten them
> That's eno- to send us poor travellers to Hell
> Much less to Mr. Workmans Asylum.
>
> In Sunshine or shade
> They were still to be found
> As also if sitting upon the ground
> Sleeping or waking its still the same
> They are sure to be up to their regular game.[45]

Nearing the Assiniboine River the guides chose a different route from that taken by previous parties. Rather than cross the Assiniboine to Fort Ellice and then cross the Qu'Appelle, they ferried the Assiniboine above the confluence with the Qu'Appelle, bypassing Fort Ellice. Harry Handcock took mail from the others though and rode into Fort Ellice for the night, rejoining the next day.[46]

They were by now "a Motely crowd indeed," according to Redgrave. He was wearing "an old cotton shirt with plenty of holes (to let air in) & an old pair of dirty white pantaloons & shoes without socks with a small cap to complete my dress." The overlanders wore clothing that has changed little in the last century. Boots were generally knee-high pull-ons, though wellingtons were also popular. Pants or trousers, were baggy and comfortable, with button flies and suspenders for support. Belts, if worn, were wrapped around the pants to hold a pistol or knife and sometimes even a frying pan or cup. Shirts were also loose fitting, sometimes with large underarm gussets for freedom of movement. They did not usually have open fronts, but tie strings or buttons a few inches below the neck. As few shirts had pockets, vests were worn as receptacles for pipe, tobacco, and watch. Jackets were usually four-button dress jackets or a similar cut, but as the overlanders moved across the plains these might be augmented by a buckskin shirt, as in the case of Alexander, or a HBC wool capote. Most men were bearded and most wore a hat of some kind, from broad-brimmed sunshields to Scots bonnets.

The farther west, the more time on the plains, the less like tenderfoot easterners they looked. The altered exterior image reflected a similar change to the interior man. The easterners became overlanders ... the overlanders became westerners.

Love kept prospecting, his tracks dogged (more accurately, puppied) by Alexander. Each stream crossing was an excuse to unpack the gold pans. Usually they found a few specks of gold. "We have not the smallest doubt," George Flett wrote, "that if we could afford the time we could find gold in paying quantities here."[47]

On July 5 they passed the Touchwoods and noted the abandoned buildings. A board now pointed south toward the new post.[48]

Richard Alexander's mess. Five men. Alexander at nineteen years of age the leader; Harry and Alfred Handcock, ages eighteen and nineteen; James Carpenter, age twenty-two; and artist William G. R. Hind, the old man of the group at thirty.

"We did good miles today."

"Thirty miles he says."

"If I never see another ox's arse-end it'll be too soon."

"Why do you write in the damn book of yours each night?"

"To remember."

"Remember? My God—I just want this to end so's I can forget."

Alexander, after a flareup: "See here, Hind, this is rather difficult for me, but the boys are not happy with the way things have been going. Too much discontent. Nothing personal I suppose, you just don't fit in. So you'll have to choose another mess, you'll have to leave. Tomorrow. We'll divide with you fairly."[49]

Redgrave's diary, Friday, July 11, 1862:

> ... started 3:30 a.m. without breakfast had biscuit & collected strawberries for a beginning. It thundered and lightened fearfully and rained in torrents all night. it also hailed as large as marbles. Slept in wet clothes ... sometimes I am in water up to my knees 20 times a day ... getting very thin. ... if ever I am settled again it will be something more than Gold that will induce me again to forsake all comforts Wife family & everything one holds dear to roam over an unknown region in quest of Gold. ... I have left our camp today & now messing with Hinds it seems to me the beginning of a break up of the party I do not know how or with whom I shall go with whether with Ellis (& others) who is very kind to me or if Hinds & myself continue together at the diggings.

The two misfits formed a party of their own—Hind the temperamental artist and Redgrave the cantankerous copper. Redgrave's gruff exterior was a mask for his insecurities, self-doubts that rose to the surface each Sunday when his journal entries stretched to several pages of sermonizing with himself. On Sunday, July 13, on the south bank of the South Saskatchewan River he takes a cup of tea, spiked no doubt, and stretches out as a rifleman might (as riflemen would two decades later here at Batoche) and, with frequent pauses for navel gazing, writes.

He begins with paraphrasing the 23rd Psalm: "... who will lead us through the valley of the shadow of death where even there he will suffer no Ills to befall us where the tempter cannot come where robbers & thieves cannot exist . . ." and then slips into melancholia.

> I am then when thinking of home dissatisfied especially as I look on the scene before me with the outward un spiritual eye—for anyway life is seen but in fragments. I do not know but influence of fate seems great with me. But if I am erring I only err as the egoist [sic] and I think shape out of my ills some use that may profit myself in after years—still fate seems to me to hang like a shadow so vast on the heart that errs especially in venturing abroad to seek ones fortune and knows and reminds me of the sources of Joy only in others—I seem to go alone myself unfriended & remote—my present looks a waste before me & my past roving life a ruin—still I must now go forth to fill up my future.[50]

Red River farmers such as George Flett saw the prairies from a different perspective. Despite their interest in Saskatchewan gold, in their minds they saw the rich land over the handles of single-shared plow, not the lip of a gold pan. Flett wrote: "From Touchwood Hills to the South Branch, the soil is of the very best kind. . . . Surely it cannot be, that this extensive fertile country can long remain uninhabited.[51]

They walk surrounded by a canvas, blue-gray on top and buckskin below, seldom changing. Their days are filled with minor adventures and adapting to their new life. Redgrave complains that he is not able to mail letters home, then "2 half-breeds" pass bound for Fort Garry and Alexander forwards letters. A cart wheel collapses and Redgrave regards it destroyed until George Gunn shows him how to repair it "better than new." Evenings and Sundays are filled with mending carts, cleaning guns, washing clothes, baking bread, "trimming up a bit, for indeed we want it," as well as writing. Someone might break out a deck of cards, another a cornet or fiddle. On occasion there would be horse racing, running and jumping matches, or evening waterfowl hunts. After a few weeks' travel Alexander decided "to go through to Cariboo this fall as there is not a certainty of gold in paying quantities on the Saskatchewan, and also fear of scarcity of provisions."[52]

Love knew well the provisioning problems at Fort Edmonton. The fort was habitually short of food and Christie was antagonistic toward miners. This, and the unfounded rumor of Indians at Fort Garry, prompted a change in route. After crossing the South Saskatchewan River they would swing west toward the Eagle Hills, bypassing Fort Carlton in favor of hunting buffalo for winter provisions. As this would mean traversing Indian hunting grounds, a meeting was held and watches appointed. There was to be one captain and four men per watch and two watches per night; each watch would have to serve once every five nights. There was one other point of discussion. Mr. O'B. As he had guessed, something was going to happen. He was being dumped.

With O'Beirne safe in a cart, an armed group of the train's most capable plainsmen escorted him to the fort. Love, Flett, Gunn, Matheson, Sutherland, all hard Red River men, rode around the cart, and tagging along behind like puppies were Harry Hamilton and Richard Alexander. A Cree Indian trying to find favor came riding toward them warning that a Blackfoot had chased him. The escort scrambled. Gun covers flew off and pre-loaded guns were capped and cocked. It was a false alarm. The small party dropped O'Beirne in the lap of Fort Carlton residents, had a dinner of "green buffalo meat," and then struck across country to join up with the others. The train had progressed twenty-five miles while the small party had ridden forty.

As they swung west the tenor of the journey changed. They were joined by a Cree and his family seeking protection from the Blackfeet as far as the Eagle Hills. "Of course," Redgrave notes, "if they wanted him we should have to give him up or we might all be killed." The Cree's wife quite upset Alexander. "Saw today what a person would hardly believe Squaw picking lice from Crees head & eating them also teaching Child to do same—made me feel quite sick."[53]

Where the McMicking men had fired only in salutation and at a few ducks, the Saskatchewan Gold Expedition might well have been a gang of buffalo hunters. From the South Saskatchewan crossing they swung south of Duck Lake following the North Saskatchewan past the Elbow to Eagle Hills Creek. Here on July 18 Love shoots the first buffalo bull and the crew enjoy fresh meat instead of pemmican.

The next day Alexander and Sutherland run another bull. Alexander, the Toronto clerk, rifle to shoulder—cap on, hammer back—the crack of the rifle, the thump of the bullet, the smell of black powder, and momentary fog. He experiences his first kill, the momentary regret. He bypasses the moment of sacrifice, the symbolic bloodletting as the hunter's knife pierces the belly and the completion of the circle of life as blood soaks the earth. Alexander evades the hunter's obligation. A native, if he could have looked over Alexander's shoulder, would have spat on the ground as he read, "I cut out the tongue and as we did not know how to cut him up, that was all we took." For those who believe in the Great Balance Wheel in the Sky, the debt is paid. On returning to camp Alexander's horse steps in a badger hole, falls on his side, and snaps Alexander's rifle at the breech. This does not slow him down. When another herd is spotted he borrows Carpenter's revolver and joins the chase. Another nine fall to the guns. "We bid good-bye to pemmican for a while," Alexander wrote.

On this little expedition Harry Hamilton and A. Myers got lost. As he readies for bed Redgrave writes, "Told them not to go—fearful cold, Gold help them." The next day, a Sunday, dawned with still no sign so a fire was lit on a hill, a flag put up on a pole, and search parties sent to scour the countryside. No luck. "I cannot bear to think of having to write to Hamiltons and tell of Harry's fate," Alexander writes.

Monday. "A very nasty day, cold and rainy" with a strong wind blowing. The party waited for the lost overlanders and about 8:00 A.M. they straggled in. They were tired, wet, and hungry, having eaten only some berries and a couple of eaglets they robbed from a nest. The party moved on for a few hours, and Love shot another buffalo. "The meat is tough and not fat at this season," Alexander writes. "The best way is to make *Neeshac-ne-boop* of it, which is the Indian name for soup, with flour in it." They were now joined by another small band of Crees. As only one was mounted they suspected them to be on a horse-stealing foray. Surprisingly George Flett loaned his horse and Whitford loaned a gun and coat so a Cree could join in a buffalo chase. He kept riding and his squaw "vamosed the train also." Another buffalo cow was killed.

On July 23 in the Eagle Hills, east of Manitou Lake, Alexander finds himself in a different kind of a buffalo hunt for as he runs a cow the herd starts to move and soon he is in the center of a mass of hair, buffalo on every side. "When you are in one of these herds, the whole place seems galloping and the dust and clods of earth fly in clouds, as you pass through they still keep running the same direction so that they close in behind you, and if anything should happen of course you are made powder of." He drops the cow and then with Sutherland kills another bull. By July 25 the buffalo tally exceeds twenty-five.[54]

This day the trail leads past the north end of Manitou Lake to the Battle River crossing. They now swing north around the Blackfoot Hills to the Vermilion River. Love kills a bear and Alexander, on a Sunday hunt, loses his horse and has to walk back to camp. As he lights a fire and prepares to spend the night out a rescue party arrives.

The Vermilion River crossing takes a whole afternoon. A raft is made by lashing two carts together and then stretching a couple of tents and waterproof blankets under them. A line is stretched across the sixty-foot-wide creek and the boat hauled back and forth.

Although the last weeks of rain had swollen creeks and marshes, they did not have to put up with the continuous rain that so depressed the McMicking party, now well ahead beyond Fort Edmonton. On August 2 they pass the "Chain of Lakes," now called the Vermilion Lakes, and then passed Egg Lake, known by the Cree as *munawanis*, "the place where the eggs are gathered." Years later this will be renamed Whitford Lake for the Andrew Whitford family, kin of guide John Whitford, who settled there.[55]

Carpenter takes his turn at getting lost, and found; and Redgrave, suffering from dysentry, likely from too much green meat, says, "This day I repented my Journey & if I were back I think a certainty of gold would hardly induce me to come this way again—from a.m. til p.m. cold, wet bed & clothes bad food ... oh for the comfort of a settled life—still I must go through now and by the help of God mean to stick it till the last I am pretty tired all day walking such a road & thru Bush & water especially when my foot gives way as it sometimes does since I hurt it on the Mississippi River." A large bog that "shakes for 20 feet at a time" makes this section of trail difficult. Alexander takes the increasing rain and poor trail in stride. Redgrave tires. He is hungry enough, he says, "to eat a dead donkey." Which only shows he really is not that hungry at all, as he was soon willing to eat much worse.

The hunting was over for now. The days were filled with fords and bridge building. August 6 they crossed Beaver Creek. Though the bridges of the previous party were a small help most had been washed away. Alexander's ox ran into a tree and split his cart. A succession of troublesome creeks are crossed in the last three days.

At 1:30 in the afternoon of Friday, August 8, a dull and rainy day, the Saskatchewan Gold Expedition arrived at the Saskatchewan River across from Fort Edmonton. They left Fort Garry eight days after McMicking and were now seventeen days behind. With nothing better to do they decided to cross that afternoon. The Fort Edmonton clerk noted their arrival in the daily journal: "Arrivals of a third party of miners. Weather cloudy. Men working some today as we gave them rations. A party of sixty-three men headed by Messrs. Love and Flett arrived some for Bow River some for this place some to go by the Jasper House Pass."[56]

After a good supper and some trading Redgrave ended his journal on an upnote. "Things looking rather more cheery," Young Alexander, randy Richard: "Most of us went up to the Fort and had a dance in the large room there. We had some good fun scraping it with the half breed girls."

*L to R; Stephen Redgrave joined the small 1862 Saskatchewan Gold Expedition in an effort to find a party in which he could feel important. He traveled in company with William Hind, the artist, who documented so much of the journey in sketches, watercolors and oils. A self portrait.(BCARS 6950; PAC CN-13964)*

*Richard Alexander (BCARS)*    *George Baillie (BCARS)*    *John Bowron (BCARS)*

*Samuel Chubbock (NHS)*    *Leonard Crysler  (Author)*    *R.A. Cunningham (BCARS)*

*John Fannin (BCARS)*    *Andrew Fletcher (BCARS)*    *Alexander L. Fortune (BCARS)*

*William Fortune (BCARS)* *Joseph Halpenny (Pete Dady)* *A.O. Handcock (BCARS)*

*Robert Harkness (Author)* *John Mara (BCARS)* *Robert McMicking (BCARS)*

*Thomas McMicking (BCARS)* *Archibald McNaughton (BCARS)* *Florien Mickle (BCARS)*

*Eustace Pattison (BCARS)*    *William Rennie (BCARS)*    *Augustus Schubert (BCARS)*

*Catherine Schubert (BCARS)*    *James Schubert (BCARS)*    *John Stevenson (BCARS)*

*Archibald Thompson (BCARS)*    *George Tunstall (BCARS)*    *Robert Warren (BCARS)*

# Chapter Eleven

## McMicking Party—At Fort Edmonton

Letters from Fort Edmonton let the folks at home know what was happening with wandering sons, where they had been, where they were going. Amidst the camp noise and confusion, Dobson Prest grabbed a few spare moments between chores to write his mother a lengthy letter, explaining that it had to be written quickly as their supplies were getting low and they had to keep moving, and that it might be disjointed by distractions.

While I sit and write, the bones are sounding on one side the fiddle on another, the banjo on another, the Cornopean and Saric horn peal forth their notes together with 13 or 14 of the best singers that I ever heard....

We have divided into four messes have a tent for each mess, 6 men to a mess. Mess No. 4 used 2 bags of flour while ours mess used one. Our provisions will last us 50 days, but the way they have been wasting them they would not last half the time.... It would make [you laugh] to see our company, all with the exception of 3 persons have got their hair but as short as it is possible ... it is difficult to keep the scalp clean. The red men not having tweasers could not scalp.

Now Mamma you would like to know something about my clothes and purse. They have both held out first-rate, the company is in my debt I think as much as will pay my share of the guide-money through to Cariboo. And some private individuals are in my debt to the amount of $3.50, just as good as cash, and I have four crown pieces in my satchel, worth here, $1.25 each and loose change enough to pay our travelling female companion for my washing. I would here say that since I left I only undertook to wash once, and it was a failure, that is a job I will not undertake if I can help it.[1]

Robert Harkness, the lovelorn husband torn apart from his young wife, Sabrina, months ago, details the events of the journey, dwelling in particular on the last two weeks of rain. He has found gold here in the Saskatchewan but explains that provisions are in such short supply they can do nothing but move on.

I never was more healthy in my life But I am so altered in appearance you would hardly know me. I am tanned to about the color of a piece of sole-leather, I am as lean as old Steve Lock, as rugged as a raftsman & fit to dig with an Irishman.

In closing he adds:

Oh! with what a yearning love my thoughts wander home. Home! O Sabrina nothing but a pressing necessity induced me to leave a home blessed with all the affection the most craving heart could desire & I hope I shall not be very long absent.

As soon as the overlanders were silhouetted against the southern sky, the Reverend Mr. Woolsey had gone to visit, crossing in true missionary style in a "pemmican trough," the boats having been swept downstream by high water. Joseph E. Brazeau, in charge during Christie's absence, and assistant Mr. Alexander, waited until a boat had been brought up the next day, then "went across to convince the miners to pass by the Couonais [Kootenay] Pass, but found them obstinate and determined to go by Jasper House [Yellowhead Pass]."

Fortune and some of his friends were pleased to meet clerk Brazeau, but offended by his morality. "Here was a gentleman in authority, who had a wife in one of the southern States, living with an Indian woman, who seemed quite a superior person. We felt shocked at such conduct."[3]

The fort too was a disappointment. It was not operated with any sense of military orderliness and had the appearance of a trash heap. The dogs did not help. Fortune inventoried six hundred. "Such a howling and barking as these dogs indulged in was terrifying and disagreeable. They sometimes got out of the enclosure and played havoc with our meats and pemican." Hunniford says, "Fort Edmonton is a large and very dirty establishment ... the Language is English and French the people whites and half Breeds the fort at present is in a starving condition in consequence of the scarcity of Buffalo."[4]

Clearly the fort's people were hungry. Numerous references in the journal indicate men off work because of lack of rations or being allowed time to hunt. The overlanders could not reprovision here and careful attention had to be paid to the remaining stores. The depletion or shifting of buffalo herds was only one reason for the fort often being short of provisions. Supply routes were not always reliable. In 1860 for instance the HBC ship *Kitty* failed to reach York Factory. Fort Garry's supplies could be brought from Hudson Bay or St. Paul, but in the 1860s Edmonton's goods were still largely received via the arctic route through Hudson's Bay.

For all three parties, McMicking's, the St. Peters, and the Saskatchewan Gold Expedition, Fort Edmonton was a place of decision. The final choice of routes, mountain passes, and where to mine had been postponed. "We'll decide when we get to Fort Edmonton. We'll decide later," they had said. Later was now. Letters and journals indicated some indecision. Two days later the post clerk notes, "Called to one of their assemblies some of the miners undecided by what pass to go after our representation of the nearly impossibility of getting through."[5]

McMicking met with Brazeau, Alexander, Woolsey, Thomas Clover, and several freemen about routes. "All parties . . . agreed that the Boundary, Cootanie and Sinclair [Kananaskis] Passes were the easiest and presented the fewest difficulties; but recommended the Leather, Cow-Dung Lake, or Jasper Pass [all the Yellowhead now] for our purpose, as being the shortest and most direct way to Cariboo; altho' some of them represented the road as nearly impassable, and foresaw difficulties and dangers which they considered almost insurmountable. After thoroughly examining the matter, and carefully comparing notes we decided to try the Leather Pass."[6]

About twenty-five of the McMicking group decided to stay on and search for Saskatchewan gold, the remainder set to choosing a guide and trading oxen and carts for packhorses and saddles. "Capts Mcmicman Watty and Robertson made arrangements with Andrew Cardinal to take them as far as tete Jones Cash Men doing nothing but trading with the miners."[7]

Andrew, or André, Cardinal was one of the large Métis family living in the St. Albert–Lac Ste. Anne area. According to McMicking, Cardinal was born at Jasper House and had traveled the trail to Edmonton no less than twenty-nine times and the Yellowhead Pass several times. There was no better guide to be found.[8]

Little fur-trade work was done during the overlanders' visit to the fort, much to Brazeau's annoyance. Trading was more important. For the overlanders trading was a necessity, for the residents of the fort it was a traditional recreation begun with the visits of the first Europeans and reaching its height during the fur-trade rendezvous of the 1830s. James Sellar, though, found it a little frustrating—he was anxious to be on the move.

[From the 23rd] till the 28 was spent trading with the halfbreeds & Indians for horses and Saddles & Saddle bags to pack with. This part of the business [sic] . . . was the most wearisom of any thing we had to encounter, As they did not seem to know any thing about the value of money. They would ask 25 pounds Stirling for a horse, and take no less, & at the same time take 2 lbs Tea, 8 lbs sugar & 100 lbs flour, & which can be bought at the Fort, when they have them, for 12 dollars, and we traided for ammunition giving a Gun & a little amunition for a horse that we could not buy for less than 120 Dollars in money, & some we got for about $10 worth of old clothes. I have seen them pay to our company for a common clay pipe, so high as 50 cts while those who had any Tobacco had to watch it very close to keep them from stealing it. A number of the company bought their saddles from the H.B. Company for which they were charged $3.50 while actually were not worth more than 40¢. Another act of the keepers at Edmonton is worth notice. The first of the carts that came over they took advantage to buy for $10. & as soon as they heard that the carts were all for sale they put them down to $5- while they could not buy them out at the settlement for less than $20 such was the extortion they practised all the way through the H.B. Teritory. However they did not get any at 5 & as we determined not to traid any more with them, it took us two days longer to get an outfit.[9]

Woolsey explained that since the Palliser expedition the price of horses had increased. Earlier they could be purchased for five to ten pounds each, but Palliser had neeeded so many that prices inflated to twenty-six pounds apiece. The overlanders, who had to abandon their carts for the trail ahead, were paying twelve to twenty pounds. Woolsey suggested that future parties bring trade goods rather than cash. Hunniford turned a profit. He sold all his extras and made enough to have his baggage packed. "1 bottle brandy $5.00 1 old coat $5.00 1 pair knee boots $5.00 2 towels $00.50 1 pair rubber leggins $00.50. 1 gun shot Belt and Powder Flask $4.00. Paid the company [Huntingdon Company] $5.00 for carrying 20 lbs of Bagge promised Bill Fortune $5.00 for carrying 20 lbs which is all the Bagge I have."[10] The overlanders were getting a first-hand lesson in the law of supply and demand.

On Tuesday morning, July 29, the McMicking party, now reduced to 125 men with 140 animals, headed north for the settlement of St. Albert at Big Lake.

## McMicking Party—Fort Edmonton to Tête Jaune Cache

McMicking's departure from Fort Garry had a certain ponderous majesty; the leaving of Fort Edmonton was comic. Without carts, supplies had to be strapped to oxen, a situation the oxen were not accustomed to. As quickly as they were loaded, the beasts unloaded themselves, scattering flour, bedrolls, clothes, and tools across the landscape. Oxen ran off dragging sacks and packs. Men tried to stop them and received bumps, bruises, and hooves in various parts of their anatomy "while the horse & mule drivers would laugh fit to kill themselves." They were thankful for a short trip this day, only about ten miles to the new settlement and mission of St. Albert.

Lacombe had moved his mission here to be closer to supplies at the fort after spending several hungry winters at Lac Ste. Anne. Even though this area was settled, there was only one bridge so again the men had to haul logs and swim the creeks and rivers to get their pack animals across.

Sellar, the protestant, actually more anti-Catholic than pro anything, takes the opportunity to take a shot at the "Romanists" at Lac Ste. Anne.

Came to the Settlement on the West side of the Lake, Where Satan has his Synagogue & Parsonage & three Priests to superentend the affairs so we concluded to halt & see the Eliphant as we passed along there we made the acquaintance of three young nuns from Montreal & who were wonderfully delighted at meeting with people from the same section of the country as they were themselves, Especially as they had no opportunity of ever hearing from home, exiled, as they were from all that was near & dear, & from every species of White people save the Priests for Whoes pleasure, they were there.

A general meeting was held to "ascertain the state of the roads ahead and collect the money to pay a Guide." They had hired Felix Monroe to pack eight hundred pounds until they had used enough supplies to have room on their own animals. Felix was the halfbreed son of Hugh Monroe, a former HBC servant who now lived with the Blackfeet as War Chief Rising Wolf.[11]

William Sellar caught up with the main party soon after they left Lac Ste. Anne. He had waited with McFie at Fort Edmonton. As they had hoped, St. Peters men who arrived the next day carried mail and a May 27 issued of the *Globe*, the most up-to-date news they had received. In that issue was the announcement of James Carpenter, now with the SGE, dissolving his law partnership to head west.

When they started the morning of August 2, just west of Lac Ste. Anne, they began a tedium of days. McMicking, Putnam, and Sellar went ahead with axes and began clearing brush and building bridges so as to not to detain the stock when it came through. What faced them were two hundred miles of spruce forest and swamp with several major river crossings. Animals sank in the swamp and mud and had to be pried out. Men walked in mud knee deep, then waded waist-deep in water. The company spread out over several miles, the last straggling into camp hours after the leaders. Progress was marked by river crossings.

On the fourth James Sellar's party traveled a "desperate bad" road and arrived at the Pembina River, a rapid current 160 yards wide. On the far side of the river was burning ground that some like McMicking took to be the eruption of a volcano, but Sellar correctly surmised that is was a coal seam that had caught fire. Campfires that night used coal instead of wood, and the blacksmiths of the group proclaimed it "a superior article."

The Huntingdon party tried to cross with a raft the following morning but the current was too strong. They again learned the wisdom of having a guide. Cardinal and Monroe took the tents and rubber blankets and stretched them out on the ground. Into these they piled supplies, then folded the tops together as one would a grain sack, tied them closed with a rope, attached another rope for towing, and with two horses towed the "round boat" across the river. This performance was repeated many times, with only one pack getting damp. On the other side, James Sellar and Putnam again took the lead with axes.

On the sixth they crossed the Buffalo Dung (Lobstick) River. On the seventh Sellar gave his ax to Wattie. A felon on his finger was swelling and his hand was so sore he could not use it. By the next day it was much worse. With the sore on his finger, a boil on his leg, and lumbago in his back, Sellar felt he was on his last legs when they came to swim the Root (now Carrot) River.

Who would know that men had passed this way? How could a man leave his mark, proof of his presence? As the overlanders of the 1840s and 50s crossing the Great American Desert had carved their notes of passage on the sandstone of Independence Rock, so the overlanders of the Great Lone Land carved theirs in the bark of spruce trees. By blazing off part of the bark and using the black end of a burnt stick, or a crayon if one was available, names could be written in the patch. The resin dried and formed a varnish that preserved writing for years. Some of the men made their mark here. Ten years later their notes were read by Sandford Fleming of the Canadian Pacific Railway survey. On September 4, 1872, Fleming approached the McLeod River and on the east side found a tree note, partially obliterated:

August 10th, 1862............................................................................................
....................................................................................................................
.................................................... East Tilbury ....................................................
.................................................... and....................................................................
.................................................... Robert Campb ................................................
....................................................................................................................
.............................................for Cariboo................................................
.............................................................................a hard road to travel.[12]

McMicking found a different note of passage. Beside the trail they came on a solitary grave. On a tree was carved: "Here lie the mortal remains of James Doherty, who died while passing through these wilds in 1860.[13]

It was a river a day now. At the MacLeod on the ninth a few almost drowned. Wilcox and Gilbert had disregarded the guide's advice and tried to wade the river rather than cross on horseback or on top of the oxen's load. The rocky bottom gave poor footing. With water surging against them they came to a point were every time they tried to lift a foot they were in danger of being swept downstream. Straining "every nerve to keep their feet" they stayed in position until others rode horses to them. They grabbed handfuls of tail, threw themselves on their faces and were towed ignominiously to shore, wetter but wiser. The next day being Sunday a camp was made on the river's west bank. They ate only two meals on Sundays now, a brunch and supper.

The Huntingdon company were again anxious to move faster than the main party. On Monday they and the St. Thomas company were up at 2:20 and were ready to go by 5:15. As André Cardinal was to go with them there was some confusion and objection by those who wanted to stay in camp an extra day to rest their cattle. The argument was finally settled by Cardinal. "I am paid as guide," he said, "so I go with the first party, suppose they be only two in number."[14]

That evening Felix Monroe explained that his contract was up. He gave a horse to the company in return for their kindness and expressed his regret at not being able to go on to Cariboo. He had obviously done a commendable job and had become popular so Captain Wattie took up a collection and gave Monroe a rifle, rubber blanket, and a pair of black pants. The next morning he bid goodbye and set out over the Fort Edmonton Trail.

They crossed the James River on the thirteenth and on the fifteenth struck the Athabasca. Until now the overlanders had been traveling in a green tunnel. Above were the branches of spruce trees, broken by occasional patches of blue light; ahead was the eastern end of a westbound horse or ox, or at best another man's back; and below was water or mud;

there were no broad vistas. After two weeks of swampy struggle they could see rising ahead the majestic *"montagnes de Roche,"* as Leguarder St. Pierre first named them in 1752. It was a sight for which they were completely unprepared. They had seen no photographs, no books, no calendars, no television to foretell the vision. It was an experience impossible to recreate and difficult to imagine today.

Thomas McMicking: "On Wednesday, the 13th, precisely at 12 o'clock noon, as the train emerged from a thick spruce swamp ... we obtained the first distinct view of the Rocky Mountains. Although we were yet one hundred miles from them, their dark outline was plainly visible far above the level of the horizon, and their lofty snowclad peaks, standing out in bold relief against the blue sky beyond, and glistening in the sunlight, gave them the appearance of fleecy clouds floating in the distance. The company were enraptured at the sight of them; for whatever dangers or difficulties might possibly be in store for us among them, all were heartily tired of the endless succession of hills and streams and swamps and swamps and streams and hills and were willing to face almost any danger that would be likely to terminate or vary our toils."

Later he added: "If it be true, as has been said, that 'wherever there is vastness, there dwells sublimity,' we were presented with a view at once sublimely grand and overpowering."

Sellar did not get a commanding view until the fifteenth when he wrote: "Camped for night on the top of a very high hill, where we had a very commanding view of the Rocky Mountains. They appeared like great Lakes of water set on edge one above another & covered with white breakers."

And again Hunniford (who would have starved if like Charles Dickens he had been paid by the word), straight and to the point, "Had a splendid view of the mountains in the afternoon."

The Rockies were known to the native peoples by a variety of names. The Cree called them *as-siniwati;* the Stonies, *ni-a-ha;* and the Blackfeet, *nis-tokis.* This backbone of the continent is more than a wall of rock that must be crossed by westbound emigrants, more than a stone barrier. The mountains form not only a physical and mental barrier but, like the Mississippi, a frontier. On the other side life was, life is, different. For the overlanders the mountains had been a goal and journey's end could surely not be far ahead.

The stock weakened. A mule was left behind "from the effects of a severe wound it had got in the foreleg with a pick which was carelessly in the bottom of the saddle baggs," and a couple of days later a horse was abandoned "from a wound it had received in the breast just below the left fore leg."[15]

As they moved deeper into the rocky vastness the enclosing rock brought a depression to some of the men. After the open horizons of the plains the snow-covered peaks that leaned and towered above were claustrophobic. On Sunday the seventeenth there was the temptation to press on as most of the parties were short of food, but again they decided to trust in providence and rest. Sellar, for one, was depressed, "The day seemed long & passed off very lonely I could not keep from thinking that starvation must be the fate of many of us long e'ar we could reach the civilized World on the other side of the mountains ... while every day was bringing with it new trouble, & trail not easey to be endured."

Though Sellar seldom mentions his wife, it was her he thought of this lonely day:

> When we two parted
> In silence & tears,
> To sever for years,
> Pale grew thy cheek, & cold,
> Colder thy kiss,
> How true that moment foretold
> Trails like this!

They camped one night beneath the towering rock column of Roche Miette, the sheer cliff that walls the southern valley side, over which a voyageur by the name of Miette dangled his feet. Apocryphal or not, the story captured the men's imaginations and a few tried to duplicate the feat but succeeded only in climbing to the top of a nearby slope.[16]

On the nineteenth they reached the old crossing to Jasper House. Cardinal called a meeting. He gave the company two route choices: the south side of the Athabasca River, where they would have to ascend and descend a high, treacherous trail and cross one river; and the north side, where there was a better trail but two bad rivers to ford. It took an hour to make the decision. The poor swimmers won and the south side was chosen.

A few rods west of Roche Miette, where the rocky precipice casts a morning shadow on the trail, the Athabasca River runs hard into a rocky ridge and, after a halfhearted attempt at washing it away, veers slightly northward before resuming its eastern flow. The river's erosion had left a steep western face around which the trail must climb, beginning where the river eddied around the face, a place called Disaster Point. From here the trail climbs southward, fenced on the left by timber; on the right is the ever-increasing drop down the steeply angled rock face. This was Cardinal's treacherous trail.

The rocky path skirted the righthand fall close enough to give vertigo. Blanchford's horse missed its footing and "canted end over end about 140 feet down, packs and all, when he landed against a tree & remained there till help was afforded." Another two feet and it would have dropped over a nine-hundred-foot cliff. Footsteps became more cautious. Because of the narrowness of the trail, now only a foot wide, the packs rubbed the uphill side and threatened to push the animals over. They climbed to seventeen hundred feet and could plainly see Jasper House below them on the shores of Jasper Lake. "A perfect picture of loneliness and solitude," McMicking called it.[17]

The knee-destroying descent dropped them down to the Rocky River ford. They traveled the ridge between Talbot and Jasper lakes and camped that night on the banks of the Athabasca at the foot of the Colin Range (known to them as Fraser's Mountain), named for Colin Fraser at Lac Ste. Anne. The morning of the twentieth saw them fording the

Athabasca downstream of the Maligne. They camped at what Cardinal told them was the site of old Fort Henry, built by William Henry who was here with David Thompson during the winter of 1810–11. Henry House may have been built across the river, in which case the pile of logs they camped near was a shack built by Joseph La Rocque in 1825.[18]

Overlanders' journals portray a sense of comradeship, a feeling that here were men who stuck together through thick and thin. But this was not always the case. After the men had forded the cold Miette and camped early, a fight broke out "between two Bullies from St. Thomas." (Hunniford says in Brocklebank's Waterloo party.) For forty minutes they hammered away at each other in a "regular pitched fight." Finally the one that was losing gave up, saying that the other did not fight fair.

Sellar celebrated his birthday the next day, the twenty-second, or rather would liked to have. Instead, he got up at 2:00 A.M. to get breakfast for the ax party. The others waited with the stock until close to 9:00 A.M. before leaving and turning up the Miette River into the Yellowhead Pass. Thomas McMicking says their progress was "rather slow, both on account of the great quantity of fallen timber that obstructed our path, and the number of times we had to ford the stream. It is a mountain torrent that rushes down a rocky gorge . . . we waded it no less than seven times." By four o'clock that afternoon they were at the headwaters of the Fraser River, the Continental Divide, the boundary of Rupert's Land and the new colony of British Columbia.

It was downhill to Quesnel and Sellar mentions that the descent down the Fraser was "very great but quite gentle and regular." The gentleness was an illusion, as the axmen were soon to discover. Camp was made on the shore of Cow-Dung (now Yellowhead) Lake.

Their course traveled the north side of the Fraser River, now a small mountain stream. They chopped their way through thick timber and masses of windfall, waded creeks and rivers running high with rain water, tramped through swamps and along lake shores. And food ran low. The beef was not a complete enough diet and some of the men showed the symptoms of scurvy. "I'm so hungry I could eat a skunk from the back-end forward," one of the men said, and got his chance as skunk, crow, and porcupine were thrown into the pot.

The stock were short of feed; pasturage was poor. Oxen were killed as the pemmican ran out. Always up ahead could be heard the sound of the choppers, clearing the trail.

Moose River was crossed. Sunday followed but it was no longer a day of rest—food was too short to linger. They traveled the shore of Moose Lake, as often in as out of the water, and spent a night camped in the timber, where they had to level rocks to find a sleeping pad and all night had to avoid the hooves of oxen and horses looking for a little feed. A shale slope a little east of Cloud Cap or Robson's Mountain made added work for they could not trust their horses and had to pack supplies on their backs and then carefully guide the animals over. Cardinal told them that of the twenty-nine times he had passed the monolith he had seen the top only once. But now it was clear and they could see the ice- and snow-covered peak towering above the junction of the Fraser and Robson rivers, then known as the Grand Forks of the Fraser.

Thomas McMicking writes: "We were aroused from our slumbers on Wednesday morning by our guide shouting through the camp, 'Hurrah! for Tete Jaune Cache,' and were informed that we should reach the Cache, if not misfortune befel us, some time during the day."

James Sellar, Wednesday the twenty-seventh: "All hands were of foot at 2 a.m. . . . the travelling was very good we got on well until 3 p.m. when the horse carrying our cooking utensils & all the dishes & China Plate got tired of life & ran over the bank into the Fraser & was drowned sinking with all his cargo, & was wash up onto a sand bar about a mile below with nothing on him except his saddle. . . . At 4:15 p.m. we came to the long looked for Cass when we found a camp of the Shouswap Indians."

With huckleberry wine supplied by the Shuswaps they toasted their arrival at Tête Jaune Cache, forgetting momentarily the decision facing them.

## St. Peters Party—Fort Edmonton to Tête Jaune Cache

The dust from the McMicking party was still settling on the wooden walls of Fort Edmonton when the St. Peters men with their mules and wagons arrived on the southern riverbank on the last day of July. On the first day of August they crossed the river, amidst the confusion of a brigade of fifty-four men under Mr. Cunningham leaving with six York boats. The post encumbents must have felt invaded as this second group of gold-fevered men crossed their sanctum's moat.

At Fort Edmonton they found a few of the McMicking party in addition to the men who had decided to stay on the Saskatchewan side. William Sellar and McFie were here waiting for mail, as was Cogswell of Detroit, one of the Huntingdon party. Cogswell had decided to change parties, or perhaps had changed his mind about mining the Saskatchewan, and he joined the Americans.[19]

The hot weather cooled slightly with rain and clouds while the Americans busied themselves with preparation, selling and trading their wagons for horses. A few men went down to the Saskatchewan's gravel bars but "found only the color of gold," not enough to stay.

In the few days they spent at the fort life continued in its usual rhythm: the men were off hunting; a group of Sarcees came to trade a couple of buffalo robes for tobacco and were sent off quickly as they had brought no provisions; one of the priests came to visit. From the priest, one of Lacombe's brothers in the cloth, the St. Peters men learned that at Ste. Anne two more overlanders awaited them, one in some discomfort.

W. W. Morrow, whose head had been planted in the mud by a cart wheel on the Qu'Appelle crossing, was a slow learner. At Ste. Anne he had some trouble loading and his ox took off. Morrow tried to stop him clinging to his horns, "and for his effort received the imprint of a hoof on his face." Archibald McNaughton, also of the Montreal company, offered to stay with him at Lac Ste. Anne where the nuns of the mission could care for him, and wait for a following party. Both men were impressed with the attention and kindness of the nuns, who were interested in hearing all the two miners could tell them of their native Montreal.

These were the same Sisters of Charity that the Moore brothers had traveled with from St. Paul in 1858. They arrived at Lac Ste. Anne on September 24 after fifty-one days of walking. They opened a school and orphanage, both of which were later moved to St. Albert, where the Youville Convent was founded.[20]

The two overlanders also had the opportunity to accept the hospitality of Colin Fraser, the fifty-seven-year-old trader in charge of the HBC post at the lake. Fraser had come to Rupert's Land in 1827 as Governor Simpson's piper and had not left the country since. He loaned the men fishing tackle and books and in the evening played his celebrated pipes.[21]

The St. Peters party left Fort Edmonton on August 6 and stopped at Lac Ste. Anne to pick up McNaughton and Morrow. The priest in Lac Ste. Anne had a "box of Homoeopathic medicines," but little knowledge of how to use them. Dr. Simonton, using McNaughton as an interpreter, was able to explain how to use the various medicines, enabling the priest "to minister to the wants of his people, both bodily and spiritually." As an expression of thanks he gave the two men a bucket of milk, a welcome addition to their sparse provisions of pemmican and flour.[22]

Now numbering at least twenty-three, the St. Peters men headed west along the terrible swampy road that the McMicking party had churned into a quagmire. Again their journey is undetailed. Copland and Davis merely report: "After leaving Edmonton, up to Tete Jaune Cache, the road as a general thing was very hard on the animals on account of swamps and fallen timber. Feed for the animals, however, was good until within a couple of days of the Cache." Like McMicking's, their journey was a succession of bogs, windfall, and river crossings that kept the men muddy and wet. Provisions ran low and the men were hungry.

They reached the Cache September 8 and found that fifteen men from the earlier parties were still here. More of the Saskatchewan Gold Expedition were close behind. Their choice of routes over the mountains to Cariboo, overland south to the Thompson or down the Fraser. None was appealing, but a choice had to be made.

## Saskatchewan Gold Expedition—Fort Edmonton to Tête Jaune Cache

At Edmonton we had a ball in the large room of the Fort on the night of our arrival, the ladies the half-breeds' wives of the men of the Fort, and the dances were all reels, etc., dance with great spirit. When you wanted a partner you never spoke (of course that would have been of no use) but you touched any of the women and walked off to your place and presently the partner chosen would walk up to your side; after the dance was over the gentlemen walked to his seat the lady to hers.[23]

It was a grand time. Months from home, after weeks of walking, sleeping in rain, and buffalo hunting, they found themselves in the middle of the wilderness dancing with wild abandon with native women. "Our travelling . . . was quite pleasant. We all kept together to Fort Edmonton, and from there we scattered like sheep having no shepard; some for the Cariboo, some for Salmon River, others up the Saskatchewan River." So John Atkinson succinctly summed up the disposition of the SGE in a letter to the Reverend Mr. Corbett, who, by the time he received the news, was behind bars with lots of reading time.[24]

While half the men prepared to winter near Fort Edmonton, the rest made ready to carry on in the tracks of the McMicking and St. Peters parties. Like those before them they sold their carts for saddles and packs, the carts fetching ten dollars each, and traded for whatever provisions they could find. Extra clothes were auctioned off. Love, according to Redgrave, was "getting gold on the Saskatchewan—I think in paying quantities with a rocker."[25]

Goodbyes were to be said. Alexander bade farewell to his friend Harry Hamilton and to his hero Timoleon Love. All the Red River men plus Wonnacott, Hutchinson, Atkinson, Jonson, the Glassford brothers, and others were staying east of the Rockies—in total about half the party—becoming what Americans had called "wintering soldiers," those who stayed at army posts for the winter.[26]

It remained only to load the pack animals and drive them west. There was a moment's delay for they had to pay a man to find the horses. "Indeed it is suspect he hid them," Alexander writes. The sting of the plains was not limited to Indians.

Poor Redgrave. He was in no mood for an ostreperous ox: "First one strap & then another breaking—plates knives & forks flying in the air flour spilling on the ground ox running away frightened to death—what a desperate plight we are in I do not know what we will do if it will not pack our provisions."[27]

The ox did pack the supplies and on August 12, after only four days at the post, the tattered remnants of the SGE plodded west. They were joined by one of the McMicking group, little Andrew Fletcher, who inexplicably had been left behind by his partner McNaughton. Picture Redgrave: on his back fifty pounds, leading his miserable ox in one hand, carrying in the other a shovel with a large kettle swinging from its end. To say the least he was discontent. "This pack spade and kettle can go to Hong Kong before I'll carry them again," he grumbled.

At Lac Ste. Anne the party stopped to rest the cattle and another "Rag fair" ensues. Redgrave bartered a scarf for two large whitefish and a silk necktie for a bushel of potatoes. Anything to lighten the load. Alexander traded a cotton handkerchief for fish, another for butter, milk, and bread, and three needles, a skein of thread, and two rows of pins for a pair of moccasins.

On Sunday morning Redgrave was awakened by the sound of the church bell calling the settlers to devotions and he slips into another reminiscence, this time about those left behind and the faithful friends he has known. He concluded that his faithful Dog was the best companion he ever had. Something had gone out of Redgrave. This is his last personal Sunday sermon and his regular diary lasts only another few days. The notations continue but they are filled with information that could only have been gleaned at the journey's end. Faced with a daily exhaustion he has seldom, if ever, known he packs his journal at the bottom of his pack and tells no more of his feelings or daily toil.

They hired a guide here for sixty-dollars and board, a man named Joe—no other name—who performs much less satisfactory service than Cardinal does for the advance party. At Ste. Anne, Felix Munroe visited on his way back to Edmonton. He told them what the road ahead was like. Difficult. Miles and miles of spruce forest and swamp. Day after day rivers were forded, swamps crossed, and as animals became bogged down they had to be unloaded, pulled and pushed out, reloaded, and then the process repeated while ax parties went ahead to hew a path in a cycle that left a man scarcely time to take a deep breath of relief. And so it was for them, their journey made easier by the clearing of the vanguard and more difficult by the bottomless pits of churned-up mud. But somewhere up ahead was Cariboo.

In the next few days both Redgrave and Alexander fell into water courses and both came close to drowning. Alexander sprained his ankle and was then kicked by a horse on which he is obliged to ride. Two horses died of strangulation, caught in their tethering ropes; oxen were abandoned, lost, and dragged through swamps. The small party broke up even further, the smaller messes of five of six men leapfrogging each other down the trail. Some took the Sabbath rest; others continued. The guide was useless. He had not brought a horse, would not help with loading, slept late, ate too much, and was often behind the leaders—altogether very unguidelike.

Through all this the overlanders' photojournalist, Hind, busily sketched in his small notebook. Like the later photographers, he recorded the daily camp life and trail—an ox mired, a river crossing, the men playing cards or writing home, a thunder shower, an ox running off—all with a few, quick pencil strokes. Later he will turn many of these into watercolors, and a few into fine oil paintings.

The Rocky Mountains. The overwhelming sight and experience caused some to craft poetry, quote scripture verses, or write fervent letters home. The paradox was that the closer to paradise, El Dorado, they came the more unattainable it was. When morale, provisions, and physical strength were at their lowest came the most difficult terrain of the journey. The awe of the scenic beauty soon gave way to more pragmatic views on how to prevent starvation and scurvy.

They reached the Athabasca River on September 4 and six of the party were nominated to hurry ahead and begin building canoes at the Cache. Elected were the guide Joe; William Burgess, the first overlander to arrive in St. Paul, four months ago; David Jones, described by Redgrave as "as determined little fellow"; Philip Leader; George Thompson, "a rather old man" Alexander called him; and Richard Alexander.[28]

This small party rushed ahead up the Miette, crisscrossing the stream as the earlier parties had, getting wet over and over. They reached Cow-Dung Lake on the seventh. On Monday the eighth they woke to find themselves trapped on an island. The guide got across the stream and then Burgess paid him to carry his baggage and then himself across. Thompson and Alexander stripped to the waist and tried to cross, but were caught in the current and swept downstream. Both survived but Thompson had a fever and so they settled in to await the main party, four days later. Reduced to eating one crow and two squirrels, they were supported by the larger party as the group moved on to Moose Lake on September 11.

Alexander's horse suffered an internal injury and after bleeding from the mouth for a day had to be left. Oxen were slaughtered for food. An animal Alexander called Beelsebub "got stuck fast in a mudhole, so after working for a long while with him, I shot him and left the pack till I could return for it."[29]

The arrival at the Cache was not triumphant. Alexander staggered in on the morning of September 16 to find a few of his party already here and more scattered behind. The men limped in. Some were injured, some were suffering from the symptoms of scurvy, all were exhausted. James Carpenter was worn out, exhausted, and even to keep his diary required energy long since spent; Robert Holloway had injured his back; Alexander was still limping; Redgrave was morose.[30]

Afraid to stop the weary men set to work to build canoes, fed and aided by the Shuswaps of Tête Jaune Cache. How long to Cariboo?

## Fraser River Parties

The hot August sun burned down on the encampment of overlanders at Tête Jaune Cache. Already the willows were red and the trembling aspen leaves were tinged with gold brought on by night frost. Smoke from many small fires drifted through riverbank cottonwoods and willows, smudging blackflies and mosquitoes. It wafted across the shallow sandbars where salmon spawned and mingled with the oily smoke of Indian fires, drying the winter's food supplies. From upstream, the sound of axes and saws could be heard as they bit large chips from cedar trees born in previous centuries, trees large enough yet light enough to make log rafts. There was a sense of urgency. Cold and hunger had already touched the men and there was no trail from here to Cariboo as had been rumored. All that faced them were the waters of the Fraser.

Arrival at the Cache had brought a certain relief. There were eight to ten Shuswaps here at the McLennan River mouth (five had been killed in an avalanche earlier that spring on their way to trade at Jasper House), and they brought five forty- to sixty-pound salmon to Fortune's camp. "Think of one fish being all seventeen men could eat in three meals, and we had large appetites," he says. Others traded dried salmon, skunk, mountain sheep, and berry cakes for ammunition, shirts, handkerchiefs, needles, thread—almost any article the overlanders wanted to part with. In the oft-repeated scenario natives came to the aid of overlanders.[31]

The excitement of the first evening's camp at the Cache was tempered by the thought of the decisions to be made. The captains met while the rest of the party did their own theorizing. There were three possibilities. Should they cut and hack their way across the Premier Range to the Cariboo? Should they press overland to the headwaters of the Thompson then on to Fort Kamloops, the long way to the mines? Or should they trust the Fraser, the shortest but most dangerous route?

Sellar wrote: "There were 11 kinds of appions [sic] about the expedition, some for water, and some for land and some could not tell which way to decide, for fear they might not happen to choose the best way."

This was the moment of final choice.

In the end, what really happened was that each person was left to make his own decision and find others of the same opinion. There were thirty-six who opted for the southern Thompson River route, driving 130 animals. Thomas McMicking wrote of the Queenston party's decision:

After fully considering our situation, and the probable difficulties that might be in our way, we decided to build rafts and canoes and float down the Fraser, taking a few animals with us as security against starvation, and to send the remainder of our horses across the country southward, in the hands of a few of the company who had volunteered for that purpose.

Some of the persistent St. Thomas party, including Andrew Holes, set off down the Fraser prospecting without bothering to cross the river, searching for the stream where Timoleon Love and his group had found gold two years previously on their eastward journey.[32]

Those not prospecting or driving cattle south set to work felling trees for rafts and canoes. Turn to Sellar for a description of the rafts:

We spent our time up to the end of the week in building two rafts, one 45 feet long of flatted Cedar & one 50 feet long of dry fir & Spruce, and to keep the cattle from getting their feet through the timbers, we chinked the cracks with small poles each raft had 7 traverses on & lashed to every stick of timber with a birch 1¼ inch thick well twisted, so that it was impossible for either wind of tide to Wreak us. We then lashed them together with poles & put double oar locks on each end for each raft in case of anything happening that we should get broke apart.

The work being completed and the rafts floated downstream to their camp for Sunday morning, they then decided that they should have a dugout canoe as lifeboat. Ten men in two gangs spelled each other and by the end of the day had a thirty-foot canoe finished.[33]

The last evening's camp had about it an air of hushed anticipation. None knew what lay ahead; all knew this was the last time they would all be together. The westward journey had so far been conducted under the organization and direction of "The Committee" but now, with men separating, a final meeting was held to formally disband the organization. It was a sharp and poignant moment.

Monday morning, September 1, 1862, dawned bright and clear, the snow-covered and cloud-capped peaks of the Premier Range to the southwest foreshadowing a possible change in weather. The rafts and canoes were pulled to shore. The stock were loaded. The Huntingdon raft had on board an estimated five tons of freight, four oxen, three horses, two mules (the walking larder), and twenty-one men.

A pause before they push off. Where are they? Over four months from home now—three thousand miles and a minimum of two thousand miles of walking. If there was ever a middle of nowhere this was it. God only knew what lay down river. Hunger but no starvation has been met; some accidents but no deaths. Why did I come? each man asks. As the man who sat on the cactus replied, "It seemed like a good idea at the time." And what was ahead, what danger, how long now to gold, how long until rest, when . . . ?

"Let go the rope," cried Captain William Sellar.

"Poor white men no more," murmured the Indians.

There were several rafts floating down this river, half a dozen canoes, and even two bull boats of green hide stretched on willow. The large Huntingdon raft was piloted by William Sellar; the Queenston raft by Robert Harkness; the Ottawa men had a smaller raft with two oxen aboard; Brocklebank piloted another. William McKenzie, James Carroll, and Eustache Pattison were paddling a canoe purchased from the Indians and had been the first to leave the Cache. Young Pattison was ill. For several days he had felt a general malaise that now centered on his throat. The trip had not gone well for him. When the guide Rochette had deserted he had stolen Pattison's gun, then Pattison had lost his horse. He had been carrying a letter from J. Richard Stevenson to his brother Edward Stevenson in his pocket for four months and had only realized at Tête Jaune that the Dr. Edward Stevenson of his party was the addressee. Unfortunately in delivering the mail he did not ask for medical attention.[34]

Two canoes lashed side by side were paddled by J. Douglas, Robert Warren, and his cousin Alexander Robertson. Robertson was an engineer and land surveyor, twenty-three years old, and the son of Anne and William Robertson. His father was the keeper of the twelve-inmate Huron county jail in Goderich. Alexander was a stalwart Church of Scotland adherent and had on many occasions taken the Sunday services of the overland trek.[35]

The first week of the trip was cold and wet. Aboard the rafts, drifting at the speed of four to six miles per hour, life if somewhat monotonous was not difficult. Below the Cache the Fraser wandered across the Robson valley. Considerable rowing was necessary in the narrow, braided channel and rafts had to be levered and pried free after grounding on unavoidable gravel bars. Provisions were low again and tainted meat caused diarrhea. Fires built on board were washed out by riffles and the cold nights ashore were spent in rain-soaked clothes under sodden blankets. But this was a fine way to travel after the miles of blistered and calloused feet.

On the fourth day the double canoe with Warren, Robertson, and Douglas overtook the Huntingdon raft, "saluted us and passed confidently without any thought of danger."[36]

A couple of hours later a small bar was seen in mid-river, and two men on its shore—Warren and Douglas. The Huntingdon raft launched their canoe-lifeboat, manned by William Sellar and Alexander Fortune, and rescued the two while the raft was snubbed to shore a mile downstream. The story was told.

Soon after passing the raft, the double canoe had run into a rapid. Short and small, loaded with only three inches freeboard, the canoes swamped. Robertson, the only swimmer, struck out for shore, hollering to the others to hang on to the canoes. Grasping with hands turned to claws they clung, dipping beneath waves, fighting for breath, and all the while hearing Robertson encouraging them. They came ashore; Douglas dragged out of the water by Warren. Robertson was gone. The Huntingdon rafters searched for hours but finally gave up. Robertson was lost, "lamented by every person who knew him, as he was a favourite with every one in the whole company," Sellar wrote. Fortune noted, "There were some serious meditations for several days following. What may become of us all? Who is next to find a grave in the cold Fraser?"

Farther downstream another drama was unfolding. The early canoe party of Carroll, McKenzie, and Pattison had arrived at the Grand Canyon of the Fraser, a somber, foreboding place, and realizing it could not safely be run had attempted to line their canoe around. The current caught the boat and swept it away. Aboard were all their provisions. They now huddled on the shore to await help. It was two days before the first raft party reached them. Two days of cold and rain, without food, extra clothing, or shelter. By the time rescue came Pattison was in bad shape, scarcely able to talk or swallow.

Sellar gives the best description of the Grand Canyon of the Fraser: "As far as we could see there was two fearful kinks in the river, where the water had a very heavy fall, the River was not more than 20 yds wide, & the whole draft of water ran into an Elbow of rock which projected out from the bank which cause the current to sink and rise on the opposite side, & then roll into the center of the river with a heavy surge, where if formed a desperate whilepool, & which we very correctly supposed would lash & wreck a raft."

The companies must either run the rapids or starve where they were. In the McMicking company Harkness agreed to run the rapids with ten men if the others lightened the load by portaging. So, now with the

Queenston party, the waters of the canyon approach:

> Onward they swept like an arrow. They seemed to be rushing into the very jaws of death. Before them on the right rose a rocky reef, against which the furious flood was lashing itself into a foam, threatening instant and unavoidable destruction, and on the other side a seething and eddying whirlpool was ready to engulf in its greedy vortex any mortal who might venture into its reach. With fearful velocity they were hurried along directly toward the fatal rock. Their ruin seemed inevitable. It was a moment of painful suspense. Not a word was spoken except the necessary orders of the pilot, which were distinctly heard on shore, above the din and tumult of the scene. Now was the critical moment. Everyone bent manfully to his oar. The raft short closely past the rock, tearing away the stern row-lock, and glided safefully down into the eddy below. The issue of the ordeal was announced by an involuntary cheer from the brave hearts aboard the raft, which was heartily responded to by those on shore.

Their jubilation was earned but premature. The first rapid washed into a large bay, then narrowed again to what Sellar described as "one of the most tyriffic looking places that any of us had ever seen for a moment mostly all were overcome with terror & in a perfect state of confusion But! through the presence of mind of Wm Sellar who was pilot & two or three others who knew well the draft & pressure of water go all composed ... what troubled us most we could not see more than two hundred feet before us ... while the water foamed & lashed the rocks on either side in a most tyriffic manner. While every two or three acres the river formed in a kind of basin, where the waters rolled around in dreadful whirls, appearently resting itself, only to burst forth again with a more desperate surge below, & as the rocks towred up perpindicular on either side to the majestic height of 400 & 500 feet, Things had a rather gloomy aspect, & upon the whole appeared as though the Earth had just opened & was waiting the appointed time when it would swallow us up."

The obvious fear that the Grand Canyon of the Fraser brought to the overlanders affected their perspective. While a fearful place, the walls are half Sellar's estimated five hundred feet and while the water is dangerous it rates a three on a canoeist's scale of six. For the rafts, which all passed safely and drifted on downstream toward Fort George, it was more excitement than danger. Not so for the canoe parties. Three on the scale of six is the limit for open canoes.

Three days downstream from the canyon, nine days from Tête Jaune Cache, the rafts bump into the shore of the Fraser at Fort George. Sellar's raft arrives a day behind the others, and just in time for a funeral. Young Eustache Pattison died September 8, the day he arrived at the fort. His sore throat was diphtheria and there was little Dr. Stevenson could do. A small canoe was cut in half for a coffin and at 10:30 A.M. on the ninth he was "slowly and sadly" lowered into his grave.

Reports of other drownings were relayed. Sellar told the McMicking men of Robertson's death, and McMicking said Philip Leader, a canoeist with the SGE, had been drowned at the canyon.[37]

The journey was quickly drawing to a close and little time was spent at the miserable collection of buildings at the confluence of the Fraser and Nechako. Hunniford crams it all into his usual four lines: "September 9, Tuesday was in camp all day at Fort George received news of Mr. Robinsons [Robertson's] Death Patterson Died and was buried here today W Thompson and D Prest stole potatoes enough for two meals had potatoes and Fish for supper."

The next morning the rafts pushed off and the remaining travelers rowed toward the sun with three Indians for guides. Quesnellemouth, the gate to the goldfields, was only two days south.

Tête Jaune Cache saw more activity during the month of September 1862 than it had for the previous hundred years or would for the next half a hundred. As the McMicking party left the St. Peters men and the remainder of the Saskatchewan Gold Expedition came straggling in over a period of weeks. A few chose the Thompson route but most launched onto the waters of the Fraser in bartered or newly-built dugout canoes.

The St. Peters men arrived to find the Whitby party about to leave on their raft and with envy waved them off. Two days later they met again. The Whitby raft went only seven miles before it hit a rock. Everything was washed off the raft, even the coats, which had been laid aside as the men worked. The helmsman was knocked off but being an expert swimmer reached shore and ran upstream for help. The St. Peters party sent two canoes to make a midstream rescue and return the now destitute men to camp. The St. Peters men shared what they could and the Whitby group took the night shift with tools, hewing new canoes while the Americans slept. In a few days they were all ready to launch again.[38]

The men of the St. Peters party had little trouble with their craft. They were surprised though on the third day to hear a shout from shore and see a figure desperately flagging them down. It was a man by the name of Gauley, a gunsmith who had been traveling with his son in one of the advance canoe parties. He and his son had had an argument and Gauley Senior was put ashore. When the St. Peters men passed he had been trying to hack out a canoe with a small hatchet. They took him on to Quesnellemouth where he rejoined his son on October 4.[39]

The Saskatchewan Gold Expedition arrived at the Cache a week behind the St. Peters group, leaving a scattering of gear along the trail. Anything that was not needed had been cast off to lighten their loads. They too decided on canoes as the best means of travel. On leaving the Cache they split into smaller groups. One of these consisted of Alexander, the two Hancock brothers, Tom Jones, Andrew Fletcher, and James Carpenter. They traveled in two canoes, sometimes lashed together, more often separate. They left the Cache on September 20, expecting to be at Fort Alexander, below Prince George, in five days. Not so. On the fifth day they ran a small canyon, wrapped their canoe on a rock, swamped, and lost Fletcher's coat and a few other things. Carpenter and Alexander finished the run and then Carpenter returned and ran the canyon successfully. On day ten they reached the Grand Canyon of the Fraser.

James Carpenter sits dismally on the slate gray rock of the Grand Canyon of the Fraser. He is wet from the drizzling rain. He is sick. Carpenter had scurvy when he left Fort Edmonton and on his way to the Cache he got lower and lower in spirits and quit writing in his journal. Here at the Canyon he is exhausted and depressed, doubting he has the strength to complete the nine-hundred-mile journey to New Westminster at the coast or even get as far as the goldfields near Quesnellemouth, half that distance away. The dugout canoes are poor craft to trust to the waters but the canyon walls presented an impasse. As so often on this journey there is no choice. They would be obliged to run. He takes out his small notebook and the stub of a pencil and for the first time in weeks begins to write.

After the run Alexander records the following: "As I thought it rather dangerous I took off my boots and buckskin shirt before we started. We went at a tremendous rate for a short time when we got among some big waves and the canoe filled over the stern and went down. When it came to the surface again Carpenter was holding on the stern and I to the bow ... the water was remarkably cold. ... The canoe then turned broad side to the current and rolled over and over. I then let go and swam for it. Carpenter I never saw again."

Alexander surfaces and finds no sign of Carpenter, then has to swim across the river again to join his companions. The large canoe has been swept downstream with their line so the smaller canoe is abandoned and they begin to walk. Several miles downstream they see a canoe on the far side. Alexander decides to swim for it in the morning but notes in his diary: "If I fail and am lost I wish this book to be forwarded to my father in Scotland." Invincible no longer.

With the morning's light Alexander rethinks the plan and he and Jones paddle a couple of logs over to the small canoe. Of Carpenter they have seen no sign. Now, as if in confirmation, they find his jacket and Alfred Handcock, who had noticed Carpenter writing just before the accident, reaches inside the pocket and finds the diary. Incredulously he reads the final entry: "Tuesday, 30th September. Arrived at Canyon about 10 a.m. and was drowned running the canoe down. God help my dear wife." Mrs. Carpenter—wife of James Carpenter, lawyer, Mason, overlander, canoeist—is a widow.[40]

Alexander's party stumbled on, trying to walk, then adding two logs as sponsons, finally enlisting the aid of Indians as guides and providers when they have to run the boulder garden of the Giscome Rapids. They arrived at Fort George on October 8, eighteen days out of Tête Jaune, and still one hundred miles from Quesnellemouth. At the fort they trade a gun of Alfred Handcock's for potatoes, beaver, and salmon and Carpenter's revolver for a fine Indian canoe. That same snowy day they continue south.

There were two major rapids: Red Rock or Fort George Canyon twelve miles downstream and Cottonwood Canyon a few miles upstream of the Quesnel River. The raft parties ran them the second week of September as the leaves were beginning to turn on the riverbank aspens and cottonwoods. Red Rock was a one-mile run through islands of broken rock, difficult maneuvering for loaded rafts, but they managed the route with nothing more serious than being caught in a large eddy that soon flushed them out. Those on shore though had to walk four miles before the raft could be snubbed for reboarding.

On the left bank of the Fraser they spotted movement, men. Chinese, Wattie said. Consider now that the only overlanders to have seen Chinese were the ex-Californians. It was a small world they had come from; a broad and strange one they had entered. The small sallow-skinned, pigtailed men were a curiosity. On shore Wattie spoke, "How much gold you catch here, one man, one day?"

"Oh, some day one dollar, some day four bittee, six bittee, one day long time two dollars."

The six Chinese were crowded around a large dish of rice and bacon soup, which they quickly flicked into their mouths with chopsticks.

"How far Quesnel River?"

"Maybe twenty mile," they answered.[41]

Of Cottonwood Canyon Sellar wrote: "This Cannon is known through this country by the name of the Grand rappid & it is far too grand for my fancy especially when I have to go through it. The river then continued very swift till 5:15 when we arrived at Quesnell." It is September 11 when Sellar arrives here; likewise for the McMickings. Alexander is lagging a month behind and in between the two the rest of the parties will straggle in. Robert McMicking celebrates by getting his "supper off a table for the first time in four months, at Whitehalls Store for $1.50."

It quickly became evident by the number of hungry, worn miners returning from the creeks that mining was over for the season, and that life on the gravel was difficult. A few thought to visit that season—they had come so far to look for gold. Most were like Sellar, who sold everything he could, "at good advantage," to make enough money "to take us to some other country where we could afford to live." On the fourteenth he and a few others boarded their raft once again "& steered our course down stream." Robert McMicking and three friends were going to try to visit Williams Creek but the rest of his group "concluded to go down to Victoria & Westminster & California & other ports below.[42]

Their expedition, which began with cornets playing and friends cheering to the sound of train whistles, was not ending with a triumphal march down the streets of William's Creek, or along the gold creeks of Cariboo. It was ending with a whimper and a note of sadness for those left behind in watery graves. After five months the overlanders had arrived in Cariboo and were scattering like the fall leaves that littered the riverbank. In the words of Thomas McMicking, "It was only after we had been allowed a little time for reflection ... that we could fully realize or entirely comprehend the magnitude of the work we had accomplished."

# Thompson River Parties

When route decisions were made at Tête Jaune Cache it was generally reckoned that the Thompson route would be the easiest but the longest of the three routes to Cariboo. André Cardinal, the most faithful of all overlander guides, volunteered to accompany the group who chose this route as interpreter for the Shuswap who was to act as guide. On September 1, as the Fraser parties prepared to launch, the Thompson overlanders crossed the Fraser and began their march.[43]

There were, says McMicking, "over twenty men, together with Mrs. Schubert and family" who took this route. They were joined, or leapfrogged at various points, by members of the St. Thomas party, two from the St. Peters group, and likely some of the SGE. Dewitt's account says thirty-two left the Cache and were joined by his four men to make thirty-six. The total may have reached fifty or sixty as Baltzy suggests, but more likely was around forty.[44]

William Hugill of the Queenston party, a school teacher, took the Thompson route. Two months after the journey ended he sat down in Victoria's Overland Restaurant, owned by overlanders Morrow and Alex Fortune, and in a fine hand wrote a letter to his father. This Hugill is a frugal man. When he has filled eight pages with handwriting he turns the paper upside down and fills the margins. Those filled, he then turns the letter sideways and writes, in a slightly more open hand, across the previous lines, forming a net of words that is surprisingly easy to read. Paper is expensive; postage more so.

His party expected, he tells his father, from what the Indians had told them to find trail most of the way.

> My only reason for choosing this route in preference to the other was that nearly all the animals were going this way so that as a last recourse we could live on our animals if they were horseflesh.
>
> The remainder of our company went down the Fraser. We engaged a Shewswap to lead us to the headwaters of the Thompson in company with our other guide. Our Edmonton Guide was first class but our Shoeswap was almost useless. For three days our trail was excellent. Then we came to a country so full of fallen timber that it was almost impassable. Here our guide failed and we sent him home and Hunted our way as best we could. We arrived at the headwaters of the Thompson on the 6th.[45]

André Cardinal, and the useless Shuswap, turned and headed back at the confluence of the Albreda and Thompson rivers. Someone, Cardinal himself perhaps, carved a note in a tree indicating his return. The blaze was found the following year by Dr. Cheadle, and ten years later by the Selwyn party.[46]

The valley of the Thompson began to narrow and the grand vistas of river and mountains that had surrounded them as they traveled the high, dry ridges up the McLennan River past Cranberry Lake to the Albreda were exchanged for a conifer-wrapped channel of water. It was as well they had a guide up to this point, poor though he may have been, for here at Cranberry Lake were the headwaters of the Canoe River and the obvious route would have been to swing left down that valley to the Columbia. The outcome of their journey would have been quite different. Instead they stayed on track toward the Thompson.[47]

"From here we cut and tore and waded our way until the 7th, at the rate of about 3 miles a day, when we concluded to try rafting, the river being considerably enlarged," Hugill wrote.[48]

At this camp they slaughtered many of their stock, knowing they would have difficulty transporting them and because they were out of provisions. Kemps, Millar, and Whitley, with a sense of the moment, took a knife and carved in a tree "Slaughter Camp, Aug. 5th 1862," and their names.[49]

While this advance party had been making their way downstream, more overlanders had been arriving at the Cache. A few, including the St. Thomas men and Dewitt and his three companions, chose the Thompson route and caught up with the advance party at Slaughter Camp on the eighteenth, after seven days' travel. Dewitt estimated they were sixty miles from Tête Jaune Cache.[50]

At the camp everyone busied themselves with drying or jerking meat and building rafts and canoes. Dewitt says, "The greater number of horses were abandoned here," but does not say whether they were all slaughtered or turned loose. On the twenty-second all parties pushed off into the river, running blind as to what might lay ahead.[51]

Hugill's group included Archibald Thompson, John Fannin, and William Fortune.

Our company, who numbered 6, concluded to take one animal each. We built one raft for them and another for our baggage and ourselves. We had bow and stern oars of stearing. We set sail ... with a fleet of 4 rafts in all. We did not make much headway for two days on account of shallow water and timber. On the third day as three rafts were gliding smoothly, our baggage raft some distance in the advance next a heavy raft with about a dozen men and 7 animals I and 3 others brought up the rear. We came to a swift bend in the river and the heavy raft stuck fast on a snag. We came up immediately and knocked them of[f] and got ourselves treed in the same place. The other rafts soon went round a turn out of sight expecting us to follow immediately. But here we remained. We got to shore along a tree and started after the other raft but found the road so difficult that we abandoned the chase and camped for the night without food or blankets.

Next day we put back to our raft and found that the water had raised about 6 inches. We hunted up our horses and 3 of our boys boarded the raft and I got on the snag and lifted her off and boarded her as she left. We snubbed to the bank loaded our horses and started down the river about 3 o'clock. We came up with the other boys about 15 miles below just at dark and found that they had killed our ox.

It has seldom happened on this journey that we have exactly the same incident told by two people. Here we do. Hugill writes his father and Thompson writes his brother.

We ran down two days when we ran into a snag in the river with our raft, and the other raft out of sight so that I put the horses off in the river let them swim ashore, and tried to get the raft off but could not, so we tied it up and went down the river by land two miles but could not find the boys, so we built a fire and laid down in the bush without any blankets and it rained all night.... We stayed there till noon the next day and nobody came to our assistance so we went back to the raft.... We had a dog with us and were going to kill him. I said we would go and hunt up the horses and if we could get the raft off easy we would not kill the dog. We got it off, and down the river we went till we overtook the boys, it being dark.[52]

The stories are similar, but each man, particularly Thompson, puts himself at the center of the action and decision making. As the years passed the I's became more frequent and the action revolved more and more around the storyteller.

Hugill continues the tale. "On the 27th we made an early start and about 1 o'clock came in sight of the advance party encamped. They called for us to land telling us there was a large rapid ahead. Our baggage raft did so but our own raft with the animals was so heavy that we could not snub her. We came near shore and I and another leaped ashore with the lines and tried to haul her in but down she went in spite of us with 2 of the boys on board.

"They, seeing the foaming rapids ahead ran the raft against a rock in the middle of the river and the captain (who by the way is a shoemaker) [John Fannin] jumped onto it calling on the other to follow. Just as they had done so away went the broken raft and horses in wild confusion down the river. It stuck fast about a mile down. One of the horses was never seen.

"The others, though badly bruised were got of[f] chiefly by the exertions of A. Holes, a tall rawboned brave western American trapper. We found the rapid 8 miles long and so very rough that out of 4 rafts and 3 canoes which were let lose at the top not a vestige of any were to come through."

Behind Hugill was another party of four, including William Strachan. As the raft approached the rapids (Porte d'Enfer), Strachan and another man panicked, jumped into the river, and tried to swim for shore. Strachan drowned. The second man reached shore. The two men left on the raft brought it safely to shore two miles down.[53]

The nine-mile portage was made in wet snow and rain. The Dewitt party were helped by two Indians but the others make no mention of help. Below Porte d'Enfer they again built rafts, preparing to float again. Dewitt left ahead of Hugill and just before Hugill launched they were surprised by a party of four miners bound upstream, and later another four. Here, finally, they could get reliable information. Where were they? Two hundred miles from Fort Kamloops and five hundred from Victoria, they were told. In fact it was just over a hundred miles. Dewitt met the men farther downstream and said they "had been up a considerable distance, earlier in the season, but finding the water too high they returned to Fort Kamloops for provisions and started a second time.

They had been up to the Forks of the North River, and had prospected ... 250 miles above the fort. ... the gold was coarse and heavy but they refused to say how rich they had struck it."

They rafted another two days below Porte d'Enfer and then came to Mad River or Murchison Rapids which, while not as bad as the previous set, were too much to run. Fortunately they found a good trail here and followed it across the Clearwater River and on to Kamloops. On the way they ravaged an Indian potato patch and had a "grand feast of potatoes and Boiled beef." They passed Barrier River and Fishtrap Canyon, passing through a country that was the easiest walking they had seen since the prairies. Hugill's group and Dewitt's arrived at Fort Kamloops on October 11. Others came straggling in over the next few days.[54]

There remains one story—that of Catherine Schubert and her family. It is difficult to know quite where the Schuberts fit in. Both Dewitt and Hugill mention being with them at various points, but both of these parties walked the final miles to the fort. The Schuberts and a few others, no doubt because of Catherine's advanced pregnancy, again built rafts. Completely out of food they landed at an Indian village in search of provisions, leaving Catherine on a raft at shore, tied with a length of cowhide. An old Indian woman came down to visit and on seeing the rope took it to be the hide of her recently lost cow. She was about to take the rope and set the raft adrift when the men hurried back and pushed off.

Later they stopped again and found a village strangely silent. Then they found the inhabitants, scattered in the fields and huts, dead, victims of smallpox. They dug a few potatoes and drifted south. The Schuberts and their companions arrived at or near the fort on October 14. Augustus quickly erected a tent for Catherine who was now, as they reached a semblance of safety and civilization, experiencing the first pangs of labor. An Indian midwife was found, and the next day she stepped out of the tent smiling and cried, "It's Cumloops, it's Cumloops." As James Schubert recalls, "Father and mother were at first inclined to give this name to the baby but later decided upon Rosa. Even with the honor of being the first white child born in the interior I don't think my sister would have thanked them if they had given her the Indian name.[55]

And so the legend of Catherine Schubert was born.

This North Thompson route was to have been easier than the Fraser, but those who traveled it would have needed some convincing. Instead of the seven to ten days it took the Fraser party, the first groups of Thompson River overlanders did not arrive at Fort Kamloops on the south bank of the river for six weeks. There, in routine fashion, their arrival was recorded in the HBC journal:

October 11   A party of men have come down the North River by Raft, they are from Canada and the States and have come via Red River, Saskatchewan and Jasper House to Tete Jaune Cache, thence to the source of the North River and down to this point.
October 13   Employed five Canadians to dig up potatoes.
October 14   Employed 3 more Canadians today.

October 15   Another party of 15 more men arrived by the North Branch.
October 16   Employed 2 more men at $1.00 a day.
October 21   Some Canadians arrived this evening with a large raft of dary weather [dry wood?].
October 26   Another party is said to have arrived via the Tete Jaunes Cache and North River.[56]

This Thompson River Post, as Fort Kamloops was often called, had changed location several times here at the confluence of the North Thompson and Thompson rivers since Alexander Ross of the Pacific Fur Company had first built in 1812. Recently a new post had been built on the south side. Times had changed. No palisade was needed and the few buildings were surrounded by garden patches and hay fields. It was the nucleus of what was soon to become the city of Kamloops.[57]

For some of the Thompson River overlanders the arrival at Fort Kamloops marked the end of the arduous journey. Those who stopped here, such as Fortune and Schubert, could relax a little and worry only of the coming winter. Most though, hearing of work on the roads or in Victoria, decided to move on. The journey was less desperate. Fort Kamloops was the salutation—but there was a postscript. The fourth horseman of the apocalypse turned on his pale mount as he rode out the door and said, "Oh yes, there was one other thing." He was speaking to overlander Frank Penwarden.

Penwarden and five others of the St. Thomas party left Fort Kamloops in a canoe and paddled the eighteen-mile-long lake perhaps remarking on the dramatic change in climate and vegetation in this arid area. They squeezed out the far end into the Thompson River, past the narrows where Francisco Savona would soon build his ferry, making good time, buoyant at the thought of actually having arrived here in the promised land.

Twenty-five miles below Kamloops Lake the Thompson River bounds into an ominous black canyon. The water surges against the walls, swirls in powerful boils and whirlpools, and eventually finds its way in a series of complex currents out of the boxed rock walls to continue downstream. The St. Thomas canoe swamped; the men were dumped into the cold water. Two Indian lads on shore reached out, perhaps with their dip nets, and pulled all but one man ashore. Frank Penwarden was the fifth overlander to drown in a little over a month. Robertson, Carpenter, Leader, Strachan, Penwarden, all drowned; Pattison dead of dyphtheria. Six dead, so far. And once again the men of St. Thomas, St. Peters, and Queenston knelt in their canoes and paddled downstream. Was this journey never to end?[58]

*Quesnel, or Quesnellemouth as it was then known, at the junction of the Quesnel River and the Fraser. The overlanders who rafted the Fraser landed on the left bank of the river at Quesnellemouth in September 1862. (PAC C-64933)*

*This freight scow shooting the rapids of the Fraser's Grand Canyon, upstream of Prince George, is similar to the log rafts built by the overlanders. This one is being used to supply construction of the Grand Truck Pacific Railway in 1912. Three overlanders drowned on this section of the Fraser. Three more starved near here. (Author's collection)*

*Named after Billy Barker, an English waterman, Barkerville grew up around the site of enormous gold strikes on Williams Creek. This photo was taken in August 1868, one month before fire leveled the town. The man to the right of the telegraph pole with a leather apron is thought to be blacksmith William B. Cameron, an overlander. (Frederick Daly. BCARS 1011)*

*Richfield was the first town to be built on William's Creek. It was here overlanders and other miners applied for mining licenses. (L.A. Blanc, 1867. PAC C619939)*

James Wattie, left, and William Wattie, were two of the leading miners on Williams Creek. They supported the cultural life of the town with significant donations to the Library and the Hospital. (BCARS 48372 and G 188)

The Cameron Claim, August 20, 1863. The four men on the foreground log are l. to r.: Alexander, John and Roderick Cameron and Robert Stevenson. Standing are William Stewart, A.D. McInnes, Jim Cummings, James Steele, overlanders James Wattie (hands on hips) and William Schuyler (hand on hip with rock fork), Robert Flynn at the corner post and George Black with shovel and wheelbarrow. (C. Fulton, VCA)

# Chapter Twelve

## London, Canada West, to Fort Edmonton

With the arrival of the last Thompson River raft at Fort Kamloops on October 26 and Alexander's arrival in Quesnel on October 13, it appeared that the trek of the Overlanders of 1862 had come to a close, with all parties accounted for. Not so. While the overlanders spread over the southern portion of British Columbia in search of warmth, five men were desperately paddling two dugout canoes somewhere below the Grand Canyon of the Fraser, looking over their shoulders, for they could feel death stalking down the river behind them on winter winds. This Rennie party was the victim of procrastination.

Like previous parties these five gold-seekers had traveled across the eastern states, the prairies, and the Rockies for five months. Their misfortune stemmed from leaving home in London, Canada West, just one month too late. While McMicking, Redgrave, and others left in April, these men dallied. Not until May 15, six weeks after the optimum starting date, did the three Rennie brothers, Gilbert, William, and Thomas, join John Helstone and John R. Wright in their westward search for gold. On this day they bid goodbye to family and friends, the Rennies to their mother and Gilbert to his wife, picked up their carpet bags, and boarded the Great Western Railway for Detroit.

The Rennies had been born in Canada East and all of them—William, age thirty-one; Gilbert, twenty-nine; and Thomas, twenty-three—were shoemakers. Carefully packed in their bags were the tools needed to set up shop in the new colony.[1]

This party might have been called the "Shoemaker or Cordwainer Party" for Wright, twenty-four, was also a shoemaker, recently arrived from England with his wife and two young daughters. Helstone, also a recent immigrant, was a hospital steward.[2]

From Detroit they traveled by railway and river steamer to St. Paul, where they arrived on May 17. They outfitted here and then walked north to Fort Garry rather than take a stagecoach and risk high prices or no provisions at Fort Garry. Eleven days later, on Wednesday the twenty-eighth at 6:30 in the morning, they began their trip to Red River.

The Rennie party were only a short distance out of St. Paul when one of the oxen ignored the cries of, "Whoa back buck," and ran off with the cart, launching it into a ditch where it shattered and splintered, injuring Wright and Helstone in the process. Repairs took two days. On the thirtieth they were on their way again and five weeks later they reined up in Fort Garry.

At the settlement they reprovisioned and exchanged their oxen for fresh animals. Father Lacombe, the Roman Catholic priest from St. Albert, was at the fort with his entourage about to leave for Fort Edmonton. The Rennie party joined them, stopping only two days, just long enough to pick up mail from Gilbert's wife and from the Rennies' mother. They left on the eighth, the party including Lacombe, Father Maisonneuve, another mission priest, and about twelve Red River carts.[3]

The expanded party moved steadily west: Fort Ellice on July 21, 250 miles; August 8, Fort Carlton; August 16, Fort Pitt. They rested on Sunday, no doubt because of Lacombe's influence, and on Monday crossed the North Saskatchewan. On August 27 the carts and oxen squeaked and bellowed their way into Fort Edmonton.[4]

The Rennie party arrived at Fort Edmonton at an auspicious moment, for Lacombe carried news that Mr. Hardisty and the fall York boat brigade would arrive in a day or two. Traveling with the brigade were HBC Chief Factor Christie and the new governor, Alexander Dallas. Lost in the excitement of the governor's announced arrival, the Rennie party is not recorded in the Fort Edmonton journal. After the hundreds of miners who had passed that summer and with dozens still hanging around the fort, five more men did little to excite the post clerk. The governor would expect the fort to be in good order—there was much work to be done.

The cleaning was easy, if tedious, with the large number of servants encumbent in the post, but food was another matter. As earlier parties had discovered the post was short of day-to-day provisions, let alone food for a governor's banquet. Fortunately, when Father Lacombe arrived with the news of the brigade he offered to provide the necessary provisions. No doubt he was anxious that Dallas be received properly and be suitably impressed with the willingness of the church to help, for relations between the Company and the church were not always the best. The Company was tolerant of the church because missionaries tended to "civilize" the Indians somewhat. At the same time there was a feeling that the priests interfered too much in the fur business.

In final readiness the cannons that squatted in each corner bastion were charged with powder and wad and as the York boat brigade appeared below the fort a salute boomed across the river. The Rennie party stayed for the occasion, taking part in the celebrations and the food and grog that followed.

While they rested and recuperated for two days at Fort Edmonton they heard what had become of the overlander parties, the last of which had left the fort only a few days before their own arrival. Many of the miners were still in the vicinity of the fort, panning and sluicing for gold on the Saskatchewan or preparing to winter at the post and make an early start the following spring. Hunting parties, brigades from east and west, and freemen who traveled the plains and mountains arrived daily at the post with news of buffalo herds, hunting possibilities, other settlements, and the progress of "the miners."

On the previous Wednesday, Felix Monroe had returned from McLeod River with news that the "miners had got that far safely," a fact duly recorded in the journal. Half a mile above Fort Edmonton the Rennies met Love working the beaches and bars of the Saskatchewan. He reported that he and his party were making five dollars a day sluicing by hand, a recovery not to be scoffed at for laborers at the fort were receiving the equivalent of ten dollars per month plus room and board.[5]

By the time the Rennie party arrived, many of the overlanders who had halted at Edmonton had moved on. John Atkinson, G. B. Wonnacott, and a few others headed south on August 12 to prospect on the Bow River, accompanied by the Glassford brothers' party, which intended to cross via the Kootenay Pass to the Salmon River Mines. Others had spread out along the Saskatchewan, gradually working their way up to White Mud Fort, fifty-five miles above Fort Edmonton.[6]

Few of the miners stayed in or near the fort. Love complained in letters to the *Nor'-Wester* of Christie's measures to discourage mining on the Saskatchewan: high prices for trade goods, low trade value for anything the miners tried to sell, no accommodation in the fort, and a general "encouraging" of the miners to move on. Christie simply felt that his district would be better off without them, that an influx of miners and settlers would hasten the end of the Company's monopoly. Love's attitude was inflamed by the treatment given George Flett, Love's co-leader of the Saskatchewan Gold Expedition, by clerk Joseph Brazeau.[7]

Flett had the foresight to bring from Red River three hundred dollars' worth of trade goods, a considerable sum in 1862, with the intention of trading with Indians during the winter, when freezing prairie winds and river ice halted mining. The HBC, however, heard of his plans and set out to block him, not with a show of force but by clandestine seizure of his goods.

One week after Love and Flett arrived at Edmonton, Brazeau wrote in the daily journal: "Weather fine. Found out that Love and Flett party were to remain here and wished to trade provisions with the cercies [Sarcees] when they came, I offered them to take their goods into the fort so as to keep them from getting provisions if the Cercies came."[8]

His plan seems to have worked, at least for a time, for on September 23, he again writes of Flett: "George Flett one of the miners arrived from the Plains, the rest of his party are prospecting at Bow River, his goods are locked up in Company's store." It was going to be difficult for the enterprising freetrader to accomplish many transactions with his provisions under HBC "safekeeping."[9]

As well as those who prospected along the Saskatchewan or spread over the southern plains, there were smaller groups of men who stayed in the vicinity of Fort Edmonton preparing for prospecting the next spring. The Fort Edmonton journal records men going to the woods to find timber for boats, hunting buffalo, and cutting hay. On the August 23, eight overlanders were cutting hay in the neighborhood. Two of these men, Erastus Hall of Acton and B. H. Hutchinson of St. Thomas, took their ox cart and headed for Father Lacombe's mission at St. Albert to pick up a boat he had promised them.[10]

The Acton party had split at Fort Edmonton in the hopes of doubling their chances of success. While Burns and Dunn continued to Cariboo, Hall, Kelso, and Malcolm stayed at Edmonton. Their plans were contained in a letter Hall wrote to his father, dated July 27, 1862, at Fort Edmonton.

... if you do not hear from me for one or more years you must not imagine the Indians have lifted my scalp or any other thing has happened. I will try and make Canada in two years more and as much sooner as I get what gold satisfied me.[11]

Letter from Father Lacombe:

... when I arrived here I found a poor fellow who came to look for gold, lying on his death bed from a wound which he received from his gun when going to shoot a bird. This poor young man suffered awful pain during three weeks and then died in the bosom of the Catholic religion, having embraced the faith during his illness.[12]

James Kelso was hardened to the realities of this journey and life west of the Canadas now—perhaps. He now had to sit down with paper and quill and write a letter east. A little over a month after receiving the letter from Erastus suggesting that he not worry, Asa Hall was delivered a second letter dated Fort Edmonton, September 7, 1852, informing him of his son's death.[13]

By some strange quirk of fate Erastus Hall died at almost the same moment that A. C. Robertson was drowning in the waters of the Fraser hundreds of miles to the west.

# The Rock

There was a temptation to stay in Fort Edmonton and work the North Saskatchewan River for gold. They were sluicing five dollars a day by hand, a recovery rate not to be scoffed at for laborers at the fort received the equivalent of ten dollars per month plus room and board and the average daily workman's wage at the coast was one dollar. The Rennie party were warned. A crossing at this time of year was dangerous, yet to stay would require winter provisions, and the HBC would sell not a bean to interloping miners. Then there was their elusive goal—Cariboo. Selling their carts, they loaded goods on their four oxen and one horse and, as winter closed in, they pushed west.

They had made good time to Fort Edmonton. They were now just two weeks behind the stragglers of the Saskatchewan Gold Expedition, and there was no reason to believe that they would have trouble making the crossing of Tête Jaune Pass before winter set in as long as they kept moving at a good pace. As the Rennie party crossed Sturgeon River they saw high above them on the hill overlooking Sturgeon Lake the mission of Father Lacombe. In one of the nearby buildings lay Erastus Hall, with a little less than a week left to live. Kelso, Hutchinson, and Malcolm were here as well. The Rennie party, who certainly knew of the accident, may have stopped to visit the injured man.[14]

Beyond St. Albert the trail was alternately packed down and churned into mud by the hundreds of men, horses, and oxen that had gone before. At Lac Ste. Anne they laid over two days, remarking on the potatoes, barley, and excellent fishing and filling their stomachs on meals of baked fish, fresh vegetables, and bread. Westward the weather was clear and pleasant and, by September 8, they were camped at the Pembina River.

Once through the seemingly endless swamps and muskegs, the days of boot-sucking mud and unsure ground that plunged the unwary walker into mossy spruce bogs, and the fording of streams like the McLeod River they reached the Athabasca River and the foot of the Rockies at Jasper House. It was now September 24. Unlike their earlier counterparts they make little mention of the mountains in their later writing, the grandeur and solemnity of the rock edifices being lost in the horror and despondency at the thought of what lay on the other side. At that night's camp a foreboding snowfall laid down six inches of misery.

Above Jasper House they crossed the Athabasca by raft on the twenty-eighth, avoiding the difficult Disaster Point traverse. A guide hired at Jasper House showed them the valley of the Miette and, pressing on, they crossed Yellowhead Pass, passed the base of Mount Robson and the Grand Forks of the Fraser, and reached Tête Jaune Cache, which they described as an "old deserted station of the HBC Company," on October 4, a Saturday. Richard Alexander and his small group had left the Cache exactly two weeks before.

Despite the lateness of the season the five overlanders found no snow at Tête Jaune Cache, but lots of blackflies for the cold had not yet given them enough of a frostbite to kill them off. The campground was well trampled down. The remains of slaughtered oxen, hides, bones, broken packsaddles, wood chips, a few broken tools, and a few names carved in trees marked the launching point. From the native Shuswaps who were still here for the salmon run they traded a canoe in exchange for a horse and then set to work to build a second. Suitable cottonwoods were only found far from camp now, the readily accessible trees having been taken earlier. While some worked with axes, adzes, and fire to hollow out the canoe others killed the four oxen, their walking larder, and jerked the meat. Eleven frosty days passed.

On October 17, as the cold fall winds whistled winter up the Fraser, they lashed their two canoes together and pushed off into the Fraser River. The water was low and fast and the men paddled quickly, not stopping to prospect the numerous bars and creeks along the way. A little over a week down the river lay the end of their rainbow. Through the meandering bends framed with golden-leaved cottonwoods and red willow, beneath the towering peaks of the Park Range on the north and the Premier Range on the south, past ranges and peaks as yet uncharted and unnamed, past flats that would not be homesteaded for another half century and benches that would one day echo to the sound of loggers, they drifted and paddled the ever-broadening current.

On their third day they reached Goat River Rapids and the canoes' lashing gave way, separating the boats and putting them in danger of capsizing. They repaired the craft and continued on. On the twenty-fifth they reached the Grand Canyon of the Fraser, which fortunately they had been warned of. They lined the canoes and portaged all their gear over a high hill over the old HBC portage on the north side of the canyon, a three-day ordeal.

Below the canyon they laboriously paddled through the slow, still water around McGregor River and then into the faster, choppy water of Giscome Canyon. As the river swung south and entered Giscome Rapids, the canoes were still lashed together, making them more stable, but less maneuverable. Giscome Rapids, seven miles of rock-studded river, is no place to be unmaneuverable. Only two days from Fort George disaster struck.

On October 29 the larger of the two canoes broadsided a half-submerged rock in the middle of the rapids. Water foamed up each side, the canoe washed back and forth with the surge and flow of the water while the smaller canoe, still lashed firmly but wallowing in the river, now filled with water. Cold water splashed in over the gunwales, soaking the baggage lying on the floor and chilling each of the five men. Rocking from side to side, paddling, pushing against the entrapping rock, shifting the load from one canoe to another—all had no effect. The canoe remained firmly stuck. Hours past. Snow began to fall. The sky grew dark, drawing the cold curtain of night around the five men huddled in the middle of the river.

Day two of the predicament. In the predawn cold the frightened, frigid men listened to the surging of the river's waters, the ominous thumping of float ice colliding with their canoes. At first light they made a more desperate effort to reach shore. The rapids precluded swimming so after a breakfast of dried meat Helstone, Wright, and William Rennie volunteered to take the small canoe and try to reach shore. They unloaded most of their goods, leaving only some rope and blankets. Then they cut the lashing that held the two craft together. As they climbed aboard, a large chunk of ice smashed into the canoe and capsized it. As it went over, Helstone and Rennie reached out and grasped the large canoe still fast on the rocks and clambered aboard. Wright was swept downstream, clutching the canoe for buoyancy, desperately dodging rocks. To let go was to drown.

One and a half miles downstream he was swept into an eddy and managed to crawl ashore. Cold and numb he let the canoe drift off. After several attempts he crawled up the rocks to dry land, staggering up the beach to a point opposite the stranded party. He waved assurances that he was all right. Those in the canoe fastened some matches to a hatchet and thew them ashore but Wright was too wet and cold to light a fire. He walked, he ran, flapping his arms to keep his blood circulating and ward off the gradual numbness that foreshadowed death. Again night fell with four men still clinging to the rock in a single canoe; the fifth man freezing on shore.

Day three. Wright had slept little during the long night. He could not keep moving and by morning was badly frostbitten. More matches and some meat had been thrown to him but still he could not start a fire.

Ropes had been lost in the capsizing so William and Thomas Rennie broke out the shoemaker's tools and cut a moose hide into thongs, from which they braided a strong rope. This was fastened to a stick and heaved ashore to Wright. Unable to grasp the rope in his frozen hands, he wrapped it around his arms and then secured it around a tree. A thin line was fastened to the boat end of the rope. Helstone volunteered to be the first to undertake the dangerous attempt to make shore. Tying the braided line around his waist, he jumped into the river, a procedure not to be recommended to river travelers. The force of the river's flow submerges whatever is on the end of the rope, in this case Helstone. Fortunately, he was close enough to shore that he could keep swimming and was swept in an arc from the rock, through the rapids, to the icy, rocky shore. The braided line was retrieved with the light cord and the three Rennies followed. All reached shore safely, but soaked.

Their clothing began to ice up. With the steadily dropping temperatures of the surrounding air and their bodies they found themselves unable to light a fire. Their situation was desperate. That night was spent huddled out of the cruel touch of the wind between cooling rocks, sitting on what buffalo robes were left, wrapped with blankets and hides.

Day four. Both John Helstone and Thomas Rennie awoke with frozen feet. Desperation lit a fire. Carefully William Rennie got a dry handkerchief out of a pocket and sprinkled some gunpowder over it. With a flint and steel he began striking sparks. The powder flashed, the cloth leapt into flame, and nearby tinder ignited. A shout of relief went up, more wood was piled on, and each man crowded close to the life-giving warmth of the burning driftwood. Their hopes soared with the flames.

It began to look as if the situation could be salvaged. They still had some provisions and Fort George could not be far away. Those who could still walk gathered more firewood and heaped up brush to provide shelter from the falling snow. And in the river sat the canoe, always tempting, rocking back and forth with the frozen flood.

Day five. The river had dropped even farther, exposing a large piece of rock between shore and the canoe. William and Gilbert Rennie laid a driftwood bridge out to the canoe and with the braided line pulled it to shore. That night John Wright's hands froze.

Day six. This day was spent loading all their gear into the canoe and helping the men with frozen limbs find comfortable positions in the crowded craft—all to no avail. The ice and snow had increased so much that no headway could be made, particularly as only William and Gilbert could work. Unless they had help soon they would all die here on the Fraser's shore. Wright's hands were badly frostbitten and Helstone and Thomas Rennie had frozen feet. William and Gilbert Rennie would leave the next day for Fort George and help. They estimated that it could not be more than about forty miles.

They left November 4, exactly one week after striking the rock, and took only one meal of fat, a rifle, and some ammunition, leaving ten days' provisions for the disabled threesome in camp. They expected to reach the fort in three days.

On their second day on the trail the snow began again. Heavy, wet flakes fell, the size of dinner plates, quickly making travel without snowshoes difficult. The storm continued to lay down a white blanket for several days, ever deeper, ever more difficult to push through. It was still snowing hard on the third day when William and Gilbert came to a large river. Their map showed no river between their estimated campsite and the Nechako River, the site of Fort George. This river must be the one. On the other side was help. They could make it back to the three men with time and provisions to spare. The river was too deep to ford at the mouth so they traveled upstream to where the river flowed in three channels. The first was forded, the second crossed on a fallen tree, but the third was so broad and deep that they had to build a bridge. The crossing took three days.

On the other side was disappointment. There was no sign of habitation, no trails, no old fires—nothing. The hours stretched into days. The river had not been the Stuart-Nechako, but, rather, an uncharted one. They later found it had been the Salmon, the main route to the Arctic Divide at Summit Lake. Had they arrived earlier in the season they might have found help in the form of a passing fur brigade or prospector heading for the Peace River country.

It was on the south side of the Salmon that William and Gilbert's hardships really started. A mink was shot and eaten, and a few grouse, squirrels, and small birds. Their diet of meat was augmented by a few handfuls of rose hips, high in vitamin C. There was never enough for a full stomach, and no tea, tobacco, salt, or sugar. Just the constant gnawing of semi-starvation.

The snow was up to their thighs. All day they waded through the deep drenching drifts, helped sometimes by a crust that allowed them to walk on top momentarily, a false hope broken when they plunged through into the wet snow. William's feet were frostbitten and their pace slowed to a shuffle. Gilbert supported him as they climbed over logs, clambered up hills, and slid down creek banks. It did not take the estimated three or four days to reach the fort, nor twice that long. Not until December 1 did they reach the high bluffs of the Nechako River that overlooked the site of Fort George. Twenty-eight days had passed. They could see the fort, the smoke of its fires drifting over the river, promising warmth and food, but they could not attract attention. As it was late in the day they moved back from the river and camped for the night.

The following morning the two men went down to the junction of the Nechako and Fraser and fired their rifle. Mrs. Charles, the trader's wife, saw them and sent her young brother, an Indian, to help. He took a canoe across, helping Gilbert to carefully load William, who was now virtually unable to walk.

On their way to the small outpost, located just a short distance down the Fraser from the Nechako, they passed a cabin occupied by three colored men going to Peace River. One was John Giscome whose name was given to the rapids in which the Rennie party had been wrecked. Another may well have been Dan Williams of the 1858 Hastings party. They stayed here for a day.

The next day Thomas Charles, the HBC factor, came over and took them to the fort. He listened to the story of the two men and judged that the accident had occurred about ninety miles upstream. He sent two Indians off to see if they could reach the men and help them back to the fort. They returned after just a few hours. The weather was too cold, the trail impassable, and the river not frozen solid enough for safe travel.

Where the last twenty-eight days had been a terrible physical agony the next month was one of mental anguish compounded with the frustration of impotent fury. There would be no rescue party. Charles told them he could not, or would not, send help. Without a rescue party a slow, cold, certain death waited for the Rennies' brother Thomas, John Helstone, and John Wright. Gilbert and William assuaged their consciences with the belief that given their own difficulties surely the other three could not have survived this long. There had been little food, snow had fallen, and winter had set in. Nothing could be done.

At Fort George the two Rennie brothers felt they were being pressured to leave by Mr. Charles. Food was short and two more mouths to feed were not appreciated. The Rennies, though, could not travel until William's feet healed.

On January 1 the two Rennies went to Giscome's cabin and while there were visited by four Indians. The Rennies and some of the Indians spoke French. When asked whether they had come by way of the Fraser and whether they had seen anything of the men at the river camp, the Indians replied that they had not come by the river, but by a nearer route. The following day the Indians left, saying they were returning to their village by the route they had come.

On January 26 the Rennies took heed of Charles's persuasion and left the post to head south for Quesnellemouth, one hundred miles away, giving up all hope of effecting a rescue for their companions. They sought provisions from Charles for the trip and he, always thinking of the Company, traded them twelve dried salmon and twenty pounds of potatoes for the Rennies' rifle.

When Gilbert and William Rennie were five days out from Fort George they met an HBC brigade traveling from Fort Alexandria to Fort St. James. The brigade encouraged them to keep going and supplemented their food supply, which was down to three salmon. On February 3 they forded the mouth of the Cottonwood River and a few miles farther met two Englishmen wintering on Italian Bar, who put them up for two days. They arrived at Quesnellemouth on the fifth, where "we were very kindly received by Mr. Daniel McBride, and with whom we remained two weeks working for our board."

They hiked south to Williams Lake where they chanced to meet an express driver by the name of Gowdie who passed the story to the Victoria *Colonist*. On March 21 the paper ran an item headed, "MAN'S INHUMANITY TO MAN." It briefly gave the story, editorializing on the callousness of Mr. Charles. "The very least which the gentleman in charge should have done was to use his influence among the Indians to get them to go on an errand of mercy to his helpless fellow-creatures. Under the circumstances also it was a gross case of inhumanity to compel the men who had taken refuge at the Fort to leave it in the depth of winter, to encounter the perils of the journey to Quesnellemouth." The item, which erroneously said there had been four men, including two brothers, caused quite a stir amongst the overlanders who had come down the river earlier in the season. There was some fear that perhaps the Glassford brothers had been stranded.

The newspaper items continued and were picked up by the Toronto *Globe* and some U.S. papers. From Walla Walla came a letter from the Glassfords to McKenzie announcing their safe arrival. A letter the Rennies wrote from Quesnel was printed, and later an account of their journey and their fear that all their friends were lost.

The two surviving Rennies worked out their bitter winter near Williams Lake, then in spring traveled to William's Creek. Perhaps they felt a debt at least to try for gold. Their stay was short for both men were still suffering the effects of their winter ordeal. When Gilbert's rheumatism flared up they left, on June 17, 1863, perhaps with a sense of relief, likely with a feeling of melancholy. The quest was over. But if they felt guilt it was about to increase a hundredfold, for black trapper John Giscome was cruising the area of the winter camp and his disturbing, macabre story soon reached the ears of the Rennies, and the newspapers. It was a story that would haunt the Rennies' minds and gnaw their guts for the rest of their lives.

When Gilbert and Williams reached Fort George and realized that no rescue party would be sent they reluctantly assumed, perhaps hoped, that the river party were dead. But ninety miles upstream a frosty winter hell was being lived. At the river camp the three men must have waited almost patiently for the first few days, buoyed by the hopes of rescue from Fort George. Five days they had estimated, and they had ten days' food, with plenty of firewood nearby.

Then the snow storm came. As their ears strained, listening for the sound of distant hellos they heard only the steady wash of the freezing river and the occasional croak of a solitary raven or the chattering of a tree squirrel. Even those sounds were muffled as the snow fell and time began to stand still, each day marked only by a growing hunger, diminishing strength, and the freezing nights that increased the screaming agony of frostbite and rendered them less able to search for food or firewood. They had with them in camp a spyglass, for which little use could be found; two axes, which they used little; and a Bible. Between the pages was the photo of a young lady, perhaps a sweetheart, perhaps the wife of Gilbert Rennie. The Bible may have been the most used item they had.

By the time the two Rennies reached Fort George the river camp was out of food and at least one of the men was in bad shape. It was now only a matter of time until death came out of the night, stalking into camp with the cold night air, bringing a relief from the hunger and cold. Yet they had a desire to live, so they waited and as they waited their fire burned out. There was no way to relight it.

By the end of January when the surviving Rennies left Fort George and headed south two men still lived at the river camp. Who and how the first one died will never be known, but two were still alive. The Indians the Rennies had spoken to at Fort George did not return to their village but headed up the river. They found the camp and were horrified to see two of the men eating the third. They later said that all but the legs had been eaten and when approached with the offer of lighting a fire the two survivors drew their pistols, forcing the Indians to leave. The Indians, like most native peoples, lived in mortal fear of cannibals and needed little persuasion. They did not return to the fort to tell the story but went to their village. The maddened men at the river camp did not realize their only hope of salvation had passed. Their fear of dying and their incredible guilt forced reason from their minds. They thought Indians could not be trusted. Over two months had passed.

A second man died, or perhaps was killed, and he too was eaten in a savage effort to avert death. In the tenth week of isolation, when Gilbert and William were at Quesnellemouth and while newspapers were berating factor Thomas, the Indians who had gone to their village returned to kill the devils who ate human flesh. They found one man still alive. He judged them correctly this time and struggled to escape on rotting limbs. His ordeal was ended by swift hatchet blows. They left him there but gathered anything of use from the camp, believing they had done the right thing, and faded into the spruce forest. Thomas Rennie, John Helstone, and John R. Wright would never see the goldfields of British Columbia.

HBC factor Charles had become suspicious when his wife was told certain stories by the Indians and he persuaded Giscome to try to locate the camp on his way east. Giscome, accompanied by some of the Indians who had raided the camp, located the site, about fifty miles above the fort, and found two bodies. In one corner of the shelter lay the carefully packed bones of one of the men, among them the skull of what appeared to be a young man, whom Giscome assumed to be Rennie. Nearby was the skull of what he thought to be an older man with the marks of eight ax blows still evident. Outside the camp was a patch of hair that he somehow identified as Rennie's. The bones were collected and buried, with a note left explaining the circumstances to anyone who might chance to pass.

Later an Indian saw Giscome writing a note to Charles and became annoyed that he was being blamed somehow for the third death. Giscome tried to appease the natives and was told that the body of the third man could be shown to him. It was found about three or four hundred yards from the camp on the other side of a small rise, naked and marked with hatchet blows. Gradually Giscome was told where all the possessions were and he was given some to take back. A Bible and photograph, two axes, a spyglass, shoemakers' tools, some camp utensils, and young Rennie's jacket. It had nine holes in the back and one under the right arm, all apparently made with a knife. Nothing could be learned of the death of the third member of the party. Giscome buried the grisly remains of the Fraser River tragedy, and carried the burdensome story out to civilization. He concluded his report by saying he had some letters from Gilbert's wife and the Rennies' mother that he would like to return.

For Gilbert and William Rennie the evidence of the river camp cannibalism and death struggle and their own premature acceptance of their companions' death would drive a wedge between them and feed doubts that in the long, cold nights of future winters would squeeze their souls.

These last tragic members of the overlander parties disappear into the throngs of men on the roads and trails of British Columbia. These men had come to see the Elephant. Some had beaten it; others had lost. The last of the Overlanders of 1862 had arrived in the Golden West.[15]

## In the Colonies in 1862

While the overlanders made their way west from prairie green-up to Indian summer, the Cariboo gold rush had surged ahead with the discovery of tons of gold. The strike that lured the overlanders was Antler Creek, the narrow green canyon where gold had, literally, been picked off the creek bed. As always there were latecomers who pushed on. Dutch Bill Deitz was one. He and a small party hiked upstream, across the broad plateau called Bald Mountain, and down into another watershed.

One night, while the others sat by the fire, Dutch Bill took a pan of gravel from a high ledge. With cold, aching hands he washed it and found a dollar's worth of gold. His companions were not impressed, but agreed to name the creek for him after he promised, "If you vill call it by me, I vill hoppen for you de very first case of vine vot come into de country." William's Creek it was.

The transformation this post-glacial stream underwent in the next year was nothing less than a boom. With thousands of men wandering the hills, no strike remained a secret long. But while the initial enthusiasm was high, William's Creek gold did not give itself up easily. Digging stopped at a layer of hard, blue clay—bedrock miners assumed.

Then at Abbott and Jordan's claim, a few hundred yards below the collection of green-timber buildings called Richfield, a pick broke through the clay. Gold-filled gravel lay beneath. No longer was this "Humbug Creek." Combined with the Lowhee strike of Richard Willoughby and the Lightning Creek strike, both only a few miles away, gold began to pour from Cariboo. That winter over two million dollars' worth reached Victoria.

By the summer of 1862 men were spread all along William's Creek, scratching at the gravel. One man, an English riverman who had been scratching for gold in North America since 1846, decided to dig deep. He was an irascible little forty-two-year-old who gave the appearance of having been hit on the head with a large mallet, a Norfolkman by the name of Billy Barker. Barker, in partnership with seven others, staked eight hundred feet on August 13, 1862. A few days later they struck gold near bedrock, at forty feet, the deepest anyone had dug. In forty-eight hours they brought up over one thousand dollars in gold, each shovelful often bearing half gold and half gravel. Around this immense strike a town grew—Barkerville.[16]

During this summer William's Creek was at once a place of unimaginable wealth and destitution. Who could have imagined a man earning thirty dollars a month being worth hundreds of thousands overnight. And who of the miners would have imagined himself living in a brush lean-to without money for coffee or tobacco. By September flat-broke, worn-out miners were streaming down the rough trail from Richfield, over Bald Mountain, down Lightning Creek, past Cottonwood House to Quesnellemouth, so named to distinguish it from the upriver town of Quesnel Forks. They arrived at the riverside town as the overlanders' rafts nudged the shore.

Upon reaching what was ostensibly journey's end at Quesnellemouth or Fort Kamloops the overlanders, now referred to as The Overlanders, scattered like dandelion seeds before a morning downriver wind. Some took root, some landed on rocky ground, a few withered, and others faded from sight.

Contrary to popular belief at least a few of The Overlanders made a try for the goldfields that autumn. Robert and Thomas McMicking, joined by their brother-in-law Chubbock, William Halpenny, John Pinkerton, and Sam Rogers ventured on a quick journey toward the goldfields. At Cottonwood they "saw lots of persons just coming from the mines making their way as fast as possible down to the Ocean Most of them about straped. Work in the mines so dull that old miners couldn't get work to do after mining for themselves all Season and spending what little they had are trying to get a few day's work to help them down to the Ocean for the winter but without avail." The McMickings and Chubbock turned back but the others went on "to see and be seen."[17]

William Halpenny arrived to find that departing miners meant work was available. When he reached the town, the "Cariboo" Cameron Claim hit water at the fourteen-foot level. Halpenny was hired to help work on the claim.[18]

The other two men to see the creeks were Alexander Fortune and James Wattie, who left Quesnellemouth Monday, September 15, leading their trusty ox. Despite the overall weariness and lack of funds these two felt "it would be a disappointment not to see for ourselves when within sixty miles of William's Creek." Wattie was also anxious to see his old friend John Angus Cameron.[19]

On the trail they met only two remarkable parties. The first was packer Barron, whom Dr. Thibodo and John Jessop had met three years earlier near Walla Walla. He told them of a trail he had followed west, through the Chilcotin country to the coast at the Indian village of Bella Coola. The second party of note sent them fleeing into the bush with an ox who was beside itself with fright at the sight of the strange pack train. It was the Cariboo Camels, the evil-smelling beasts of burden, that so upset other pack trains and were found so ill-suited to the terrain that their use was soon discontinued.

The two overlanders spent only eight days on the creeks. They were impressed with the wealth. "On the west bank of the Creek about half a mile up stream from Black Jack tunnel, near the canon, the famous Steele claim and the Abbot claim and several others were taking out very rich pay. Also above the town [Richfield] several claims were proving rich. ... We saw a few men making riches in a short time, much gambling and life of low character." They met a troubled Cameron at his claim and found that Sophie Cameron was lying ill of typhoid. She was one of many to sicken in an epidemic that raged up and down the creek, a result of poor sanitation and lack of sufficient medical care. Wattie had seen enough. He would be back, of that he was sure, but the necessary provisions could not be purchased to overwinter.

Wattie and Fortune headed back to Quesnellemouth, to find some of the Saskatchewan Gold Expedition, the original Toronto party, just arriving. Joscelyn said, "Remember how corpulent I was at Fort Garry? Look at me now." Although his method of dieting was not one to be recommended he was now "decently slim."[20]

They picked up William Wattie and set out to follow Barron's trail west. Walking across Rupert's Land had not been enough. They crossed the Chilcotin grassland and the coast range to Bella Coola, hired some Indians to take them to Fort Rupert on Vancouver's Island, and then caught a steamboat south to Victoria. Fortune soon went into business with Morrow in opening the Overland Restaurant and the Watties went to work at a Puget Sound lumber mill for the winter.

While the tenacious few had taken their goldfield trip, others were oozing south. Sellar for example sold everything, including his ox, on which he made over 100 percent profit. The raft they floated on brought twenty-five dollars and the tent ten dollars. Like most others he did not try to reach the goldfields that season but moved south, picking up odd jobs along the way, such as cutting forty cords of wood for one hundred dollars, an eight-day job. At New Westminster he found no work; at Victoria no work. On November 18 he and Gage boarded the steamer *Sierra Nevada* bound for San Francisco.[21]

Several others headed for California. With the whimsy that had begun their journey the Phillips brothers thought "Why not?" and steamed south to spend five years in the Sierra Nevada mines. Leonard Crysler made a fast trip south, passing through Victoria soon after the first brideship, the *Tynemouth*, arrived with sixty marriageable women for the female-starved colony. By November 6 he too was in San Francisco and wrote his family concluding that "California is played out, Cariboo is a fizzle and that I would have done better to have taken Mrs. Enoch's advice and stayed at home 'where I need never do nothen and just had the best.' "[22]

While a few headed for warmer climes, others stayed in the Cariboo as long as they could find work. Many hired on with the road crew of Sergeant McMurphy, Royal Engineer. Robert McMicking joined at forty dollars per month and board or fifty-seven dollars if working Sundays. The next day he changed his job to that of cook at fifty dollars per month. McMicking was joined by other road builders: John Hunniford, John Bowron, William Schyuler, Thompson, William Sellar, Dobson Prest, and Stephen Redgrave.[23]

Sergeant McMurphy, R.E., wrote in his diary on September 25, "We have a great many Canadians with us working that came overland." And on the 28th, "A party of Overland Canadians has taken 2½ miles of road to make at Bridge Creek. They get 450 dollars per Mile." They had cut trail for hundreds of miles through the Rockies—a few more would not hurt.[24]

Others, such as Harry Handcock, found work at road houses or building cabins; Johnnie Brown became a barkeeper at Lillooet; the Schuberts wintered at Kamloops; Hugill and others of the Thompson River party worked on southern sections of the road. Alexander and friends, reluctant to spend their last thirty-five dollars, begged their way down the road. "It is not begging," Alexander explains. "You just tell them you are broke and hungry and of course you get a meal." Though a beggar he is not above the odd derogatory comment. When he stopped at the Blue Tent House, run by Henry Felker and his family, he was less than impressed. "Got a little meat and bread there to serve for breakfast and dinner. Man and his wife and family here—wife a regular shrew and children pests; German."[25]

By the time Alexander and Handcock reached New Westminster they were destitute, as were many overlanders. John Robson, *British Columbian* editor, loaned them five dollars and offered work at room and board plus five dollars per month, but it was not enough. They had too many debts. They got rooms on the security of Alexander's watch, but when he tried to pawn it the jeweler said it was too rusty to be worth more than its weight in silver—three dollars. They finally took a job splitting cordwood and built a shanty on the edge of the small town and to pass the winter.

Alexander summarizes his narrative: "Fletcher and Tunstall have gone down to Victoria. Purdy, Tife, Hind and Coffein, Wright and Collins are down at Frisco.

"This then is the nature of the journey occupying a space of nearly seven months, which was to have been accomplished in a period of six weeks."

The journey may have been long but it was inexpensive. Hunniford itemizes his "Bill of expenses" at a total of $98.75. McMicking is more detailed. His fares were $36.65; the "outfit," i.e. tools, tent, etc., was $31.00; provisions, $12.00; groceries, $5.00; and incidental expenses, $8.00, for a total of $97.65. If these figures are accurate they had reached the mines for just $100, compared to the sea voyage where passage to Victoria alone was $300. McMicking adds that the mining tools were the only article "found to be unnecessary." In summary he wrote: "It is certainly cheap, healthy and practicable; but these advantages are more than counter balanced by the difference of time between this and the ocean route." While he did not want to encourage the use of the "Overland Route" as a means of reaching the goldfields, the journey had, McMicking felt, shown the practicability of a road or railroad across the country.

As winter rains washed the mountain slopes of the lower Fraser and the small coastal communities began to celebrate another Christmas season the last of The Overlanders dragged their weary feet in. The poem Thomas Phillip had written at the journey's outset is a fitting close:

> We are the voices of the wandering wind,
> which moan for rest,
> but rest can never find . . .

"*In Jones tent. Jones playing at cards. Carpenter.*"  This sketch by Hind shows James Carpenter just one month before he drowned on the Fraser.

# The Overlanders in Historical Perspective
## An epilogue

*"I am at present working at the Carpenter's trade and I think I will be for another month. Joseph Halpenny is working with me. You will please give the other Overlanders the following information. I reported Peter McIntyre dead which is not the case, he recovered. Nearly all the Overlanders were sick in Cariboo last season. There were only 5 or 6 who escaped disease. Physicians say that the hardships they suffered on the overland journey was the cause. The man Burden [Berdan] that beat his horse to death died on Williams Creek, also William Hugill. David Byers was put in hospital by J. Halpenny the day Joe left. Byers having been sick all summer and so reduced that there is no hope of his recovery. [Byers died in early 1864.] Joseph Hough has been sick on Williams Creek for a long time, sometimes better, sometimes worse. The last I heard poor Joe's means had run out and he was forced to go to the hospital. Ephriam Harper is the only overlander that struck anything in Cariboo. He struck it late in the Fall very rich, should it hold out he will likely do well."*
Letter from Dobson Prest to his brother, Victoria, December 25, 1863

Reading the correspondence, journals, and newspapers of the late 1860s leaves little doubt that the Overlanders, these people who had arrived in British Columbia by this unusual, difficult route, had a profound effect on the development of Canada west of the Great Lakes.

Consider that during the period from 1858 to 1863 these 350 people, the various parties of Overlanders, accomplished the following:
- Drew attention to Minnesota expansionists' efforts and emphasized the need for an all-British route across Canada.
- Demonstrated the economic development that would follow any immigration route west
- Drew attention to and followed a Canadian immigration route across the Canadian Shield, the longed-for all-British route west.
- Made the first crossing of the southern plains in over three decades.
- Were the first western immigrants to use the HBC fur brigade trails for any economy other than the fur trade.
- Were the first immigrants to utilize the HBC posts as provisioning points, helping to drag the monopoly into the 19th century.
- Drew gold seekers and settlers from the Red River colony to the Fort

Edmonton area, likely advancing this settlement by a decade or more.
- Rediscovered Rocky Mountain passes and showed they could be used for future trails, roads and railroads, notably the Yellowhead, Sinclair and Kootenay passes.
- Opened the Yellowhead Pass to immigration and public awareness. Much of this activity was centered on the small party with Timoleon Love at its core.
- These were the first immigrant parties, some with women and children, to arrive via an overland route, remarkable at the time.
- Showed that passage through the native nations of the plains was possible without the losses common in the United States.
- The newspaper accounts of their journeys, and their eastern connections, brought the news of their journey, the goldfields of B.C. and the need for an all-British route west to the front pages of newspapers and to the discussion floor of legislatures and parliaments.
- Their journey strengthened British or Canadian sovereignty.
- As individuals they had a significant effect on the development of the Cariboo in particular and British Columbia in general.
- Their journey, linked with the wealth of B.C.'s goldfields, sparked the demand for a trans-Canada route.
- This journey had the effect of advancing the need for a railway and therefore confederation, forward by at least a decade.

The arrival of these 200 overlanders in 1862 can be likened to forty thousand young, hardened craftsmen arriving in present-day British Columbia by some new means of transportation. (Based on an 1862 populations of approximately 20,000 and a present day population of more than 2.5 million.)

Contrary to historians from the 1930s–50s, most of the Overlanders did go to Cariboo to search for gold. Of course, they did not go directly to Williams Creek in the fall of 1862. They were exhausted, starving and broke, and winter was sweeping in over the coastal mountains. Mining was over for the year.

Many of the pre-1862 Overlanders disappeared in terms of documentation, their small parties absorbed in the anonymity of the goldfields or the Pacific west. However, from the 250 known Overlanders of 1862 we can draw these figures:

Sixty stayed in Edmonton or went south into the plains. Five were guides. Ten died enroute, leaving 175 to reach B.C. in the fall of 1862. Ten or 20 went south to the U.S. or home to Canada immediately. Of those remaining close to 100 are documented through licenses, letters, journals and mining records, as going to Cariboo for the 1863 season. Also, a few who had wintered in California returned.

The prevalent myth that they scurried home, lost interest or took up other work is clearly wrong.

Despite the effect the Overlanders specifically and the goldrush in general had on the development of B.C. and Canada, little can be found in academic journals or general history books, which tend to leap precipitously from the fur trade era to Confederation. Except for grade school curriculum, the eastern lust for western wealth and the fact that Canada clearly wanted "the golden fields of British Columbia" and was willing to give a railway in return is generally ignored. It is difficult to find more than passing reference to the Overlanders or the Cariboo goldfields in any contemporary history of the west.

Over and over again the Cariboo Sentinel, the British Colonist, the Toronto Globe and others argued for the need to connect Canada and the Colonies. For example on September 9, 1867 the Sentinel editorialized with passion on the budget approval for a road making the final link in a route from Halifax to Fort Garry. Waddington's road through Bute inlet was expected to reach completion soon. "It only remains to open the road from the Upper Fraser through the Yellowhead Pass, as proposed by Sir James Douglas, and over the plains…in all 230 miles, to have a communication with Fort Garry. This achieved the whole line will be open between Bute Inlet and Halifax."

Their frontier optimism was misplaced. It was 20 years before the railway reached the west coast in July 1886. The Trans-Canada highway was years away.

Despite the efforts of Overlanders such as Thomas McMicking, who wrote eloquently and frequently on the need for east-west routes, the main routes of commerce were north-south. There were passionate arguments by Overlanders and other westerners that not only did B.C. not need links with Canada but that Cariboo did not need B.C. A railroad would only draw wealth out of B.C. it was argued. Goods, cattle, sheep and horses from Washington and Oregon, and California merchandise, came from the south. "You need us; we don't need you," was a common 1860s sentiment. It is an argument still echoed in the 21st century, 150 years later, an argument with its roots in Cariboo gold and Overland journeys.

Those Overlanders who stayed became a part of the literature, the myth, the folklore of pioneer British Columbia. Their journey marked them. Their obituaries recorded that this man was "an Overlander."

They began businesses on the coast, such as the Morrow's Overlander restaurant in Victoria and Heron's saddlery. Men like John Bowron and George Tunstall became Gold Commissioner and Government Agent.

Robert McMicking was a pioneer of the BC Telephone Company. His brother Thomas was a town clerk and deputy sheriff. John Jessop founded the New Westminster Times and Victoria Press. He helped frame the BC Education Act and was the first superintendent of Education.

George Wallace founded the Cariboo Sentinel newspaper in Barkerville and was followed by editor/publisher Robert Holloway. John Mara was elected to the B.C. Legislature and Speaker of the House.

The Mickles, McQueen, Cooney and the Moores became leading interior stockmen, and the Schuberts were prominent settlers in the Okanagan.

John Fannin the shoemaker wrote music and used his love of natural history to found the B.C. Provincial Museum, now the Royal B.C. Museum. William Fortune began the first flour mill in the interior of B.C., near Kamloops.

Museum. William Fortune began the first flour mill in the interior of B.C., near Kamloops.

Thomas Graham was a prominent mill owner and architect in New Westminster where he built the attorney general's house, the original Royal Columbian Hospital and Capt. Irving's house, now a museum.

Dan Williams explored the Peace Country and became a legend in his own right. Alfred Perry kept exploring and led Walter Moberly to Roger's Pass as the CPR route. Moberly is remembered, Perry forgotten.

In Cariboo, Overlanders began the newspaper, William Rennie was a shoemaker, Colin McCollum had a tailor's shop, Archibald McNaughton and Andrew Fletcher were merchants. The Wattie brothers were successful miners and donated significantly to the cultural life of the creek. Dr. Edward Stevenson practiced in Barkerville. Many others stayed as miners.

There were those who continued to seek gold, who stayed in Cariboo: John Pinkerton, Samuel Rogers, John Malcolm, Sam Kyse, Archibald McNaughton, Andrew Fletcher, W. H. G. Thompson, Andrew Weldon and many more.

Some died within a year or two, such as D.F. McLaurin, John Jones, William Hugill, David Byers, E.W.W. Linton, Thomas McMicking.

And Timoleon Love? He lies in an unmarked grave in Cranbrook, British Columbia.

They were farmers, merchants, musicians, husbands, artisans, teamsters, artists, tailors and labourers who built the province.

Recognizing the effect these 150 people had on the development of British Columbia, one might compare their recognition to the similar, though significantly larger, immigrations to Oregon and California. There every camp and death and event is marked and recorded. We might wonder where are the monuments to these Canadians and Americans who opened the Canadian route, the markers to their trek, their contributions.

There is a stone cairn in Jasper National Park, one Stop of Interest on the Thompson River, the Overlander's bridge in Kamloops and a scattering of businesses incorporating the word Overlanders. Barkerville recognizes the Overlanders and the city of Quesnel has a sign on their Riverside Walk. O'Keefe Historic Ranch in Vernon has preserved the Schubert's house and history.

Generally the Overlanders are remarkable in our lack of familiarity, our lack of memorials. Where are the markers for the ten dead Overlanders? Where the marker for Slaughter camp, or the Tete Jaune Camp or the numerous prairie camps? Where is the broad recognition of these pioneers?

How Canadian, eh?

*"It seems there are quite a number of raw Canadians newly come out this year which proves that the newspapers have not quit lying, nor are the fools all dead yet."*
Robert Harkness, Barkerville, to his wife Sabrina, May 31, 1864

# Appendix One

## Overlander Rosters

The following party rosters are compiled from the journals and letters of the overlanders, newspapers, and Wade's *The Overlanders of '62*. Many rosters are incomplete as indicated by the totals given beside the name. In 1858–59 there was considerable blending during the winter and spring so some men will appear on two lists. In the case of those men who traveled with the Palliser and Hector expeditions the only names listed are those of overlanders.

**OVERLANDER PARTY ROSTERS 1858 and 1859**
**Caldwell**
    Caldwell, William N. (Billy)
    Cheever, James
    Dignan, John Pat
    Harris, Nelson
    Hind, E. (Ned)
    Kennedy, Duncan P.
    McCullough, George (McCully)
    Reed, George N.
**Faribault**
    Amesbury, William
    Emihiser, Ira
    Gibson, Joe
    Hall, J. J.
    Hind, E. (Ned)
    Houck, Joseph S.
    Jones, John W.
    Palmer, John
    Sanford, John
    Schaeffter, John (Dutch John)
    Smith, James Elnathan (Ellhi)
**Goodrich**
    Goodrich, Charles
    Hammond, Fletcher M.
    Smith, W. Ellis
**Hastings**
    Cook, George
    Hammond, Fletcher M.
    Johns, R. W.
    Loveland, C. A.
    Martin, [?]
    Maxwell, James
    McLaurin, D. F.
    Robinson, M.
    Williams, Daniel T.
**Hector**
    Burnham, George C.
    McLaurin, D. F.

## APPENDIX ONE

**Holmes**
  Holmes, Thomas
**Jessop**
  Duff, Elijah
  Jessop, John
**Mankato**
  Brewster, [?]
  Gibson, Joe
  Hall, J. J.
  Hodgson, G. W.
**Moulton**
  Bunker, W. E. (Billy)
  Clorine, [?]
  Duff, Elijah
  Jessop, John
  Koffman, [?]
  Moulton, J. C.
  Reese, [?]
**New Brunswick**
  Bohanan, Shubeal
  Brown, Z. B. (James)
  Campbell, John A. (Big John)
  Campbell, Thomas
  Cooney, Charles
  Dillman, James
  Edgar, William
  Fairweather, William
  Foster, A. C.
  Graham, Thomas
  Harding, Anning
  Harding, Dwight
  Henshaw, Albert
  Henshaw, David
  Howard, D. W.
  Johnson, H. S.
  Johnson, J. G.
  Kerr, James
  Montgomery, Charles W.
  Moore, John Pearsey
  Moore, Samuel
  Robinson, J. A.
  Smith, B. Y.
  Sweeny, Wm.
  Windle, James
**Nobles**
  Anderson, Dr. Charles L.
  Caldwell, William N. (Billy)
  Cheever, James
  Dignan, John Pat
  Gooderich, Dr. J. C.
  Hamilton, John W.
  Harris, Nelson
  Kennedy, Duncan P.
  Lynch, Thomas (Judge)
  Marble, Manton
  McCullough, George (McCully)
  Nobles, Col. William H.
  Palmer, John (Boney)
  Reed, George N.
  Sandont, John B.
  Smith, Henry
  Taylor, James Wilkes
  Thibodo, Dr. Augustus J.
  Thompson, W. W.
  Wheelock, Joseph Albert
  Young, John
**Palliser**
  Cook, George
  Maxwell, James
  Williams, Daniel T.
**St. Paul**
  Burnham, George C.
  Goodrich, Charles
  Smith, W. Ellis
**Tête Jaune**
  Brewster, [?]
  Linton, E. W. W.
  Loveland, C. A.
  Pambrun, Pierre Chrysologue Jr.
  Perry, Alfred (Mountaineer)
  Sanford, J. R.
**Thibodo**
  Hamilton, John W.
  Lynch, Thomas (Judge)
  Palmer, John (Boney)
  Reed, George N.
  Sandont, John B.
  Smith, Henry
  Thibodo, Dr. Agustus J.
  Thompson, W. W.
  Young, John

**OVERLANDER PARTY ROSTERS FOR 1861**
**Reid (5)**
  Contu, F.
  Jones, William
  Leith, George
  Reid, Dr. Alexander P.

# APPENDIX ONE 253

## OVERLANDER PARTY ROSTERS 1862

Where an individual was tallied in more than one party his affiliation is given as of Fort Garry. There was, however, frequent crossover. The hometown groups within the larger McMicking party are those listed by Thomas McMicking. In the subsequent organization some of these were absorbed into other parties. The first figure after the name is the party total given by McMicking. The second figure is the maximum figure given by any journalist.

### McMicking (138–160)
Acton (6)
    Burns, John B.
    Dunn, Thomas
    Hall, Erastus C.
    Kelso, James
    Malcolm, John
Chatham (3)
Goderich (5)
    Douglas, J.
    Robertson, Alexander C. (rep.)
    Warren, Robert
Huntingdon (19–24)
    Anderson, Arthur
    Anderson, James
    Blanchford, Harry
    Bowron, John
    Cameron, William Birnie
    Clarke, Michael
    Clyde, Alexander
    Cogswell, [?]
    Cunningham, Robert A.
    Dunsmour, David
    Edgar, Robert
    Fortune, Alexander Leslie
    Gage, William
    Hall, J. C.
    Irwin, William
    McFie, A.
    McIntosh, James
    McIntyre, Peter
    Merriat, W. [Economy]
    Nicols, John
    Oney, Daniel [Olney?]
    Perkins, — [?]
    Phillip, Thomas
    Phillip, William W.
    Reid, George
    Schuyler, William B.
    Sellar, James M.
    Sellar, William
    Stevenson, John
    Tunstall, George C.
    Wallace, George
    Watson, Hugh
    Watson, John
    Wattie, James (rep.)
    Wattie, William
    White, Joe
London (5)
    Strachan, T. [Wm.] [S]
    Urlin, Adolphus N.
    Urlin, Alfred John
Montreal (7)
    Heron, Robert
    McNaughton, Archibald
    Morrow, W. W. (rep.)
Ogdensburg (7)
    Phillip, Thomas (rep.)
    Phillip, William W.
Ottawa (8)
    Glassford, J. P.
    Glassford, William
    Halpenny, John
    Halpenny, Joseph T. (rep.)
    Halpenny, William
Queenston (24)
    Bowland, John (treasurer)
    Brown, A.
    Brownlee, Robert W.
    Chubbock, Samuel W.
    Crysler, Leonard
    Cumner, Simeon E.
    Duffin, P.
    Ensign, Justus
    Fannin, John
    Fitzgerald, Fred
    Fortune, William C.
    Gilbert, Wm. [Robt?]
    Harkness, Robert
    Hugill, William
    Hunniford, John
    McConnel, Arch.
    McMicking, Robert Burns
    McMicking, Thomas M.
    Marlow, Peter
    Monroe, Felix (guide)
    Murphy, Thomas
    Nellas, J. W. G.

Prest, Dobson E.
Putnam, I. C.
Robinson, Joseph [James]
Rose, James [I. A. ?]
Stevenson, Dr. Edward
Thompson, Archibald
Thompson, Wm. Henry Guelph (rep.)
Wilcox, James
Wood, R. H.
Red River (7)
   André (Schubert's farm hand)
   Pierre (Schubert's farm hand)
   Schubert, Augustus
   Schubert, Mrs. Catherine
   Schubert, Augustus Jr.
   Schubert, James
   Schubert, Mary Jane
St. Thomas (21)
   Berdan, Isaac Freeborn S.
   Berdan, Samuel E.
   Crandall, Mark
   Cutler, John R.
   Dodd, John
   English, John
   Fowler, Jacob
   Hamm, M. Andrew
   Holes, Andrew
   Hutchinson, A. F. [B. H.] (rep.)
   McAlpine, Daniel
   McCollum, C.
   McQueen, Isaac Brock
   Mains, Brock
   Mead, Rollin P.
   Nicol, Albert G. [Nicoll]
   Penwarden, Frank
   Prior, Stoughton
   Wallis, Mark
   Weldon, Andrew
Scarborough (5)
   Hough, Joseph Z.
Toronto (7)
   McKenzie, James
   Wallace, George (rep.)
   Wonnacott, G. B.
Waterloo (6)
   Brocklebank, W. (rep.)
Whitby (6)
   McPherson, Dr. James G.
   Otta, Charley
   Simpson, Donald [George?] (rep.)
McMicking — Unknown Hometown Party
   Anson, [?]

[Bouche?], James
Bowse, Thomas
Byers, David
Campbell, Robert
Cardinal, André (guide)
Fallon, John
Gauley, Robert and son
Hardy, F. F.
Kemps, [?] [Kempth, John?]
Kyse, Samuel
Leet, J. J. [Leck?]
Lockwood, Charles
Marshall, W.
Miller, A. H. [Hugh?]
Monroe, Felix (guide)
Pinkerton, Jack
Rachette, Charles (guide)
Shaw, John
Whitley, Spencer P.
**Rennie**
   Helstone, John
   Rennie, Gilbert
   Rennie, Thomas
   Rennie, William
   Wright, John R.
**Saskatchewan Gold Expedition (69)**
   Alexander, Richard Henry
   Atkinson, John
   Ballantyne, Sam (guide)
   Beatty, [?]
   Brown, Johnnie W.
   Burgess, William R.
   Carpenter, James C.
   Carroll, James
   Caydon, [?]
   Cofferin, George
   Collins, George
   Ellis, M.
   Fletcher, Andrew
   Flett, George Jr.
   Frederick, Walter
   Gunn, George
   Hamilton, Henry [Harry]
   Handcock, Afred Ormsby
   Handcock, Harry W.
   Hind, William
   Holloway, Robert
   Jones, Dave
   Jones, Tom
   Jonson, [?]
   Joslin and/or Jocelyn, Joshing
   Leader, Philip
   Love, Timoleon

McBeath, Hector
McKenzie, William
McLean, John W.
MacRae, John
McRonock, [?]
Mara, John A.
Matheson, Donald
Myers, A.
O'Beirne, Eugene Francis
Pattison, Eustache
Redgrave, Stephen
Smith, Big Thomas
Sutherland, George
Thompson, George
Tife, C. E.
Turner, Wrathman
Wessels, Allen
Whiteford, John
Wonnacott, G. B.
Wright, John (son of Wm.)
Wright, Wm.
Woman 1
Woman 2
Woman 3
Boy
Girl

**St. Peters**
Camehl, Christian
Camehl, Henry
Couplin, William L.
Davis, E. Page
Dewitt, H. C.
Fisher, Capt. A. D.
Gardner, J. R.
Hanscome, M. G.
Hart, [L. J. ?]
Little, Thomas [John]
Miner, Alonzo
Miner, D.
Simonton, Dr. William B.

**Unknown Affiliation**
Ashton, Charles
Baillie, George
Barnes, R. S.
Bell, W. R.
Borthwick, A. [Alex?]
Brodlunk, William

Cormack, Richard S.
Earl, James
Farguharson, Donald
Farmer, George
Folley, William
Glen, John Jr.
Glen, John Sr.
Harper, Ephram S.
Harrison, William
Kenkey, H. [Keonkey, A. ?]
Lane, James M.
Little, Thomas [John]
McCormick, William G.
McIntyre, Norman
McKenzie, William
McQuarrie, Daniel
Mickle, George
Mickle, Hiram Florien
Mickle, Wheeler Adam
Morton, Thomas
Polly, William J.
Purdy, [Daniel?]
Robinson, Henry W.
Rogers, Samuel Augustus
Ross, John S.
Shaw, John
Tompkins, Dr.
Torrance, Joseph
Urlin, Adolphus N.
Urlin, Alfred John
Weir, J.
Weston, George A.
Willis, J.

**OVERLANDER PARTY ROSTER 1863**

This party spent the winter of 1862-63 at Fort Edmonton and headed for Cariboo the following spring.

**Hutchinson**
Hutchinson, A. F. [B. H.]
Kelso, James
Kyse, Samuel
Malcolm, John

# Appendix Two

This roster of overlanders known to have traveled with various parties has been compiled from newspaper accounts, journals, letters, Wade's *Overlanders of '62*, and other archival material. Biograpical material as been compiled from similar sources as well as Canada census records for 1861 and 1881, directories of businesses, Gold Commissioner's records in British Columbia, Hudson's Bay Company records, and numerous other printed sources.

The information is listed and abbreviated in the following order. Name; date of trek; hometown at time of trek; party and, in the case of 1859 overlanders, their second affiliation; birth date and place (B.); origin; age at time of trek; religion; date married (M.), spouse (and spouse's birth date if known) and number of children; pre-journey occupation (P. occ.); occupation post-journey (Occ.); residences post-journey and dates, abbreviated by state if not in B.C. (R.); dates of death (D.); and place buried if known (Bd.). Any particular notes of interest are then added. In the occupation category the word "yeoman" will be noted, a term for landowner used in the 1861 census.

An asterisk before names indicates they spent time in Cariboo, the original destination. Most of this information comes from the issuance of mining certificates, recorded in the Gold Commissioner's records, as well as directories, voters' lists, and census records.

A note to family researchers. Information on individuals which has been collected often far exceeds the space limitations of any book and the author welcomes further information or inquiries from those searching for family.

## OVERLANDERS OF 1858–61

Amesbury, William. 1858. Faribault, Minn. Faribault party. R. Colville, Wash., 1859.
Anderson, Dr. Charles L. 1859. St. Paul, Minn. Nobles party. B. Va. R. Nev. 1860s; Santa Cruz, Cal.
Bohanan, Shubeal. 1858–59, N. B., Canada. New Brunswick party. Occ. lumberman.

Brewster, [?]. 1858. Mankato, Minn. Mankato-Tête Jaune parties. R. [B.C., 1858?].

Brown, Z. B. (James). 1858–59. N. B., Canada. New Brunswick party. Occ. lumberman.

Bunker, W. E. (Billy). 1858. [St. Paul Minn.?] Moulton party.

Burnham, George C. 1858. St. Paul, Minn. St. Paul-Hector parties. Occ. miner. R. Cal., Minn., 1858; B.C., Similkameen, 1859.

Caldwell, William N. (Billy). 1858. St. Paul, Minn. Nobles-Caldwell parties.

Campbell, John A. (Big John). 1858–59. N.B., Canada. New Brunswick party. Occ. lumberman.

Campbell, Thomas. 1858–59. N.B., Canada. New Brunswick party. Occ. lumberman.

Cheever, James. 1858. St. Paul, Minn. Nobles-Caldwell parties.

Clorine, [?]. 1858. [St. Paul, Minn.?]. Moulton party.

Contu, F. 1861. Reid party.

Cook, George. 1858. Hastings, Minn. Hastings-Palliser parties. R. Wash. 1859.

*Cooney, Charles. 1858–59. St. Paul, Minn. New Brunswick party. B. March 17, 1835, Banagher, Ireland. Age: 24. M. 1867, Betsy Allard, dau. of Jos. Allard, HBC. Occ. leather-dresser; miner, 1860; packer, 1869; stockman. R. B.C., Fraser, 1860; Cariboo, 1862; Tranquille, 1869–1917. D. May 13, 1917.

Dignan, John Pat. 1858. St. Paul, Minn. Nobles-Caldwell parties. Occ. prop. of billiard saloon.

Dillman, James. 1858–59. N.B., Canada. New Brunswick party. Occ. lumberman.

Duff, Elijah. 1858. Belleville, Canada West. Jessop-Moulton parties. B. August 15, 1823, Canada East. English. Age: 36. P. occ. British army officer. Occ. packer; stockman, hotelman. R. Wash., Colfax and Spokane. Duff and his two brothers established a ranch on the Snake River and later in Whitman county. In 1887 they went into the hotel business in Colfax. Duff never married, "his heart having remained to a Canadian girl." D. June 26, 1920, Spokane. Bd. Colfax.

Edgar, William. 1858–59. N.B., Canada. New Brunswick party. Occ. lumberman.

Emihiser, Ira. 1858. Faribault, Minn. Faribault party. R. Colville, Wash., 1858.

Fairweather, William. 1858–59. N.B., Canada. New Brunswick party. Occ. lumberman.

Foster, A. C. 1858–59. N.B., Canada. New Brunswick party. Occ. lumberman.

Gibson, Joe. 1858. Mankato, Minn. Mankato-Faribault parties. B. [?]. "Young" in 1858. R. Walla Walla, Wash., 1859.

Gooderich, Dr. J. D. 1858. St. Paul, Minn. Nobles party. Occ. physician.

Goodrich, Charles. 1858. St. Paul, Minn. St. Paul-Goodrich parties. R. St. Paul, 1858; Dalles, Wash., 1859.

Graham, Thomas. 1858–59. N.B., Canada. New Brunswick party. B. [1837?]. Age: 22. Thomas Graham became a prominent millowner and architect in New Westminster, where he built the attorney general's house, the original Royal Columbian hospital, and the Capt. Irving home, now a museum. In 1869 he migrated south to California where he died in San Diego in 1899.

Hall, J. J. 1858. Mankato, Minn. Mankato-Faribault parties. R. Walla Walla, Wash., 1859.

Hamilton, John W. 1858. New York. Nobles-Thibodo parties. B. 1830. Age: 29. Occ. reporter; bookkeeper, 1859. R. Portland, Ore., 1859.

Hammond, Fletcher M. 1858. Hastings, Minn. Hastings-Goodrich parties. B. 1836. O. Age: 22. P. occ. merchant. R. Portland, Ore., 1860.

Harding, Anning. 1858–59. N.B., Canada. New Brunswick party. Occ. lumberman.

Harding, Dwight. 1858–59. N.B., Canada. New Brunswick party. Occ. lumberman.
Harris, Nelson. 1858. St. Paul, Minn. Nobles-Caldwell parties. Occ. barkeeper, 1859.
Henshaw, Albert, 1858–59. N.B., Canada. New Brunswick party. Occ. lumberman.
Henshaw, David. 1858–59. N.B., Canada. New Brunswick party. Occ. lumberman.
Hind, Edward (Ned). 1858. Faribault, Minn. Faribault-Caldwell parties. Occ. saddler. R. Cal., 1849; Ft. Edm., 1858; Wash., 1859; B.C. [New West., 1862?].
Hodgson, G. W. 1858. Mankato., Minn. Mankato party.
Holmes, Thomas. 1858–62. Shakopee, Minn. Holmes party. B. 1804, Bergerstown, Pa. Age: 54. Occ. real estate dealer; promoter; Indian trader. Holmes led several more wagon trains west. See Helen White, *Ho! For the Gold Fields*. D. 1888, Cullman, Alta.
Houck, Joseph S. 1858. Faribault, Minn. Faribault party. R. Colville, Wash., 1859.
Howard, D. W. 1858–59. N. B., Canada. New Brunswick party. Occ. lumberman.
*Jessop, John. 1858. Whitby, Canada West. Jessop-Moulton parties. B. June 29, 1829, Norfolk, Engl. English. Age: 30. Methodist. M. March 31, 1868, Victoria, B.C. to Margaret Fausett, dau. of Wm. Faucett, Ireland. P. occ. school teacher. Jessop reached the goldfields but returned in debt so took up journalism again. He founded the *Times* in New Westminster and the *Press* in Victoria, both unsuccessful. He then returned to teaching. He was instrumental in framing the first education act of B.C. and in 1872 became the first superintendent of schools for the province. He resigned in 1878, a victim of government change. He was later appointed provincial immigration agent. Jessop died on the street, with his boots on, March 30, 1901, in Victoria.
Johns, R. W. 1858. Hastings, Minn. Hastings party. R. B.C., Victoria, 1859.
Johnson, H. S. 1858–59; N. B., Canada. New Brunswick party.
Johnson, J. G. 1858–59; N. B., Canada. New Brunswick party. Occ. lumberman.
Jones, John W. 1858; Faribault, Minn. Faribault party. B. Nov. 7, 1831, Pleasant Grove, I. American. Age: 27. P. occ. clerk. Occ. printer. After a short sojourn in Portland Ore., in 1860 Jones headed for the silver strikes in Nevada in 1862, where he worked for various newspapers. In 1868 he moved to San Francisco where his escape came in alcohol. Early on the morning of Dec. 12, 1868, he jumped, or fell, from his boarding house window while suffering the effects of three days of drinking. He died within two hours. He is buried at Laural Hill.
Jones, William. 1861. Reid party.
Kennedy, Duncan P. 1858; St. Paul, Minn. Nobles-Caldwell parties. Occ. trader.
Kerr, James. 1858–59; N. B., Canada. New Brunswick party. Occ. lumberman.
Koffman, [?]. 1858. [St. Paul, Minn.?]. Moulton party.
Leith, George. 1861. Reid party.
Linton, E. W. W. 1858. Tête Jaune party. Occ. tailor. R. New West., 1861; Victoria, B.C., 1865. D. Dec. 25, 1865, Victoria, of drowning.
*Loveland, C. A. 1858. Hastings, Minn. Hastings-Tête Jaune parties. Occ. miner. R. B.C., Cariboo, 1859. Returned to Wisconsin and visited Edmonton in 1896.
Lynch, Thomas (Judge). 1859. St. Paul, Minn. Nobles-Thibodo parties. B. 1835. Age: 24. Occ. clerk.
McCullough, George (McCully). 1858. St. Paul, Minn. Nobles-Caldwell parties.

*McLaurin, D. F. 1858. Hastings, Minn. Hastings-Hector parties. B. Glasgow, Scot. Scottish. Occ. miner. R. Cal.; Australia; Minn., 1858; B.C., Cariboo, 1860; Red River and Ft. Edm., 1861. D. Sept. 13, 1861, Red River.
Marble, Manton, 1858. New York. Nobles party. Occ. reporter.
Martin,[?]. 1858. Hastings, Minn. Hastings party. D. March, 1858. Ft. Pitt. Bd. Ft. Pitt.
Maxwell, James. 1858. Hastings, Minn. Hastings-Palliser parties. R. Wash., 1859.
Montgomery, Charles W. 1858–59. N. B., Canada. New Brunswick party. Occ. lumberman.
*Moore, John Pearsey. 1858–59. Grey Co., Canada West. New Brunswick party. B. 1823, Grey Co. Irish. Age: 36. Baptist. M. Agnes Whiteford. Occ. miner; stockman. R. B.C., Cariboo, 1859–67; Nicola, 1867–81. D. Nov. 4, 1881, Nicola.
*Moore, Samuel. 1858–59. Grey Co., Canada West. New Brunswick party. B. 1821, Montreal, Canada East. Irish. Age: 38. Presbyterian. M. April 10, 1873, Grey Co., Mary Ann Whiteford, 1856–81. Occ. miner; packer; stockman. R. B.C., Cariboo, 1860–67; Nicola, 1868–1900. Samuel and John Moore became well-known stockmen in the Nicola area where they ran the Beaver Ranch.
Moulton, J. C. 1858. St. Paul, Minn. Moulton party.
Nobles, Col. William H. 1858. St. Paul, Minn. Nobles party. 1816. New York. Age: 43. Methodist. M. Pre-1848, Miss Parker. P. occ. machinist; blacksmith; wagonmaker, 1848. R. Ill.; Minn.; Cal.; Minn. Nobles served in the Civil War as Lt. Col. of the 79th New York regiment. He resigned that commission prematurely and returned to St. Paul where he died in poverty in 1876. He left a wife and two children in Calfornia and a son in St. Paul.
Palmer, John. 1858. Faribault, Minn. Faribault party. R. Colville, Wash., 1859.
Palmer, John (Boney). 1858. [St. Paul, Minn.?]. Nobles-Thibodo parties. B. 1832. Age: 27.
Pambrun, Pierre Chrysologue Jr. 1858. Lac La Biche. Tête Jaune party. B. 1823, Ft. Walla Walla, Ore. Canadian. Age: 36. Occ. freetrader. R. Lac La Biche, Red River. D. 1902.
*Perry, Alfred. 1858. B. Eastern USA. Little is known of Perry's early life but after he arrived in B.C. he became a "well-known" explorer and worked for a time as Walter Moberly's assistant. He was murdered by an Indian on the north shore of Burrard Inlet near Moodyville just before another expedition, on the night of July 29, 1869.
Reed, George N. 1858. St. Paul, Minn. Nobles-Thibodo parties. Occ. clerk.
Reese, [?]. 1858. [St. Paul, Minn.?]. Moulton party.
[*?] Reid, Dr. Alexander P. 1861. London, Canada West. Reid party. Occ. medical doctor. R. B.C., Victoria, 1862.
Robinson, [?]. 1858. Hastings, Minn. Hastings party. R. Ore. 1860; Minn., 1860.
Robinson, J. A. 1858–59. N. B., Canada. New Brunswick party. Occ. lumberman.
Sandont, John B. 1858. Rivière du Loup, Canada East. Nobles-Thibodo parties. B. 1835, Canada. Age: 24. R. Walla Walla, Wash., 1859.
Sanford, J. R. 1858. Faribault, Minn. Faribault-Tête Jaune parties.
Schaeffter, John (Dutch John). 1858. Faribault, Minn. Faribault party. R. Walla Walla, Wash., 1858.
Smith, B. Y. 1858–59. N. B., Canada. New Brunswick party. Occ. lumberman.
Smith, Henry. 1858. Nobles-Thibodo parties. B. 1838. [Cree ?]. Age: 21.
Smith, James Elnathan [Ellhi]. 1858. Faribault, Minn. Faribault party. B. Sept. 15, [?]. R. Walla Walla, Wash., 1859.

Smith, W. Ellis. 1858–64. St. Paul, Minn. St. Paul-Goodrich parties. Occ. surveyor; engineer. R. B.C., [1859?]; Minn.; Mont., 1864.
Sweeny, Wm. 1858–59. N. B., Canada. New Brunswick party. Occ. lumberman.
Taylor, James Wilkes. 1858. St. Paul, Minn. Nobles party. B. Nov. 6, 1819, Starkey, N.Y. English. Age: 40. M. 1845, Chloe Sweeting Langford. Occ. lawyer; special government agent. R. N.Y.; Ohio; Minn., 1856. D. 1893.
Thibodo, Dr. Augustus J. 1858. Kingston, Canada West. Nobles-Thibodo parties. B. 1834. Canadian. Age: 24. M. July 20, 1864, San Francisco, Cal. P. occ. medical doctor. Occ. medical doctor; Indian agent. R. Walla Walla, Wash., 1874; Ore.; Nev.; Ariz.; Ida. After moving around the U.S.A. Thibodo returned to Kingston, Ont., where he was an active member of the Masonic St. John's lodge. He died there Dec. 7, 1909.
Thompson, W. W. 1859. St. Paul, Minn. Nobles-Thibodo parties. B. 1839. Age: 20. Occ. real estate.
Wheelock, Joseph Albert. 1858. St. Paul, Minn. Nobles party. B. Feb. 8, 1831, Bridgetown, N.S. Age: 28. M. May 14, 1861, Concord, N.H., Katherine French, d. of Theodore French. Occ. editor, 1861–90. R. Minn. D. May 9, 1906.
Williams, Daniel T. 1858. Hastings, Minn. [Hastings?]-Palliser parties. Occ. slave; miner. "Nigger Dan" reached B.C. and may have stayed at Fort George with John Giscome. By 1869 he was in the Peace River area where over the years he developed a feud with HBC trader Kennedy and shots were fired. He was charged and sentenced to jail. Upon release he returned to mining in the Finlay River area and died there during the winter of 1886–87. The feud story is found in W. F. Butler, *The Wild North Land* (Edmonton: Hurtig, 1973. Reprint of 1873 edition) and an imaginative story in Peter Freuchen, *The Legend of Daniel Williams* (New York: J. Messner, 1956).
Windle, James. 1858–59. N. B., Canada. New Brunswick party. Occ. lumberman.
Young, John. 1859. [St. Paul, Minn.?]. Nobles-Thibodo parties. B. 1839, Ky. Age: 20. Occ. real estate.

## OVERLANDERS OF 1862

In 1862 there were approximately 250 known overlanders; 243 are listed.

*Alexander, Richard Henry. Toronto. SGE party. B. March 26, 1844, Edinburgh, Scot. Scottish. Age: 18. M. 1867, Emma Rammadge, 4 children. P. occ. clerk. Alexander packed and mined in Cariboo for a season, then worked in Victoria at a wholesale warehouse until 1870 when he became manager of Hasting's Mill in Vancouver. He served on city council in 1887–88 and died in Vancouver, Jan. 29, 1915.
Anderson, Arthur. Huntingdon. Huntingdon party. M. [?] McAdam. R. Kan., 1886. D. 1886.
*Anderson, James. Huntingdon. Huntingdon party. R. B.C., Cariboo; William's Ck., Nov., 1864. Returned east. D. 1910, Huntingdon.
Anson, [?]. [McMicking party?].
Ashton, Charles. R. Spallumcheen, 1887–88.
Atkinson, John. Red River settlement. SGE party. R. Ft. Edm., 1862.
*Baillie, George. B. 1843. Age: 19. M. Minnie Toy, d. of Pete Toy of Toy Bar. Occ. musician; saloon operator; rancher; hotel owner. R. Camerontown; Lillooet. D. B.C., 1887.
Ballantyne, Sam. Ft. Edm. SGE party. Rupert's Land. Halfbreed. P. occ. guide. R. Ft. Edm.
Barnes, R. S.

APPENDIX TWO    261

Beatty, [?]. SGE party. Occ. miner. R. B.C.
Bell, W. R. Occ. [stonecutter?]. R. [Victoria, 1863?].
*Berdan, Isaac Freeborn S. Southwold twp., Canada West. St. Thomas party. B. 1829, Upper Canada. U.E.L. age: 33. Evangelical Mission. M. 1855, Jannett, 1 son. P. occ. yeoman. Occ. farmer; miner. D. 1863, William's Ck. of typhoid.
*Berdan, Samuel E. Southwold twp., Canada West. St. Thomas party. B. 1825, Upper Canada. U.E.L. Age: 37. Evangelical Mission. M. [1852?], Catherine, 2 children. P. occ. yeoman. Occ. farmer; miner. R. B.C., Cariboo.
*Blanchford, Harry. Huntingdon. Huntingdon party. B. 1837-40, Lower Canada. English. Age: 22, C. of E. M. 1879, Indian girl, Mary. P. occ. blacksmith. Occ. blacksmith. R. Cariboo; William's Ck., Nov. 1864; Lytton, 1881.
Borthwick, A. [Alex?].
[Bouche?], James. McMicking party.
Bowland, John. Niagara. Queenston party treasurer. B. 1823, Ireland. Irish. Age: 39. Methodist. M. pre-1850, C. E., b. 1831, 6 children. P. occ. grocer. Occ. Overland Restaurant. R. Victoria, 1863; Queenston; Denver, Col.
*Bowron, John. Huntingdon. Huntingdon party. B. March 10, 1837, Huntingdon, Canada East. English. Age: 25. C. of E. M. first, Aug. 16, 1869, Emily P. Edwards; second, 1897, Eliz. Watson. Bowron stayed in Cariboo where he became the leading civil servant, taking positions as postmaster, mining recorder, and Gold Commissioner. He retired in Victoria where he died Sept. 6, 1906. The Bowron Lake Provincial Park is named for him.
Bowse, Thomas. McMicking party.
Brocklebank, W. Waterloo. Waterloo party rep.
Brodlunk, William.
[*?] Brown, A. Queenston party. Several Alexander Browns were issued mining certificates at Richfield in the spring of 1863.
*Brown, Johnnie W. SGE party. Occ. miner, R. B.C., Cariboo. Five J. Browns received mining certificates in the spring of 1863.
Brownlee, Robert W. St. Catharines. Queenston party. B. 1841, Upper Canada. Irish. Age: 21. Wesleyan. P. occ. clerk. R. B.C., New Westminster, Jan. 1863.
Burgess, William R. Toronto. SGE party. B. 1835, Toronto. English. Age: 27. Unitarian. P. occ. merchant. R. [Barkerville?].
Burns, John B. Acton. Acton party. B. 1829, Canada West. Age: 33. Methodist. P. occ. farmer. Occ. foreman. R. B.C., Lillooet. D. Hamilton, Ont.
*Byers, David. [McMicking party?]. B. Canada. R. B.C., Cariboo; William's Ck. D. Feb. 1864, William's Ck.
Camehl, Christian. St. Peters. St. Peters party.
Camehl, Henry. St. Peters. St. Peters party.
*Cameron, William Birnie. Huntingdon. Huntingdon party. B. Feb. 1839, Lottingstone, Scot. Scottish. Age: 23. Catholic. M. first, 1879, Elizabeth Gardiner; second, Agnes Blachford. P. Occ. blacksmith. Occ. blacksmith; school board, 1885-1909. R. B.C., Cariboo; Dewittville; Huntingdon, 1909. D. Jan. 27, 1919, Huntingdon, P.Q.
Campbell, Robert. McMicking party.
Cardinal, André. McMicking party. B. 1829, Jasper House. Métis. Age: 33. Catholic. Occ. guide.
Carpenter, James C. Toronto. SGE party. B. pre-1839. Occ. lawyer. R. Toronto. D. Sept. 30, 1862, Fraser River.
Carroll, James. Toronto. SGE party. B. 1833, Ireland. Irish. Age: 29. Catholic. M. pre-1861, Ellen, b. 1837, Ireland. P. occ. laborer.
Caydon, [?]. SGE party.

Chubbock, Samuel W. Niagara twp. Queenston party. B. 1839, Upper Canada. American. Age: 23. Methodist. M. pre-March, 1868, Anne E. LeCompte. P. occ. telegrapher. Chubbock, McMicking's brother-in-law, soon moved to Gold Hill, Nev., where he ran a bookstore and post office and served as telegrapher. He was active socially and served two terms in the Nevada Senate, 1874–79, and was appointed lieut. governor August, 1899. He resigned a few months later to take a new position with Wells Fargo in Oakland, Cal., where he retired in 1919. He died there Nov. 8, 1921.

Clarke, Michael. Huntingdon. Huntingdon party. R. B.C., [Cariboo?].

Clyde, Alexander. Huntingdon. Huntingdon party. B. 1833, Lower Canada. Age: 29. Evangelical Mission. M. pre-1856, Fanny, b. 1834, 4 children. P. occ. blacksmith. Occ. blacksmith.

*Cofferin, George. [SGE party?]. Occ. miner; [blacksmith?]. R. B.C., Cariboo; Camerontown, 1863–65.

Cogswell, [?]. Huntingdon. Huntingdon party.

*Collins, George, SGE party. R. B.C., Cariboo, 1863.

*Cormack, Richard S. B. 1825. Age: 37. Occ. owned and operated thirteen Mile House, 1865. R. B.C., Cariboo; William's Ck., 1863.

Couplin, William L. St. Peters. St. Peters party.

*Crandall, Mark. St. Thomas. St. Thomas party. Occ. miner. R. B.C., Cariboo, 1863–64. Associated with Weldon and Simonton in Tiger claim on William's Ck. *See* Cutler.

Crysler, Leonard. Niagara. Queenston party. B. Nov. 16, 1836, Niagara. Canadian. U.E.L. Age: 25. Evangelical Mission. M. 1870, Margery Clement, 2 children. Occ. medical doctor. R. Cal., 1862; Canada West, 1863–85. D. Jan. 13, 1885, St. Davids. Bd. St. Catharines.

Cumner, Simeon E. St. Davids. Queenston party. B. Canada. American. D. Cal.

Cunningham, Robert A. Huntingdon. Huntingdon party. B. 1830. Age: 32. Occ. miner; special agent, Barnum's circus. D. 1915 or 1916.

*Cutler, John R. St. Thomas. St. Thomas party. Occ. miner. R. B.C., Cariboo, 1863. Applied for mining certificate July 4, 1863, with Crandall, Nicol, and Prior.

*Davis, E. Page. St. Peters. St. Peters party. B. 1832, N.Y. Age: 30. M. Harriet, b. 1831. P. occ. attorney. Occ. U.S. customs; miner. R. B.C., Cariboo, 1863.

Dewitt, H. C. St. Peters. St. Peters party.

Dodd, John. St. Thomas. St. Thomas party. R. Canada West, 1864. Though Dodd was the titular head of the St. Thomas party he did not stay with them in Cariboo. Most of the party, however, remained in two tight groups and registered for mining licences on July 4 and 8, 1863, more than a year after they left home.

Douglas, J. [Goderich?]. Goderich party.

Duffin, P. St. Catharines. Queenston party.

*Dunn, Thomas. Acton. Acton party. Occ. miner. R. Ft. Edm. 1863; B.C., Cariboo, 1863. D. 1868, Lillooet.

Dunsmour, David, Huntingdon. Huntingdon party. B. 1840, Lower Canada. Irish. Age: 22. P. occ. laborer.

Earl, James.

Edgar, Robert. Huntingdon. Huntingdon party.

Ellis, M. Toronto. SGE party. R. returned east.

English, John. St. Thomas. St. Thomas party. B. 1831. Irish. Age: 31. Unitarian. M. [1867?], Ann, b. 1845, Engl. Occ. blacksmith. R. Yale, 1868–81.

*Ensign, Justus. Queenston. Queenston party. Occ. miner. R. B.C., Cariboo.

Fallon, John. McMicking party.

*Fannin, John. Kemptville. Queenston party. B. July 27, 1837, Kemptville, Ont. Irish. Age: 25. C. of E. P. occ. shoemaker. Occ. shoemaker; taxidermist; guide; civil servant. R. B.C., Cariboo; Hastings; Victoria. John Fannin mined in Cariboo with Archibald Thompson for several years. He is best remembered for his avid natural history interest which resulted in many papers for the Natural History Society and his forming the B.C. Provincial Museum. He has a creek, a lake, a group of mountains, and a mountain sheep *(ovis fannini)* named for him. He died June 20, 1904, and is buried in Victoria.
Farguharson, Donald.
*Farmer, George. Occ. miner. R. B.C., Cariboo, 1863.
Fisher, Capt. A. D. St. Peters. St. Peters party.
Fitzgerald, Fred. St. Catharines. Queenston party.
*Fletcher, Andrew. Montreal. SGE party. B. 1841, Quebec. English. Age: 21. Presbyterian. Occ. miner; merchant. R. B.C., Cariboo; Stanley, 1863-88. D. May, 1913, [Phoenix, B.C.?].
Flett, George Jr. Red River settlement. SGE party. B. 1823, Rupert's Land. Scottish-Métis. Presbyterian. M. Nov. 26, 1840, Mary Ross, 2 children. P. occ. farmer. Occ. farmer; Presbyterian missionary, 1866. R. Red River; Ft. Edm.; Prince Albert, 1866.
Folley, William.
*Fortune, Alexander Leslie. Huntingdon. Huntingdon party. B. Jan. 20, 1831, St. Anicet, Lower Canada. Scottish. Age: 31. Presbyterian. M. Sept. 1861, Bathia Ross. P. occ. theological student. After working on the Cariboo road, Fortune went into business with Morrow in the Overland Restaurant, Victoria. He later mined in Barkerville and the Big Bend mines before settling near Spallumcheen. Twelve years after his trek he brought out his wife and together they built a fine farm. He died July 5, 1915, and is buried in the Lansdowne Cemetery.
Fortune, William C. St. Davids. Queenston party. B. 1838, Yorkshire, Engl. English. Age: 24. C. of E. M. Lytton, B.C., Jane McWha, b. 1842, Ireland. P. occ. tanner. After working for the HBC for several years William, no relation to Alexander, settled at Tranquille, near Kamloops. Here he built the first flour mill in the interior and later the steamer *Lady Dufferin*, which ran the Thompson River for fourteen years. He died Dec. 1, 1914, and is buried in Kamloops.
Fowler, Jacob. Yarmouth twp. St. Thomas party. b. 1824, England. English. Age: 37. Baptist. M. [1850?], Sarah, b. 1830, Upper Canada, 2 children. P. occ. farmer
Frederick, Walter. SGE party. Occ. miner. R. Ft. Edm., 1862.
*Gage, William. Huntingdon. Huntingdon party. R. B.C., Cariboo, 1863-68.
Gardner, J. R. St. Peters. St. Peters party.
Gauley, Robert, and son. McMicking party. Occ: gunsmith. R. New West., 1862.
Gilbert, Wm. [Robt?]. Queenston. Queenston party.
Glassford, J. P. Ottawa. Ottawa party. B. 1841, Ottawa. Age: 21. Methodist. P. occ: carpenter. R. Walla Walla, Wash., March, 1863.
Glassford, William. Ottawa. Ottawa party. B. 1834, Ottawa. Age: 28, Methodist. M. pre [1859?], 1 daughter. P. occ. carpenter. R. Walla Walla, Wash., March, 1863.
[*?] Glen, John Jr.
*Glen, John Sr. Occ. miner. R. B.C., Cariboo, 1863-72.
Gunn, George. Red River settlement. SGE party. B. Red River. Scottish. Occ. farmer. R. Ft. Edm.
Hall, Erastus C. Acton. Acton party. B. 1839. Canadian. Age: 23. Wesleyan Methodist. P. occ. clerk. D. Sept. 4, 1862, St. Albert. Bd. St. Albert.

Hall, J. C. Huntingdon. Huntingdon party.
Halpenny, John. Ottawa. Ottawa party. Irish. Occ. miner.
Halpenny, Joseph T. Ottawa. Ottawa party. B. 1844. Irish. Age: 18. Methodist. Occ. miner; carpenter. R. B.C., Cariboo; Victoria, 1881.
Halpenny, William. Ottawa. Ottawa party. B. 1830, Brockville, Ont. Irish. Age: 32, Methodist. M. [1860?], Lois, b. 1842, [widow?]. Occ. miner; guide. R. B.C., Cariboo; Victoria, 1881. William was working on the Cameron claim when gold was struck. He was associated with the Beaver claim and he ran a boarding house on Lightning Creek. He died on Nov. 7, 1896, in Victoria, where he was buried.
Hamilton, Henry [Harry]. Toronto. SGE party. R. Ft. Edm., 1863.
Hamm, M. Andrew. St. Thomas. St. Thomas party. Occ. miner. R. B.C., Cariboo.
*Handcock, Alfred Ormsby. Toronto. SGE party. B. May 23, 1843, St. Malo, France. Irish. Age: 19. C. of E. M. May 13, 1872, Bloomington, S.D., Sophia Ester, several children. P. occ. student. Occ. cordwood cutter; teamster; sawyer. R. B.C., New West.; Cariboo, 1863; Ida.; Neb.; Cd.; Bloomington, S.D., 1869. D. Jan. 9, 1926. Bd. Blue View Cemetery, Vermilion, S.D.
Handcock, Harry W. Toronto. SGE party. B. 1841, Ireland. Irish. Age: 21. C. of E. M. post-1863, Mexico. Occ. waiter. R. Victoria; Mexico. Bd. Mexico.
Hanscome, M. G. St. Peters. St. Peters party.
Hardy, F. F. McMicking party.
*Harkness, Robert. Iroquois. Queenston party. B. 1833, Dundas, Canada West. Irish. Age: 29. Presbyterian. M. June 25, 1856, Sabrina Wood, 6 children. P. occ. merchant. Harkness worked in Cariboo for three summers, then returned to Sabrina. He taught school, bought a hotel, and in 1882, in partnership with his son, bought the *Picton Times* which he operated until his death in 1884.
*Harper, Ephram S. B. 1839, Canada West. Irish. Age: 23. Presbyterian. Occ. miner; millwright; carpenter. R. B.C., Cariboo; Barkerville, 1885. Dobson Prest wrote in 1863 that Harper was the only overlander to strike gold. He later ran a mill on William's Creek.
Harrison, William.
Hart, [L. J.?]. St. Peters. St. Peters party.
Helstone, John. London. Rennie party. B. [1812?], Engl. English. Age: 50. Congregationalist. M. pre-1861, Catherine, b. 1830, Ireland. P. occ. hospital steward. D. Oct., 1862 on Fraser River.
*Heron, Robert. Montreal. Montreal, party. B. 1837, Montreal, Canada East. Canadian. Age: 25. Spiritualist. Occ. saddler. R. B.C., Cariboo, 1863; Victoria, 1877–89.
Hind, William. Toronto. SGE party. B. 1832, Engl. English. Age: 30. P. occ. artist. Occ. artist. R. Victoria, 1863; N.B., 1870. After years as a professional artist Hind worked for the Intercolonial Railway in New Brunswick. After his death in Sussex in 1888 his paintings were lost. They were rediscovered by B.C. Provincial Librarian John Hosie in 1927.
*Holes, Andrew. Moorehead, Minn. St. Thomas party. B. Feb. 10, 1836, Ithaca, N.Y. American. Age: 26. M. 1870. Occ. kiln-worker; land agent. R. B.C., Cariboo; Moorehead, Minn. Applied for a mining certificate in 1863 with four other St. Thomas men.
*Holloway, Robert. SGE party. B. 1833, Norwich, Engl. English. Age: 29. Episcopalian. M. [1860?], Margaret, b. 1843, 9 children. Occ. editor and proprietor of *Cariboo Sentinal* 1868–75, then editor of *Colonist* and *Standard*. R. B.C., Cariboo; Barkerville; Richfield; Victoria. D. May 21, 1909, Victoria. Bd. Victoria.
*Hough, Joseph Z. Scarborough party. B. 1829, U.S. American. Age: 33. Wesleyan Methodist. P. occ. engineer. Occ. engineer; restaurant and saloon owner.

R. B.C., Cariboo; Barkerville, 1863–81. Hough was a partner in Barkerville's Eldorado Saloon and an active member of the Cariboo Amateur Dramatic Association.

Hugill, William. Fullerton. Queenston party. B. 1838. English. Age: 24. Wesleyan Methodist. P. occ. teacher. Occ. miner. After wintering in Victoria in 1862–63 Hugill wrote his family saying, "If you do not hear from me again for a considerable time don't feel uneasy," and headed for the creeks. That was the last his family heard of him until a 1972 television show mentioned his grave in Barkerville. The stone reads, *"In memory of William Hugill. Late of Fullerton, Canada West, who died August 31, 1863, aged 25. Blessed are the pure in heart, for they shall see God. Inscribed as a token of ESTEEM by his Overland companions."*

Hunniford, John. St. Catharines. Queenston party. B. Portadown, Armagh, Ireland. Irish. M. pre–1858, Letitia Hardy, 3 children. Occ. roadworker; seaman; lumberman; merchant. R. Victoria, 1862; San Francisco, 1863; St. Catharines, 1864.

*Hutchinson, A. F. [B. H.]. Bayham. St. Thomas-Hutchinson parties. Occ. HBC, 1863. R. Ft. Edm., 1863. After wintering in Edmonton Hutchinson, Malcolm, Kelso, Kyse, and one other man came through to Cariboo in the spring of 1863. Dr. Cheadle in his *North-West Passage by Land*, 1865 (facsmile edition Toronto: Coles Publishing Co., 1970) and his journal follows their footsteps and remarks on their journey.

Irwin, William. Huntingdon. Huntingdon party.

Jones, Dave. Toronto. SGE party.

Jones, Tom. Toronto. SGE party. B. [1844?], Upper Canada. Irish. Age: 18. Roman Catholic.

Jonson, [?]. SGE party.

Joslin and/or Jocelyn, Joshing. SGE party.

*Kelso, James. Acton. Acton-Hutchinson parties. B. 1834, Scot. Scottish. Age: 28. Presbyterian. Occ. miner; blacksmith, 1881. R. B.C., Cariboo; Barkerville, 1863; Keithly Ck., 1881–83.

Kemps, [?]. [Kempth, John?]. McMicking party.

Kenkey, H. [Keonkey, A.?].

*Kyse, Samuel. McMicking-Hutchinson parties. B. 1823. American. Methodist. Occ. miner, 1863–87. R. Ft. Edm., 1863; B.C., Cariboo; Keithly Ck., 186[?]–87.

Lane, James M.

Leader, Philip. Huron city. SGE party. D. drowned on Fraser, Sept.–Oct., 1862.

Leet, J. J. [Leck?]. [McMicking party?]. R. left for San Francisco, Jan. 1863.

Little, Thomas. [John]. [St. Peters?]. [St. Peters party?].

*Lockwood, Charles. Canada. [McMicking party?]. Occ. miner. R. B.C., Victoria, 1862; Cariboo, 1863.

*Love, Timoleon. Red River settlement. SGE party. B. Oct. 1, 1827, Lancaster, Ky. American. Age: 35, Protestant. P. occ. gunsmith; soldier; miner. Occ. gunsmith; carpenter; miner. R. B.C., Cariboo, Ft. Steele, 1897. D. Feb. 18, 1905, Cranbrook, B.C. Bd. Cranbrook.

*McAlpine, Daniel. Southwold, Canada West. St. Thomas party. B. 1839, Upper Canada. Scottish. Age: 23. Baptist, P. occ. yeoman. R. B.C., Cariboo, 1863. Most of the St. Thomas men stuck together, and on July 8, 1863, McAlpine applied for a mining license with four others.

McBeath, Hector. Red River settlement. SGE party. Occ. HBC, 1863. R. Ft. Edm.

*McCollum, C. Southwold, Canada West. St. Thomas party, B. 1835, Scot. Scottish. Age: 27. Baptist. P. occ. merchant; tailor. Occ. tailor, 1868. R. B.C., Cariboo; Barkerville, 1863–1868. McCollum ran a tailor's shop in Barkerville which later became Joe Denny's saloon.

McConnel, Arch. Niagara twp. Queenston party. b. 1836, Ireland. Irish. Age: 26. Presbyterian. M. pre–1858, [E. M.?], B. 1840, 2 children. P. occ. blacksmith.

*McCormick, William G. Canada. Occ. miner. R. B.C., Cariboo; Barkerville, 1870; Jack of Clubs Ck., 1888. D. Aug. 1, 1890. Bd. Barkerville cemetery.

McFie, A. [Huntingdon?] [Huntingdon party?] R. St. Paul.

*McIntosh, James Huntingdon. Huntingdon party. Occ. miner. R. B.C., Cariboo, 1863.

*McIntyre, Norman. Occ. miner. R. B.C., Cariboo; Barkerville. Associated with the Ferguson Co. on Conklin Gulch. He left with "a good swap of dust" and returned east in 1874.

*McIntyre, Peter. Huntingdon. Huntingdon party. B. 1834. Age: 28, Occ. miner; teamster; rancher. R. Okanagan, 1880s. D. Feb. 12, 1925, aged 91.

McKenzie, James. Toronto. Toronto party. B. Scotland. Scottish. Occ. Overland Restaurant, 1863, R. Victoria, 1863.

*McKenzie, William. Occ. miner. R. B.C., Cariboo, 1868–76.

McLean, John W. SGE party. R. Ft. Edm., Feb. 3, 1863.

McMicking, Robert Burns. Stamford. Queenston party. B. July 7, 1843, Upper Canada. Scottish. Age: 19. Presbyterian. M. 1869, Margaret B. Leighton. Robert worked for the ill-fated Collins Overland Telegraph for several years, then the Western Telegraph Union, and in 1871 was appointed superintendent of the Government Telegraph Lines. He became general manager of the B.C. Telephone Co. in 1904. He died Nov. 27, 1915, Victoria.

McMicking, Thomas M. Queenston. Queenston party leader. B. April 16, 1829, Stamford, Canada West. Scottish. Age: 33. Presbyterian. M. July 12, 1853, Laura Chubbock, 4 children. P. occ. merchant. He worked at a shingle mill for the winter and was appointed town clerk in 1864 and deputy sheriff in 1866 in New Westminster where his family joined him. On August 25, 1866, his son William fell into the Fraser River. Thomas jumped in to rescue him but both were swept under a log boom and drowned. His funeral was the largest the town had seen.

*McNaughton, Archibald. Montreal. Montreal-St. Peters parties. B. Montreal, March 16, 1843. Scottish. Age: 19. Presbyterian. M. first, Margaret Peebles; second, 1890, Elizabeth McGregor. Occ. miner; assessor, 1884; HBC, 1884; postmaster, 1887; merchant. R. B.C., Cariboo; Quesnel, 1868–84. McNaughton and Fletcher went into business together as merchants in Stanley on Lightning Ck. D. July 21, 1900.

McPherson, Dr. James G. Whitby. Whitby party. B. 1843, Upper Canada. Scottish. Age: 20. Church of Scotland, P. occ. medical student.

McQuarrie, Daniel. B. 1840, Scot. Scottish. Age: 22. Presbyterian. M. [1877?], Jessie Kellie, b. 1854, 3 children. Occ. shoemaker. R. Yale, 1881; Kamloops, 1890.

*McQueen, Isaac Brock. Fingal. St. Thomas party. B. 1830, Brockville, Canada West. Scottish. Age: 31. Wesleyan. M. [commonlaw?], Susan Grant, halfbreed, 4 children. P. occ. yeoman. Occ. HBC; stockman, 1881. R. B.C., Cariboo, 1863; Kamloops, 1865–95. D. Oct. 11, 1895. Bd. at his ranch on N. Thompson.

MacRae, John. SGE party.

McRonock, [?]. SGE party.

Mains, Brock. St. Thomas, St. Thomas party.

*Malcolm, John. Acton. Acton–Hutchison parties. B. 1838, Banff, Scot. Scottish. Age: 24. Protestant. Occ. HBC; bookkeeper; miner. R. Ft. Edm., 1863; B.C., Cariboo; Barkerville, 1863; Harvey Ck., 1868–87. Malcolm was secretary of the

Wessels Co. He was a partner in the Foster claim, which produced 550 ounces of gold in three weeks. D. 1910. Bd. Barkerville.

Mara, John A. Toronto. SGE party. B. July 21, 1840, Toronto. Irish. Age: 21. Wesleyan Methodist. M. Jan. 6, 1883; Alice Barnard, 2 children. P. occ. clerk. Mara went into business supplying Big Bend country miners, then opened a store in Kamloops. A strong confederationist, he served as a member of the legislative assembly in 1871 and in 1883–86, when he was speaker of the House. He took a ship, the *Stikine Chief*, to the Klondike rush but it sank. He died in Victoria in Feb. 1920.

Marlow, Peter. Queenston. Queenston party. B. 1830, Pa. Age: 32. M. 1858, 7 children. P. occ. farmer. Occ. farmer; miner; sawyer. R. B.C., Cariboo; Ontario, 1865. D. Sept. 28, 1912. Bd. Grimsby, Ont.

Marshall, W. Acton. [McMicking party?].

Matheson, Donald. Kildonan, Red River settlement. SGE party. B. May 22, 1835, Red River. Scottish. Age: 27. M. pre–1871, Christina Sutherland, b. Apr. 29, 1845. P. occ. guide for Earl of Southesk. Occ. HBC, 1863. R. Ft. Edm., 1863 to post-1874.

Mead, Rollin P. St. Thomas. St. Thomas party.

Merriat, W. [Economy]. Huntingdon. Huntingdon party. B. Engl. English.

Mickle, George. Scottish.

Mickle, Hiram Florien. B. Jan. 22, 1833, Canada. Scottish. Age: 29. Church of Scotland. M. pre–1881, Lucinda. Occ. blacksmith. R. B.C., Nicola Valley. D. July 21, 1883, Nicola. Bd. United Church, Nicola.

Mickle, Wheeler Adam. B. 1843, Essex Co., Upper Canada. Scottish. Age: 19. C. of E. M. Oct. 12, 1870, L. Julia Thomson, b. 1843, 4 children. Occ. blacksmith; teamster; stockman. R. B.C., Nicola Valley, 1870–80; Calgary, Alta., 1881–1918. D. April 26, 1918, Cochrane, Alta.

Miller, A. H. [Hugh?]. McMicking party. A. H. Miller applied for a mining certificate in May 1863. An A. Miller had a saloon in Barkerville.

Miner, Alonzo. St. Peters. St. Peters party.

Miner, D. St. Peters. St. Peters party.

Monroe, Felix. Lac Ste. Anne. Queenston party guide. Rupert's Land. English–Métis. Occ. guide. R. Ft. Edm.

Morrow, W. W. Montreal. Montreal party rep. P. occ. merchant. Occ. restauranter; miner. R. Victoria, 1863; Kootenay, 1875.

Morton, Thomas.

*Murphy, Thomas. Stamford. Queenston party. Occ. miner. R. B.C., Cariboo, 1863–69.

Myers, A. Toronto. SGE party. Occ. cabinet maker, [1863?]. R. Victoria, 1863.

Nellas, J. W. G. Queenston. Queenston party.

*Nicol, Albert G. [Nicoll]. St. Paul. St. Thomas party. R. B.C., Cariboo, 1863.

*Nicols, John. Huntingdon. Huntingdon party. Occ. miner. R. B.C., Cariboo.

O'Beirne, Eugene Francis. Red River settlement. SGE party. B. 1809–11, Clooneen, Ireland. Irish. Age: 51. Catholic–Protestant. Occ. lecturer; con-man. R. B.C., 1863; Australia, 1864.

*Oney, Daniel. [Olney?]. Huntingdon. Huntingdon party. B. 1837, U.S.A. Age: 25. Wesleyan. M. pre–1860, Elizabeth, b. 1837, 1 child. R. B.C., Cariboo, 1863.

Otta, Charley. Whitby. Whitby party. B. 1835, Engl. English. Age: 27. P. occ. bookbinder. Occ. bookbinder. R. B.C., [Victoria?], 1863.

Pattison, Eustache. Toronto. SGE party. B. Launceston, Cornwall, Engl. English. Age: 19. D. Sept. 8, 1862, Ft. George. Bd. Ft. George.

Penwarden, Frank. St. Thomas. St. Thomas party. D. Oct., 1862, Thompson River.

Perkins, [?]. Huntingdon. Huntingdon party.
Phillip, Thomas. Huntingdon. Huntingdon party. Irish.
Phillip, William W. Huntingdon. Huntingdon party. B. March 17, 1840, Ormstown, Canada East. Irish. Age: 22. R. San Francisco, 1863; U.S.A.; San Diego, 1916.
*Pinkerton, Jack. Leeds County, Canada West. McMicking party. B. 1839, Westport, Leeds Co. Irish. Age: 23. Methodist. M. 1875, Westport, Ont., Margaret Blair, b. 1859, 4 children. Occ. miner. R. B.C., Cariboo; Barkerville, 1862–1917; Vancouver, 1917–20. D. Feb. 23, 1920, Vancouver.
*Polly, William J. Occ. miner. R. B.C., Cariboo.
Prest, Dobson E. Queenston. Queenston party. P. occ. carpenter. Occ. miner. R. Victoria, 1863; Gold Hill, Nev. D. Truckee, Cal., 1885.
*Prior, Stoughton. Southwold twp., Canada West. St. Thomas party. B. 1830, United States. Age: 32. Baptist. M. pre-1852, Mary, b. 1833, Upper Canada, 4 children. P. occ. farmer. Occ. miner. R. B.C., Cariboo. *See* Cutler.
*Purdy, [Daniel?] Occ. miner. R. B.C., Cariboo.
*Putnam, I. C. Ingersoll. Queenston party. Occ. miner. R. B.C., Cariboo.
Rachette, Charles. McMicking party. Guide.
*Redgrave, Stephen. Toronto. SGE party. B. 1831, Crick, Northamptonshire, Engl. English. Age: 31. C. of E. M. 1849, Birmingham, Engl., Martha Susan Lincoln, 6 children. P. occ. police offer. Redgrave spent his first winter as cook for the Victoria police station. He was constable on William's Creek in 1865, but resigned over a pay dispute. He moved to Virginia and bought the Redgrave Farm, returning to B.C. in 1873. In 1884 he became sheriff of Kootenay. Redgrave often "mis-remembered" his role, placing himself at the center. Life was not stable. His wife died and he remarried, in 1894, but that lasted only four years. His son was convicted of attempted murder in 1893. Redgrave died in Golden, B.C., March 25, 1903, and is buried in Golden Municipal Cemetery.
Reid, George. Huntingdon. Huntingdon party. B. 1841, New Erin, Canada East. Age: 21. Evangelical Mission. Occ. blacksmith.
Rennie, Gilbert. London. Rennie party. B. 1833, Canada East. Scottish. Age: 29. Presbyterian. M. pre-1859, Mary Butler, b. 1839, Engl., 1 son. P. occ. shoemaker; cordwainer. R. B.C., Cariboo, 1863; Canada West, 1864.
Rennie, Thomas. London. Rennie party. B. 1839, Canada East. Scottish. Age: 23. Free Church of Scotland. P. occ. shoemaker. D. Oct. 1862, Fraser River.
*Rennie, William. London. Rennie party. B. 1831, Scot. Scottish. Age: 31. Free Church of Scotland. M. Aug. 29, 1880, Mrs. Catherine Evans, b. 1841, Wales. P. occ. shoemaker. Gilbert Rennie returned east after one season in Cariboo, but William returned to Barkerville where he was shoemaker until at least 1886. After that nothing is known of him or his wife.
Robertson, Alexander C. Goderich. Goderich party rep. B. 1839. Age: 23. Church of Scotland. P. occ. surveyor. D. Sept. 4, 1862, Fraser River.
*Robinson, Henry W. Occ. miner. R. B.C., Cariboo, Nov. 4, 1862.
Robinson, Joseph [James]. Queenston. Queenston party. B. 1822. Age: 40. M. Jan. 1, 1848, Mary Dixon. Occ. farmer. R. Ont. D. 1911. Bd. Buffalo, NY.
*Rogers, Samuel Augustus. B. Northern Ireland, 1840. Age: 22. Presbyterian. Occ. merchant; sheriff; MLA. R. Barkerville. D. June 4, 1911. Bd. Barkerville.
*Rose, James [I. A.?]. St. Davids. Queenston party. M. 1873, St. Davids, R. B.C., Cariboo, 1863; Cal., 1873. D. Berkeley, Cal.
*Ross, John S. Occ. miner. R. B.C., Cariboo, May 9, 1863.
*Schubert, Augustus. Red River settlement. Red River party. B. Dresden, Germany, 1827. German. Age: 35. Presbyterian. M. Springfield, Mass., 1856, Catherine O'Hare. Occ. tavern keeper; miner; farmer. R. St. Paul, 1856; Red

River, 1860. After wintering at Fort Kamloops the Schuberts moved to Lillooet while Augustus spent about fifteen summers in Cariboo. There he was convicted of "claim jumping" and forced to remove his stakes from the ground of the Perseverance Co. Two more children were born. Catherine became matron of the Cache Creek Board Schooling. They took up land in the Spallumcheen Valley and moved there in 1883. Many descendants still reside in the valley. Augustus died in Armstrong on July 10, 1908. He is buried there.

Schubert, Augustus Jr. Red River settlement. Red River party. B. St. Paul, Minn. Dec. 23, 1856. German. Age: 26. Catholic. Occ. farmer. R. Lytton–Cache Ck., 1881. D. Nov. 10, 1946.

Schubert, Mrs. Catherine. Red River settlement. Red River party. B. April 23, 1835. Irish. Age: 27. Catholic. M. Springfield, Mass., 1856, Augustus Schubert. D. July 18, 1918.

Schubert, James Armstrong. Red River settlement. Red River party. B. St. Paul, Aug., 1860. German. Age: 2. Occ. carpenter; builder; merchant. R. Penticton; Hedley; Tulameen, 1913–38. D. March 17, 1938.

Schubert, Mary Jane. Red River settlement. Red River party. B. St. Paul, Minn. March 7, 1858. German. Age: 4. M. Jan. 26, 1874, Lillooet, Richard Hoey. D. Winnipeg, 1876.

André—Schubert's farm hand. Red River settlement. Red River party.

Pierre—Schubert's farm hand. Red River settlement. Red River party.

*Schuyler, William B. Huntingdon. Huntingdon party. B. 1839, Upper Canada. American. Age: 23. C. of E. Occ. miner. Schuyler, Bowron's cousin, resided with Bowron in Barkerville until 1886 when he returned east. He died in California in 1923.

*Sellar, James M. Huntingdon. Huntingdon party. B. Aug. 22, 1834, Huntingdon, Canada East. Age: 27. M. 1860, Mary Jane [?]. B. 1842. Occ. miner. R. San Francisco, 1862; B.C., Cariboo, 1863; Huntingdon; Toronto; S.D., Minn. D. Minneapolis, Minn.

Sellar, William. Huntingdon. Huntingdon party. B. pre–1834, Huntingdon, Canada East. M., 1 son.

*Shaw, John. B. Scotland, 1830. Scottish. Age: 32. Presbyterian. Occ. miner. R. B.C., Cariboo.

*Simonton, Dr. William B. St. Peters party. P. occ. U.S. Army surgeon. Occ. medical doctor. Simonton mined on William's Creek with the Tiger Company, of which four of the seven partners were overlanders. He left in 1865 and moved to Salem, Ore., and was not heard of again.

Simpson, Donald [George?]. Whitby party rep.

Smith, Big Thomas. Toronto. SGE party.

*Stevenson, Dr. Edward. Belleville. Queenston party. Occ. medical doctor. Stevenson practiced in New Westminster and Cariboo for a couple of years and then moved to California. He returned to Victoria in 1883 and was last heard of there in 1889.

Stevenson, John. Huntingdon. Huntingdon party. B. Sept. 25, 1827, Glasgow, Scot. Scottish. Age: 35. P. occ. cabinet maker; farmer. Occ. farmer. D. March 15, 1915, Huntingdon.

Strachan, T. [Wm.] [S]. Seaforth, Huron Co. London party. P. occ. clerk. D. Oct., 1862, Thompson River.

Sutherland, George. Red River settlement. SGE party. R. Ft. Edm., 1863; Red River, 1863.

*Thompson, Archibald. Stamford twp. Queenston party. B. Jan. 6, 1830, Niagara. Scottish. Age: 32. Presbyterian. M. first, 1853, Miss Brown, 1 child; second, 1875, Miss Gilchrist. P. occ. blacksmith. Occ. blacksmith; bridge superintendent. R. Victoria; Cal.; Niagara. D. April 23, 1909, Stamford.

[*?]Thompson, George, Toronto. SGE party. Occ. miner. R. B.C., Cariboo.

*Thompson, Wm. Henry Guelph. Niagara. Queenston party rep., (lieut.). B. 1836, Canada West. Scottish. Age: 26. Free Thinker. Occ. miner. R. B.C., Barkerville; Cariboo, 1886; Horsefly, 1909. Thompson had good claims on Conklin Gulch along William's Ck. and served on the hospital board. D. 1912.

*Tife, C. E. [SGE party?]. R. B.C., New West., Nov., 1862; Cariboo; Barkerville, Nov., 1864.

Tompkins, Dr.

Torrance, Joseph. B. Scotland. Scottish. Age: 24. Occ. policeman. R. B.C., Victoria. D. Jan. 27, 1871, Victoria.

*Tunstall, George C. Huntingdon. Huntingdon party. B. Dec. 5, 1836, Montreal. Canadian. Age: 26. C. of E. M. 1865, Miss Annie Morgan, 2 children. Tunstall mined in Cariboo for many years. In 1879 he was government agent at Kamloops and in 1885–89 Gold Commissioner for Similkameen, later a magistrate. He died Jan. 6, 1911.

Turner, Wrathman. Toronto. SGE party.

Urlin, Adolphus N. Southwold, Canada West. B. 1816, London, Engl. English. Age: 46. M. 1839, Agnes Elizabeth Kelly, 1 son. P. occ. farmer. Occ. farmer. R. B.C., 1863; Canada West, 1864.

Urlin, Alfred John. Southwold, Canada West. B. 1840, Southwold. English. Age: 22. M. Missoula, Mont. 2 daughters. P. occ. farmer. R. B.C., Missoula.

*Wallace, George. Toronto. Huntingdon party. B. Ireland. Irish. C. of E. M. c. 1880, Montreal, Miss Moss, d. June, 1883, 2 sons. After working for and owning newspapers in Victoria, Wallace founded the *Cariboo Sentinel* in Barkerville in 1865. He sold out after only a year and tried to start another in Big Bend. He was a member of the provincial legislature in 1867 but left B.C. in 1871. He managed a troupe of Japanese jugglers and later toured Europe with the Siamese twins. Married, he moved to England and returned bankrupt, then worked for several newspapers. He died a few years after his wife in Montreal in May 1887.

Wallis, Mark. Southwold twp., Canada West. St. Thomas party. B. 1844, Upper Canada. English. Age: 18. Baptist. R. Spallumcheen, B.C. D. Ontario.

*Warren, Robert. Acton. Goderich party. B. Oct. 13, 1823, Kingussie, Scot. Scottish. Age: 38. Knox Church. P. occ. farmer. Occ. miner. R. B.C., Cariboo. Returned to Acton and farming in 1866. D. Nov. 1, 1889. Bd. Fairview Cemetary, Acton.

Watson, Hugh. Huntingdon. Huntingdon party.

Watson, John. Huntingdon. Huntingdon party.

*Wattie, James. Huntingdon. Huntingdon party rep. B. Dec. 1829, Strathdon, Scot. Scottish. Age: 33. M. 1858, Miss Janet Morrison, 3 children. P. occ. miner, Cal. Occ. miner; owner, woolen mill. R. B.C., Cariboo; William's Ck., 1864. Though on the creeks only a short time, the Watties had a significant effect on the social life. They had a claim adjoining the Cameron claim and shares in the Cameron Co. James used his profits to help build the William's Creek hospital and the Reading Room. He was also managing director of the Bedrock Drain Co. He was given a testimonial and gold watch when he left in Nov. 1864. He returned east to Huntingdon and then operated a woolen mill at Valleyfield, Quebec. He retired in 1890 and died in Nov. 1907.

*Wattie, William. Huntingdon. Huntingdon party. B. May 8, 1842. Scottish. Age: 20. M. first, 1870, Elizabeth Gibson; second, Emma Smith. P. occ. machinist. Occ. miner, machinist. R. B.C., Cariboo; William's Ck.; Worcester, Mass. After leaving William's Creek, William returned to his trade of machinist and

patented over sixty weaving industry devices. He died on April 24, 1918.
*Weir, J. Occ. miner. R. B.C., Cariboo.
*Weldon, Andrew. Southwold twp., Canada West. St. Thomas party. B. 1817, United States. Age: [45?]. M. pre-1844, Linissa, b. 1846, Ireland, 7 children. P. occ. yeoman. Occ. miner. R. B.C., Cariboo, 1864. Weldon lived in Barkerville where he was associated with Crandall and Simonton in the Tiger Co. His house was later used as the Wesleyan parsonage.
*Wessels, Allen. SGE party. Occ. miner, 1963–64; hotelman, John Bull Hotel, Victoria, 1864. R. B.C., Cariboo; William's Ck., 1864; Victoria, 1865. Allen was likely the owner of the Wessels Co. for whom John Malcolm was secretary.
Weston, George A.
White, Joe. Huntingdon. Huntingdon party.
Whiteford, John. Red River. SGE party guide. B. Rupert's Land, bapt. May 23, 1824. Métis. Anglican. Occ. guide.
Whitley, Spencer P. McMicking party.
Wilcox, James. Stamford twp. Queenston party. B. 1830, Scot. Scottish. Age: 32. Evangelical Mission. M. pre–1858, Margaret, b. 1840, two children. P. occ. miller. Occ. miner and a parter in the Union Co. R. B.C., Cariboo; William's Ck., 1864.
Willis, J.
Wonnacott, G. B. Belleville, Toronto party.
*Wood, R. H. Niagara. Queenston party. M., 1 daughter, Johanna E. Wood. P. occ. farmer. Occ. miner; court clerk, 1863–68. R. B.C., Cariboo, 1863; Victoria.
[*?]Wright, John. (son of Wm.). [SGE party?]. B. 1850, Canada West. Irish. Age: 12. Methodist. M. [1877?], Alice Rowebottom, b. 1861. Occ. dairyman. R. B.C., Cariboo; Williams Lake, 1881.
Wright, John R. London. Rennie party. B. 1837, Engl. English. Age: 25. C. of E. M. pre-1857, Elizabeth, b. 1838, Engl., 2 daughters. P. occ. shoemaker. D. Oct., 1862, Fraser River.
[*?]Wright, Wm. (and son John). [SGE party?]. B. [Ireland?]. Irish. Methodist. M. [widower?]. Occ. miner; roadhouse owner. R. B.C., Cariboo, 137 Mile House.

# Addendum to the 2000 Edition

As with any book of research or history the story continues to evolve long after the last pages are set in type. "Overlanders" is no exception.

In a letter, January 7, 1979, Isabel Walker wrote of Archibald Thompson that, "Some years before his death he collected the letters he had sent to his brothers and sent them to B.C. to someone who had requested them." These letters appeared to have disappeared and evaded all research efforts.

Dr. Wade, in his "Overlanders of 1862", published in 1932, refers to several groups of documents that later could not be found. On page 289, footnote 43, reference is made to Archibald Thompson letters in the collection of Dr. Wade "now unfortunately lost." The loss of these and other papers such as "the Wattie journal" in the Wade collection meant that certain aspects of the Overlander story had to be drawn from Wade's version of the events, resulting in less immediacy and more conjecture. But history keeps unfolding.

In 1987 Kamloops dump scavengers came across a collection of papers they recognized should not be trash. They contacted Ken Faverholdt, then curator of the Kamloops museum, who recognized what had been found, the lost Dr. M.S. Wade collection of Overlander papers, trashed by unconcerned descendants.

In the collection were several Archibald Thompson letters, reminiscences of A.L. Fortune, lecture notes of William Wattie, the diary excerpts of James Wattie and the original of a Wrathman Turner letter from Edmonton, reprinted in the Globe. Identified as coming from the Dr. Wade estate, they now reside in the Kamloops B.C. Museum and Archives in the M.S. Wade Collection.

While these papers do not alter the story, they provide detail formerly only available in Wade's secondary source. For those interested they provide a more complete story of the Wattie journey to Bella Coola and their encounters with Chilcotin and coastal First Nations groups and details from Thompson of the Thompson River journey. Fortune's notes refer mostly to later years.

As research becomes easier with increased microfilm availability, more computer databases and the massive amount of material now available on the Internet, the detail becomes more readily available. However, despite that, the story of the overlanders has not changed, will not change.

What have become more accessible are the vital statistics and documents that record the specific events in an Overlander's life, births, marriages, and deaths. The Overlanders have remained of importance and interest to me. As information was uncovered it was added to their files. These updates to biographical information are covered with some first edition errata in the following pages.

Further information, maps and photographs not reproduced in this book will be found on our Overlanders website at: http://goldrushbc.com/overlanders.

Those interested in further Overlander genealogical research should check the BC Archives website and link to BC Vital Statistics, which only became available in the last few years

# Notes to the 2000 Edition

### Chapter Three
Page 51. The date in paragraph two should be November 12, not the 2nd.

### Chapter Four — The Man from Brechin
In 1988 Quesnel researcher Lana Fox drew my attention to an advertisement and note in the October 11, 1873 issue of the *Cariboo Sentinel*.

"Attention is called to the advertisement in today's issue asking for information of Alexander Hebenton, a native of Brechin, Scotland, who came to this province overland in 1858, and worked at his trade [joiner] in Victoria in that year. " The advertisement added, "it is supposed he left for the gold fields."

In November 1999 I posted a note on an Internet Scottish genealogy site, looking for Hebenton. That day I had a response from George Hebenton in Glasgow, Scotland, with a wealth of information about the family of the "Man From Brechin", a 24-year-old from a large family centered on Brechin.

The identity of the "Man from Brechin" is known; his fate remains a mystery.

### Chapter Seven – Across the Rocky Mountains
This chapter details in part the travels of the Hastings (Minnesota) Party whose winter quarters were Moose Woods and Fort Pitt. A gunfight over provisions left Fletcher Hammond wounded and his partner Martin dead.

While it was known that HBC Factor Wm. Christie of Fort Edmonton took dispositions from the Hastings party and HBC servants these could not be located, as detailed in footnote 3 of Chapter Seven.

The collection of papers was located by chance in the BC Archives some years after publication. Hammond, described as "the prisoner", and the papers were, according to Christie's notes, turned over to his party "to deliver him to the authorities on the West side of the Rocky Mountains ... to stand his trial for the murder of John K. Martin."

There is no record of a trial. Hammond was last heard of in Portland, Oregon, in 1860. However, the papers must have been delivered to BC Colonial administration for them to appear in the BC Archives.

The papers do add some details of the event and party members and makeup. The argument was over a few dollars that Martin still owed Hammond for provisions. Martin wanted to leave the party and take provisions. When he began taking pemmican Hammond challenged him. Martin drew a revolver and fired. Hammond returned fire and killed Martin.

Martin, we now know, was John K. Martin, who joined the party after they left Hastings, Minnesota. Hammond was 22 years old, born in Ohio. Maxwell's

Christian name was Wyman Maxwell Jr., not James. Robert McDougall was also a member of either the Hastings or McLaurin party

**Chapter Twelve**
Page 239 refers to "a cabin occupied by three colored men going to Peace River". It is now evident that these men were Dan Williams, John B. McLean and Henry McDame, all former Cariboo miners.

# Update to Appendix Two rosters and biographical information

### 1858-1861
**Cooney, Charles,** appears in the 1881 census for Kamloops, record number 3144.
**Jessop, John.** Jessop's wife Margaret Fausett was on the brideship Tynemouth.
**Jones, John W.** is buried at Laurel Hill cemetery in San Francisco, California.

### 1862
*****Alexander, Richard Henry.** His wife, Emma Tammadge [not Rammadge] was on the brideship Tynemouth. He ran in Vancouver, B.C.'s first election but was defeated.
*****Baillie, George,** died in New Westminster, B.C. on November.29, 1887.
*****Halpenny, John.** Born c 1848, Ottawa. At 14, the youngest overlander next to the Schubert children. Married, Oct 1872, Nancy Kellough. In B.C. in 1885. Died Ontario.
*****Halpenny, Joseph Giltrap.** Born July 12, 1843, Canada. Age 18. Married 1871, Oregon, Elizabeth Gilmore. Returned to Alberni, B.C. 1881. Died 1916, Buried in Alberni.
*****Halpenny, William.** See notes. Married Lois Chapman. See also p.174. When he died the *Colonist* incorrectly reported he was the last Overlanders.
*****Hamm, Andrew,** went to Cariboo.
*****Harkness, Robert,** died October 23, 1883, Ontario.
*****Heron, Robert,** died June 14, 1904, Victoria.
*****Hough, Joseph,** spent time quartz mining in California.
*****Hugill, William,** did go to Cariboo and is buried there.
*****McCormick, William.** It appears Overlander McCormick was not the Barkerville William G. McCormick, according to correspondence from the latter's family.
*****McQuarrie, Daniel,** died Oct. 8, 1911.
*****Miller, A.H.,** went to Cariboo
*****Oney, Daniel,** died in 1873 with an estate of $6.50, B.C. Sessional Report, 1877.
*****Rennie, Gilbert,** went to Cariboo before returning home.

*Shaw, John.** Shaw remained in Barkerville until his death March 12, 1898.

*Stevenson, Dr.,** has the first name Eady, not Edward. He moved to Vancouver and died in Victoria Nov. 13, 1909.

**Turner, Wrathman,** born 1837, settled near Burnaby Lake, near Vancouver B.C. He died September 9, 1913.

**Young, James.** In his 1970 book *Bella Coola,* Cliff Kopas devotes several pages to the journal of a James Young who he says went to Bella Coola with the Wattie brothers and A.L. Fortune. However, neither Wattie nor Fortune makes mention of Young and both specify the count as three men, not four. Kopas has no footnotes and his records, as Dr. Wades were, are lost. There was a John Young who crossed in 1859 with the Nobles-Thibodo party but nothing more is known about him.

**Nelson, Frank.** When we moved to Pioneer Ranch outside Williams Lake, B.C. in 1995 we were told by the family most associated with the ranch, the Wiggins, that they believed it had first been settled by "Frank Nelson, an Overlander". The coincidence seemed too strong. We have confirmed his settling here in 1876, but unfortunately not that he was an Overlander.

# Overlanders who died in route.

### Brechin party – 1858
Guide John Flett and 13 unnamed died, all from Indian attacks.

### Hastings-1858
Martin, [?] – Gunfight with party member at Fort Pitt

### 1862
Carpenter, James C. – Drowned on Fraser, Sept. 30, 1862
Hall, Erastus – accidental self-inflicted gunshot wound, Sept. 4, 1862, St. Albert
Helstone, John – Starvation, Oct. 1862, Fraser River
Leader, Philip, - drowned on Fraser, Sept.-Oct. 1862
Pattison, Eustache – Dyptheria, Sept. 8, 1862, Fort George
Penwarden, Frank – Drowned on Thompson, Oct. 1862
Rennie, Thomas – Starvation, Oct. 1862, Fraser River
Robertson, Alexander – Drowned on Fraser, Sept 4, 1862
Strachan, T. – Drowned on Thompson, Oct. 1862
Wright, John R. – Starvation, Oct. 1862, Fraser River

# Notes

The following abbreviations are used throughout the Notes and Bibliography.

| | |
|---|---|
| CAV | Vancouver City Archives |
| DAR | Daughters of the American Revolution |
| HBCA | Hudson's Bay Company Archives |
| MiHS | Minnesota Historical Society |
| MoHS | Montana Historical Society |
| OMI | Oblate of Mary Immaculate |
| PAA | Provincial Archives Alberta |
| PABC | Provincial Archives British Columbia |
| PAM | Provincial Archives Manitoba |
| SC/UBC | Special Collections Division, University of British Columbia |
| SFU | Simon Fraser University |
| VPL | Vancouver Public Library |
| PAC | Public Archives Canada |
| USNA | U.S. National Archives |

## Chapter One

1. *Pioneer and Democrat*, Olympia, Washington, March 5, 1858.
2. Thomas Seward, "A miner's experience on the Pacific Slope," Victoria *Colonist*, February 26, 1905.
3. Waddington, *The Fraser River Mines*.
4. *Daily Alta California*, April 21, 1858.
5. State of California, pamphlet, *Sutter's Fort*.
6. Elsie G. Turnbull, "First Gold in British Columbia," *B.C. Historical News*. See also: Spry, *Palliser Papers*; Avery, *Washington: A History*; Ormsby, *British Columbia: A History*.

7. *Daily Alta California*, April 21, 1858; Akrigg, *Chronicles*, vol. 2, p. 105.
8. Taylor, *Northwest British America*.
9. Spry, *The Palliser Expedition*.
10. Hind, *Narrative*, vol. 1, pp. xiii–xv.
11. *Parliamentary Debates*, 3rd Series, vol. 151, p. 1102, quoted in Ormsby.
12. Ormsby.
13. White, *Ho! For the Gold Fields*.
14. John Prebble, *The Highland Clearances*. Harmondsworth, England: Penguin Books, 1982; Gilman, Gilman, and Stultz, *Red River Trails*.
15. Gilman. The names of the trails are those used in *Red River Trails*, though these names may not have been in use at the time of the overlanders' travels.
16. St. Paul, *Pioneer and Democrat*, July 2, 1858.
17. *St. Croix Valley Old Settlers' Association Obituary Record*, vol. 4, MiHS.
18. Blegen, "James W. Taylor, A Biographical Sketch," pp. 153–95.
19. Flandrau, *Encyclopedia of Biography of Minnesota*, vol. 1, p. 490.
20. St. Paul, *Pioneer and Democrat*, July 10, 1858.
21. Ibid., July 11, 1858.
22. Bird was the country-born son of HBC factor James Bird. Jamey Jock was born about 1790 and while still a young man joined the HBC and was sent to live with the Peigans of the Blackfoot confederation to entice them to trade. He had crossed the Rockies many times. John E. Wickman, "James Bird Jr.," *The Mountain Men*. California: Arthur Clark Co., 1968.
23. Bird's Bears River Pass is likely the Marias Pass, long sought by westbound explorers. Chief Mountain Pass is the South Kootenay west of the readily identifiable monolith of Chief Mountain near Glacier National Park. Bad Back Fat Pass is unknown, although James Doty of the Stevens expedition refers to a creek or river of that name in his 1855 explorations. Medicine Rock Pass is the North Kootenay Pass, although the rock itself has not been identified. Crows Lodge Pass is the modern Crows Nest Pass.
24. St. Paul *Pioneer and Democrat*, July 14, 1858.

## Chapter Two

1. See party rosters in appendix 1.
2. Letter to editor of *Venago Spectator*, Pennsylvania, quoted by Giddens, *Minnesota History*, Summer 1979, p. 216.
3. *Globe*, June 30, 1859. *Victoria Gazette*, September 22, 1858. Jones journal, *see* bibliography. All quotes and information are from this journal unless otherwise noted. This journal was evidently copied from a diary and, while accurate to the spirit, Jones draws conclusions obviously not possible until after the journey. In addition, portions of the journal are virtually word-for-word with the account by Jim Smith for the *New York Commercial Advertiser*, written before Jones recopied his journal. It is possible, however, that Smith copied Jones.
4. Letter from J. Jones to Colonel McKenny, published in the *Chatfield Democrat*, July 2, 1859.
5. John Jones had been somewhat of a mystery until just before publication. The Faribault *Central Republican*, August 4, 1858, p. 1, says that "another, (Mr. Jones,) was connected with Capt. R. B. Marcy's exploration of Red River of Louisiana in 1852." There was indeed a John Jones with Marcy's expedition. This individual was born in London. In 1852 he was a private and

according to U.S. Army records he stayed with the U.S. Infantry's Company D of the 5th Regiment from 1837 until 1861. See U.S.A. War Office Records: enlistment papers, muster role, and letter. To support the view that this was the John Jones of the Faribault overlanders there are his journal references to the swamps of Louisiana and the Gulf of Mexico and his interest in all things military. However, the recent discovery of a John W. Jones obituary in Nevada papers such as the *Reese River Review*, December 18, 1868; the *Mountain Champion*, December 26, 1868; and the *San Francisco Bulletin* seem to indicate that two men have been confused. The John W. from Faribault was a native of Pleasant Grove, Iowa, and about thirty-seven years old, born on November 7, about 1821. Marcy's John Jones, according to enlistment papers, was born in either 1813, 1816, or 1817, depending on which series of papers is correct, and, in 1858, was stationed in Utah. It seems evident that the editor of the *Central Republican* mistook the Faribault Jones for another he knew or had heard of.

6. St. Paul *Pioneer and Democrat*, September 15, 1858; White, *Ho! For the Gold Fields*; Faribault *Central Republican*, August 4, 1858; Spry, *Palliser Papers*.
7. The route from St. Cloud to the Otter Tail Crossing is now paralleled by Interstate 94, except the highway is five to fifteen miles north.
8. Morton, *Manitoba: A History*.
9. It arrived in 1878, by which time it had been sold, resold, and renamed the St. Paul Minneapolis and Manitoba Railway Company. Spry, *Palliser Papers*, p. 100; Folwell, *Minnesota*.
10. Bowsfield, *Canadian Dictionary of Biography*, vol. 10, p. 628.
11. Jim E. Smith, letter in St. Paul *Pioneer and Democrat*, September 15, 1858. Unless otherwise indicated, notes on Smith's movements are from this letter.
12. Palliser had passed in April and found the ruins smoking, the site abandoned, a scene to become a classic a century later in John Ford Westerns. Palliser caught up to the survivors a day later and gave them food, a gun, and ammunition. Spry, *Palliser Papers*, p. 171.
13. Adam was one of a large family born to Michael Klyne, a trader at Jasper House in 1825 and postmaster in 1835. Also spelled Klein, Kline, Cline, and Clyne. Spry, *Palliser Papers*, p. 96. See also Hind, *Narrative*, p. 156, and Southesk, *Saskatchewan and The Rocky Mountains*, p. 35.
14. Hime photos in Huyda, *Camera in the Interior*.
15. Francis, *Battle for the West*.
16. Although there is no direct proof that Major Seton was the officer to whom Jones refers, evidence suggests this conclusion. Jones says the officer was "in charge," and Seton's subsequent actions fit with the Jones conversation. Seton's sketch book in the PAC indicates he was at Thunder Bay, Fort William, on May 31, 1857. By July he was visiting with Captain Palliser at Upper Fort Garry. See Spry, *Palliser Papers*, p. xxi. For documents on Seton's service and resignation, and information on the Royal Canadian Rifles, See p. 829 A. S. Morton, *A History of the Canadian West to 1870–71*, edited by Lewis G. Thomas (Toronto: University of Toronto Press, 1973); Public Records Office, London, England; War Office, 25/632 pp. 8 and 171; Colonial Office, 6/26. f96–98v.; PAC, Seton sketch book; letter from William McTavish to Sir George Simpson, HBCA D 5/47 f338–38b.
17. Ross, *Beyond the River and the Bay*, p. 68.
18. St. Paul *Pioneer and Democrat*, April 19, 1860; *Edmonton Bulletin*, October 8, 1896.
19. Hind, *Narrative*, p. viii.

20. "Bear Ellice," as he was known in the trade, a Northwester, had been instrumental in the amalgamation of the two companies. In 1858 he was the Right Honorable Edward Ellice, HBC Deputy Governor, one of the oldest members of the fur trade. Spry, *Palliser Papers*, p. xxi.
21. Pierre Chrysologue Pambrun Jr. was born in the Red River settlement in 1823, the second son of P. C. Pambrun Sr. and Catherine Humperville. Pambrun Sr. was French Canadian, a former British Army officer who joined the HBC as a clerk in 1815 and, after a career spread across Rupert's Land and the Columbia River country, had risen to Chief Trader in 1839. "Kitty" Humperville was the country-born daughter of Thomas Humperville and a Cree woman. Pambrun Jr. had been with his father when he served in the Oregon Territory, and likely returned to Red River when his father died in 1841.
22. HBCA, B63/a/4 1858-68, p. 15.
23. Holmes, *Mountain Men*, p. 239. See this for a more complete biography on Pierre Chrysologue Pambrun Sr.; *see also* HBCA, *Fort Edmonton Journal* B60/a/30 f51d.
24. Jones's journal, p. 33; Spry, *Palliser Papers*, p. 390 and p. xxxv-vi; McKay was the son of John Richards McKay, born in 1790 and for part of 1858 stationed at Touchwood Hills Post.
25. R. C. Russel in "Notes and Correspondence," *Saskatchewan History*, vol. 2, no. 3 (Autumn 1949): 38-39. John R. McKay may have been in charge at this time as the Northern Department minutes 1821-31 indicate he was posted here in 1858. Minutes of council of Northern Department of Rupert's Land, 1821-31, app. p. 446.
26. Hind, *Narrative* vol. 1, p. 411; Spry, *Palliser Papers*.
27. The hut that was marked on Palliser's map and recorded by Hector as being McMurray's trading post. It was a temporary establishment of the HBC built in the winter of 1857 to oppose freetraders. McMurray arrived in November of 1857 and by December 17 had only been able to build a small hut for storage, still living in a skin lodge. Obviously by the time Jones passed, "Fort Pike" had been abandoned. Spry, *Palliser Papers*, p. 190.
28. James Simpson entered the HBC in 1844, but is not mentioned in Company records after 1860. According to the *Palliser Papers* (Spry ed.) he was at Fort Pitt in December 1857 and March 1859; *see* pp. 192 and 390.
29. Sylvia van Kirk, lecture, Simon Fraser University, October 23, 1979, "Putting Women into History"; Francis, *Battle for the West*.

## Chapter Three

1. HBCA *Fort Edmonton Journal*, B60/a/30 1858-60; hereafter cited as *Fort Edmonton Journal*.
2. Dialogue is based on Jones's journal.
3. MacGregor, *Edmonton*.
4. *Fort Edmonton Journal*, B60/a/30.
5. Spry, *Palliser Papers*, p. 201.
6. For a discussion of the guide Rossette see notes to chapter 10, for he also guided and deserted the 1862 overlanders.
7. Dempsey, *The Rundle Journals*, p. 263; *Indian Tribes of Alberta*.
8. Dempsey, *Indian Tribes of Alberta*. Hall mentions the Stonies were very religious. They had received their instruction from Wesleyan missionary Rev.

Robert T. Rundle, who had adapted the Cree syllabic alphabet developed by the Rev. James Evans to Stoney and Blackfoot and given them prayer and study books.
9. Spry, *Palliser Papers*.
10. Dempsey, "A History of Rocky Mountain House."
11. When Blakiston came through in August he too noticed the carts and reported that they were left by Sinclair's emigrant party of 1854. He does not say how he knew, but it was in this vicinity that Sinclair's men dismantled their carts and made packsaddles for the mountain crossing. Fording the Bow brought travelers to its south side near the mouth of the Kananaskis River, which flowed northwards from headwaters in the high mountains of the Continental Divide.
12. Southesk, *Saskatchewan and the Rocky Mountains*.
13. Baptiste Gabriel, Palliser's guide, had attempted to find this route as a short cut to Bow Fort that summer of 1858, but became lost and gave it up. Spry, *Palliser Papers*, p. 265.
14. Although this theory of the Blackfeet versus the Kutenais is one of the basic tenets of Plains Indian ethno-history, it has been challenged by Claude E. Schaeffer in "Plains Kutenai, An Ethnological Evaluation," published posthumously in *Alberta History*, Autumn 1982. Schaeffer feels that smallpox played a large role in the tribe's shifting and that after a severe epidemic in the late 1700s the Kutenais were diminished and the Blackfeet moved into the attractive foothill vacuum. Jamey Jock Bird, who lived with the Peigans for many years, said the Kutenais used the North Kootenay Pass for eastward travel, and Crows Lodge or Crows Nest Pass for westward travel, dragging sleds on the ice of the Crows Lodge lakes. The "half-breed Kutenai," as he called them, a mix of Kutenai and Flathead, used the South Kootenay Pass.
15. George Bird Grinnell, "The Crown of the Continent," *Century Magazine*, September 1901, pp. 663–64.
16. J. E. Smith, St. Paul *Pioneer and Democrat*, September 23, 1859.
17. Kootenay Post had for several years been located south at the mouth of Rainy Creek, then moved upstream to the mouth of the Fisher. After the 1846 U.S./British Boundary Treaty, Edward Berland moved the post upstream to the Tobacco Plains, east of the river about five miles south of the new boundary. This location left it open to Blackfoot attack so the post was moved to the west side, first to the mouth of Dirge Creek (now Dodge) and later the mouth of Young Creek. In 1852 Edward Berland died and John Linklater took over as trader and in about 1857 moved the post back to its original site. O. W. Johnson, *Flathead and Kootenay*, pp. 331–32.
18. Ibid.
19. Spry, *Palliser Papers*, pp. 328 and 464.
20. Jones's journal; Spry, *Palliser Papers*, p. 571.
21. O. W. Johnson, *Flathead and Kootenay*.
22. Jones's journal; Spry, *Palliser Papers*, p. 464. It is possible that Linklater was not alone at the Tobacco Plains. John V. Campbell, who came to the Oregon Territory with Sinclair in 1854, says that he was in Colville until the fall of 1858, "when I was hired by Mr. Angus McDonald to go up to the Tobacco Plains to be assistant trader to Mr. John Linklater. The following March I went back to Colville." See *Washington Historical Quarterly*, vol. 8, no. 3. No overlander party records him being at this post.
23. St. Paul *Pioneer and Democrat*, July 25, 1860. Also *Globe*, August 10, 1859;

*Globe,* April 5, 1862; *Edmonton Bulletin,* October 8, 1896; *Hastings Democrat,* July 7, 1860; Spry, *Palliser Papers.* D. F. McLaurin was a native of Glasgow, Scotland, who had first sought gold as a California forty-niner, had gone on the Australian rush of 1851, and then returned to Hastings in 1856. J. J. Hargrave, *Red River* (Montreal: J. Lovell, 1871); J. W. Taylor, *Globe,* April 5, 1862. D. C. Loveland was a Minnesotan with family in nearby Galena. "Nigger Dan" Williams was an ex-slave who recognized only two authorities: Jesus Christ and Queen Victoria. He was later a legend in the Peace River country of Canada. Fletcher Hammond, twenty-two, married to Sarah, was a Hastings man. Spry, *Palliser Papers; Hastings Democrat,* July 7, 1860.
24. St. Paul *Pioneer and Democrat,* September 15, 1858; May 17, 1859. *Globe,* August 10, 1859. Hind, *Reports on the North West Territory,* Overlander information does not appear in Hind's *Narrative* version, nor in his "Rough Notes," 19 July–6 August, 1858; nor in his "Notebook" no. 13, 9 August–23 August, 1858, [Fort la Corne to Fort Ellice]; although his notes are for the most part illegible.
25. The party were traveling with a trader, possibly the McGillis who had been reported in the Jackfish Lake area the previous winter. Spry, *Palliser Papers,* p. 191n.
26. St. Paul *Pioneer and Democrat,* May 17, 1859.
27. Born in Bergerstown, Pennsylvania, in 1804, Tom Holmes spent the early years of his life as an Indian trader in the upper Mississippi–Great Lakes frontier called the North West. Holmes's keen eye had marked land suitable for farming and townsites. By 1849 he was living in Sauk Rapid and had been elected to the territorial legislature. When the townsite mania of the 1850s swept the region he was ready. He pre-empted a tract of land and laid out a town that became Chicago and followed with others in the Mississippi region: Milwaukee and Janesville and an idefinite number of towns in Wisconsin. In spite of his obvious talent as a developer or real estate promoter, Old Tom Holmes valued most the skills of his frontier life. He once said, "While I can only just about write my name now, I can skin a musk-rat quicker than an Indian." St Paul *Pioneer and Democrat,* March 7, 1860; July 25, 1858. White, *Ho! For the Gold Fields.* p. 25.
28. Wade, *The Overlanders of '62.*
29. OMI Records, G–I–360; *Lac Ste. Anne—Chronique du R. P. Fourmond, O.M. 1846–73,* PAA.
30. See party rosters for a complete listing of this party. Not all the New Brunswick overlanders agreed with moving west in the autumn of the year. Two young men, James Quigg, twenty-six, and Elijah Dunphy, twenty-five, and possibly one woman, Catherine Dungan, thirty-three, decided to stay in St. Anthony. Elijah Dunphy and Catherine Dungan, a widow, both born in New Brunswick, headed west four years later with James Fisk's wagon train. Dunphy settled at Helena, Montana, and Mrs. Dungan began a ranch at Ten Mile Creek, Montana. James Quigg worked in St. Anthony as a lumberman until 1863, when following the lead of Dunphy and Dungan he too went west with a Montana-bound Fisk train. Colin Inkster, *Winnipeg Free Press,* June 30, 1934; St. Paul *Pioneer and Democrat,* September 23, 1859; White, *Ho! For the Gold Fields.*
31. St. Paul *Pioneer and Democrat,* September 23, 1859.

## Chapter Four

1. *Guide Book for British Columbia by a Successful Digger,* n.d, n.p.

2. Descriptions of Victoria are from the *British Colonist*, October, 1859; Gregson, *Victoria*; R. B. Johnson, *Very Far West Indeed*; and photos of the 1858 period.
3. All block quotations are from the 1860 *Globe* unless otherwise credited.
4. Hind, *Narrative*, vol. 2, pp. 126–27.
5. Ibid., pp. 125–26.
6. Ibid., p. 417.
7. It appears from other overlander journals that this would have been the route taken.

## Chapter Five

1. Ormsby, *British Columbia: A History*; Waddington, *The Fraser River Mines*; Akrigg, *Chronicles*, vol. 2.
2. *Oshawa Vindicator*, March 1862.
3. *Canadian Album*.
4. Alice Munro, *The Newcomers*.
5. Kerr, *Biographical Dictionary*.
6. F. H. Johnson, *John Jessop*.
7. *Canadian Album*.
8. DAR, *Family Records and Reminiscences of Washington Pioneers*, vol. 6, p. 222.
9. Victoria *Colonist*, 1890.
10. Jessop's diary is lost as are early copies of the *Oshawa Vindicator*. Jessop's route is traced through summaries in the Victoria *Colonist* in 1890, the *Vindicator* in 1862, two *Vindicator* letters in *The Globe*, 1859, and diaries of other parties. Unless noted, information is from these accounts.
11. *Globe*, March 14, 1862; Jessop, *Oshawa Vindicator*, March 1862.
12. Harmon, *Journal*, pp. 18–19.
13. Grant, *Ocean to Ocean*, p. 21.
14. Harmon, p. 105; Ross, *Beyond The River and The Bay*, pp. 107–8, p. 179; Innes, *The Fur Trade in Canada*.
15. Morse, *Fur Trade Canoe Routes*.
16. Route descriptions from Fort William to Fort Garry are taken from Jessop, Hind, Morse, and the author's experience on portions of the route.
17. By 1872, when Sandford Fleming's C.P.R. survey party came through, forty-five-mile road had been constructed to Shebandowan Lake, from where vessels made their way north to Lac des Milles Lacs. Grant, *Ocean to Ocean*.
18. Hind, *Narrative*.
19. Their route was through the heart of what is now Quetico Provincial Park in Ontario. Pine Portage is 594 yards long, between Pickerel and Doré lakes. Jessop's Bruce Lake is likely the bay that forms in an arm of Pickerel Lake.
20. Hind and others record it as being 750 yards long, though modern maps of Quetico show it as 1452 yards.
21. *National Atlas of Canada*.
22. Remembering this in 1890 he mistakenly nicknamed Fort Frances, Hungry Hall, in fact the name of the post at the mouth of Rainy River.
23. Grant, p. 51.
24. A new post was built here two years after Jessop passed. It became the present town of Kenora, Ontario.
25. Southesk, *Saskatchewan and The Rocky Mountains*.

## Chapter Six

1. Marble, "Red River and Beyond."
2. Babcock, "Gateway to the Northwest," p. 251.
3. St. Paul *Pioneer and Democrat*, April 24, 1859.
4. Thibodo, "Diary—1859," p. 293; *Globe*, June 14, 1859; St. Paul *Pioneer and Democrat*, April 24, 1859.
5. St. Paul *Pioneer and Democrat*, May 17, 1859.
6. Thibodo, "Diary—1859," pp. 293 and 313; St. Paul *Pioneer and Democrat*, June 24, 1859; Babcock.
7. Brode, "Diary of Augustus Thibodo."
8. Ibid.
9. St. Paul *Pioneer and Democrat*, June 3, 1859.
10. Thibodo "Diary—1859."
11. Marble.
12. *St. Paul Daily Times*, May 24, 26, 27, 1859; *St Cloud Democrat*, June 16, 1859.
13. *St. Paul Daily Times*, May 24, 1859.
14. Gilman, Gilman, and Stultz, *Red River Trails*, pp. 69–70.
15. Joseph A. Wheelock, St. Paul *Pioneer and Democrat*, July 7, 1859.
16. Ibid.
17. Thibodo, "Diary—1859."
18. Ibid. Palmer should not be confused with John Palmer who traveled with John Jones. No evidence suggests they are the same person.
19. Gilman, *Red River Trails*.
20. Fort Abercrombie brochure, State of Minnesota.
21. Thibodo, "Diary—1859."
22. Marble.
23. Wheelock, "Diary."
24. Marble.
25. Ibid.
26. Bellecourt had only a short time left in the Red River area. He was about to be recalled once again, to serve the Acadians of Prince Edward Island. He never returned to the Red River valley. *Canadian Pictoral Biography*, n.p., n.d.
27. Marble, p. 589.
28. Michael Klyne Jr. was the son of Michael Klyne [Klein, Clyne], born, 1781, fur trader at Jasper House in 1825–35. Adam, who had a road house and ferry at Scratching River, north of Pembina, was Michael Jr.'s brother. *See* chapter 2. PAC MG25, G62, p. 514.
29. St. Paul *Pioneer and Democrat*, March 15, 1860.
30. Thibodo, "Diary—1859," p. 303.
31. Marble.
32. St. Paul *Pioneer and Democrat*, March 15, 1860.

## Chapter Seven

1. Spry, *Palliser Papers*; St. Paul *Pioneer and Democrat*; *Fort Edmonton Journal*.
2. *Edmonton Bulletin*; *Fort Edmonton Journal*, B60/a/30.
3. *Edmonton Bulletin*. On a spring trip to Fort Pitt, Christie and Hector took dispositions regarding the killing of Martin. No record of these dispositions has been found by either the author or Shirlee Anne Smith of the HBC archives.

4. *Fort Edmonton Journal*, B60/a/30 f49d, 50–51. Loveland's account in the *Edmonton Bulletin* indicates he took the Tête Jaune Pass.
5. *Fort Edmonton Journal*, B60/a/30 f49d. In *The Overlanders of 1862* Wade says a party left Fort Garry with a guide around the end of May and crossed via this pass but only one man, Linton, reached Victoria. While not a contemporary, Wade did know many of the overlanders when they were in later life and may have heard stories of this crossing. Colin Inkster, whose father employed several overlanders in Red River, also reports a similar group, but, like Wade, gives no sources. If Wade is correct, only Linton reached Victoria. After a short mining venture and term as a tailor he drowned visiting friends at a lighthouse on Christmas Day. Perry headed for the Cariboo and Pambrun was back in Fort Edmonton by January 1862 and later that year told Dr. Cheadle that he had crossed the Rockies several times and "had found gold in a small stream near Jasper House, having been confirmed in his discovery by Perry, the miner."
6. Spry, *Palliser Papers*, pp. 387–89; *Fort Edmonton Journal*, B60/a/30 p. 48.
7. Spry, *Palliser Papers*, p. 390.
8. *Globe*, August 10, 1859 p. 3; *Fort Edmonton Journal*, B60/a/30 f51d.
9. Spry, *Palliser Papers*, p. 393; *Fort Edmonton Journal*, B60/a/30; Fletcher Hammond, *Hastings Democrat*, July 7, 1860.
10. Spry, *Palliser Papers*, p. 400.
11. *Globe*, November 11, 1869.
12. Lord Southesk had written of this group on July 8 when he traversed the country north and west of Qu'Appelle Post: "The only tracks of any sort that we noticed were those of some Americans who, having started for Fraser River without a guide, had here lost themselves in the desert." It is possible that this was not Holmes but the party of four that Goodrich met at Old Bow Fort. *Saskatchewan and The Rocky Mountains*, p. 72.
13. Thibodo, "Diary—1859," p. 334; Fletcher Hammond, *Hastings Democrat*, July 7, 1860.
14. Goodrich went to the Dalles, then faded away, as do most of the men. Fletcher Hammond was in Portland the next spring. W. Ellis Smith later returned to Minnesota and joined another wagon train west with Captain Fisk in 1864. Holmes also returned, and led two wagon trains of American emigrants west via the Stevens route in 1862 and 1864. White, *Ho! For the Gold Fields*; Fletcher Hammond, *Hastings Democrat*, July 7, 1860.
15. Spry, *Palliser Papers*, p. 396.
16. Ibid., p. 393.
17. A description of Palliser's route and adventures is found in Spry's *Palliser Expedition* and *Palliser Papers*.
18. Spry, *Palliser Expedition*.
19. Spry, *Palliser Papers*.
20. Ibid., p. 469.
21. See note 42, chapter 10.
22. Cooney migrated to the USA at age eighteen in 1853. He worked briefly in New York, then moved to Trois Rivières, Quebec, where he worked as a leather dresser for three years. In 1857 he went west to St. Paul and worked on the railway survey.
23. *Fort Edmonton Journal*, B60/a/30.
24. Spry, *Palliser Papers*, p. 434.
25. Wade, *The Overlanders of '62*; *Globe*, February 18, 1860.
26. Thibodo, "Diary—1859."

27. *Fort Edmonton Journal*, B60/a/30 f61d.
28. Southesk, p. 144.
29. *Fort Edmonton Journal*, B60/a/30 f68 and 68d.
30. Southesk, pp. 262–63.
31. *Globe*, September 2, 1859.
32. Ibid.
33. As Jessop's letters from this period are lost, only brief information on their plains journey is available but they followed a route along the South Saskatchewan River (a few days ahead of Thibodo who remarked on their cart tracks). *See* chapter 6 notes for information on Jessop's accounts. All quotes from Jessop unless otherwise noted.
34. Hind, *Narrative*.
35. Thibodo, "Diary—1859."
36. Ibid. Duff joined the American-British Boundary Commission that winter and the following summer worked as a transit man leaving the commission at Boundary Pass (by which John Jones had crossed the Rockies in the autumn of 1860) to winter in Walla Walla. He was joined in the spring of 1861 by his two brothers R. H. and Thomas Duff and began running pack trains while mining at Pierce City during the summer. Florence Camp on the Salmon River was discovered that summer and miners deserted Pierce City for the new diggings. Provisions were short at the new camp and, were it not for the help of the Indians on whose land they were trespassing, they would have starved. In December 1861 Elijah Duff and his brothers loaded their pack train at the new city of Lewiston and headed south on an "impossible journey" over the mountains. Elijah Duff though had faced more difficult terrain with greater hazards on his cross country journey two years previously—Duff had crossed the Rockies. So on Christmas Day he arrived in Florence, a rough Santa Claus, loaded with provisions for hungry miners. DAR, *Family Records and Reminiscences of Washington Pioneers*. vol. 6, pp. 222-23.
37. Southesk, p. 53. Southesk spells the name *Numme* and says the Fort Ellice records read *Denoummee*.
38. Spry, *Palliser Papers*.
39. Harmon, *Journal*, p. 76.
40. The plains grizzly is now extinct.
41. See examples of this in other parties, and particularly in *The Plains Across*, by Unrah.
42. Thibodo's journal description and Linklater's explanation indicate that the pass used was actually south of what is now South Kootenay Pass, perhaps Akamina or even farther south of the 49th parallel. Newspapers had reported deaths in the Jones party by the fall of 1859, and Hector gave a dramatic report after his October visit to Kootenay Post, two weeks before Thibodo, incorrectly reporting one death. St. Paul *Pioneer and Democrat*, September 11, 1859. Spry, *Palliser Papers*, p. 465.
43. Thibodo, "Diary—1859;" O. W. Johnson *Flathead and Kootenay*. Thibodo spells the name *Minetry*.
44. Victoria *Colonist*, January 25, 1861.
45. St. Paul *Pioneer and Democrat*, March 15, 1860. Dr. Augustus Thibodo spent the winter of 1859–60 in Walla Walla to refinance his quest, hanging out his shingle at McAulif's store and then moving to the home of a Mr. Ingersoll. In February 1860 he wrote in his diary: ". . . have done very well since I have been here and should I be able to collect all I have made will have a good

outfit in the spring to start for the diggings. I expect to leave here in 3 weeks for the upper mines." By April, when his diary ends, he had still not reached the Dalles for supplies. Thibodo did go north however. During the summer of 1860 he went to the Similkameen mines, Fort Kamloops, and Fort Alexandria on the Fraser, visiting all the nearby mining fields. In winter he returned to Walla Walla and the post of resident physician at the Nez Percé Indian Agency at Lapwai. *Pioneer and Democrat,* Olympia, Washington, May 3, 1861.

46. *Pioneer and Democrat,* Olympia, Washington, February 4, 1860.

## Chapter Eight

1. Ormsby, *British Columbia: A History,* p. 182.
2. *Fort Edmonton Journal,* B60/a/31 f44d; USNA, Records of the Adjutant General's Office, Discharge papers.
3. St. Paul *Press,* July 14, 1861; PABC, Gold Commissioners' reports; Perry, *British Columbian,* June 6, 1861; Cheadle, *Journal,* pp. 140–41; Unrah, *The Plains Across; See* this book chapters 2 and 3; McLaurin, *Globe,* April 5, 1862; and Cowie, "The Life Story of Tom Clover." This is found in the Manitoba archives scrapbook with the notation *Manitoba Press,* May 19, 1917; however, the date is incorrect and the source cannot be found. *Nor'-Wester,* July 15, 1861; HBCA, B60/a/31; *Globe,* April 5, 1862. Reports on this party vary. Most state four members. Cheadle, p. 140, however, says Love and four others. The Victoria *Colonist,* June 6, 1861, says Perry and four others and *Fort Edmonton Journal* entries concur. The confusion came from Parker's death, which left four members.
4. Moberly, *When Fur was King.*
5. *Fort Edmonton Journal,* B60/a/31 f43.
6. Ibid., f43, 44, and f68d.
7. *Nor'-Wester,* July 15, 1861; *Fort Edmonton Journal,* B60/a/31 f68d.
8. *Nor'-Wester,* March 5, 1862. Clover returned to Fort Edmonton and married the daughter of Paulette Paul, "the famous strong man of the Saskatchewan brigade." Cowie, "The Life Story of Tom Clover"; Kane, *Wanderings of an Artist,* pp. 73–74.
9. *Nor'-Wester,* March 5, 1862.
10. *Fort Edmonton Journal,* B60/a/31 f61, f68d, f81d.
11. Gladstone's diary, *Lethbridge Herald,* August 19, 1958.
12. Moberly. St. Paul *Pioneer and Democrat,* July 21, 1861. At Fort George he was told his letters were at Fort St. James and brother Walter at Peace River, so re-engaged as Fraser Lake clerk for three years. In 1864 he mined in Cariboo. He returned to the HBC, became factor in 1894, and settled at Duck Lake.
13. *British Columbian,* June 6, 1862.
14. *Nor'-Wester,* March-April, 1861.
15. *Nor'-Wester,* July 15, 1861. *Globe,* June 27, 1862.
16. *Globe,* March 6, 1862.
17. *Globe,* June 27, 1862.
18. McDonald, *British Columbia and Vancouver's Island.*
19. *Globe,* June 27, 1862.
20. Lewis, ed., "The Sinclair Party," p. 22.
21. *Fort Edmonton Journal,* B60/a/32 f8. Victoria *Colonist,* June 6, 1861.
22. *Fort Edmonton Journal,* B60/a/31 1860–61 f42d.
23. McDonald.

24. *Fort Edmonton Journal*, B60/a/32 f8.
25. Elsewhere Reid says that he was paid a horse, Reid's double barreled rifle, and fifty dollars [ten pounds] in gold, approximately the equivalent of twenty-five pounds. McDonald; *Globe*, June 27, 1862. Baptiste Gabriel served with Palliser during 1858. Palliser described him as being "a first rate rider and smart little hunter," but as a sometimes-guide, he once attempted a short cut that led into fallen timber and meant back-tracking many miles. With Palliser, Baptiste crossed the Kananaskis Pass to the Kootenay River, and returned via the Wigwam River and Railway Pass to Fort Edmonton in September 1858. Spry, *Palliser Papers*, p. 174, n.260–66.
26. Reid and his companions were only the fourth group of whitemen to follow this route. Governor Simpson was first in 1847, then missionary Reverend Rundle in 1847 and Dr. Hector in 1858.
27. Spry, *Palliser Papers*, p. lxxxix.
28. McDonald.

## Chapter Nine

1. White, *Ho! For the Gold Fields*.
2. *Montreal Witness*, March 5, 1862.
3. Flett was the Métis son of George Flett, late a Scots servant of the HBC, and Margaret Whitford, a Métis. He was born in 1823 in Rupert's Land and by 1862 had a son and daughter by Mary Ross. The Flett family was well established in Red River, George having a farm fifteen miles west of Fort Garry. PAC, MG25, G62, Hind, *Narrative*, vol. 1, p. 148.
4. Redgrave, "Journal." Unless otherwise specified all Redgrave quotes are from this source.
5. Harkness, "Correspondence Outward." All Harkness quotes are from these letters.
6. Phillips, "Reminiscences, 1840–1916."
7. Rordans and Finch, *Upper Canada Law List 1862*, 4th ed., Toronto, 1862, pp. 93 and 120.
8. Vancouver *Daily Province*, October 25, 1924.
9. Fortune, "Overland Route to Cariboo."
10. A. B. Guthrie, *The Way West*. New York: Houghton Mifflin, 1952.
11. Sellar, "Diary—1862," Unless otherwise noted Huntingdon party references are Sellar's. Census 1861, Huntingdon County; David Millne, Scot, Innkeeper, age sixty-nine; wife Margaret, age fifty-two.
12. Wade, *The Overlanders of '62*. Biographical details of many men are taken from Wade's appendices. *See also* letters, journals, and bibliography.
13. Fortune, "Overland Route to Cariboo."
14. See party rosters in appendix 1 for a complete list. Party associations were a transitory affiliation for some and may change with location. A. L. Fortune, for instance, says Peter McIntyre was with the Ottawa party.
15. Many who boarded with Redgrave shifted to other less traumatic groups, and thus the roster is unclear. *See* party rosters, appendix 1.
16. Harper, Russell J. "William Hind and the Overlanders," *Beaver*, Winter 1971; and *William G. R. Hind*, Willistead Art Gallery of Windsor, 1967; and Stanton, *Impression of an Age*.
17. T. McMicking, *Overland from Canada to British Columbia*.
18. T. McMicking, *British Columbian*, December 1862.
19. John Bowland, letter to *Christian Guardian*, May 28, 1862, p. 86.

20. The *Frank Steele* was named for a noted Minnesota pioneer. Built in Hampton, Ky., she was 175-by-28 feet with a 5½-foot draft. She ran the Minnesota River trade for the Davidson Line until spring of 1860, then transferred to the La Crosse–St. Paul run. the *Keokuk* was a side-wheel packet, wood hull with texas, 177x27x5 feet; built in Brownsville. Originally ran St. Louis to Keokuk, later in the Minnesota Packet Company and then in the Davidson Line, La Crosse to St. Paul, under Captain J. R. Hatcher. It was sunk at Baton Rouge. Information from Steamship Museum, Winona, Minnesota.
21. *St. Paul Press*, April 19, 1862.
22. The original twelve from St. Thomas were joined by seven others. One was Isaac Brock McQueen, son of Colonel McQueen who served under General Brock in the War of 1812. The family had lived in the St. Thomas area for over half a century.
23. *St. Paul Press*, May 1862.
24. See *St. Paul Press* and St. Paul *Pioneer and Democrat*; White, *Ho! For the Gold Fields*; and overlander journals.
25. For notes on Wallace post-1862 see biographical notes. *See also:* James K. Nesbitt, "Japanese Jugglers Make Victorian Rich," Victoria *Colonist*, December 2, 1956, and vertical file, PABC.
26. The term *humbug* comes from the worthless Dublin mint money with which King James II of England flooded the land. It was a popular nineteenth-century word for worthless.
27. John Bowland, letter to *Christian Guardian*, May 28, 1862, p. 86; William Hugill, letter to *Globe*, December 27, 1862; Harkness, undated letter fragment in "Correspondence Outward."
28. John Bowland, letter to *Christian Guardian*, May 28, 1862, p. 86.
29. Gilman, Gilman, and Stultz, *The Red River Trails*; Fortune, "Overland Route to Cariboo."
30. Harold J. Abrahams, "Extinct Medical Schools of Nineteenth Century Philadelphia," *Transactions and Studies of the College of Physicians of Philadelphia*, 4 ser., vol. 30, no. 2, October 1962, p. 108.
31. Record Group 94, Records of the Adjutant General's Office, 1780s–1917, Medical Officers and Physicians, USNA; St. Paul *Pioneer and Democrat*, May 10, 1862, p. 1.
32. See V. H. Cady to J. L. Macdonald, June 1, 1862, quoted in White, *Ho! For the Gold Fields*, p. 36–37. For example, the Montana-bound Holmes train included a Philip Lovell, born 1840 in Yorkshire, England, a likely crossover. The later Fisk train had on its roster Elijah Dunphy and Mrs. Catherine Dungan, who appear to have stayed in St. Anthony as remnants of the 1858–59 New Brunswick party. (James Quigg, another New Brunswick dropout, crossed with Fisk the following year.) There were also several who may have been from the ill-fated British Overland Transit Company scheme: William Hall of London, England; Robert Halliday of London, England; and Nathaniel L. Shaw of Liverpool. Canadian James Marsden, born 1843 in Toronto, also joined Fisk. Alonzo Miner left St. Peters with his brother D. Miner, Thomas Little, and M. L. French and his three sons, bound for Cariboo. French and sons switched to the Holmes train. Alonzo appears on the Holmes train roster, although we know he arrived in Fort Garry aboard the SS *International* with other overlanders. He had trouble making up his mind. *St. Peters Tribune*, May 21, 1862. For information on Holmes and Fisk parties *see* White, *Ho! For the Gold Fields*.

33. G. E. Johnson, *Here-There-Everywhere*. His name is also misspelled; Wade and Leduc incorrectly spelled it *Hales*.
34. Old Settlers' Association, "Proceedings," 1898. Unpublished typescript in Moorehead, Minnesota. The site of old Georgetown is two miles north of the present town on County Road 36.
35. The HBC warehouse has been reconstructed, incorrectly according to old photos, at a wayside rest where County Road 36 crosses the Red River.
36. Barris, *Fire Canoe*; "Old Commodores and Captains of the Prairie Fleet," *Manitoba Free Press*, December 1, 1923.
37. Barris, *Fire Canoe*; *Nor'-Wester*, May 28, 1862; R. McMicking, "Diary—1862-63."
38. John McLean was a Scot, born in Perthshire, 1815, settled in Ontario in 1837. After reading H. Y. Hind's report he decided to move to Red River. Metcalfe, *The Tread of the Pioneers*, pp. 187-8.
39. Frank Penwarden, *Canadian Home Journal*, July 17, 1862.
40. See Alexander, "Diary—1862," and "Narrative." *Gregg* is the spelling used by Alexander and by the *Nor'-Wester*, although later Alexander uses Greig.
41. A discrepancy in Sellar's diary leaves some confusion. Sunday was May 25, although Sellar notes it as the twenty-sixth. He also writes the twenty-seventh twice, the second one being correctly the Tuesday.
42. Quoted in Friesen, *The Canadian Prairies*, p. 10.
43. Unrah, *The Plains Across*.
44. An example of the erroneous linking is found in the foreword of Florence McNeil's *The Overlanders*, a volume of poetry where she says they were "lured by fraudulent advertising." The story of the BCOTC has been misrepresented since Wade's book on the overlanders which appears to link the two. More likely the error lies with the book's editor, for Wade died before publication. The overlanders previously discussed had no connection with the company.
45. *Nor'-Wester*, July 9, 1863.
46. Waite, "Sleigh, Burrows Willcocks Arthur," *Dictionary of Canadian Biography*, vol. 9; Boase, *Modern English Biography*.
47. *Nor'-Wester*, November 17, 1862.
48. Letters in BCOTC vertical file, PABC.
49. *Globe*, June 24, 1862.
50. Mcdonald, *British Columbia and Vancouver's Island*; *New York Times*, August 22, 1862.
51. *St. Catharines Evening Journal*, June 24, 1862; *Toronto Leader*, November 18, 1862. The Rossin House burned down on November 14, 1862.
52. *New York Times*, August 15, 1862. When George Wallace passed in May he intimated he was agent of "a transportation company." If he had a connection with the BCOTC he wisely kept it a secret.
53. *St. Paul Press*, July 3, 1862; *Globe*, July 15, 1862.
54. *Nor'-Wester*, July 9, 1862.
55. Mr. M. Roberts, Keeper of Enquiry Services, Guildhall Library, searched unsuccessfully there and in the Corporation of London Record Office, Guildhall Police Court Records, and the *Daily Telegraph* Library.
56. Victoria *Colonist*, May 15, 1869; Boase, *Modern English Biography*.

## Chapter Ten

1. *Nor'-Wester*, March 3–May 23, 1863.

2. Wade, *The Overlanders of '62*, pp. 173–74; Schubert, "Reminiscences," 41a; St. Paul *Pioneer and Democrat*, November 25, 1860.
3. In 1856 St. Paul was experiencing unprecedented immigration. The year before the population had been less than five thousand but in 1855 river steamers disembarked thirty thousand passengers. St. Paul *Pioneer and Democrat*, November 25, 1860.
4. The offence for which Schubert was fined is not known. *St. Paul Press*, June 1, 1861, p. 2.
5. The overblown story of Catherine Schubert has been told in many versions, all based in a great part on family memories rather than documentation. Two examples are Metcalf, *Catherine Schubert*, and Scott, *The Trek of the Overlanders*. Both of these booklets have a great deal of unsubstantiated dialogue and no bibliography or footnotes.
6. Palliser mentions such an instance in May 1859: "In addition . . . were several women and children, who begged accompany us in hopes of food." Spry, *Palliser Papers*, p. 396.
7. Campbell, "The Sinclair Party." In the trans-Mississippi migrations the average was one woman for sixteen men. The women were mainly with those parties going to settle, not to mine. The "Canadian" overlanders averaged one woman in sixty-four men. Holliday, *The World Rushed In*, pp. 354–55.
8. For Tschudi's list see Macfie, *Vancouver Island and British Columbia*, p. 379.
9. Houghton, *The Victorian Frame of Mind*.
10. The old man who refused was likely Jamey Jock Bird. A. L. Fortune, *The British Columbian*, January 31, 1863.
11. Which of at least three Charles Racettes in Red River this was, is unclear. It seems certain that he was the Jones party guide, equally certain that he had guided for Palliser. *See* Jones party at Fort Edmonton. Genealogy from notes in PAC, MG25, G62. Isaac Cowie, "Plain Tales from the Plains"; *Free Press*, November 25, 1911.
12. T. McMicking, "An Account of a Journey."
13. *Globe*, June 26, 1862.
14. The latter a raincoat named for Charles Macintosh (1766–1843), the inventor. James Carpenter, *Globe*, July 24, 1862.
15. Alexander, "Narrative," p. 8; James Ross, ed. of *Nor'-Wester*, in *Globe*, July 14, 1862.
16. T. McMicking, "An Account of a Journey."
17. Sellar is the only diarist to give a complete account of the bylaws and watch formation.
18. Marcy suggested elections and rules in *The Prairie Traveller*. For an example of the elaborate bylaws of California overlanders see those of the Wolverine Rangers in Holliday, *The World Rushed In*, p. 461.
19. See Holliday, *The World Rushed In*, and Sellar, "Diary—1862." Since at least fourteen of this company mined in Cariboo they may in fact have had some as yet undiscovered written agreement binding them together.
20. For a recent discussion on the Plains Indians' culture see Friesen, *The Canadian Prairies*. For accounts of the problems American wagon trains had at this same time see White, *Ho! For the Gold Fields*.
21. Leduc, p. xxiv in T. McMicking, *Overland From Canada to British Columbia*. Leduc seems to discount the Indian danger by editing McMicking's quote.
22. *See* Sellar at St. Albert, chapter 11, section 2, this book.
23. For a somewhat differing view of Sellar see Wade, *The Overlanders of '62*, and Leduc, ed., *Overland From Canada to British Columbia*, by T. McMicking.

24. Fortune, "Overland Route," p. 15.
25. T. McMicking, "An Account of a Journey," p. 15.
26. Two and a half months later Dr. Cheadle and Viscount Milton stopped here and remarked on the site being "covered with marks of old camp fires, the skulls of numberless ducks and geese." Cheadle, *Journal*, p. 53.
27. Quote from Sellar, "Diary—1862." A note on the music: *Castles in the Air* was written by James Ballantine, next to Robert Burns one of the most notable of Scots songwriters. It was a popular song of the day and frequently referred to by overlanders. James Anderson, "the Bard of Cariboo," later put new words to it. The lyrics of *The Old Oaken Bucket* were printed in the *Pioneer and Democrat*, Olympia, Washington, April, 1859. The words to *The Yellow Rose of Texas* were found in R. B. McMicking's sparse diary.
28. Leduc, ed., *Overland From Canada to British Columbia*.
29. Note the greasing of the carts. Common practice was not to grease the axles and hub for this attracted dust and grime.
30. Wrathman Turner with the SGE wrote: "On the 5th of July we passed Touchwood Hill Fort, an old building which is fast falling to the ground, the occupants having removed to a new one lately built." *Globe*, January 14, 1863. Voorhis, *Historic Forts and Trading Posts*. Voorhis says the post was closed temporarily in August of 1862, but obviously it was abandoned earlier. Voorhis also says a new HBC post opened in 1879 a few miles south, but again overlanders seem to indicate it was open the summer of 1862. The Carlton Trail east of the Touchwoods followed much the route of present-day Saskatchewan Highway 15 and the Canadian National Railway. At Hudson's Bay Lake, where the later post was built, it angled northwestward through the hills and can only be followed on foot. Beyond the lakes and hills the roads of present-day Saskatchewan run north-south and east-west, so again the trail, which took a diagonal line, can only be traced by foot. The Touchwood Hills are now the site of several Indian Reserves.
31. See Palliser's map *in* Spry, *Palliser Papers*.
32. Kelso's drowning is based on various journal entries, and the author's experience in a similar situation.
33. Russell, *What's In A Name?*
34. R. McMicking, "Diary," p. 23.
35. T. McMicking, "An Account of a Journey," p. 25.
36. *St. Peters Tribune*, April 2, 1862. *See* party rosters, appendix 1.
37. *St. Peters Tribune*, May 28, 1862.
38. Accounts of the St. Peters party include those from the *St. Peters Tribune* in the text, and *The British Colonist*, October 17, 1862. A third evidently exists but cannot be found, for the March 28, 1863, *St. Peters Tribune* refers to a letter from H. C. Dewitt which "owing to its great length we postpone its publication until next week. He gives a full account of the trip and the country." The letter was evidently not published; it was not found despite searching issues for several months. Hopefully the Dewitt account will one day be found.
39. *Fort Edmonton Journal*, B60/a/32 f40.
40. Leonard Crysler letter, Fort Garry, May 31, 1862; quoted in Crysler, *History of the Crysler Family*, p. 59.
41. James Carpenter, letter, *Globe*, June 24, 1862.
42. The complete roster of the party is found in appendix 2. The numerous Red River families with similar surnames has made positive identification of individuals elusive, if not impossible. Flett is the only one positively identi-

fied. McBeath's relationship is not confirmed. Whit[e]ford, the guide, was related to Flett. James Peter Whitford married an Indian woman, Sara; they had a daughter, Peggy, George Flett's mother. James Peter also had four sons: James Jr., Peter (1), George, and Francis. James Jr., born 1796, went to Oregon with the Sinclair party of 1851 accompanied by his wife Mary (née Spence) and family, including son Peter (2), age about thirty. In 1857 a returning group was led by Peter (2) according to Erasmus in *Buffalo Days and Nights*. A Peter Whiteford is reported killed in the foothills of the Rockies in October of 1863; *Fort Edmonton Journal*, B60/a/33 f55. James Jr. had older sons named John, baptized May 23, 1824; and James, baptized August 10, 1831. A James Whiteford is in British Columbia, October 1861 (*British Columbian*), likely the guide who led the New Brunswick party of 1859 across. Peter (1), born 1796, married Christy (née Spence), sister of his brother's wife. They had twelve children including a son John, baptized August 23, 1846, married to Jane Cook (born 1851). Based on family movements and age it appears that the John Whitford guiding the overlanders in 1862 was the eldest son of James Whitford Jr. who stayed behind when his father and family went to Oregon. His brother, then, would have guided the New Brunswickers. PAC, MG25, G62. Campbell, "The Sinclair Party."
43. For the complete story of O'B., as he was often referred to, and other Irishmen often confused with him see Tweed, "On the Trail of Mr. O'B."
44. Redgrave, "Journal," p. 223.
45. Ibid., p. 209.
46. Alexander, "Diary," p. 15.
47. George Flett, *Nor'-Wester*, August 30, 1862.
48. Hind, *Narrative*, vol. 1, p. 414; Alexander, "Diary," p. 18.
49. Alexander, "Diary."
50. Redgrave, "Journal," pp. 229–31.
51. George Flett, *Nor'-Wester*, August 30, 1862.
52. Alexander, "Diary," July 1.
53. They were joined by Samuel Ballendine, an HBC Fort Edmonton Métis with mail for Love. He traveled with the Palliser expedition in 1858–59 and went west as far as Colville, returning to Fort Edmonton in October, 1859. Alexander, "Diary," July 16; Spry, *Palliser Papers*, p. 473.
54. Alexander, "Narrative"; letter of November 23, 1862.
55. Holmgren and Holmgren, *2000 Place Names of Alberta*. The route from Vermilion Lakes to Edmonton followed much the same course later taken by the Canadian Pacific Railway.
56. *Fort Edmonton Journal*, B60/a/32 f40d.

## Chapter Eleven

1. Prest, "Correspondence Outward," July 22, 1862. Prest's wash lady is a mystery. Leduc, ed., *Overland From Canada to British Columbia*, p. 85 n.1, says quite clearly, "Prest reported that Catherine Schubert did his washing." Prest's letter is not as definite. Catherine Schubert was seven months pregnant with three small children and a husband so it seems unlikely she would look for extra work. It is possible that a halfbreed woman accompanied the group to help with camp chores. As is evident in Sellar's journal and Prest's letters, men held with disdain the chores of cooking and washing and went to great lengths to avoid such work, making a servant more likely.

2. *Fort Edmonton Journal*, B60/a/32 f39. Thomas Woolsey, the Wesleyan minister whom Dodd referred to, was fifty-four years old and not entirely suited to missionary life. The difficult position would have been better served by a younger man of more positive outlook. Woolsey, though, kept up regular correspondence with newspapers and on occasion parents or friends inquiring about prairie travelers.
3. The woman Fortune refers to is Marguerite Brabant. She and Brazeau had eight children. Whether they were married in the legal sense or were living *à la façon du pays*—commonlaw—is not known. See earlier reference to Brazeau: Fortune, "Overland Route," p. 38. Fortune does not name Brazeau, but he was an American and no one else "in authority" fits the bill. PAC, MG25, G62, p. 345. Mr. Alexander had been with the HBC only a year. A young man, he was the son of Rev. Dr. Alexander of Edinburgh. *See* Alexander, "Diary," p. 30.
4. Hunniford, "Journal," 1862, p. 20.
5. Ibid.
6. T. McMicking, "An Account of a Journey."
7. *Fort Edmonton Journal*, B60/a/32 f40.
8. The identity of Andrew Cardinal is unclear. Leduc quotes OMI records indicating that he was André Cardinal, born 1829, son of Jacques Cardinal and Marguerite or Marianne Desjarlais; employed by HBC and in charge of Jasper House in 1855–56. Southesk refers to an André Cardinal in 1859 near Edmonton. However, *The Rundle Journals*, p. 344, edited by Hugh Dempsey, show a son Andrew (the name used in HBC records) born to Mary and Andrew Cardinal in December 1840 and baptized at Edmonton a month later. Andrew may be Rundle's anglicizing of André, or there may be two or three Cardinals with similar names. McMicking says he was born at Jasper House and refers to him as André. Leduc's Cardinal is likely the overlander guide.
9. Sellar, "Diary."
10. Hunniford, "Journal," p. 20.
11. Hugh Monroe, born 1798 (or 1784) in Trois Rivières, became an HBC servant and was sent to the Blackfeet to learn their language and enhance the trade. He remained there the rest of his life. He had at least three sons: Piscan, Oliver, and Felix. Felix had ridden with Palliser in 1859 and then worked for the HBC as interpreter. *See* Spry, *Palliser Papers* and MoHS vertical files.
12. Grant, *Ocean to Ocean*, p. 206.
13. T. McMicking records the name as Mokerty. McNaughton, *Overland to Cariboo*, p. 68, gives the inscription noted.
14. Sellar, "Diary."
15. Ibid., pp. 149-51.
16. Kane, *Wanderings of an Artist*.
17. The original Jasper House was built at the north end of Brûlé Lake in 1813. The post seen in 1862 was built by Michael Kline, the father of the guide the 1859 Nobles expedition had hired at St. Joseph.
18. For a discussion on Henry House see Leduc, ed., *Overland From Canada to British Columbia*, p. 106 and James McGregor, *Overland by Yellowhead*. This is the site of present-day Jasper, Alberta.
19. Sellar, "Diary," p. 113. The *British Colonist*, October 17, 1862.
20. Sister Alphonse died 1879; Emery, 1885; and Lamy, 1892. *Lac Ste. Anne Codex historicus, 1844–1961*, Notes sur la Mission de St. Albert; OMI records, PAA, 5GI 360.
21. Fraser and his Métis wife, Nancy Beaudry, had eight daughters and five

sons. One married William Borwick, the Fort Edmonton blacksmith whom Thomas Clover had known; another remarried to Edward McGillivary. A son married Joseph Brazeau's daughter Sophie, and four of his children married into the Rowand family. Spry, *Palliser Papers*; Cheadle's *Journal*, pp. 147–48; *Nor'-Wester*, March 5, 1862. Family information: PAC, MG25, G62, pp. 345–47.
22. McNaughton, *Overland to Cariboo*. The following year, 1863, Dr. Cheadle mentions giving Colin Fraser similar advice. Cheadle, *Journal*, p. 148.
23. Alexander, "Narrative," p. 15.
24. *Nor'-Wester*, June 11, 1863.
25. Redgrave, "Journal," p. 261.
26. Unrah, *The Plains Across*, p. 231.
27. Redgrave, "Journal," p. 262.
28. Ibid., p. 274. Alexander, "Diary," pp. 36–37.
29. Alexander, "Diary," p. 39.
30. Ibid., p. 40.
31. Sellar, "Diary," p. 169. Fortune, "Overland Route."
32. Thomas McMicking mentions Andrew Holes and "four or five others" in his account for September 2. Wade and Leduc also confuse Dewitt with this St. Thomas party. Dewitt was H. C. Dewitt of the St. Peters party. On September 11 two members of the St. Peters party, joined by two others, left the Cache on the southern route. *See* Copland–Davis account in the Victoria *Colonist*, October 17, 1862, mentioned by neither of the above authors. The same account says the main party left fourteen days before the St. Peters men arrived, about August 27, and were followed ten days later by "another party of thirteen." This latter group was likely the St. Thomas party, which varied between eleven and twelve members at various times. In his own account, *Colonist*, November 3, 1862, Dewitt says he and three others left the Cache and in a few days joined the main Thompson party.
33. Sellar, "Diary," p. 172.
34. Dr. Edward Stevenson letter, Toronto *Leader*, December 12, 1862.
35. Canada Census 1861, C 1035, Huron Co., Goderich, p. 67.
36. Fortune, "Overland Route," p. 54.
37. Thomas McMicking refers to Leader's death, the circumstances were similar to Carpenter's; "An Account of a Journey," p. 44. The *British Columbian*, October 25, 1862, lists Leader drowned with Alexander, Fletcher, Jones, Carpenter, and Alfred Handcock. It later corrected the news to Leader and Carpenter.
38. McNaughton, *Overland To Cariboo*.
39. Victoria *Colonist*, October 17, 1862.
40. Toronto *Leader*, June 15, 1863.
41. Fortune, "Overland Route."
42. R. McMicking, "Diary," p. 55.
43. Details of the southern journey are scant. No dairy has emerged and all we have are the stories told to McMicking and later printed in the *British Columbian*, a brief account by Dewitt of the later St. Peters party, letters from Archibald Thompson (edited by Dr. Wade and now unfortunately lost), and recently discovered letters of William Hugill. The other source is the reminiscences of James Schubert. Considering, however, that he was two years old at the time, these papers represent more what he remembers being told years after the journey than his own memories.
44. Victoria *Colonist*, November 3, 1862.

45. William Hugill, Victoria, B.C., letter to father, December 15, 1862, A.L.S., 8 p., Hugill papers.
46. Cheadle, *Journal*; Selwyn, *Journal*; Birrell, ed., Baltzly, *Journal*.
47. When Rev. Grant was passing here with Sandford Fleming in 1872 they met overlander John Glen heading upstream—still searching ten years later. Grant, *Ocean to Ocean*, p. 267.
48. Hugill papers. Hugill's date is difficult to read and could read seventh, eleventh, or seventeenth. They were six miles south of the junction, so the seventh seems correct.
49. Selwyn, *Journal*, and Birrell, ed., *Baltzly Journal*. The date Baltzly gives, August 5, is likely incorrect for it was approximately September 5 when the first Thompson parties arrived. While little is known of the three men he mentions, they were part of the main overlander movement. A. H. [Hugh?] Miller and S. [Stephen?] P. Whitley were aboard the maiden voyage of the SS *International*. In 1983 the author found what may have been Slaughter Camp, a quiet grove of cedar and hemlock squeezed between the North Thompson River and Highway 5. In the grove are many ancient stumps which one can imagine were cut by the overlanders. Archeological work could prove or disprove the location, which is historically worthy of preservation.
50. Selwyn paced it off at 78½.
51. When Dr. Cheadle came through here on July 29 the next summer he found a "great number of trees cut down, a number of pack saddles and harness" and other litter.
52. Archibald Thompson to brother, Victoria, December 7, 1862, quoted in Wade, *The Overlanders of '62*, p. 112.
53. William Hugill, Victoria, to brothers Charles, January 1, 1863, A.L.S., Hugill papers. This set of rapids was the formidable Porte d'Enfer, Hells Gate. It was not named until the following year, by the Dr. Cheadle party, and should not be confused with the turbulent Hell's Gate on the Fraser, which is in fact much easier to run in a boat. Here the Thompson, which is normally thirty to sixty yards wide, narrows, makes a sudden turn through a canyon, and squeezes its autumn flow of fifteen thousand cubic feet of water per second through a gap just over two arm spans in width. See *Historical Streamflow Summary, British Columbia*. Ottawa: Inland Waters Directorate, Water Resources Branch, 1977.
54. One hundred years later, on a bluff overlooking Fish Trap Canyon the following sign was erected: "It had been an epic struggle against the wilderness for the goldseekers from eastern Canada. They had crossed the Rockies, trekked through pathless forests, and won the swift rapids of the North Thompson River. The open country now offered hope and safe passage. Ragged and starved, they reached Kamloops where many became pioneer farmers."
55. Notes of conversation with James Armstrong Schubert, Tulameen, July 18, 1930, Schubert "Reminiscences." Leduc, ed., *Overland From Canada to British Columbia* by T., McMicking, says Catherine denied this often printed version, and had the child on her own.
56. Balf, *The Overlanders*..
57. Balf, *Kamloops: A History*.
58. Hugill papers; Dewitt, Victoria *Colonist*; T. McMicking, "An Account of a Journey."

## Chapter Twelve

1. Canada Census, 1861, London, Canada West; 1881, British Columbia; E. A. 188, A, no. 10. Gilbert was married to Mary Butler and had a year-old son, Gilbert S.
2. See 1861 Census, London. *British Columbian*, July 11, 1863. All further references are from this issue, or those listed in note 25.
3. *Nor'-Wester*, July 9, 1862.
4. Lacombe had gone ahead and arrived the day before. *Fort Edmonton Journal*, B60/a/32 f41.
5. *Nor'-Wester*, April 13, 1863.
6. Ibid., June 11, 1863.
7. Ibid., August 18, 1862.
8. *Fort Edmonton Journal*, B60/a/32 f41.
9. Ibid.
10. Ibid.
11. Correspondence of Hall and Kelso in author's collection.
12. Father Lacombe to Dear Sergeant, April 26, 1863; doc. 4; PAM.
13. James Kelso to Asa Hall, September 7, 1863, author's collection. In 1977 James B. Stanton visited the St. Albert cemetery. Only a smooth green grass slope could be seen. Inquiries at the mission told him the area had been "de-consecrated and re-contoured."
14. Ibid.
15. The Rennie story is found in the following sources: letter from William Rennie to friend, *British Colonist*, April 6, 1863; Goudie's report, British Colonist, March 21, 1863; William and Gilbert Rennie to editor, The *British Columbian*, July 11, 1863; *British Colonist*, July 11, 1863; and Giscome's report, *British Colonist*, December 14, 1863. Some of these items were picked up by the *Victoria Chronicle, Nor'-wester,* and the *Globe*.
16. Recent research has shown that Barker was not a naval deserter from Cornwall, as he is usually described. *See* Bishop Hill's diary, SC/UBC.
17. It is unclear how far the McMickings traveled. Robert says they went to Cottonwood on Lightning Creek. Cottonwood is on the Cottonwood or Swift River. Lightning Creek is farther east. R. B. McMicking, "Diary"; Dobson Prest, Victoria, letter to father; December 14, 1862, PABC, EB P42. It is remarkable that neither Rogers nor Pinkerton ever left William's Creek. They died in 1920 and 1911 respectively. John Pinkerton, letter, 1905, in vertical file, PABC photo A-3784, taken in 1906, shows a group of Barkerville old-timers. Above the figure of Rogers is the note, 1862, his arrival year.
18. Stevenson and Walker, *Stories of Early British Columbia*.
19. James Wattie is clearly identifiable in the Cameron's wedding photo, PABC.
20. Hunniford, "Journal," p. 65. Wade refers to a Wattie manuscript in his book, *The Overlanders of '62*, but like the Thompson letters, it has since disappeared.
21. Sellar, "Diary."
22. Leonard Crysler, San Francisco, letter to family, November 6, 1862, quoted in J. Crysler, *History of The Crysler Family*.
23. Alexander, "Diary"; Prest, "Correspondence Outward," letter, December 14, 1862; Hunniford, "Journal," p. 14.
24. McMurphy, "Diary."
25. Alexander, "Diary"; Wade, *The Overlanders of '62*; and May Williams, "Cariboo Pioneer," *Colonist*, September 4, 1956, indicate this was Henry Felker.

# Bibliography

## Unpublished Sources

Alexander, Richard Henry. "Narrative of Incidents and Personal Adventures in a Journey Across the Rockies." Typescript. PABC.
———. "Diary—April 29, 1862–December 9, 1862." Typescript. CAV.
Cuthbert, W. "Diary—1862." Typescript. MoHS.
Fortune, Alexander Leslie. "Overland Route to Cariboo." Typescript. Northwest History Room, VPL.
———. 'Collection of Addresses and Narratives." Typescript. SC/UBC.
Gardiner, R. W. "Life of the Late W. B. Cameron, An Overlander of 1862." Typescript. PABC.
Hall, Erastus. *Papers.* Author's collection.
Harkness, Robert. "Correspondence Outward: personal letters to his wife, 1862–65." *Harkness Papers.* PABC.
Helmcken, John Sebastian. "Reminiscenses of John S. Helmcken." Typescript. SFU.
Hind, Henry Youle. "Rough notes by H. Y. Hind, 19 July–6 Aug., 1858." Manuscript. PAM.
———. "Notebook no. 3, 9 Aug.–23 Aug., 1858." Manuscript. PAM.
Hugill, William. *Papers.* Author's collection.
Hunniford, John. "Journal and Observations of John Hunniford, 1862." Typescript. SC/UBC.
Jones, John W. "A Diary of a Trip in 1858–1859 from Minnesota to Oregon." Manuscript. Graff Collection, Newberry Library, Chicago.
Lambert, Gwen. "Wheeler and Julia Mickle—My Grandparents." Typescript. Author's collection.
Love, Timoleon. *Papers.* Author's collection.
McMicking, Robert Burns. "Diary of Robert Burns McMicking, April 23, 1862–April 29, 1863." Typescript. PABC.
McMicking, Thomas. "An account of a journey overland from Canada to British Columbia–1862." *The British Columbian,* Nov. 1862–Jan. 1863. Typescript. SC/UBCL.

McMurphy, Sgt. "Diary." PABC.
Phillips, W. W. "Reminiscenses—1840-1916." Typescript. PABC.
Prest, Dobson. "Correspondence Outwards, 1862-1863." *Prest Papers*. PABC.
Redgrave, Stephen. "Journals and Sundry Papers, 1852-1875." Typescript. PABC.
Schubert, James Armstrong. "Reminiscences: Notes of Conversation with James Armstrong Schubert, recorded by R. Hartley." Typescript. PABC.
Sellar, John M. "Diary, April 22, 1862-Nov. 22, 1862." Typescript. PABC.
Taylor, James W. *James Taylor Papers*. MiHS.
Walker, Isabel. "Particulars of Thompson and McMicking Families." Typescript. Author's collection.
Wheelock, Joseph A. "Diary of a Trip with Nobles' Expedition." Typescript. *Wheelock Family Papers*. MiHS.

## Primary Published Sources

Baltzly, Benjamin. *Photos and Journal of an Expedition Through British Columbia in 1871*. Edited by Andrew Birrell. Toronto: Coach House Press, 1978.
Birrell, Andrew, ed. *Photos and Journal of an Expedition Through British Columbia in 1871*, by Benjamin Baltzly. Toronto: Coach House Press, 1978.
Bowsfield, Hartwell. *The James Wickes Taylor Correspondence, 1859-70*. Altona: Manitoba Record Society Publications, 1968.
Brode, Howard S., ed. "Diary of Dr. Augustus J. Thibodo, 1859." *Pacific Northwest Quarterly*, July 1940.
Cheadle, Walter B. *Cheadle's Journal of Trip Across Canada, 1863-63*. Edmonton: M. G. Hurtig Ltd., 1971.
Crysler, John M. *History of the Crysler Family*. Niagara: John M. Crysler, 1936.
Dempsey, Hugh A., ed. *The Rundle Journals, 1840-1848*. Calgary: Historical Society of Alberta and Glenbow Alberta Institute, 1977.
Erasmus, Peter. *Buffalo Days and Nights*. Calgary: Glenbow Alberta Institute, 1976.
Fortune, Alexander Leslie. "The Overlanders." *Okanagan Historical Society Report* (1957): 80.
Frost, Robert. "Fraser River Gold Rush Adventures." *Washington Historical Quarterly*, vol. 22, 1931.
Griesbach, W. A., ed. "The Narrative of James Gibbons (Part 1)." *Alberta Historical Review*, 6, no. 3 (Summer 1958): 1-6.
Gladstone, William. "William Gladstone Diary, 1858-1860." *Lethbridge Herald*, 19 Aug. 1958.
Grant, Rev. George M. *Ocean to Ocean*. Toronto: James Campbell and Son, 1873. Reprint. Toronto: Coles Publishing Co., 1970.
Harmon, Daniel Williams. *The Journal of Daniel Williams Harmon—Sixteen Years In the Indian Country*. Toronto: Macmillan of Canada Ltd., 1957.
Hind, Henry Youle. *Reports on the North-West Territory*. Toronto: Legislative Assembly, John Lovell, 1859.
———. *A Sketch of an Overland Route to British Columbia*. Toronto: W. C. Chewett and Co., 1862.
———. *Narrative of the Canadian Red River Exploring Expedition of 1857 and Assiniboine and Saskatchewan Expedition of 1858*. 2 vols. in 1. Edmonton: M. G. Hurtig Ltd., 1971.

Inkster, Colin. "Visits of 'Overlanders' of 1859 and 1862 to Fort Garry." *Winnipeg Free Press*, 30 June 1934.
Jessop, John. "Over the Plains in 1859." Victoria *Daily Colonist*, 1 January 1890.
Kane, Paul. *Wanderings of an Artist*. Edmonton: M. G. Hurtig Ltd., 1968.
Marble, Manton. "To Red River and Beyond." *Harper's New Monthly Magazine*, August–February, 1861.
Milton, Viscount and Cheadle, W. B. *The North-West Passage by Land*. London: Cassell, Petter, and Galpin, 1865. Reprint. Toronto: Coles Publishing Co., 1970.
Moberly, Henry John. *When Fur was King*. Toronto: J. M. Dent and Sons Ltd., 1929.
McNaughton, Margaret. *Overland to Cariboo*. Toronto: William Briggs, 1896. Reprint. Vancouver: J. J. Douglas, 1973.
Selwyn, Alfred R. C. *Journal and Report of Preliminary Explorations in British Columbia*. Ottawa: Geological Survey, 1872.
Southesk, The Earl of. *Saskatchewan and the Rocky Mountains*. Edmonton: M. G. Hurtig Ltd., 1969.
Spry, Irene M., ed. *The Palliser Papers*. Toronto: The Champlin Society, 1968.
Taylor, James W. *Northwest British America and its Relations to Minnesota*. St. Paul: Legislature of Minnesota, 1860.
Thibodo, Dr. Augustus J., Howard S. Brode ed. "Diary of the Northwest Exploring Expedition of 1859." *Pacific Northwest Quarterly*, July 1940.
———. "Nez Percé Mines—A Report." *Pioneer and Democrat*, Olympia, Washington, 3 May 1861.
Unrah, John D. Jr. *The Plains Across*. Urbana: University of Illinois Press, 1979.
Wade, Mark Sweeten. *The Overlanders of '62*, Victoria: PABC, 1931.
White, Helen McCann. *Ho! For the Gold Fields*. St. Paul: MiHS, 1966.

## Secondary Published Sources

Akrigg, G. P. V., and Akrigg, H. B. *British Columbia Chronicle, 1778–1846*. Vancouver: Discovery Press, 1975.
Allard, Jason O. "When Gold Was King." *MacLean's Magazine*, 15 May 1929.
Armstrong, Audrey. *Harness In The Parlour*. Toronto: Musson Book Co., 1974.
*Atlas of Dundas County*. Stormont, Dundas, and Glengarry, Belden, 1879.
Avery, Mary W. *Washington: A History of the Evergreen State*. Seattle: University of Washington Press, 1961.
Babcock, Willoughby M. "Gateway To The Northwest." *Minnesota History* 35 (June 1957): 245–61.
Bailey, A. *St. Paul Directory for 1863*. vol. 1. St. Paul: A. Bailey Publishing, 1863.
Balf, Mary. *Kamloops: A History of the District up to 1914*. Kamloops: Kamloops Museum, 1969.
———. *The Overlanders and other North Thompson Travellers*. Kamloops: Kamloops Museum, 1973.
———. "1867 Was a Cold Winter." Kamloops *Daily Sentinel*, 6 Nov. 1971.
———. "McQueen Lake Named After Pioneer." Kamloops *Daily Sentinel*, 30 Oct. 1971.
Bancroft, H. H. *History of British Columbia*. San Francisco: The History Company, 1890.
———. *History of Oregon*. San Francisco: The History Company, 1886–91.

Barris, Theodore. *Fire Canoe.* Toronto: McClelland and Stewart, 1977.
Begg, Alexander. *History of British Columbia.* Montreal: Wm. Briggs, 1894.
Berry, J. P. "Clover Bar in the Making, 1881–1931." Clipping in vertical file, PAA.
Berton, Pierre. *The National Dream.* Toronto: McClelland and Stewart, 1970.
Best, Geoffrey. *Mid-Victorian Britain.* London, England: Weidenfeld and Nicolson, 1971.
Blegen, Theodore. "James W. Taylor, A Biographical Sketch." *Minnesota Historical Bulletin* 1 (Nov. 1915): 153–95.
Boase, F. *Modern English Biography.* New York: Barnes and Noble Inc., 1965.
Bowsfield, Hartwell. "Rolette, Joseph." *Dictionary of Canadian Biography.* vol. 10. Toronto: Toronto University Press, 1976.
Brown, Dee. *Bury My Heart at Wounded Knee.* New York: Holt Reinhart and Winston Inc., 1971.
Brown, Jennifer. "Ultimate Respectability: Fur-Trade Children in the Civilized World." *Beaver* (Winter 1977): 4–10.
Bryce, George. *The Scotsman in Canada.* Toronto: Musson Book Co., 1911.
Butler, William Francis. *The Great Lone Land.* Rutland: Charles E. Tuttle Co., 1968.
Campbell, J. V. "The Sinclair Party." *The Washington Historical Quarterly* 8, no. 3, July 1916.
Campbell, Marjorie Wilkins. *The Saskatchewan.* Toronto: Clarke Irwin and Co., 1965.
Campbell, R. N. "John Bowron." Newspaper clipping, 9 June 1928. PABC.
Campbell, Susan. *Fort William.* Fort William: Ontario Ministry of Culture and Recreation, 1976.
Castle, Henry A. *History of St. Paul and Vicinity.* vol. 1. Chicago and New York: Lewis Publishing Co., 1912.
Champagne, Reverend Antoine. *The Verendryes and Their Successors.* Winnipeg: Manitoba Historical Society, 1968.
*The Canadian Album: Men of Canada.* Vol. 4. Brantford, Bradley, and Garretson and Co., 1895.
Cowie, Isaac. "Life Story of Tom Clover." *Winnipeg Free Press,* 19 May 1917.
Cox, Ross. *The Columbia River.* Norman: University of Oklahoma Press, 1957.
DeGroot, Henry. *British Columbia; its Condition & Prospects, Soil, Climate and Mineral Resources.* San Francisco: Alta Californian Job Office, 1859.
Dempsey, Hugh A. "A History of Rocky Mountain House." Canadian Historic Sites, no. 6. Ottawa: *Department of Indian Affairs and Northern Development,* 1973.
———. "The Overlanders in Alberta, 1862." *Alberta Historical Review* 14 no. 3 (Summer 1966): 1–13.
———. *Indian Tribes of Alberta.* Calgary: Glenbow Museum, 1979.
Domer, John. *New British Gold Fields: A Guide to British Columbia and Vancouver Island.* London: Angell, 1858.
Downs, Art. *Paddlewheels on the Frontier.* Surrey: Foremost Publishing Co. Ltd., 1967.
Dryden, Cecil. *Dryden's History of Washington.* Portland: Binfords and Mort, 1968.
Emmerson, John. *British Columbia and Vancouver Island: Voyages, Travels, and Adventures.* Durham: Wm. Ainsley, 1865.
Flandrau, Judge Charles E. *Encyclopedia of Biography of Minnesota.* Chicago: The Century Publishing and Engraving Co., 1900.

Folwell, William Watts. *Minnesota*. Boston and New York: Houghton Mifflin Co., 1908.
Forman, Grant, ed. *Adventure on Red River: Report on the Exploration*, by Capt. R. B. Marcy. Norman: University of Oklahoma Press, 1968.
Francis, Daniel. *Battle for the West*. Edmonton: M. G. Hurtig Ltd., 1982.
Friesen, Gerald. *The Canadian Prairies: A History*. Toronto: University of Toronto Press, 1984.
Fromhold, A. J. "Alberta Kananaskis Wilderness Area." *Canadian Geographic* (Dec. 1978/Jan. 1979): 40.
Giddens, Paul H. "Impressions of Minnesota Territory by a Pennsylvania Visitor of 1857." *Minnesota History*, Summer 1979.
Gilman, Carolyn. "Perceptions of the Prairie: Cultural Contrasts on the Red River Trails." *Minnesota History* 46, no. 3 (Fall 1978): 112–220.
Gilman, Rhoda R.; Gilman, Carolyn; and Stultz, Deborah M. *The Red River Trails*. St. Paul: MiHS, 1979.
Goosen, N. Jaye. "William MacTavish." *Dictionary of Canadian Biography*. Vol. 9. Toronto: University of Toronto Press, 1976.
———. "A Wearer of Moccasins: James McKay." *Beaver* (Autumn 1978): 44–53.
Gosnell, R. E. *A History of British Columbia*. Lewis Publishing Co., 1906.
Gregson, Harry. *A History of Victoria 1842–1970*. Victoria: Victoria Observer Publishing Co. Ltd., n.d.
Hague, Harlan. "Eden Ravished." *The American West* 14, no. 3 (May-June 1977): 30.
Hardy, W. G., ed. *Alberta: A Natural History*. Edmonton: M. G. Hurtig Ltd., 1967.
Harrison, R. W. "John Malcolm." *Vancouver Sun*, 30 Sept. 1947.
Hazlitt, William Carew. *The Great Gold Fields of Cariboo*. London: Routledge, Warne, and Routledge, 1862. Reprint. Klanak Press, 1974.
Healy, W. J. *Women of Red River*. Winnipeg: The Women's Canadian Club of Winnipeg, 1977.
Holliday, J. S. *The World Rushed In*. New York: Simon and Shuster, 1981.
Holmgren, Eric J. and Patricia M. *2,000 Place Names of Alberta*. Saskatoon: Modern Press, 1972.
Hopwood, Victor G., ed. *David Thompson's Travels in Western North America 1784–1812*. Toronto: MacMillan of Canada, 1971.
Howay, Frederick W. *The Early History of the Fraser River Mines*. Memoir no. 6. Victoria: PABC.
———. "The Overland Journey of the Argonauts of 1862." Royal Society of Canada. *Proceedings and Transactions*. Series 3, vol. 13, 1920.
——— and Scholefield, E.O.S. *British Columbia from the Earliest Times to the Present*. 4 vols. Vancouver, 1914.
Holmes, Kenneth L. "Pierre Chrysologue Pambrun." In *The Mountain Men and the Fur Trade*. Glendale: The Arthur H. Clark Co., 1966.
Houghton, Walter E. *The Victorian Frame of Mind: 1830–1870*. New Haven and London: Yale University Press, 1957.
Huyda, Richard J. *Camera in the Interior: 1858. H. L. Hime—Photographer*. Toronto: The Coach House Press, 1975.
Innis, Harold A. *The Fur Trade in Canada*. Rev. ed. Toronto: University of Toronto Press, 1956.
Johnson, F. Henry. *John Jessop: Gold Seeker and Educator*. Vancouver: Mitchell Press Ltd., 1971.
Johnson, Glenn E. *Here—There—Everywhere Clay County, Minnesota*. Moorehead: Johnson, 1972.

Johnson, Olga Weydemeyer. *Flathead and Kootenay*. Glendale: The Arthur H. Clark Co., 1969.
Johnson, R. Bryon. *Very Far West Indeed*. London: Sampson, Low, 1872.
Johnson, Rev. Charles. "The Overlanders—1862: A Poem." *Kamloops News Advertiser*, 13 April 1966.
Josephy, Alvin M. Jr. "David Thompson." In *Mountain Men and The Fur Trade*. Vol. 3. Glendale: Arthur H. Clark Co., 1966.
Kelly, Fanny. *My Captivity Among The Sioux Indians*. New York: Corinth Books, 1962.
Kerr, J. B. *Biographical Dictionary of Well Known British Columbians*. Vancouver: Kerr and Begg, 1895.
King, Dr. D. J. "Many Overlanders of 1862 Were Outstanding Men". *Kamloops Sentinel*, n.d.
Leduc, Joanne, ed. *Overland From Canada to British Columbia*. By Thomas McMicking. Vancouver: University of British Columbia Press, 1981.
Lewis, William S., ed. "The Sinclair Party—An Emigration Overland." By John V. Campbell. The *Washington Historical Society Quarterly* 8, no. 3, July 1916.
Lugrin, N. De Bertrand. *The Pioneer Women of Vancouver Island 1843–1866*. Victoria: Women's Canadian Club, 1928.
McCloy, T. R. "McKay, John Richards." *Canadian Dictionary of Biography*. Vol. 10, p. 475. Toronto: University of Toronto Press, 1976.
McDonald, Duncan George Forbes, C. E. *British Columbia and Vancouver's Island*. London, England: Longman, Green, Longman, Roberts and Green, 1862.
Macfie, Matthew. *Vancouver Island and British Columbia*. London, England: Longman, Green, Longman, Roberts and Green, 1865.
MacGregor, J. G. *Edmonton: A History*. Edmonton: M. G. Hurtig Ltd., 1967.
MacGregor, James. *Overland by Yellowhead*. Saskatoon: Western Producer Prairie Book Service, 1974.
McKelvie, B. A. "Overland to Cariboo." Vancouver *Daily Province*, 1 Dec. 1923.
———. "Peter McIntyre Recalls Thrilling Days of Overland Expedition of 1862". Vancouver *Province*, 25 Oct. 1924.
McMicking, Thomas. *Overland from Canada to British Columbia*. Edited by Joanne Leduc. Vancouver: University of British Columbia Press, 1981.
Mallandaine, Edward. *First Victoria Directory*. Victoria: E. Mallandaine, 1863.
Marcy, Randolph B. *Adventure on Red River: Report on the Exploration*. Edited by Grant Forman. Norman: University Oklahoma Press, 1968.
Marcy, Randolph B. *The Prairie Traveller: A Handbook for Overland Expeditions*. New York: Harper and Bros., 1859. Reprint. Corner House Publishers, 1968.
Metcalf, Vicky. *Catherine Schubert*. Toronto: Fitzhenry & Whiteside Ltd., 1978.
Metcalfe, J. H. *The Tread of the Pioneers*. Toronto: Ryerson Press, 1932.
Monaghan, Jay., ed. *The Book of the American West*. New York: Crown Publishers Inc., 1963.
Morse, Eric W. *Fur Trade Canoe Routes of Canada: Then and Now*. Ottawa: Queen's Printer, 1969.
Morton, James. *The Enterprising Mr. Moody, The Bumptious Captain Stamp*. North Vancouver: J. J. Douglas Ltd., 1977.
Morton, W. L. *Manitoba: A History*. Toronto: University of Toronto Press, 1970.
Ormsby, Margaret. *British Columbia: A History*. Toronto: Macmillan of Canada Ltd., 1958.
Peltier, Jerome. "Antoine Plante." In *The Mountain Men and the Fur Trade*, 291. Glendale: Arthur H. Clarke Co., 1969.

Peterson, F. Ross. *Idaho—A Bicentennial History.* New York: W. W. Norton and Co. Inc., 1976.
Pike, E. Royston. *Human Documents of the Victorian Golden Age.* London, England: George Allen and Unwin Ltd., 1967.
Ross, Eric. *Beyond the River and the Bay.* Toronto: University of Toronto Press, 1970.
Russell, E. T. *What's in a Name?* Saskatoon, Western Producer Prairie Books, 1975.
Russell, R. C. *The Carlton Trail.* Saskatoon: Western Producer Prairie Books, 1971.
Sampson, William R. "Lane, Richard." *Dictionary of Canadian Biography,* vol. 9, p. 624. Toronto: University of Toronto Press, 1976.
Schaeffer, Claude E. "Plains Kutenai—An Ethnological Evaluation." *Alberta History* 30, no. 4 (Autumn 1982): 1–9.
Scholefield, E. O. S. *British Columbia from the Earliest Times to Present.* Chicago: S. J. Clarke Publishing Co., n.d.
———, and Gosnell, R. E. *A History of British Columbia.* Vancouver, 1913.
Scott, Irene G. *The Trek of the Overlanders.* Toronto: Burns and MacEachern Ltd., 1968.
Spry, Irene M. *The Palliser Expedition.* Toronto: Macmillan of Canada Ltd., 1963.
Stanton, James B. *Impression of an Age.* Occasional Paper no. 1. Vancouver: Centennial Museum, 1969.
Stevenson, Robert, and Walker, Wymond W. *Stories of Early British Columbia.* Vancouver: News Advertiser, 1914.
Strickland, Jack. "Link with Early B.C. Breaks." Vancouver *Daily Province,* 29 March 1947.
Thomas, Gregory. "Fire and the Fur Trade." *Beaver* (Autumn 1977): 32–39.
Thomas, Lewis G., ed. *The Prairie West to 1905: A Canadian Source Book.* Toronto: Oxford University Press, 1975.
Turner, Allen R. "McKay, James." *Dictionary of Canadian Biography.* Vol. 10, pp. 473–75. Toronto: University of Toronto Press, 1976.
Turner, John and Semling, C. K., eds., *History of Clay and Norman Counties, Minnesota.* Indianapolis: B. F. Bowen and Co., 1918.
Tweed, Tommy. "On the Trail of Mr. O'B." *Alberta History* 23, no. 2 (Spring 1975): 4–13.
*Upper Canada Law List, 1862.* Toronto: Rordans and Finch, 1862.
Voorhis, Ernest. *Historic Forts and Trading Posts of the French Regime and of the English Fur Trading Companies.* Ottawa: Department of the Interior, 1930.
Waddington, Alfred. *The Fraser River Mines Vindicated.* Victoria, 1858.
Waite, P. B. "Sleigh, Burrows Willcocks Arthur." *Dictionary of Canadian Biography.* Vol. 9. Toronto: University of Toronto Press, 1976.
Walkem, W. Wymond. *Stories of Early British Columbia.* Vancouver: News Advertiser, 1914.
White, Leslie A., ed. *Lewis Henry Morgan's Indian Journals, 1859–62.* Ann Arbor: University of Michigan Press, 1959.
Woolliams, Nina G. *Cattle Ranch.* Vancouver: Douglas and McIntyre, 1979.
Ziebarth, Marily and Ominsky, Alan. *Fort Snelling—Anchor Post of the Northwest.* St. Paul: MiHS, 1970.

# Index

Abbott and Jordan Claim (on William's Creek), 243
Alexander, Richard, 40, 156, 167, 189, 194, 196, 215
Alphonse, Sister, 60
Amesbury, William, 12
Anderson, Dr. C. L. (Smithsonian representative), 91
Annexation, American, 116
Antler Creek, 141
Assiniboine and Saskatchewan Exploring Expedition, 6
Athabasca Pass, 90
Atkinson, John, 191, 213, 233

Bald Mountain, 243
Ballendine, Sam, 287n.53
Ballie, George, 179
Baltzly, 290n.49
Barber, Edmund Lorenzo (partner of Love), 189
Barker, Billy, 243
Barkerville, 229, 243, 247
Barron, W. H.: near Walla Walla, 119, 128; on Cariboo Trail, 244
Batoche, 184
Bauerman, Dr. H., 164
Beads, John, 58
Bear's Hip Bone (Blackfoot chief), 46
Bears River Pass, 272n.23
Beaudry, Nancy, 288n.21
Bellecourt, Fr. George-Antoine, 17, 99, 278n.26

Berland, Edward, 275n.17
Big Hills, 30
Biographical information, 254–269
Bird, Jamey Jock, 10, 50, 170, 189, 272n.22, 275n.14; as partner of Love, 189
Black, Rev. John, 167
Black, John (judge), 157
Black Jack Tunnel, 244
Blakely, Capt. Russell, 95, 150
Blakiston, Captain, 44, 50–51, 275n.11
Blakiston Creek, 118
Blanchford, Harry, 154
Blinding the trail, 30, 46
Blue Tent House, 245
Bonner, Edwin (ferryman), 55
Borwick, William, 289n.11
Bosquet, Louis, 58
Botineau, Pierre, 170
Boundary Commission Survey, 112, 139
Bovine party, 93; splits, 97
Bow River, prospecting, 233
Bow River Expedition, 69
Bowland, John, 148, 152, 156
Bowron, John, 37, 245
Brabant, Marguerite, 288n.3
Brazeau, Joseph E. (Fort Edmonton clerk), 203, 233
Brazeau, Sophie, 289n.21
Brechin, the Man from, 66; arrives at Victoria, 70
Brechin, Scotland, 66

## INDEX

Brewster, 34, 110
Brisco, Captain, 27
British Columbia, formation of, 6
British Columbia Postal and Steam Navigation Service, 164
British Columbia Overland Transit Co., 161–65, 283n.32, 284n.44
British imperialism, 77–80 passim
British North American Exploring Exp., 5
British overland route, 77
Brocklebank (pilot of raft), 217
Brown, George (editor of *Globe*), 142
Brown, Johnnie, 245
Brown, Thomas, 63, 139
Brown, Mrs. Thomas, son born, 170
Buffalo: chips, 16, 135; hunt, 99–100, 201; meat, 184
Bull's Head (Blackfoot chief), 46
Bunker, W. E. "Billy," 93
Burbank brothers: and HBC, 96; and BCOTC, 164
Burden, 247
Burgess, William R., 149, 215
Burnham, George C., 14, 59, 113
Burns, 234
Byers, David, 247

Caldwell, William N., 91; fight with Wheelock, 98
Caldwell party, 114–15, 249
California miners: Burnham, 112; Clover, Love, McLaurin, 142; Wattie, 153; Wattie and Putnam, 175
Cameron, John Angus "Cariboo," 230, 244
Cameron, Sophie, 244
Cameron, William, B., 154
Cameron Claim, 230, 244
Canadian Red River Exploring Expedition, 5
Canadian Royal Rifles, 21
Canadian Shield Overland Route, 79, 82
Cardinal, Andrew [André]. *See under* Guides
Cariboo Camels, 244
Cariboo [St. Peters] party, 187
Carlton Trail, 5, 10, 25, 27, 134
Carpenter, James, 167, 172, 194, 197, 206, 215; drowns, 221
Carroll, James, 217

Chalemptta, 56
Charles, Thomas (Fort George trader), 239
Cheadle, Dr., 290n.51
Cheever, James, 91
Chesterfield House (on South Saskatchewan), 69, 123
Chief Mountain, 117
Chief Mountain Pass, 272n.23
Chinese, on Fraser, 222
Christie, Gov. Alexander, 21
Christie, Chief Factor William, 41, 43, 72, 171, 232–33
Christmas Eve, 57
Chubbock, Samuel, 243
Clearwater River, 132
Clorine, 93
Clover, Thomas, 132, 281n.8
Cochrane, Archdeacon, 191
Cofferin, George, 246
Cogswell, 211
Collingwood, Henry Isaac, 162–65
Collins, George, 246
*Colonist*, 77
Colville, 139
Colville Valley, 63, 70
Continental Divide, 210
Contu, F., 134
Cook, with Palliser, 111
Coon Creek Incident, 98
Cooney, Charles, 113
Corbett, Rev. Griffith Owen, 213; preaches to overlanders, 167; abortion of Maria Thomas, 168
Coteau des Prairies, 67
Coteau du Missouri, 67
Cottonwood Canyon, 221–22
Cottonwood House, 243
Cow-Dung Lake, 215
Cranberry Lake, 223
Crowe, Gabriel (Fort Edmonton clerk), 41
Crows Lodge Pass, 272n.23
Crowsnest River, forded, 50
Crysler, Leonard, 158, 172, 245
Cut Arm Creek, 181

*Daily Telegraph*, 163
Dallas, Gov. Alexander Grant, 156, 171
Dallas, Mrs., 158
Dancing, 99
Davidson, John, 155
Davis, E. Page, 188

De Smet, Father, 54, 126
Dead Man's Hill, 48
Dead Man's River, 48
Dease, John, 59
Deep Creek, 56, 62, 64
Deux Rivières Portage, 83
Devil's Head Mountain, 47
Devils Lake Settlement, 44
Dewitt, H. C., 224, 289; account of journey, 286n.38
Dietz, Dutch Bill, 242
Dignan, John Pat, 91
Dodd, John, 177
Doherty, James, grave of, 207
Doty, James, 272n.23
Douglas, David, 7
Douglas, James, 3, 163; named governor, 6
Ducks Lake, 55, 56, 57, 61, 119, 127
Duff, Elijah, 79, 280n.36
Dungan, Catherine, 276n.30
Dunleavy, Peter, 130
Dunn, Thomas, 234
Dunphy, Elijah, 276n.30

Eagle Hills, 197
Edgar, William, 113
Ellice, Edward, Sr., 26, 274n.20
Emery, Sister, 60
Emihiser, Ira, 12
Erasmus, Peter, 171; with Hector, 110

Fairweather, William, 113
Fannin, John, 39, 179, 187, 224
Faribault, 12
Faribault party, 249; bateau party, 15, 17; reaches Fort Edmonton, 35; in North Kootenay Pass, 51; split at Deep Creek, 56; wintering, 61
Felker, Henry, 245
Fenner, N. J., 163
Fidler, Peter, 69
Finnis, Aldermann, tries BCOTC, 165
Firearms, 23, 160; gunfight, 108; hunting, 100; navy pistol, 44; revolver, 48; Sharps rifle, 127
Fisk, James, 141, 151
Fisk wagon train, 283n.32
Fletch, John. *See under* Guides
Fletcher, Andrew, 213, 246, 248
Flett, George, 143, 166, 190, 195, 233, 282n.3
Flett, Mrs. Robert, son born, 170

Fording, 27, 48, 50
Fort Abercrombie, 96
Fort Alexander, 86
Fort Benton, 67, 122
Fort Carlton, 31, 32, 74, 135, 184; description by Sellar, 177
Fort Colville, 76, 119
Fort Edmonton, 75, 195, 212, 231–34; description of, 41–43; hunger at, 203
Fort Ellice, 67, 73, 102, 180; description of, 26
Fort Frances, 85
Fort Garry, 20, 73, 166, 199; Jones's impression of, 21; description of, by Sellar, 177
Fort George, 75, 238
Fort Henry, 210
Fort Kamloops, 76, 227
Fort Kootenay, 118, 275n.17; description of, 53
Fort Langley, 3–4
Fort Pike, 32, 274n.27
Fort Pitt, 74; description of, 32; winter at, 109; description of, by Sellar, 185–86
Fort Shepard, 119
Fort Snelling, 9
Fort Union, 67
Fort Walla Walla, 64, 128
Fortune, Alexander, 37, 152, 167, 168, 171, 244
Fortune, William, 39, 224
Fraser, Colin, 212
Fraser River, 1; gold discoveries, 4; convention, 9; parties, 215
Freemen, Jones's description of, 44–45

Gabriel, Baptiste. *See under* Guides
Gage, William, 245
Gambitz, S., 163
Gauley, and son on Fraser, 220
Gibson, Joe: joins Faribault party, 34; frostbitten, 53; with Linklater, 63
Giscome, John, 239, 242
Giscome Rapids, 236
Gladman, George, 5
Glassford brothers, 213, 240
Goat River Rapids, 236
Gold discoveries, 151; California, 2; Ophir, Australia, 2; Nez Percé mines, 3
Goodard, A., 162
Gooderich, Dr. J. D., 91

Goodrich, Charles, 14, 59, 279n.14
Goodrich-Hastings party, at Fort Pitt and at Fort Edmonton, 110–11
Goodrich party, 249
Gowdie (expressman), 240
Graham's Point, 15
Grand Canyon of the Fraser, description of, 218–19
Grand Forks, 18
Grand Portage route, 82, 84
Great Migration, 7
Great Savanne Portage, 82
Green, Robert, 163
Gregg, L. B., 159
Grey Nuns, 60
Grizzly bear, plains, 123
Grott, George, 189
Guides: Cardinal, Andrew [André], 204, 223; desertion by, 47, 138, 181; Fletch, John, 68; at Fort Kootenay, 111; Gabriel, Baptiste, 137; hiring, 170; Indian, 82, 127; Joe, 214; Kutenai, 118, 125; McKay, James, 96, 170; Mitchelle (Iroquois), 186; Nomm'e, Pierre, 120; Monroe, Felix, 206, 207, 214; Racette [Rochette] [Rossette], Charles, 45, 47, 171, 181, 285n.11; Stoney, 48, 115, 137; Whit[e]ford, John [James], 113, 170, 171, 197
Guide books, 28
Gunn, George, 196
Gunsmith, 23

Halfbreeds, 170
Hall, Asa, 234
Hall, Erastus, 234; death of, 235
Hall, J. J., at Fort Edmonton, 42
Halpenny, Joseph, 247
Halpenny, William, 243
Hamilton, Harry, 191, 196, 213
Hamilton, John W. (New York *Tribune* correspondent), 91
Hamilton, W. W., resigns as leader, 124
Hamilton, William (mountainman), 54
Hammond, Fletcher, gunfight, 108, 279n.14
Handcock, Alfred, 194, 221
Handcock, Harry, 167, 194, 245
Hanscome, M. G., 188
Hardisty, Richard, 232

Harkness, Robert, 152, 156, 182, 202, 217; description of, 143–44
Harper, Ephriam, 247
Harriott, J. E., 48
Harris, Nelson, 91
Hastings party, 58, 249
Hayward, James, 164–65
Hector, Dr., 44, 110, 112
Hector party, 249
Helstone, John, 231–42
Henshaw, Albert (leader of New Brunswickers), 61
Henson, James, 163–65
Highland Clearances, 8
Himes, H. L., 164–65
Hind, 246
Hind, Edward (Ned), 12, 31, 41, 110, 114
Hind, Henry Youle, 5–6, 59, 67, 82
Hind, William G. R., 40, 167, 194
Hodgson, G. W., 42
Holes, Andrew, 154, 216
Holloway, Robert, 215
Holmes, Thomas, 60, 151, 279n.14
Holmes party, 60, 250
Holmes wagon train, 283n.32
Horses, 22; accidents, 53, 208, 209
Houck, Joseph S., elected leader, 25
Hough, Joseph, 12, 247
Hudson's Bay Company, 5, 87, 240
Hugill, William, 152, 223, 245; on Thompson River, 224–25; death of, 247
Hunniford, John, 149, 182, 183, 186, 187, 208
Hunting, 47, 116–17, 122, 124; antelope, 49; buffalo, 16, 97, 100, 116, 196
Hutchinson, 213
Hutchinson party, 253

Independence, Missouri, 7
Indians: assistance to overlanders, 55, 125, 137; battles, 136; battles with overlanders, 70; captives, 68; cruelty of, 68; equality with Europeans, 176; harassment of overlanders, 69; molestation by, 10; overlanders' fear of, 176; stealing horses, 118, 176; territories of, 50; trading with, 43–44; warring, 186
Indian Tribes: Assiniboine, 48; Blackfeet, 46, 67–69, 136; Blood, 70;

Chippewa, 19, 155; Cree, 29, 136, 196; Dahcotas, 97; Kutenai, 50, 55, 118, 275n.14; Lower Kutenai, 56; Oglalla Sioux, 68; Sarcee, 46, 211; Shuswap, 211, 216, 235; Snare, 48; Spokane, 56; Stoney, 48, 274n.8; Sioux, 14, 97, 159, 168-69
Inkster, John (of Red River), 61, 113
Islington Mission, 86

Jackfish Lake, 185
Jasper House, 209, 288n.17
Jasper House Pass, 203
Jessop, John, 37, 78, 277n.10
Jessop party, 250
Jones, David, 215
Jones, John, 12, 14, 272n.5; impression of Fort Garry, 21; fights Hind, 25; as racist, 34; at Fort Edmonton, 41; gets lost, 47; birthday, 49; psychic powers, 62; arrives at Colville Valley, 63
Jones, Tom, 179
Jones, William, 134
Jonson, 213
Joscelyn [Joslin], 244
Journey, shipboard, 78

Kam-Dog route, 82, 84
Kaministikwia River, 81
Kananaskis Pass, 137; Goodrich-Hastings party at, 110; see also Sinclair Pass
Kananaskis Valley, 49
Kane, Paul, 7, 164
Kelso, James, 234, 248; near drowning, 184
Kemps, 224
Kennedy, Duncan P., 91
King George's Men, 46
Kittson, Norman, 17
Kittson, Norman (financial agent), 91
Klyne, Adam, 19
Klyne family, 273n.13
Klyne, Michael, 100
Koffman, 93
Kootanais Pass, 10
Kootenay Pass, 45, 60, 203
Kootenay Trail, 46, 55; description of, 50
Kyse, Sam, 248

La Vérendrye, 80, 178
Lac Ste. Anne, 205
Lacombe, Father, 232, 234
Lake Agassiz, 15, 86, 101, 179
Lamy, Sister, 60
Langley, Edward, 163
Leader, Philip, 215; drowns, 219
Leather Pass, 204
Leith, George, 134
Letendre, Xavier [Batoche], 184
Lightning Creek, 243
Linklater, John, 118, 125, 275n.17; description of, 54; to Fort Colville, 63
Linton, E. W. W., 110, 279n.5
Little Saskatchewan River, 26
Little Touchwood Hills, 182
London *Times*, 161
Louch, Mr., 27
Love, Timoleon, 142, 166, 171, 213, 233; with Saskatchewan Gold Expedition, 189-98; description of, 130-31
Loveland, C. A. [D. C. and C. D.], 110, 127
Lower Fort Garry, 20, 87
Lowhee Gold Strike, 243
Lull, Capt. Cornelius P. V., 157
Lumbering, at Red River, 113
Lumbermen, 61
Luxor Pass, 138
Lynch, Thomas, 91
Lytton, Sir Edward Bulwer, 6

McBeath, Hector, 191
McBeath, Robert (councillor of Assiniboia), 191
McBride, Daniel, 240
McCullough, George, 91
McDermott, Andrew, of Red River, 61, 113, 133
MacDonald, Benjamin, 130
McDonald, Rev. R., 87
McFetridge, James, 17
McFie, 206
McFitridge, Jim (customs inspector), 98
McGillivary, Edward, 289n.21
McGillivray, William, 81
McIntyre, Peter, 247
McKay, James. *See under* Guides
McKay, John R., 274n.24
McKenzie, 240
McKenzie, Robert, 155

McKenzie, William, 217
McLaurin, D. F., 127, 132; with Palliser, 111, 113; death of, 189
McLean, Mrs. John, 158
McLellan, John (governor's piper), 156
McLennan River, 216
MacLeod River, 207
McLeod, Martin, 9, 10, 11
McMicking, Robert, 38, 243
McMicking, Thomas, 38, 173, 243; as leader, 173–87; on Fraser, 216–22
McMicking party, 251–52; Fort Ellice to Fort Edmonton, 180–87; to Fort Ellice, 174–180; at Fort Edmonton 202–5; Fort Edmonton to Tête Jaune Cache, 205–11
McMurphy, Sergeant, 245
McMurray's trading post, 274n.27
McNaughton, Archibald, 212, 248
McQueen, Isaac Brock, 283n.22
McTavish, Mr., *see* MacTavish, William
MacTavish, William (HBC factor), 21, 167, 171
Mad River Rapids, 226
Maisonneuve, Father, 232
Malcolm, John, 248
Mangles, Frederick, 163
Mankato party, 27, 250
Marble, Manton (*Harper's Weekly* correspondent), 91
Marcy, Capt. Randolph, 28
Marias Pass, 90
Marshall, James, 2
Martin, dies in gunfight, 108
Martin, John, 162
Matheson, 196
Matheson, Donald, 191
Maxwell, with Palliser, 111
Medicine Rock Pass, 10–11, 50, 272n.23
Menetry, Fr. Joseph, 126
Merchants: American, 77; St. Paul, 87
Merriman, John L., 150
Métis, 170
Mickle, Wheeler, 174
Miette, Roche, 209
Miette River, 215
Migrations, 7
Military, adventurers, 27
Millar, 224
Miner, Alonzo, 188, 283n.32
Miner, D., 188

Miners, 222; description of, 2, 65. *See also* California miners
Minnesota Stage Company, 94; and HBC, 96
Minnesota expansionists, 7, 166
Mitchell, William R., 27
Mitchelle (Iroquois). *See under* Guides
Moberly, 281n.12
Moberly, Henry, 131
Mondieu, Joseph, 91
Monroe, Felix. *See under* Guides
Monroe, Hugh, 288n.11; with Blackfeet, 206
Montgomery, Charles, 114
Montreal canoe, 81
Moore, Benjamin, 162
Moore brothers, 60
Moose River, 210
Moose Woods, 59; in winter, 108
Morrow, William W., 180, 211
Mosquitoes, 16, 17, 134, 183, 193
Moulton, Joseph C., leads expedition, 93
Moulton party, 250
Moulton-Jessop party, 115
Mount Robson, 210
Mountainmen, 170
Mountains, gloom and danger of, 49
Murchison Rapids, 226
Murphy, Thomas, 156; quarrels with Hunniford, 183
Murray, Alexander, 155
Myers, A., lost, 196

New Brunswick party, 61, 113, 250
New Caledonia, 4
Nez Percé, 3
Nicols, John, 153, 185
Nobles, Col. William, 8–9; leads party, 90; description of, 9; quits party, 102
Nobles party, 250; disagreements, 95
Nomm'e, Pierre. *See under* Guides
Nooning, 28
North Canoe, 81
North Kootenay Pass, 11, 50, 51, 272n.23; Palliser travels, 112
Northrup, Capt. Anson, 96
Northwestern Exploring Expedition, 89–103; dissolves, 102
Notes of passage, 126, 223; of Faribault party, 48; of Bunker, 119; of Thibodo and Hamilton, 125; of Robert Campbell, 206

## INDEX

O'Bierne, Eugene Francis, 191, 196
Old Bow Fort [Peigan Post], 48
Oldman River, forded, 50
Olmstead, General S. B., 91; to lead party, 90; resigns, 92
Ophir, Australia, 2
*Oshawa Vindicator*, criticizes Jessop, 120
Overlanders, 7; accidents, 180, 184, 236–39; biographical information, 254–69; bylaws, 124, 175, 181–82, 191; clothing, 193–94; deaths, 227; discipline, 183, 191; equipment, 91; expedition difficulties, 94; expenses, 246; fares, 151; fights, 25, 98, 210; hometown parties and reps, 174–75; joint-stock companies, 175; leaders, 25; lost, 47; medical problems, 121, 124; music, 156, 179, 286n.27; party formation, 173; party representatives, 174–75; provisions and supplies, 150, 172; resting on Sabbath, 183, 187; stage journey, 152; trading, 27, 120, 121, 204, 211, 213–14, 221, 239–40; trail routine, 178; travel, 28–29, 92, 93, 178; travel on Fraser, 214–22; wagon breakdowns, 95
Overland routes, 9, 80, 102, 141–42; description of, 67; journeys, 7
Oxen, 15, 22, 205; stolen, 32; travel, 29

Paddlers Lake. *See* Ducks Lake
Palliser, Capt. John, 5, 44; route of, 48–49
Palliser expedition, 67; overlanders join, 111
Palliser party, 250
Palmer, John, 12
Palmer, John (Nobles party), 96
Pambrun, Pierre Chrysologue Jr., 25, 30, 274n.21
Panama route, 77
Parker, Gilbert, 131
Parker, Lucius, 95
Party rosters, 249–53
Passes, discovery of, 51
Pattison, Eustache, 40, 217; dies, 219
Paul, Paulette, 281n.8
Pembina, 17; description of, 98; dance at, 99
Pembina River, 206
Pemmican, 22

Pend Oreille Lake, 127
Penwarden, Frank, 158; drowns on Thompson, 227
Perroway, Mr., 63
Perry, Alfred, 110, 131, 133, 279n.5
Peters, Mr., 95
Phillip, Thomas, 154, 184, 246
Phillip, William, 154
Pine Portage, 83
Pinkerton, John, 243, 248
Plains, description of, 177–78
Plainsmen, 25
Plante, Antoine (ferryman), 64, 127
Porte d'Enfer, 226, 290n.53
Premier Range, 216
Prest, Dobson, 180, 202, 245, 247
Prices, 23, 172
Ptarmigan, 49
Purden, Arthur, 135
Purden, James, 155
Purdy, 246
Putnam, 206

Qu'Appelle Mission, 121
Qu'Appelle Post, 121
Qu'Appelle River, fording, 27
Queen Charlotte Islands, 2, 6
Quesnel Forks, 131
Quesnellemouth, 220, 221, 228, 243
Quigg, James, 276n.30
Quill Plains, 30, 182

Racette, Charles. *See under* Guides
Racette, George "Shaman," 171
Rae, Dr., 164
Rainy River Post, 86
Ramsey, Gov. Alexander, 10
Rat Portage Post, 86
Red River Métis, battle with Sioux, 159
Red River party, 286n.42
Red River, travel down, 17–18
Red River settlement, 8, 20, 60; social mores, 168; stores, 23
Red River Trail, 15, 153
Red River cart, 14; trains, 8, 28
Redgrave, Stephen, 40, 173, 191, 213, 245; description of, 143, 193; resigns leadership, 152; joins with Hind, 195
Reed, George N., 91, 184
Reese, 93
Reid, Dr. Alexander, 133, 164
Reid party, 250

Remas, Father, 61
Rennie, Gilbert, 231–42
Rennie, Thomas, 231–42
Rennie, William, 231–42, 247
Rennie party, 231–42, 252
Richfield, 229, 244
River crossings, 32, 180, 183–84, 215; Little Saskatchewan, 26; Pembina River, 206
Robertson, A. C., 234; elected captain, 186; drowns, 218
Robson, John, 245
Robson's Mountain, 210
Rochette, Charles. See under Guides
Rocky Mountains, 106, 208, 214
Rogers, Samuel, 243, 248
Rolette, Joseph, Jr., 17, 57; at trading post, 97; hosts dance, 99
Ross, James (editor of Nor'-Wester), 166
Rossette. See under Guides
Rossin House, Toronto, 164
Rosters, 249–53
Rowand, John, 42
Rowand family, 288n.21
Rundle, Rev. Robert T., 274n.8; with Sarcees, 46
Ryerson, Egerton, 79
Ryerson's Normal School, 79

St. Albert, 189, 212
St. Arneaux, Louis, 136
St. Joseph, 17, 159
St. Paul, merchants, 7, 149
St. Paul party, 59, 250
St. Peters party, 253; Fort Edmonton to Tête Jaune Cache, 211–12; Fort Garry to Fort Edmonton, 187–89
St. Thomas party, 149, 289n.32
San Francisco, 1
Sandont, John B., 91; elected leader of party, 124
Sanford, John R., 12, 110; stops at Fort Edmonton, 44
Saskatchewan Elbow, 69
Saskatchewan Exploring Expedition, 67
Saskatchewan Gold, 142, 212
Saskatchewan Gold Expedition, 169, 252–53; Fort Garry to Fort Edmonton, 189–98; mess breakups, 194; Fort Edmonton to Tête Jaune Cache, 212–15
Sault Ste. Marie, 80
Savona, Francisco, 227

Schaeffter, "Dutch" John, 12
Schubert, Augustus, Jr., 168
Schubert, Catherine [O'Hare] 39, 287n.1; description of, 168; gives birth, 226
Schubert, Francis Augustus, 39; description of, 168
Schubert, James, 168
Schubert, Mary Jane, 168
Schubert, Rosa, 226
Schubert family, 223–26
Schyuler, William, 230, 245
Scratching River, ferry, 19
Scratching River, 160
Selkirk, Thomas Douglas, Earl of, 8
Sellar, James, 174, 186, 216; description of, 176; view of Rockies, 208
Sellar, William, 177, 206, 218, 245
Sergeant, Mr., 24
Seton, Maj. George, 21, 273n.16
Settee, Rev. James, 180
Shakopee, Minn., 60
Sheffield, Mr., 95
Similkameen gold, 113
Simonton, Dr. William B., 188, 212; description of, 153
Simpson, Governor Sir George, 20, 23, 31, 173; describes Fort Edmonton, 43; illegitimate children, 20, 33–34; on trail, 96
Simpson, James, 33, 59, 274n.28
Sinclair, Betsy, Simpson's mistress, 34
Sinclair, James, 7
Sinclair settlers, 7
Sinclair Pass, 45, 46, 138. See also Kananaskis Pass
Sioux War, 160
Sisters of Charity, 60, 212
Slaughter Camp, 224, 290n.49
Sleigh, Burrows Willocks Arthur, description, 162–65
Sleigh, William, 163
Smith, Henry, 91
Smith, James Elnathan [Ellhi], 12, 14, 18; at Ducks Lake, 56, 63, 127; arrives at Fort Colville, 64
Smith, W. Ellis, 14, 59, 279n.14
Snake, 3
Souris River, description of, 101
South Kootenay Pass, 116, 272n.23
South Saskatchewan River, 31; Elbow of, 116, 122

Southesk, Earl of, 49, 164
Southgate, Thomas, 163
Spokane Garry (Spokane Chief), 56
SS *Albatross*, 163
SS *Anson Northrup*, 87, 93, 155
SS *Commodore*, 1–2
SS *Frank Steele*, 148, 283n.20
SS *Freighter*, 155
SS *International*, 106, 155, 157
SS *Keokuk*, 148, 283n.20
SS *Northern Belle*, 148
SS *Otter*, 3
SS *Pioneer*, 96, 134, 155
SS *Rescue*, 79, 80
SS *Sierra Nevada*, 245
SS *Tynemouth*, 245
SS *United Kingdom*, 162
Steamboats, 19
Stevens, Col. John H., 10
Stevens route, 67, 116, 154
Stevenson, Dr. Edward, 180, 217
Stone Fort, 20
Strachan, William, 184
Sullivan, John William (of Palliser expedition), 112
Supplies, 9
Sutherland, George, 191, 196
Sutter, John, 2
Sweeny, Michael, dies in Schubert's grog shop, 169
Sykes, Sir Francis, 95

Tache, Bishop, 157, 171
Tait, Robbie, 190
Taylor, James W., 141; secretary, 91; lost, 97
Tête Jaune Cache, 211, 235
Tête Jaune party, 110, 250
Thibodo, Dr. Augustus J., 37, 91, 280n.45; at Snake River ferry, 119; at Walla Walla, 128
Thibodo party, 250
Thomas, Maria (servant of Rev. Corbett), 168
Thompson, 245
Thompson, George, 215
Thompson, S., 162
Thompson W. H. G., 248
Thompson, W. W., 91
Thompson, William, 183
Thompson River: deaths, 227; gold discoveries, 3; parties, 223–27, 289n.32

Thunder Bay, 81
Thunder Breeding Hills, 69
Tife, C. E., 246
Touchwood Hills, 29, 182; fort, 286n.30; house, 182
Trading, 135; at Fort Edmonton, 41–42; with Sarcees, 46; "pain-killer," 59; at Fort Kootenay, 126
Trails, blinding, 30
Transportation: companies, 151, 161; methods of, 7
Tunstall, 246

Valentine's Day, 62
Vermilion River, 197
Victoria, 70; description of, 65
Victorian Society, 167–70

Walla Walla, description of, 139
Wallace, George, description of, 151
Warren, Robert, 217
Waterton River, 118
Wattie, James, 38, 159, 230, 244, 291n.19; elected captain, 153
Wattie, William, 38, 244
Whatcom Trail, 77
Wheelock, Joseph Albert, 9, 149; *Pioneer and Democrat* correspondent, 91; fight with Caldwell, 98
Whiskey trading, Pambrun, 33
Whitefords. *See under* Guides
Whitford family, 286n.42
Whitford, Andrew, 197
Whitford, James. *See under* Guides
Whitford, John. *See under* Guides
Whitley, Spencer P., 224
Whyte, Joseph, 154
Williams, Dan, 239; with Palliser, 111, 113
William's Creek, gold discoveries on, 243
Willoughby, Richard, 243
Wolf's Track or Trail, 46
Women: in camp, 98; in fur trade, 33; to goldfields, 142; left behind, 15; with overlanders, 169–70; social position, 24; on trail, 95; with wagon trains, 285n.7
Wonnacott, 213
Wonnacott, G. B., 233
Wood, Sabrina Jane, 143

Woolsey, Rev. Thomas, 134, 142, 203, 204–5, 288n.2
Wright, John R., 231–42, 246

Yellowhead Highway, 28

Yellowhead Pass, 203
York Boat brigade, 232
Young, John, 91
Youville Convent, 212

# Music of the Overlanders
## Reclaimed Music & Stories of British Columbia's 1860s gold rush

## THE BOOK

Richard Thomas Wright & Cathryn Wellner

**CASTLES in the AIR**

Music & Stories of British Columbia's 1860s gold rush

A companion to

Complete lyrics, song sheet sources, historic photos and documents.
ISBN 0-9696887-5-X, $12.95.

## & THE CD

Companion CD includes Rough but Honest Miner, Dancing Girls of Cariboo, Hard Times & many more songs & narrations. 22 tracks & over 60 min.
ISBN 0-9696887-4-1, $24.95

BUY BOTH for $32.95 and SAVE $4.95!

Check your favorite book & CD store or order from
Winter Quarters Press, Box 15 Miocene, Williams Lake, BC, V2G 2P3 (250) 296-4432; fax 296-4429. To order call 1-800-583-2880 or e-mail order@goldrushbc.com

**http://goldrushbc.com**